LANGUAGE IDEOLOGIES

Language Ideologies

Critical Perspectives
on the Official English Movement

Volume 1

Education and the Social Implications
of Official Language

Edited by

ROSEANN DUEÑAS GONZÁLEZ
University of Arizona

with

ILDIKÓ MELIS
University of Arizona

 National Council of Teachers of English
1111 W. Kenyon Road, Urbana, Illinois 61801-1096

 Lawrence Erlbaum Associates, Inc.
10 Industrial Avenue, Mahwah, New Jersey 07430

Staff Editor: Bonny Graham
Interior Design: Jenny Jensen Greenleaf
Cover Design: Carlton Bruett

NCTE Stock Number: 26677-3050

Lawrence Erlbaum Associates, Inc. ISBN 0-8058-3967-4

Library of Congress Cataloging-in-Publication Data

Language ideologies: critical perspectives on the official English movement
/ edited by Roseann Dueñas González with Ildikó Melis.
    p. cm.
    Includes bibliographical references and index.
    Contents: v. 1. Education and the social implications of official language
    ISBN 0-8141-2667-7 (pbk.)
    1. Language policy—United States. 2. Language and education—
United States. 3. English language—Study and teaching—United States.
4. English language—Political aspects—United States. 5. Pluralism
(Social sciences)—United States. I. González, Roseann Dueñas.
II. Melis, Ildikó.

P119.32.U6 L358 2000
428'.0071'073—dc21
                                                          00-055887

I dedicate this book to my mother, Maria Luisa Sazueta Dueñas, who believed in all the languages of knowledge. She prayed in her eloquent Spanish, read the Bible in English and Spanish, listened to the Mexican radio station, watched gothic novelas on Spanish television, read her favorite literature in Spanish, baby-talked to my children in Spanish, read the newspaper and health books in English, scolded me in Spanish, and read the English dictionary for fun! In her beautiful Spanish and broken English, she instilled in me my fundamental belief in social justice and taught me, by example, that we are all accountable for our actions toward each other, and that doing the right thing is always the most difficult thing to do.

CONTENTS

Contents

FOREWORD

JIM CUMMINS
University of Toronto

Language ideologies represent statements of identity. They range along a continuum from coercive to collaborative in nature. In the former case, they are articulated as an expression of discursive power by dominant groups with the intent of eradicating, or at least curtailing, manifestations of linguistic diversity. The transformation of these ideologies into language policies, as illustrated in California by Proposition 227 and its predecessor Proposition 187, carries material consequences for all those who do not speak the dominant language at home. Students are denied rights to instruction through their home language, and the possibilities for children to develop bilingualism and biliteracy are dramatically reduced. These ideologies and policies are one among many manifestations of coercive relations of power where power is exercised by dominant groups to the detriment of less powerful groups in the society. They express who belongs and who does not belong; who is an insider and who is on the outside looking in. They set the rules for entry and the conditions for staying. They make clear who are the landlords and who are the tenants. They communicate clearly an absence of rights to those who do not conform to the codes of belonging.

By contrast, language ideologies and policies that cluster along the collaborative end of the continuum emphasize what Richard Ruiz (1984) has termed *language as right* and *language as resource* orientations. The Australian National Policy on Languages (Lo Bianco 1987) represents an exceptional example of these orientations, albeit one that remains contested. The Official English movement justifies its existence on the grounds that national unity is threatened by the multitude of languages that immigrant groups have brought to the United States. Elevation of English to "official" status would somehow stem the tide of fragmentation, presumably by legitimating a prohibition on the use of any other language for "official" purposes (such as schooling). The Official English movement raises the specter of ethnic enclaves maintaining their cultures and languages outside the mainstream of society, loyal only to the ethnic community, refusing to meld their differences as previous generations of immigrants are presumed to have done. Maintenance of language and culture is constructed as opting out of becoming American. Multiculturalism, multicultural education, and bilingual education are vilified as expressions of thinly veiled separatist manifestos. Cracks in the edifice of nationhood, visible only through the lens of Official English, demand immediate action to repair the damage that has already been effected by unbridled immigration and its associated linguistic and cultural proliferation.

If this sounds like paranoid xenophobia, it is. Diversity has been constructed as "the enemy within," far more potent than any external enemy in its threat to the fabric of nationhood. Within this xenophobic discourse, Spanish-English bilingual education is seriously viewed (by reasonably intelligent people) as a potential catalyst for Quebec-style separation. It is also viewed by these same reasonably intelligent people as *the* cause of underachievement among bilingual students, despite the fact that only a small proportion of English-language learners are in any form of bilingual education (Gándara 1999).

Xenophobic discourse, broadcast into every classroom in states such as California, constricts the ways in which identities are negotiated between teachers and students and the opportunities for learning that culturally and linguistically diverse students experience. The potency of the indoctrination process, and its potential to warp rationality, can be appreciated when a historian as eminent as Arthur Schlesinger Jr. makes the following observations about bilingualism and its consequences:

> Bilingualism shuts doors. It nourishes self-ghettoization, and ghettoization nourishes racial antagonism. . . . Using some language other than English dooms people to second-class citizen-

ship in American society. . . . Monolingual education opens
doors to the larger world. . . . [I]nstitutionalized bilingualism
remains another source of the fragmentation of America,
another threat to the dream of "one people." (1991, 108–109)

The claims that "bilingualism shuts doors" and "monolingual education opens doors to the wider world," are laughable if viewed in isolation, particularly in the context of current global interdependence and the frequently expressed needs of U.S. business for multilingual "human resources." Schlesinger's statement also displays an inexcusable abdication of intellectual responsibility in that he feels no need to invoke any empirical data to support his claims. As the data reviewed in this volume and many others illustrate, far from "shutting doors," bilingualism is associated with enhanced linguistic, cognitive, and academic development when both languages are encouraged to develop. Schlesinger simply assumes that "bilingualism" means inadequate knowledge of English despite the fact that a simple one-minute consultation of any dictionary could have corrected his assumption. He also blithely stigmatizes the victim rather than problematizing the power structure in U.S. society which, he asserts, dooms those who use some language other than English to second-class citizenship. He presumably is not against the learning of "foreign" languages by native speakers of English, but he evades the obvious question of why bilingualism is good for the rich but bad for the poor.

Schlesinger's comments become interpretable only in the context of a societal discourse that is profoundly disquieted by the fact that the sounds of the Other have now become audible and the hues of the U.S. social landscape have darkened noticeably.

In previous times, reflections in the mirror of national identity were maintained in a sanitized condition by the complementary policies of exclusion and assimilation. The terms "exclusion" and "assimilation" may appear to be opposites insofar as exclusion focuses on segregation of subordinated groups from the mainstream of schools and society while assimilation strives for total integration into society. In reality, however, they have functioned as two sides of the same coin: both orientations aspire to make subordinated groups invisible and inaudible.

Minority groups constructed as "racially different" historically were subjected to exclusionary rather than assimilationist
policies for the simple reason that disappearance could not readily be achieved through assimilation. In addition, if assimilationist
policies were applied to "racial" minorities, it would imply inter-
marriage across "races" within the same "melting pot." This
mixing of races would implode the myths of racial superiority
that have characterized most dominant groups in societies around
the world.

How do we challenge the discourse of paranoia? Clearly, we
need to recognize that Proposition 227 and the ideology of Official English are about power, who has it and who intends to keep
it. They are about intimidation and racism, and we must recognize these realities if we are to fight them. We should also recognize, however, that the United States has probably the strongest
legal protections (on paper) regarding equity in education of any
country in the industrialized world. These legal protections provide potent tools for community groups to challenge discrimination in various spheres of education. Thus one arena for dialogue
(albeit conflictual dialogue) is in the courts.

Bilingual education has held its own in the court system but
has fared much less well in the court of public opinion orchestrated by the media. In order to communicate more effectively in
the public arena, we need to develop a clear strategy for what I
will term collaborative dialogue (Cummins in press; Moraes
1996). A starting point is to refrain from dismissing all opposition to bilingual education as xenophobic and racist, because a
large proportion of those who supported Proposition 227 do not
see themselves as racist and do not act in overtly racist ways in
their ordinary lives. They portray themselves as concerned with
rationality, effectiveness, and cost. They are either unaware or
have been disinformed regarding the research on bilingual education. Typically, in the absence of any real understanding of the
research, these opponents of bilingual education revert to the
commonsense view that bilingual children should be immersed in
English as self-evidently the best way to learn the language and
succeed academically. Collaborative dialogue with this group is
an essential part of the challenge to coercive relations of power.

Challenging Coercive Relations of Power through Collaborative Dialogue

Collaborative dialogue aims to expose the structures of disinformation concealed in media sound bites and patently contradictory reviews of research. It also strives to identify shared vested interests between privileged and less privileged societal groups as a way of imploding the "Us versus Them" divisions which are the foundation of xenophobic discourses. Collaborative dialogue includes the following four components:

◆ Recognition that dominant groups are no more homogeneous than subordinated groups and that to dismiss all those who enjoy privileged status in our society as oppressors amounts to essentialization, which will curtail rather than promote the dialogic process; we need to identify and reach out to those within dominant groups who are prepared to engage in meaningful dialogue

◆ Identification of shared goals and common vested interests that transcend more superficial Us versus Them divisions between dominant and subordinated communities

◆ Demystification of research findings related to the issues under dispute (e.g., bilingual education) and exposure of contradictions and inconsistencies inherent in both academic attempts to distort these research findings and in the media discourse related to diversity

◆ Promotion of programs that explicitly challenge Us versus Them divisions and demonstrate in concrete ways the advantages for all in establishing collaborative relations of power

Each of these components can be illustrated briefly.

1. Identification of the possibilities for dialogue. If we consider the fact that approximately 70 percent of those who voted in California's Proposition 187 plebiscite in 1994 were in favor of severe restrictions on the use of languages other than English, and 61 percent supported Proposition 227 in 1998, we might well be apprehensive about the impact of further "democratic" action on minority rights in general and bilingual education in particular.

We should recognize, however, that a large proportion of those who supported these two propositions see themselves as support- ive of "the common good" despite the fact that they have bought (or been indoctrinated) into the discourse of xenophobia. If we dismiss all those who support anti-immigrant initiatives as racists or oppressors, then the possibilities of change through democratic action are remote indeed. If we are to challenge the discourse of xenophobia and work toward a saner and more tolerant society, we must communicate and engage in dialogue with many of those who currently see diversity as a threat. In fact, we must join forces with them to articulate a vision of our society where there is cooperation rather than competition across cultural boundaries and where cultural and linguistic differences enrich rather than fragment the whole.

2. Recognition of common goals and shared vested interests. Among the common goals in which all members of society have a vested interest are the following:

◆ *Promote academic achievement for all.* At a time when both corporations and nations acknowledge that intellectual resources are paramount to their future progress, it should not be difficult to agree on the desirability of maximizing the aca- demic and intellectual potential of all students. Every dropout carries a huge price tag for society: these students' potential to contribute to the economic and social well-being of their soci- ety remains unrealized, costs for social services ranging from welfare to incarceration increase, and tax revenues these indi- viduals might have generated are lost. Students from subordi- nated groups are massively overrepresented among statistics of school failure. Initiatives such as bilingual and multicultural education should thus be examined not only through an ideo- logical lens but also as dispassionately as possible for their potential to reverse underachievement and realize the intellec- tual and academic resources of the nation.

◆ *Develop society's cultural and linguistic resources.* At a time of dramatically increased global interdependence, the cultural and linguistic resources of any nation assume particular signifi- cance. The ability to work together to solve problems across cultural, linguistic, racial, and national boundaries is not only part of the "job description" sent out by corporate America, but it is also essential for social cohesion in both domestic and international arenas. As Robert Hughes (1993) succinctly put it, "In the world that is coming, if you can't navigate difference, you've had it" (100). From this perspective, it makes no economic or other form of sense for a society to squander its cultural and linguistic resources when for a minimal investment they could so easily be developed.

3. Demystification of research findings. The suspicion that bilingual education is some form of "Hispanic/Latino Plot" to destabilize the nation is fueled by the apparent counterintuitive nature of its rationale. This rationale suggests that English proficiency will be better developed if children are taught, for part of the instructional day, in Spanish (or some other language) rather than in English. It makes more sense to many skeptics to argue that success in learning English is more likely to be assured if instructional time in English is maximized. As several contributors to this volume note, however, this "time-on-task" or "maximum-exposure" hypothesis is totally at variance with *all* the research findings from bilingual programs around the world that involve either minority- or majority-language students. Despite the empirical support for bilingual programs and the fact that some form of bilingual education is implemented in almost every country around the world, there has been a sustained attempt in the United States since the early 1980s to discredit both the rationale and the empirical foundation of bilingual programs (e.g., Rossell and Baker 1996).

It is not difficult to expose the superficial logic and sociopolitical functions of the attempt to undermine the empirical basis of bilingual education (Cummins 1999; Krashen 1996). For example, Rossell and Baker argue for a monolingual program, taught by monolingual teachers, aimed at promoting monolingualism, on the basis of the success of a fully bilingual program (Canadian French immersion), taught by bilingual teachers, whose goal is bilingualism. Blatant contradictions in Keith Baker's writings are also not difficult to find. For example, he described the El Paso Independent School District program in 1992 as "a Spanish-English dual immersion program" whose positive results support the "claims of bilingual education advocates that most bilingual education programs do not use enough of the native language"

(Baker 1992, 6). Yet six years later, he describes exactly the same program as a "structured English immersion" program whose positive results illustrate "the harm that bilingual education programs do to learning English" (Baker 1998, 201).

This type of patently contradictory antibilingual discourse becomes interpretable when seen as the discourse of the courtroom lawyer whose goal is to present the most persuasive case for her or his client with little regard for the truth. In these courtroom situations, lawyers frequently attempt to obscure the facts so that reasonable doubt is created in the jury. In a climate of xenophobia, all that is needed to confirm the paranoia in relation to "Hispanic/Latino activists" is to create sound bites: "In reading, 83% of the studies showed TBE [transitional bilingual education] to be worse than structured immersion" (Rossell and Baker 1996, 21). Despite their total lack of credibility (Cummins 1999, in press; Krashen 1996), these sound bites then get recycled through the media and into the discourse of policymakers, providing "scientific proof" for what was obvious anyway to reasonable observers: namely, bilingual education doesn't work and simply constitutes at best a make-work program for Hispanics/Latinos, and at worst a plot to undermine American values.

Even among policymakers and members of the public who try to look at both sides of the issue, the sound bite's morsel of truth highlights the fact that the experts disagree. Thus decision makers must invoke other criteria, such as "common sense" or "American values," as a basis for action. One way of highlighting the coercive intent of these supposedly objective analyses of the research is to expose their internal logical contradictions and inconsistencies to empirical data (Cummins 1999, in press; Krashen Chapter 6, this volume).

4. Promotion of programs that challenge Us versus Them discourse. The Achilles heel of bilingual education opponents is the success of dual-language or two-way bilingual immersion programs. According to the "maximum-exposure/time-on-task" argument, these programs should be a disaster for language-minority students since they involve much less English instruction than the vast majority of transitional bilingual education or all-English (structured immersion) programs. In fact, minority-language students in these programs consistently attain or come very close to grade norms in English academic skills by grade 6 or 7 (Cummins in press; Thomas and Collier 1997). It is ironic that these two-way programs have been explicitly endorsed by two of the most prominent *opponents* of bilingual education: Rosalie Pedalino Porter and Charles Glenn.

According to Porter (1990), a two-way or dual-immersion program is "particularly appealing because it not only enhances the prestige of the minority language but also offers a rich opportunity for expanding genuine bilingualism to the majority population." Such programs promise "mutual learning, enrichment, and respect." They are also "considered to be the best possible vehicles for integration of language minority students, since these students are grouped with English-speakers for natural and equal exchange of skills." Furthermore, two-way programs are "the best opportunity for families that are seriously committed to genuine bilingualism for their children," and these programs "do not cost any more than the average single-language classes to maintain" (154–56).

There is clearly an Orwellian doublethink process going on here involving the simultaneous endorsement of (a) English only immersion programs as the most promising option for bilingual students' academic success because they provide maximum English exposure (time-on-task); and (b) two-way bilingual immersion programs that typically entail *less* English-medium and more first-language instruction than any other bilingual education option. Nevertheless, the identification of points of agreement between opponents and advocates of bilingual education provides a starting point for collaborative dialogue on the basis of the fact that both groups endorse exactly the same form of program option (two-way bilingual) as much superior to the usual form of bilingual education (quick-exit transitional bilingual).

Charles Glenn, a well-respected Massachusetts academic and administrator, has also been critical of bilingual programs that segregate bilingual students from the mainstream, but, like Porter, he has been one of the strongest and most consistent advocates of two-way bilingual immersion as *the best* program alternative for all students. His own five children have attended a two-way bilingual program. He notes, for example:

> More than any other model of education for linguistic minority pupils, two-way bilingual programs meet the diverse expectations that we set for our schools. Properly designed and implemented, they offer a language-rich environment with high expectations for every child, in a climate of cross-cultural respect. Linguistic minority pupils are stimulated in their use of English, while being encouraged to value and employ their home language as well. (Glenn 1990, 5)

> The best setting for educating a linguistic minority pupil—and one of the best for educating *any* pupil—is a school in which two languages are used without apology and where becoming proficient in both is considered a significant intellectual and cultural achievement. (Glenn and LaLyre 1991, 43)

In summary, the four stages just outlined clearly show the possibilities for collaborative dialogue in the bilingual education debate. Two-way bilingual programs have expanded rapidly in the United States during the past five years (to a current level of close to three hundred). They clearly chart positive directions for educational enrichment for *all* students. To focus on these programs, and their endorsement by supposed opponents of bilingual education, is probably the most effective strategy for transforming the discourse from a pattern of coercive relations of power to one of collaborative relations of power.

Conclusion

However disdainful some academics might be of the media's sound bite discourse through which coercive power relations are perpetuated, the reality is that this is the primary discursive arena for the political process. I believe that it is irresponsible to abandon this arena to the forces of racism and xenophobia. In the absence of dialogue, the "democratic" voice of the dominant majority, infused with prerecorded sound bite formulas, will ensure that the coercive status quo remains intact.

Dialogue, by contrast, has at least the potential to identify concerns and priorities shared by various sectors of society, expose the superficial logic and sociopolitical manipulation underlying opposition to programs such as bilingual education, and finally work toward concrete social and educational changes that overturn xenophobic Us versus Them perspectives and implement programs that are self-evidently for the common good. Collaborative dialogue of this type has the potential to cause sound bites to implode, because their apparent logic can be sustained only in the absence of dialogue.

Works Cited

Baker, Keith. 1992. "Review of *Forked Tongue.*" *Bilingual Basics* (Winter/Spring): 6–7.

———. 1998. "Structured English Immersion: Breakthrough in Teaching Limited-English-Proficient Students." *Phi Delta Kappan* 80(3): 199–204.

Cummins, Jim. 1999. "The Ethics of Doublethink: Language Rights and the Debate on Bilingual Education." *TESOL Journal* 8(3): 13–17.

———. (in press). *Language, Power, and Pedagogy: Bilingual Children in the Crossfire.* Clevedon, Eng.: Multilingual Matters.

Gándara, Patricia. 1999. *Review of Research on Instruction of Limited English Proficient Students: A Report to the California Legislature.* Santa Barbara: University of California, Linguistic Minority Research Institute.

Glenn, Charles. 1990. "Introduction." In *Two-Way Integrated Bilingual Education.* Boston: Massachusetts Department of Education, Office of Educational Equity.

Glenn, Charles, and I. LaLyre. 1991. "Integrated Bilingual Education in the USA." In K. Jaspaert and S. Kroon, eds., *Ethnic Minority Languages and Education.* Amsterdam: Swets & Zeitlinger.

Hughes, Robert. 1993. *Culture of Complaint: The Fraying of America.* New York: Warner Books.

Krashen, Stephen D. 1996. *Under Attack: The Case against Bilingual Education.* Culver City, CA: Language Education Associates.

Lo Bianco, Joseph. 1987. *National Policy on Languages.* Canberra: Australian Government Publishing Service, Commonwealth Department of Education.

Moraes, Marcia. 1996. *Bilingual Education: A Dialogue with the Bakhtin Circle.* Albany: State University of New York Press.

Porter, Rosalie. 1990. *Forked Tongue: The Politics of Bilingual Education.* New York: Basic Books.

Rossell, Christine, and Keith Baker. 1996. "The Educational Effectiveness of Bilingual Education." *Research in the Teaching of English* 30: 7–74.

Ruiz, Richard. 1984. "Orientations in Language Planning." *NABE Journal* 8(2): 15–34.

Schlesinger, Arthur Jr. 1991. *The Disuniting of America.* New York: W. W. Norton.

Thomas, W. P., and Virginia Collier. 1997. *School Effectiveness for Language Minority Students.* Washington, D.C.: National Clearinghouse for Bilingual Education.

ACKNOWLEDGMENTS

This book grew out of three interests. First, in my work as director of the National Council of Teachers of English (NCTE) Commission on Language from 1993 to 1996, we struggled with the misconceptions surrounding the English Only controversy held by many educators—that it was no longer a threat, that it was an old story, that it had no real effects on the lives of students and teachers. Often sessions concerning the English Only movement planned by the Commission were not as well attended as we had hoped. But all of this changed when California Propositions 187 and 227 passed, and it became clear that English Only had begun to affect teachers' and students' lives in California in a very real way. We were stunned by the inhumanity of these events and concerned that this was a national trend that could spread to other states with large language minority populations. The Commission sponsored panels and wrote resolutions opposing these hostile propositions directed against minority children, and as a group we immediately recognized the pressing need for a new volume on English Only. *Not Only English: Affirming America's Multilingual Heritage*, NCTE's first book on the English Only controversy, is now nearly a decade old, and a new volume seems essential to explore the path this virulent movement took in the 1990s. When I stepped down as director, I took the project with me to work on. I would like to thank the Commission on Language for its constant encouragement and dedication to the completion of *Language Ideologies: Critical Perspectives on the Official English Movement*, which resulted in two volumes of excellent essays, proving that such a collection was indeed timely.

Second, the Conference on College Composition and Communication's (CCCC) Language Policy Committee, chaired by

Geneva Smitherman, University Distinguished Professor of English at Michigan State University, had been working steadily for many years to explore the sociolinguistic and sociopolitical dimensions of the official language movement and to counter its monolingual, monolithic perspectives through the development and dissemination of an inclusive language policy that embraces the natural language of all groups in the United States. Five of the essays in this collection emanate from that panel's work in 1997. I am very grateful to Geneva Smitherman for her cooperation and assistance on this project and to another member of the CCCC Language Policy Committee, Gail Okawa, assistant professor of English at Youngstown State University, who kindly collected the papers given at that panel for my review.

Third, this book is born out of my own experience. For a Chicana who grew up in the '50s in Arizona, the English Only movement conjures up a nightmare of the bad old days that many of us desire to forget but cannot entirely put out of our minds. Being a Mexican American child in Phoenix in the '50s meant understanding my family's and my place in the world; knowing that, for whatever reason, we were often not welcome in the majority milieu; knowing that there were certain places we could and could not go; and knowing that our Spanish language (and even our brand of English) was suspect and a constant object of attack. I quickly realized that "Sorry, I don't speak Mexican" was a polite cover for "Mexicans aren't served here," a familiar refrain from my youth.

I knew from my earliest moment that my family and I were different. It wasn't just that Santa Claus didn't come in the morning as he did for all the other kids (he must have come some time during *Misa de Gallo* [Midnight mass] because when we came home from mass at about 1:30 A.M. and ate our *tamales*, our presents were already under the tree). It wasn't just that we looked different, especially me—I had black hair and wore two big braids tied in bright ribbons woven in and out. It wasn't just that I didn't celebrate birthdays with a dozen classmates, party hats, and favors. All my aunts and uncles came over, and Mama served *menudo* or *tostadas* while my cousins and I played together and the grown-ups listened to their Spanish *boleros* and *cumbias*, danced, and drank *cuba libres*. There was no "pin the tail on the donkey"; instead, we had a beautiful *piñata*. And it also wasn't that we were called "dirty Mexicans" a few times in school or at the park. I think our most important difference was that we spoke Spanish and our own brand of English. My dad spoke only Spanish (except for swear words in English, as well as construction terms that he learned to survive on his job). Being a hod carrier didn't give him a lot of English practice, especially since he worked with a primarily Spanish-speaking crew, and laboring eight to twelve hours in the sun didn't leave him much energy to attend English class either. He left that to Mama.

And Mama did that with a vengeance. By the time I was five, Mama faithfully attended English classes at the Friendly House, a nonprofit agency in Phoenix that assisted immigrants to become citizens, offering citizenship and ESL classes. That's what she did on Tuesday and Thursday afternoons. She took off her apron and her housedress, put on her fancy downtown clothes, walked to the corner, got on the bus, and headed downtown for two hours of English oral practice, reading, and writing. She had waited years for the opportunity since the classes had always been full. And she had also waited for me to be old enough to stay with my older sisters and brother. Every day Mama did her homework, which consisted of writing out English sentences and doing assigned readings. On top of that work, Mama assigned herself the job of reading the newspaper. I watched her, every morning, spread the *Arizona Republic* on the kitchen table and begin reading it voraciously, looking up every word she didn't know in the huge, navy blue, 1948 unabridged *Webster's* that I sometimes used as a stool. She read every article, every column, every obituary, every comic—often asking me to listen so that I could tell her why it was funny. I was five then and knew enough English to help Mama read. Why did I know English? Because my teenage brothers and sisters did, because my friends in the neighborhood did, and because Mama tried her best to speak only English to me, so that, in her words, I wouldn't be mistreated in school the way her other children had been. She was doing her best to protect me by forcing me to become proficient enough in English to enter the culture of the school without the harassment and hostility my sisters and brother had encountered there.

My two older sisters and my brother had been corporally and verbally punished for speaking Spanish in school—spanked, rapped on the knuckles, made to pay fines, put in the corner, kept in from lunch, and ridiculed by both students and teachers (besides being forcibly sprayed for lice). My sisters and brother were all put into 1C, the infamous "English Only" isolation classroom for Mexicans who didn't know English. In this class, all content learning was prohibited. The purpose of the class was to teach English in English to a group of wide-eyed and confused Mexican children who didn't understand a word the teacher was saying until quite late in the year. The problem was that most children didn't get out of 1C in a year, or even two. Some children stayed there for three years, stuck in a holding tank until they had learned to speak English well enough to be mainstreamed. For one to three long years, these children lost the opportunity to learn in all of the conceptual areas of knowledge that they were biologically and mentally ready to learn at that age, had they been given the chance to learn in their own language. The educational outcome for my brother and sisters and for most other children treated in this manner was grim. It was no wonder that Hispanic/Latino children dropped out long before eighth grade and that graduation from high school was considered a wondrous achievement. English Only 1C was the wholesale discriminatory approach to educating Hispanics/Latinos that the Bilingual Education Act of 1968 sought to remedy—providing educational access for Hispanic/Latino and other language-minority children to help them begin learning immediately in the language they knew so that their school experience would be enriching rather than disabling. For good reason, this educational approach embraced Spanish and the Mexican American culture rather than shunning it or ignoring it completely.

Despite the fact that there has never been an adequate number of bilingual education programs, there has been an improvement in the educational achievement of language minorities, among them the many fortunate Hispanic/Latino children who have been saved from the pain of facing a new language and culture on the first day of school—who have been given the chance to learn in the code they know best and to master English as they progress in their education. For many socioeconomic and sociopolitical reasons, Hispanic/Latino children are still near the bottom of the educational ladder in the United States. If the only assistance they receive in the way of bilingual education is taken away, however, our society will regress to the bad old days of English Only, when blatant and subtle exclusion was intimately linked with the suppression of language.

For all of these reasons, I felt compelled to develop this collection and am grateful to a number of people who so graciously helped along the way. First, I would like to thank Agnese Nelms Haury, a local philanthropist and friend who assisted us financially in the preparation of the manuscript. I am deeply grateful for her deep and abiding commitment to social justice and the variety of projects in which she has shown an interest throughout the years.

I thank my son, Roberto José González, Truman Scholar and first-year law student at Stanford University, for his astute and critical readings of many of the articles in process and my introduction. His wide reading and intellectual curiosity about the radicalized politics of the language wars both inspired and aided me in my work. My daughter Marisa, A.B. Duke Scholar and sophomore at Duke University, I thank for her special insight and pride in her culture and language, and to my husband Bob, thank you especially for all the support and understanding during the many hectic months of work on this collection.

Many thanks go to Julie Gray, our technical assistant and proofreader extraordinaire, for her critical contribution in the preparation of the manuscript. Without her expert work, we would not have been able to finalize this project. I would also like to thank Patty Mathews for her helpful comments and suggestions and John Bichsel for his careful manuscript reading and editing. I am also indebted to my staff at the National Center for Interpretation, Testing, Research, and Policy for their great support in many important arenas—unlocking attachments we could not open; retyping tables that could not be transferred electronically; and delivering paper, disks, and toner for our voluminous drafts. Thanks to Socorro Hurtado, Jonathan Levy, and Armando Valles.

We also appreciate the thoughtful contributions of our authors, who took the time to produce articles that have special meaning for this volume. Their responsiveness to our suggestions and questions was heartening and truly made this otherwise formidable task pleasant. We extend our most sincere thanks to all of our contributors for their great cooperation, collaboration, and faith in us. I am honored to have worked with such a stellar group of scholars.

We are exceedingly grateful for the support and encouragement from Michael Greer, former NCTE Senior Editor of Books, and Karen Smith, former NCTE Associate Executive Director, both of whom remained excited about and committed to this volume despite our roving deadlines. Since putting such an extensive work together required a lot of time, we also had the pleasure of working with Zarina Hock, current Senior Editor at NCTE. NCTE is fortunate to have staff members who are so committed to equity and social justice and do the work of the Council so thoughtfully.

To my co-editor, graduate student, research assistant, and dear friend Ildikó Melis, I express my deepest thanks for making a tremendous commitment of time and energy to this project and for doing a magnificent job of library research and editing, working with authors, proofreading, and providing insightful comments on all the essays and my introduction in process. One of my greatest pleasures has been to renew my friendship with Ildikó. After her initial stay in the United States in 1988 as a student in the ESL graduate program and my teaching assistant at the University of Arizona, she returned from Hungary in 1996 to the University of Arizona to pursue a doctorate degree in rhetoric and composition. Her intensity, depth, and breadth of cross-disciplinary reading and her insight as a reader are remarkable, and her dedication to this project was pivotal to its completion. I am honored to count Ildikó Melis among the colleagues and friends I most respect and admire—she is a true scholar dedicated to discovering and revealing truths for the purpose of bettering the world we live in.

INTRODUCTION

ROSEANN DUEÑAS GONZÁLEZ
University of Arizona

*You're abusing that child and you're relegating her to
the position of housemaid.*

TEXAS JUDGE SAMUEL KISER,
August 1995, to Latina mother
Marta Laureano for speaking Spanish
at home to her five-year-old daughter

It has been almost two decades since Senator S. I. Hayakawa
first proposed that English become the official language of the
United States. Joining forces with the primary originator of the
group U.S. English, John H. Tanton, Hayakawa and Tanton
together fueled an incendiary movement that has steadily gathered momentum, putting in place Official English Language
statutes and amendments in twenty states across the United
States, proposing a series of English Language amendments at the
federal level, and transforming the sociopolitical landscape of the
United States by instigating anti-immigrant, antibilingual education and anti–affirmative action sentiments and initiatives.[1]
Through a highly financed campaign employing an "odd mixture
of shallow information, misinformation, tangled logic, illogic,
and xenophobia" (Donahue 1985, 100), U.S. English, as well as
other similar groups, has staged an incessant battle against a relatively powerless enemy—minority language speakers in the
United States, in particular Latinos and Asians.[2]

Some scholars recognize that the controversy surrounding Official English camouflages deeper, more systematic problems rooted in the political, social, racial, and economic structure of our nation. Unfortunately, many scholars, teachers, journalists, and politicians have underestimated the movement as the inconsequential voice of an aberrant few and have not vigorously labored against it. They are ignorant of the real danger of the official language movement—"its strategic and unrelenting use of a series of prevalent myths and stereotypes upon which it predicates its ideology" (González, Schott, and Vásquez 1988) in order to scapegoat and vilify minority populations of the United States. Because Spanish is the most widely spoken language in the United States after English, Latinos have been the main locus of anxieties over the status of English. U.S. English has created a viable enemy for "mainstream" America, one that many could, for one reason or another, rally against. U.S. English accomplished its goal by playing on and fueling an irrational fear of Latino language and culture—a Hispanophobia, as Ana Celia Zentella (1997) puts it. U.S. English documents frequently portray Spanish speakers as reluctant to learn English and assimilate into the "mainstream" culture. These documents warn readers that Latinos "pollute" the United States and threaten the economic, social, and political fabric of our society with their "prolific presence."

The mailings, newsletters, media coverage, Web sites, fundraising, and celebrity of the U.S. English movement are formidable and pervasive—difficult for politically uninformed or uncommitted scholars to debate but easy for the general public to accept. U.S. English effectively uses numerous myths and distortions to assert its major propositions and appeal to a broad audience. The most prominent of these is that foreign-language use will fragment and ultimately disunite the United States. This apocalyptic image resonated well with a society reeling from the sting of an economic downturn in the late 1980s, fearful of its fate in an increasingly globalized economy and disturbed by the changing racial, ethnic, and linguistic complexion of the populace. Another distortion is that the English language is in jeopardy—a ludicrous claim in the face of solid evidence that English is the indisputable lingua franca of business and technology around the world and that its hegemony is firmly grounded both in the United States and internationally. (There are approximately 600 million English speakers in the world, including those who speak English as a second or foreign language.) Proponents of the official language movement also promote the misconception that language minorities in the United States refuse to learn English. Although this assertion is untenable in the face of a demonstrable language shift, it has captured the imagination of a significant number of "mainstream" Americans whose own limited language and cultural experience provide them with little reason to disbelieve such claims. In reality, Latinos and other language-minority communities view learning English as indispensable for economic survival, so much so that the demand for ESL classes is vastly undermet across the nation. Learning English is a high priority for immigrants, an obvious key to the American dream in which they hope to participate. Those who have the financial means begin their studies before they arrive, while others labor intensely to learn enough to survive. So rapid and permanent is this English learning by immigrants by the second or third generation that Kenji Hakuta (1986) has aptly described this process as a hydraulic mechanism by which English is learned and the primary language is displaced entirely. This lamentable fact controverts a major precept of English Only, laying bare the movement's shallow intellectual foundations.

Language and Ideologies

Dynamism and multiculturalism are irreversible features of modern societies, and their rapid emergence threatens the survival of static and homogeneous cultural and social ideals. Stuart Hall (1997) believes that modernity is a perpetual struggle between those who constantly have to move, change, and evolve and those who use various ideologies of nationalism or racism to maintain "some system of supremacy . . . against this multicultural drift" (297). As a result, all modern societies, including the United States, develop various sites where the battle between the old and the new systems is waged in the form of contesting cultural values and assumptions.

The controversy over Official English is an important site of these cultural wars and polymorphous social struggles waged over the "essence" of America, over what forms of cultural and social life are valued and which are marginalized. The social ideologies promulgated by this movement have tapped into the nativist ideal of a homogenous, unified U.S. culture, drawing symbolic dividing lines between those who do and those who do not belong in this country. It is clear that the official language movement has identified a group that allegedly does not belong—Spanish-speaking Latinos, which then implicates Latinos as a whole.

The current backlash dynamics of politics in the United States has particularly heightened the ideological significance of language issues, reminiscent of the more overtly threatening forms of historical colonialism. The official language movement utilizes the discourses of colonialism, an ideology that, in order to dominate, disempowers some social groups through subjugation and "subjectification." Arteaga interprets English Only ideology from the perspective of colonial discourse criticism and sees Chicanos/Latinos as subjects of internal colonization in which, as defined by Rodolfo Acuña, "the dominant and subordinate populations are intermingled, so that there is no geographically distinct metropolis separate from the colony" (qtd. in Barrera 1979, 194). Latinos as well as other language minorities in the United States are identified as Other and are dominated by the oppressive practices of linguistic and racial politics of English Only, which "valorizes English and suppresses expression both in and about Spanish. English is elevated from the status of one language among languages . . . to that of sole and pervasive language in general. This is coupled with the simultaneous erasure of Spanish through the restriction of its use" (Arteaga 1994, 13). In a colonialist perspective, language, color, and religion represent some of the markers employed to subjugate people. For Hispanics/Latinos, language use is the central trait over which the dominant group can exert control.

The rollback of civil rights, which began in the late 1980s during the Reagan and Bush administrations and which is concomitant with the manifestations of exclusionary colonialist discourse, was a defining characteristic of the 1990s, undermining affirmative action programs in California, Texas, and Washington and increasing the risk of their curtailment nationwide. A major facet of this erosion is the successful attack against bilingual education peddled in California under the ominous slogan "English for the Children" that is expected to spill over into Arizona and other states with large language-minority populations.

This retreat from equity and social justice has been accompanied by the deterioration of the racial climate in the United States, evidenced by the fact that the number of racial hate groups and crimes was high in the 1990s. In 1998, for example, 7,947 hate crimes were reported to the FBI, of which 5,076 incidents were related to race, ethnicity, or national origin (FBI 1998). According to the Southern Poverty Law Center, in 1998 there were 537 racial hate groups engaged in racist behavior, an increase from 474 in 1997. These increases were fueled by the addition of 27 chapters of the Ku Klux Klan and 33 chapters of the Council of Conservative Citizens, a group that has called itself moderate but revealed itself as holding starkly racist views (United Nations 2000, 2–3). Just as the Council of Conservative Citizens and other white supremacist organizations have adopted "patriot" or antigovernment platforms, the official language movement masks its agenda with the "patriot" discourse of guardianship of English. Throughout U.S. history, such groups have taken refuge behind the cover of patriotism for the purpose of marginalizing minorities. After all, as cultural studies scholar Stuart Hall puts it, what can be objectionable about some Americans "defending a certain kind of 'Americanness,'" or "what could possibly be racist about" the claim that American children should speak "American language" in schools? (Hall 1997, 297).

It may well be that the official language movement attracts those in our society who find themselves threatened by the dramatic increase in the non-White population of the United States but who are reluctant to support more overt manifestations of racism. The 1990 census showed a 58 percent increase in Latinos, while the Asian population more than doubled (108 percent). The projections for 2020 are even more striking: Latinos and African Americans will comprise one-half of the U.S. population, and for the first time, the Latinos will constitute the largest minority group. The vitality and the visibility of the Hispanic/Latino culture, along with the increasingly multicultural complexion of our society, have generated new anxieties in the dominant culture, whose members may be eager to maintain their competitiveness, yet may not be willing to learn the new skills required in a multicultural social environment. Undoubtedly, the fear that persons of color will displace the hegemony of the White majority has contributed significantly to the conscious and unconscious decision making concerning issues of language difference. As cultural theorist Giroux (1992) warns, "populations traditionally defined as the Other are moving from the margin to the center and challenging the ethnocentric view that people of color can be relegated to the periphery of everyday life" (111). Because outright racism is still considered unacceptable by polite society, however, language is the most tenable channel for these Americans to vent more subtly their racist hostility. The official language movement offers a quasi-respectable ideology for legitimizing discriminatory measures against minority groups: the demand that the entire U.S. population speak the same language—and that its members speak that language correctly—seemingly cultivates unity and integration.

The real harm of the English Only movement is that it has fostered a climate in which the expression of prejudiced, jingoistic ideas is encouraged, cloaked in the patriotic rhetoric of "protecting English and the unity of our country." Even though Latinos have been "disappeared," their Spanish locates them. The cultural invisibility of Latinos promoted by the national media and the majority society is disturbed by the presence of the Latino voice speaking in Spanish. Over the past decade, the English Only movement has steadily intensified negative attitudes toward speakers of Spanish and other languages. Moreover, its ideology has nurtured a climate in which accents and other forms of variety in linguistic expression, including syntactic, lexical, or rhetorical varieties, are discriminated against or overtly ostracized. For example, the Oakland Ebonics proposal of 1998, which was a reasoned attempt to assist children to achieve academically and learn standard English through a shared understanding of their language variety, produced nationwide hysteria. Lost in the disproportionate response was the reason for the proposal: children were failing to connect with the school culture and needed assistance.

These developments reflect the crisis in the intellectual and sociocultural rationale for the civil rights/antiracist programs, a rationale which has suffered numerous defeats in the discursive struggles and contestations over the terms of the race/equity debate in the United States. Currently, conservative forces dominate the U.S. discourse on race, and society has largely accepted either tacitly or explicitly the "end of racism" hypothesis, which reduces racism to matters of individuals and bad attitudes, and promotes belief in the moral illegitimacy of race-conscious programs. Furthermore, this discourse solidifies what Stuart Hall calls a "racist common sense," which in turn legitimizes racial inequities by stigmatizing minority cultures and by racially coding issues such as crime and poverty. As teachers and intellectuals, we need to affirm and deepen the justification for policies that combat past and present forms of racism, discrimination, and exclusion. We need to see our dangerous potential to be accomplices in these ideological maneuvers as we set our own language policy in the classroom and in our daily encounters with "other" languages, dialects, accents, or rhetorical styles.

Linguistic Rights and Wrongs

As evidenced by Judge Kiser's admonitions in August 1995, quoted at the beginning of this introduction, the English Only movement has poisoned the national conversation about race, civil rights, and justice: it has made discussions on language a seemingly legitimate platform for delivering an exclusionary or anti-immigrant message. The disingenuous concern about English and the future of those who do not speak it has become an acceptable vehicle for people of every socioeconomic and professional level to express racist perspectives. T-shirts shout out slogans to Speak English Only; bars display signs advising customers that "Only English Is Spoken Here"; customers are not served because they speak Spanish; persons who do not speak English are denied the opportunity to apply for a driver's license; school boards, administrators, and teachers do not support children's need for bilingual education or for texts that connect to their cultural and linguistic reality. As these conflicts intensify, they also pose a challenge for our courts, which do not seem to be prepared to decide what should be considered right or wrong in matters of language use and policy. An increasing number of court cases have been filed by Americans who were fired for speaking their home language in the workplace, and the judges and juries who hear these cases often decide against these persons' right to use the language of their choice. Americans for whom English is a second language lack sufficient protection under the law because there is no explicit regulation prohibiting discrimination based on language. Furthermore, the courts have never recognized the essential nexus between national origin and language, nor do they consider language discrimination as a form of race discrimination. Therefore, even though English only rules in the workplace disproportionately and unfairly burden Hispanics/Latinos and other minorities, these rules are upheld at a disturbing rate (see Guadalupe Valdés's and Juan Perea's chapters in *Language Ideologies: Volume 2: History, Theory, and Policy* for more detail).

Outside the strictures of the legal domain, sociolinguistics offers three insightful perspectives from which multi- and bilingualism can be approached. As Ruiz (1984) proposes, language can be viewed as a problem, a potential source of social and political conflict. In this framework, the less dominant language is suppressed, and monolingualism is enforced. But language can also be looked on as a right. In this perspective, individuals' choice of language is similar to their choice of religion or expression and deserves the same equal protection under the law. Finally, language can be regarded as an asset or resource—a unique treasure trove of human insight and cognition. This approach values and encourages the learning and use of diverse languages. The conventional view in the United States, however, is that language is a problem, and the recent emergence of English Only propositions both confirms and exacerbates this position. On the other hand, those who refuse to see multilingualism as a problem have been hopeful that the right to use a language of one's choice is sufficiently protected by the constitutionally guaranteed rights to free speech or by civil rights law.

But as legal scholar Bill Piatt points out, the latter scenario has proven to be less than dependable. The same person's right to use a language other than English might be legally guaranteed in one situation (say, in a bar where she is having a conversation) but denied in another (she can be fired from her job for speaking Spanish, or her children can be flunked out of school for not speaking standard English). In addition, some businesses hire bilingual employees to better serve minority clients, yet their knowledge of another language is not rewarded; it is taken for granted. Piatt (1995) expresses concern that, since there is no explicitly defined "right to language" in the United States, language poses a problem in the courts that the conventional system of rights cannot adequately address: "It is as though the threads have not been woven into the fabric of the law, but rather surface as the bothersome loose ends to be plucked off when inconvenient" (886).

This lack of fit between law and language use obviously imperils the equal treatment of multilingual individuals. This situation warrants, according to Piatt, the creation of statutory provisions protecting language rights, or at least the establishment of a general principle that applies to all cases of enforced monolingualism. Before imposing monolingualism on multilingual individuals, the proponents of such policy must have the burden of demonstrating that the danger to person and property caused by the use of another language outweighs the individual's right to free expression (Piatt 1995, 905).

On the international level, proponents of human rights have also attempted to provide some general principles that would address the grievances of language and ethnic minorities throughout the world. The 1984 United Nations International Covenant on Civil and Political Rights, for example, followed the well-established path of *individual* civil rights and declared that "persons belonging to ethnic, religious or linguistic minorities" should not be denied the right "to enjoy their own culture, to profess and practice their own religion, or to use their own language" (§27). More recently, however, these rights have also been recognized as *collective* rights. This shift in conceptualization was driven by the recognition that an individual's freedom to choose a language is determined by that individual's complex socioeconomic and institutional context that values and rewards some languages or language varieties while stigmatizing, marginalizing, or excluding others. The declaration of linguistic human rights was primarily motivated by an increasing international concern about the large-scale loss of minority languages and cultures in the world. Its advocates often use the argument that endangered cultures and languages, like endangered species or historic landmarks, are assets of the global heritage, and therefore deserve equal if not more protection.

The adoption of principles from the linguistic human rights framework has been impeded by the fact that the declaration has never been signed by the United States, nor has there been significant public demand for such ratification. As Guadalupe Valdés (see *Volume 2: History, Theory, and Policy*) and others point out, however, the gap between "civil rights" and "human rights" is not as unbridgeable as it may seem, and the specification of language rights in a system of civil rights is not inconceivable. But the reconsideration of language rights will demand a shift of perspective in U.S. society. Unless we, just like the international community advocating linguistic human rights, accept that multilingualism is an asset and that monolingualism is not a prerequisite of social unity, the extension of legal protection to cover language discrimination will not take place.

The English Only movement is more likely to violate human rights than to protect them. Moreover, it is probably the only movement in the world designed to promote an already dominant language. Therefore, English Only cannot logically be viewed as anything but a convenient mechanism to revoke any and all legislative initiatives designed to make the transition of immigrants into the "mainstream" both easier and consistent with U.S. standards of justice and fairness. The purpose of English Only, though never expressed, is to eradicate the few institutions in place in our society designed to bridge the linguistic gap for limited English speakers. It has created a hostile environment for Spanish speakers and other linguistic minorities that further marginalizes them and that aims to block their access to education, to the justice system, to employment, to the political process, and to social services (González 1990).

As Americans, we like to think that we are concerned about the violation of human rights in other parts of the world, but we do not feel the same kind of empathy for children and adults who come to this country seeking opportunity and fairness, and we are often reluctant to grant them the consideration we would wish for ourselves if we were in the same situation. Every day children who speak other languages attempt to join the school culture. For many of these children, school means a set of negative experiences culminating in poor achievement, alienation, and eventual dropout. But as Earl Shorris (1992) reminds us, these children do not "drop out"; they have simply never entered the school culture. They are turned away by school administrators and classroom teachers whose own linguistic, educational, and cultural experiences have not prepared them to understand the obstacles these children encounter as they struggle not only to become socially and linguistically acceptable but also to learn a whole new way of perceiving reality through the lens of a new language and culture. As we are reminded by Sonia Nieto, school culture is but a microcosm of the larger society, in which teachers (and administrators to some degree) function within particular structures over which they have very little power (Nieto 1996). Teachers of language-minority students, however, can monitor and eradicate unintentional and intentional discrimination through self-awareness. Such self-examination may lead teachers to understand how these children would greatly benefit from bilingual instruction so that they can learn subject matter in an understandable code while they are learning English. At the very least, the children deserve a culturally and linguistically sensitive curriculum as well as respect and tolerance of their difference, because the lack of this affirmation hurts personal as well as academic development. Gloria Anzaldúa (1987) characterizes her painful experiences with English as "linguistic terrorism": "[I]f you want to really hurt me, talk badly about my language. . . . I am my language. Until I can take pride in my language, I cannot take pride in myself" (59).

Why do we question that a child's primary language plays a crucial role in his or her education? Why do we refuse to accept that employees have the right to speak their home language on the job under reasonable conditions? Why do we fail to see the plain humanity of assisting non-English speakers to participate in the political process by providing a bilingual ballot? For linguistic rights to be respected, and for all members of our society to be protected from language discrimination, it is time to reconsider the ideal of unity as it is promoted by English Only advocates and to challenge the notion of a homogeneous U.S. nationalism, to rethink, as David Saldivar (1997) suggests in *Border Matters*, the "linear narratives of immigration, assimilation, and nationhood . . . in terms of multifaceted migrations across borders" (1). As Iris M. Young (1990) points out, homogeneous nations are not necessarily harmonious nations. The maintenance of homogeneity requires assimilation to the dominant values and puts the unassimilated groups at a serious disadvantage. The demand that "persons transform their sense of identity in order to assimilate," says Young, is "an unreasonable and unjust requirement of citizenship," not to mention that it is likely to become an infinite source of hostility and conflict (178). Perhaps we need to enunciate that unity—as it is promoted by English Only advocates of "one nation, one language"—is obsolete, unfair, and needs to be challenged. Maybe it is time to recognize that it is more important to understand each other than to speak the same language. Such an understanding can be based on a common vision of an egalitarian United States that embraces everyone irrespective of their language by providing access to the benefits and privileges of U.S. civic culture. As constitutional scholar Kenneth L. Karst (1986) stresses, "the only vision of America capable of being shared by all of us is a vision in which all of us belong" (368).

Hispanophobia

Modern societies are irreversibly diverse, or, as Stuart Hall (1997) puts it, they are "hybridized and mongrelized to their roots." This causes anxiety in some groups, which therefore need a "defense against living with difference." This anxiety explains why modern societies witness many forms of what Hall calls a "retreat into the bunker of cultural and racist nationalism" (297).

The English Only movement has particularly scapegoated Hispanics/Latinos, advancing a new wave of Hispanophobia through false accusations and more openly hostile linguistic restrictions. The most recent incarnations of the U.S. English campaign, however, are more careful about directly evoking these "mainstream" anxieties. In fact, few movements with racist, nativist tendencies have been so comfortable and successful while speaking in the name of the groups that their agenda targets. The official language movement, despite some notable exceptions, has been diligent in distancing itself from racism and nativism. The prominent place that Hispanics/Latinos occupy in the movement's public relations has been no small factor in its disavowal of racist motives. Because its ostensive concerns have to do with such venerable American values as unity, citizenship, and the melting pot, the Official English movement has been remarkably successful in creating the impression that it has nothing to do with racism or xenophobia.

The conspicuous presence of several Hispanic/Latino spokespersons in the English Only movement, such as Richard Rodriguez, Linda Chavez, and Jaime Escalante, has been effectively used to throw hesitant potential followers off the racist scent. The "our best supporters are Hispanic Americans" ploy continues to work, year after year; only the mascots change. The most enduring symbol has been Richard Rodriguez, the Hispanic American journalist well known for his works depicting his bilingual childhood (*Hunger of Memory* 1982; *Days of Obligation: An Argument with My Mexican Father* 1992). Richard Rodriguez did much to confer legitimacy on the English Only movement, using his private culture/private language, public identity/public language dichotomy as a central theme. His impressive prose earned him a stable and token place in anthologies widely used in high schools and universities, and he has tantalized a large readership with his emotional narrative of an immigrant finding himself, at the end of a painful journey, an English-speaking Hispanic American who is completely estranged from who he was, whose intimacy with his Spanish-speaking family and culture has been lost and turned into faded memories. In 1986, at the National Council of Teachers of English Annual Convention, a huge crowd of English teachers filled the ballroom to hear Rodriguez tell them that English is the "glue" that keeps this country together. Rodriguez was even more emblematic of English Only rhetoric when he argued that all immigrants come to the United States by their own choice and therefore have an obligation to learn English even at the expense of their own language and culture. More recently, however, Rodriguez has reversed his position on the English Only movement because he recognized the destructive consequences of having supported it.

Because most Americans lack any serious second-language learning experience (beyond the usual skirmishes with a foreign language requirement in high school and college), it is difficult for "mainstream" America to understand that it takes time for a child or teenager to learn a second language well enough to succeed in school, and that adults take even more time to learn a foreign language well enough to work, to vote, and to participate in the justice system without depending on their first language. Rodriguez's emotional memoirs provide a vivid account of the affective and cognitive burdens of linguistic and cultural assimilation. But no matter how compelling it is, his narrative is only one of the many stories language minorities can tell us about how the domains of public and private language, culture, and identity conflict or overlap in their lives. Moreover, there are minorities who do not wish to experience the painful loss Rodriguez believes to be inevitable, and who do not see their cultural/linguistic identity as a problem to be overcome but rather as an asset to build on. There are Americans who want to redefine the dividing line between private and public language. For Gloria Anzaldúa (1987), Chicanos are a "complex heterogeneous people" who speak many languages and switch codes many times as they move along the domains of work, family, and school, yet they also maintain a unified identity and language. "For some of us," says Anzaldúa, "language is a homeland closer than the Southwest" (55–56). Apparently, some Spanish-speaking Americans have found better ways to counter Hispanophobia than by self-denial. It is our responsibility as teachers and educators to listen to their voices, especially at times when they are hard to hear through the general noise of English Only.

Purpose of the Book

As we enter a new millennium, we contemplate the major issues that enable us to move forward—or prevent us from doing so—as a nation of diverse peoples toward the construction of a democracy that takes into account the rights and needs of all of its members. The official language movement embraces a set of ideologies and policies that are counterproductive to our work as educators and nation builders because it devalues the language and presence of minority persons in our society and in our most important societal institutions—the schools, the workplace, the government, the judicial system, and the voting booth. For this reason, we have gathered a set of essays and present them in *Language Ideologies: Critical Perspectives on the Official English Movement* in two volumes to shed new light on and reinvigorate the scrutiny of this movement. We divided the essays into two groups, the first one examining how an official language—and the assumptions that motivate such policy—would affect education, and society in general (*Volume 1: Education and the Social Implications of Official Language*). The second group of essays comprises various theoretical, historical, and political aspects of the Official English movement, including some international comparisons (*Volume 2: History, Theory, and Policy*). The division of essays does not represent separation. In fact, we believe that the two volumes supplement each other well and are equally important. Those educators, language specialists, or ESL specialists who start with Volume 1 will find just as much theory and research in these essays as those who begin with Volume 2 because they are interested in issues of social justice or in the relationship between language and ideology. Likewise, the educator, language specialist, or ESL specialist will find these broader issues just as relevant as the ones discussed in Volume 1, which are more directly related to the world of classrooms.

As we have pointed out, the resurrection of debates over Official English is often concurrent with social anxiety about the economic condition and national security of our country, or with the presence and social visibility of immigrants. The idea that the United States should declare English as its official language has had its ebbs and flows. The fervor of the advocates subsides whenever there is something more interesting at hand to divert attention, such as a political scandal, an international conflict, a scientific breakthrough, or another outbreak of gunfire in our public schools. As time goes by, however, the flares of excitement about Official English seem to have a cumulative effect. Consequently, as Dennis Baron states in Volume 2, "the U.S. is moving closer than it ever has to accepting some sort of formal language policy at the federal level." The possible realization of this prediction compels us to consider the valuable insights assembled in these essays.

Overview of Volume 1

Volume 1: Education and the Social Implications of Official Language was designed for educators, administrators, ESL experts, scholars, and all those who are concerned about language as a source and product of discrimination in our schools and society. The Update section contains a demographic overview provided by Dorothy Waggoner, who uses data from the last U.S. census to demonstrate the changing linguistic and ethnic composition of the U.S. population. James Crawford analyzes a recent political event, the dubious victory of English Only in California. Crawford points out some new and alarming features in the rhetoric of California English Only and raises the issue of the responsibility of the media in promoting the belief that less bilingual education will lead to more and better English. Finally, Carol Schmid interprets the history of bilingual education and language conflicts in the United States as the outcome of interplay between larger social forces of power and domination.

The Research and Politics section begins with a report by Eugene E. García, who writes from the unique position of education administrator and scholar. His chapter shows how administrators' pursuit of efficient, cost effective, and tangible educational outcomes is challenged by the complexities of research about what good education entails. Thomas Scovel provides a meticulous and rational analysis of "the younger, the better" myth that has been the dominant assumption of the public and the media about language acquisition both in the United States and in many other parts of the world, no matter how much contrary evidence has been accumulated in linguistic research. Similarly, Stephen D. Krashen's analysis of the conflicting definitions and evaluations of bilingual education reveals that the public is seriously misinformed about the potential and the actual success of these programs.

English Only does make a difference, but as each of the three chapters in the Politics, Economy, and the Classroom section shows, such politics can only make things worse. Elliot L. Judd argues that ESL education is already in a disadvantaged position, especially ESL for adult immigrants. The relatively powerless group of adult immigrants does not have much influence on the distribution of resources, and as a result, there is already a waiting list for those who want to better their socioeconomic opportunities by improving their English. English Only can only create a hostile environment in which both learning the language and assimilation become more painful and difficult. Elsa Roberts Auerbach's essay takes us into the ESL classroom where English Only has been a policy for a long time, although no theory of language acquisition or pedagogy of language learning has ever proved that the best way of learning English is to silence, humiliate, or ignore competence in another language. In fact, as Auerbach's research shows, quite the contrary is the case: adult learners benefit from relying on their first language as a source, and respect for difference in general helps learners overcome anxiety in the classroom. Arturo Gonzalez studied the relationship between economic success and the acquisition of English skills and found that English-language acquisition is economically driven, yet not all of the four basic language skills are equally rewarded on the job market. Economists, school administrators, and language experts can draw many important conclusions from Gonzalez's findings, yet none of these implications indicates that legal enforcement of language use would be beneficial.

Rosina Lippi-Green's chapter in the section What Difference Does Difference Make? leads a series of discussions on the social value of linguistic difference. Lippi-Green demonstrates how the definitions of the African American Variety of English (AAVE) move out of the linguistic realm into the cultural and political realms for the simple reason that leadership and success are associated with standard English (SE). The assumption that AAVE is inferior cannot be substantiated in any meaningful linguistic terms, yet it dominates the perception of the public as well as that of many AAVE speakers. Lippi-Green's essay points out that social perception overrules linguistic description, and it also eliminates distinctions between language and variety that linguists have been painstakingly trying to define. AAVE is a variety of English, but it does not enjoy more social prestige than the dispossessed Spanish of the speakers who are the subjects of Frances R. Aparicio's chapter. One of Aparicio's insightful contributions is the demonstration of how the same language (Spanish) has different social prestige depending on whether it is laboriously learned as a foreign language by English speakers (advantage) or learned in the home of Spanish-speaking immigrants (disadvantage). Three other essays in this section discuss linguistic difference in terms of pedagogy and classroom experience. Gail Okawa argues that language awareness, in the broad sense of including awareness of social values attached to language, should be an essential component of teacher training. Victoria Cliett and Louise Rodríguez Connal struggle with diversity and linguistic difference in the writing classroom. Cliett confronts her learners with a three-dimensional model of language that allows for expression of diversity and individual variety; Connal uses transcultural experience as a model of teaching students respect for difference in language and expression in general.

Victor Villanueva's afterword summarizes what the reader can learn from this book. In fact, as he states, there is nothing new in these essays that one would not intuit and that has not been verified by research. Yet we need to revisit the myths that recurrently influence public opinion because apparently new generations do not necessarily learn from the lessons of the past. Villanueva closes his essay on a few personal notes about the losses and gains involved in being bilingual. These ideas deserve attention, more thought, and more discussion from all of us who care about the linguistic and cultural assets of the future generations:

> One gives up nothing by being adept at two languages or more. One gains. So many have had to give up so much to be part of the United States. It was the price when going back meant prison or famine, at best an expensive and long trip on a steamship. That price is no longer necessary. Why deny the children of a richness because it had been denied to the parents? The story that begins "my grandfather had to" is wrongheaded. We don't limit on the basis of our ancestors' limits. We break through the limitations of the past.

Notes

1. For an updated list of these statutes and bills, see Crawford's Web site: *http://ourworld.compuserve.com/homepages/JWCrawford/lang-leg.htm.*

2. All chapters in this book have been edited to conform to NCTE's house style for books, including editing the names of various racial and ethnic groups in the United States in accordance with sensitive and bias-free usage. We deviate from this practice only when the authors refer to specific studies, where changing these names would misrepresent results. In all other cases, names of racial and ethnic groups have been changed to comply with *The Dictionary of Bias-Free Usage* and NCTE's Policy Statement on People of Color, among other sources.

Works Cited

Anzaldúa, Gloria. 1987. *Borderlands/La frontera: The New Mestiza.* San Francisco: Aunt Lute.

Arteaga, Alfred. 1994. "Introduction: Here and Now." In Alfred Arteaga, ed., *An Other Tongue: Nation and Ethnicity in the Linguistic Borderlands.* Durham: Duke University Press.

Barrera, Mario. 1979. *Race and Class in the Southwest: A Theory of Racial Inequality.* Notre Dame: University of Notre Dame Press.

Donahue, Thomas S. 1985. "'U.S. English': Its Life and Works." *International Journal of the Sociology of Language* 56: 99–112.

Federal Bureau of Investigation. 1998. *Unified Crime Reports* [Online]: http://www.fbi.gov/ucr/hr97all.pdf.

Giroux, Henry A. 1992. *Border Crossings: Cultural Workers and the Politics of Education.* New York: Routledge.

González, Roseann D. 1990. "In the Aftermath of the ELA: Stripping Language Minorities of Their Rights." In Harvey A. Daniels, ed., *Not Only English: Affirming America's Multilingual Heritage.* Urbana, IL: National Council of Teachers of English. 49–60.

González, Roseann D., Alice Schott, and Victoria Vásquez. 1988. "The English Language Amendment: Examining Myths." *English Journal* 77(3): 24–30.

Hakuta, Kenji. 1986. *Mirror of Language: The Debate on Bilingualism.* New York: Basic Books.

Hall, Stuart. 1997. "Subjects in History: Making Diasporic Identities." In Wahneema Lubiano, ed., *The House That Race Built: Black Americans, U.S. Terrain.* New York: Pantheon Books. 289–301.

Karst, Kenneth L. 1986. "Paths to Belonging: The Constitution and Cultural Identity." *North Carolina Law Review* 64: 303–77.

Nieto, Sonia. 1996. *Affirming Diversity: The Sociopolitical Context of Multicultural Education.* New York: Longman.

Piatt, Bill. 1995. "Toward Domestic Recognition of a Human Right to Language." In Antoinette Sedillo Lopez, ed., *Latino Language and Education: Communication and the Dream Deferred.* New York: Garland Publishing.

Ruiz, Richard. 1984. "Orientations in Language Planning." *NABE Journal* 8(2): 15–34.

Saldívar, José David. 1997. *Border Matters: Remapping American Cultural Studies.* Berkeley: University of California Press.

Shorris, Earl. 1992. *Latinos: A Biography of the People.* New York: W.W. Norton.

Southern Poverty Law Center. 1998. "The Year in Hate" [Online]. SPLC Intelligence Report: Winter. http://www.splcenter.orgcgi-bin/goframe.pl?dirname=/.&pagename=sitemap.html.

United Nations. 1984. *International Covenant on Civil and Political Rights* [Online]: http://www.oil.ca/rights/iccpr.html.

———. 2000. "Mainstreaming Hate: CCC Reveals Its True Color: White" [Online]: http://www.splcenter.org.

Young, Iris M. 1990. *Justice and the Politics of Difference.* Princeton, NJ: Princeton University Press.

Zentella, Ana Celia. 1997. "The Hispanophobia of the Official English Movement in the US." *International Journal of the Sociology of Language* (127): 71–86.

I

UPDATE

The debate as to whether English should be the official language of the United States has a long history, and those who have been following these public discussions are already familiar with most of the issues these discussions have brought to the surface. On the other hand, because of this long history, new generations of students and educators have come of age and require an introduction to this continuing cultural battle. The chapters in the Update section represent a balance between a review of history and a presentation of what is relatively new. Dorothy Waggoner's work is based on the 1980 and 1990 decennial census data, which show a dramatic increase in the number of both minority and foreign-born populations in the United States. Waggoner's analysis of the numbers confirms that diversity is and has for a century been a fact in our country. Although it will take a while until similar data of the 2000 census are available for analysis, Waggoner's conclusions are not likely to be undermined by new statistics. As she argues, limited English proficiency will only be a problem in the United States if the educational system refuses to reflect the demographic changes and if society in general fails "to incorporate the linguistic and cultural strength of all our population in everything we do."

James Crawford's chapter examines the change in official English rhetorical strategies. The target of his analysis is a relatively recent and controversial victory of English Only politics, demonstrated by the passing of Proposition 227 in California. The California law was not about making English the official language; such an amendment had already been passed in the state. Instead, by imposing "a draconian approach to teaching English in schools," Proposition 227 was "an act of hostility against California's minority population." In addition, a particularly disturbing aspect of this legislation is, as Crawford points out, that it restricts local flexibility and parental choice and also makes resistance by educators virtually impossible. With all these concerns in mind, one might wonder how Proposition 227 could garner such overwhelming public support (61 percent Yes versus 39 percent No). One of Crawford's answers is that the proposition and its supporters took advantage of California's general anxiety about the state's latest demographic trends, and the votes were predominantly motivated by nativist and anti-immigrant attitudes. Another answer lies in the overtly simplistic rhetoric of the English for the Children initiative that successfully and deceitfully tapped into the goals and desires of language minorities and had enormous emotional appeal. Crawford analyzes the overt fallacies of this political discourse, but he also draws attention to another unsettling novelty of the California case: the ineffectual campaign strategy employed by the supporters of bilingual education failed to counter Ron Unz's rhetorical maneuvers.

In Chapter 3, Carol Schmid outlines the social and historical background of the hegemonic ideologies that today seem to control the assimilation of both adult and young learners of English in the United States. These language ideologies are true reflections of the recurrent trends of "Americanization" of both immigrant and indigenous populations because the dominant although not official language policy in the United States has, ever since the earliest days, expressed "ambivalent attitudes toward languages other than English" and because the English language has become "a symbol of what it means to be American" in the late twentieth and early twenty-first centuries. Thus one outcome of this update is that the numbers clearly show an ongoing trend of increasing diversity in the population of the United States. Next, the California case illustrates some disturbing responses to this trend: a political campaign that carefully steers away from overt hostility toward minorities while disguising its agenda in emotional narratives and slogans, and an ineffective opposition strategy that shies away from gearing the public discourse toward more positive and rational discussions of education for minorities. Finally, Carol Schmid's review points out a common thread in the U.S. history of language matters, a thread that reveals tensions and anxieties of national identity behind the issues of language. Although some of the essays in this collection point out that not all Official English proponents are motivated by racism and anti-immigrant hostility (e.g., Jim Cummins, in the preface, and James Crawford), the ultimate outcome of the information provided in the Update section is that such ideologies, as well as lack of strong support for diversity and tolerance, have always been associated with the English Only movement.

CHAPTER ONE

The Demographics of Diversity in the United States

DOROTHY WAGGONER

Increasing diversity characterizes the population of the United States. Minority racial and ethnic groups are growing, both in size and in number of different groups. Immigration is increasing, bringing people with diverse backgrounds and new languages to the United States. To some, diversity represents the fulfillment of the meaning of the United States embodied in our motto, "One from many." To others, it is a source of the fear that somehow those who are different will fracture our unity as a nation. The responses of the latter are draconian and contradictory. They want to limit the rights of immigrants, deprive immigrant children of access to public education, abolish affirmative action, and outlaw programs that help limited-English-proficient children acquire English. They want to legislate the use of English by means of the English Only and the Official English movements. But diversity is a fact. It is homegrown. Even if all immigration were to be prohibited, the country would continue to become more diverse because minority populations are increasing naturally.

This chapter provides information from the 1980 and 1990 decennial censuses and other Bureau of the Census sources to document the growth of diversity in the United States, offering the numbers and growth rates of racial/ethnic populations, the foreign born, language-minority populations, and people who speak languages other than English in their homes at the end of the twentieth century. It considers the projections of the continuing growth of minority populations and increasing diversity in the twenty-first century.

The questions asked of home speakers of non-English languages about their English-speaking ability in 1980 and 1990 provide a surrogate measure of the number of children and adults, both native-born and newcomer, needing help to acquire or improve their English proficiency and fulfill their potential in our society. The chapter, accordingly, includes information on the changing numbers of people who speak English less than very well and of those who do not speak English at all. These are the people for whom special programs are needed and will continue to be needed. What we do for home speakers of non-English languages who have difficulty in English will determine whether they become a part of our society and able to make their contribution, or whether their lack of English skills will continue to separate many of them from the opportunities and rights of U.S. citizenship. This chapter will help policymakers, school administrators, and community advocates understand the reality of diversity and consider its implications for the future.

The Growth of Racial/Ethnic Minorities

Racial and ethnic minority populations in the United States are increasing faster than the White majority population. As illustrated in Figure 1.1, between 1980 and 1990, the White population increased by about 4 percent. The Asian and Pacific Islander population, in contrast, almost doubled; the Hispanic/Latino population increased by more than half again, and the American Indian and Alaska Native population grew by a quarter.[1] In 1980 White majority people constituted 80 percent of the total population; by 1990 they were 76 percent of the total and still losing ground to the minorities (Census 1983, 1992). Table 1.1 gives the population figures for 1980 and 1990 and the ten-year growth rates for the racial/ethnic groups.

Racial/ethnic groups are younger than the White population, and the numbers of young children in the various groups are increasing at different rates, reflecting the proportions of the populations of childbearing age as well as differing fertility rates. In 1990 there were fewer White children under age fifteen than in 1980, but there were 6.1 percent more African

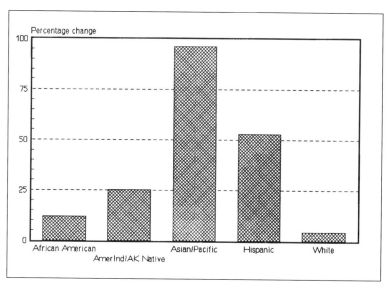

FIGURE 1.1. *Growth rates of racial/ethnic populations, 1980 to 1990.*

American children, 22.9 percent more American Indian and Alaska Native children, 38.9 percent more Hispanic/Latino children, and 81.4 percent more Asian and Pacific Islander children (Census 1983, 1993d).

The growth of the Asian and Pacific Islander population has come largely from immigration. In 1990 two-thirds of the people who identified themselves as Asians in the census were born

TABLE 1.1. Population in 1980 and 1990 and Ten-Year Growth Rates, by Racial/Ethnic Group, United States

Group	1980	1990	Growth rate
Total	226,545,805	248,709,873	9.8
African American	26,091,857	29,216,293	12.0
American Indian and Alaska Native	1,432,807	1,793,773	25.2
Asian and Pacific Islander	3,550,605	6,968,359	96.3
Hispanic	14,603,683	22,354,059	53.1
White	180,602,838	188,128,296	4.2
Other non-Hispanic	264,015	249,093	−5.7

SOURCES: U.S. Bureau of the Census, *1980 Census of Population, General Social and Economic Characteristics, United States Summary*, Washington, D.C.: U.S. Government Printing Office, 1983; U.S. Bureau of the Census, *1990 Census of Population and Housing, Summary Population and Housing Characteristics, United States*, Washington, D.C.: U.S. Government Printing Office, 1992.

abroad and more than half of them (38 percent of the total) had arrived between 1980 and 1990 (Census 1993a). The majority of Hispanics/Latinos, however, were born in this country. Nearly two-thirds of the 1990 population were native born, including people living on the mainland who were born in Puerto Rico (Census 1993c).[2] Among Whites, Blacks, American Indians, and Alaska Natives, 5 percent or fewer in 1990 were born abroad (Census 1992; Lapham 1993a).

The Foreign-Born Population

The 1980s saw increased immigration to the United States. Newcomers fled troubled areas of the world and became refugees in this country. They also came, as immigrants always have, seeking economic opportunity. Between 1980 and 1990, the number of foreign-born people increased from 14 million to 19.8 million—a growth rate of about 40 percent (Census 1984, 1993b). As Figure 1.2 illustrates, the growth rate of the foreign-born population was about the same as that of the population of people speaking

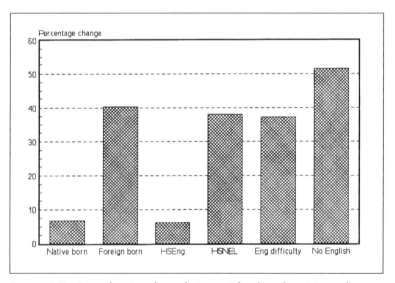

FIGURE 1.2. *Growth rates of populations with selected nativity and linguistic characteristics, 1980 to 1990.*

non-English languages at home (HSNELs in the figure), many of whom are part of the foreign-born population. The numbers of foreign-born people are still growing: they grew by another 20 percent, to 24.6 million, between 1990 and 1996, according to Bureau of the Census estimates. These increases brought the proportion of immigrants in the total population up from a low of 4.8 percent in 1970 to 9.3 percent in 1996, but still short of the proportion in 1910, when immigrants constituted 14.7 percent of the total population (Census 1997). Table 1.2 shows the estimated numbers of foreign-born people by countries of birth with at least 200,000 in the population in 1990.

Recent immigrants come from different areas of the world than immigrants who arrived in earlier years. They bring new cultures and languages to our country. At the turn of the century, the vast majority of newcomers to the United States were born in Europe. In 1980, Europe and the Soviet Union still contributed

TABLE 1.2. Estimated Numbers of Foreign-Born People in 1980 and 1990 and Ten-Year Growth Rates, by Selected Country of Birth, United States

Country of birth	1980	1990	Growth rate
Total, all countries	14,080,000	19,767,000	40.4
Mexico	2,199,000	4,298,000	95.4
Philippines	501,000	913,000	82.0
Canada	843,000	745,000	–11.6
Cuba	608,000	737,000	21.2
Germany	849,000	712,000	–16.2
United Kingdom	669,000	640,000	–4.3
Italy	832,000	581,000	–30.2
Korea	290,000	568,000	96.0
Vietnam	231,000	543,000	135.1
China	286,000	530,000	85.2
El Salvador	94,000	465,000	392.8
India	206,000	450,000	118.6
Poland	418,000	388,000	–7.1
Dominican Republic	169,000	348,000	105.7
Jamaica	197,000	334,000	69.8
Soviet Union	406,000	334,000	–17.8
Japan	222,000	290,000	30.8
Colombia	144,000	286,000	99.4
Guatemala	63,000	226,000	257.9
Haiti	92,000	225,000	143.9
Portugal	177,000	210,000	18.4

NOTE: Percentages calculated on unrounded numbers.
SOURCES: U.S. Bureau of the Census, *1980 Census of Population, Detailed Population Characteristics, United States Summary*, Washington, D.C.: U.S. Government Printing Office, 1984, and *1990 Census of Population, The Foreign-Born Population in the United States*, Washington, D.C.: U.S. Government Printing Office, 1993.

about the same proportion of the total foreign-born population as the Western Hemisphere (37 percent); Asia contributed 18 percent (Census 1984). By 1996 the Western Hemisphere accounted for more than half (52 percent), Asia for 27 percent, and European countries only for 17 percent (Census 1997), as shown in Figure 1.3.

The largest number of immigrants born in a single country come from Mexico. In 1980 people born in Mexico numbered 2.2 million and constituted 16 percent of the total foreign-born population (Census 1984). By 1996 their numbers had grown to 6.8 million, or 27 percent of the total (Census 1997). Growing even faster and swelling the numbers of Hispanics/Latinos in this country, however, are people born in El Salvador, Guatemala, and other Central American countries, and people born in the Dominican Republic. In 1980 Salvadoran-born people numbered only about 94,000; by 1990 the population had almost quadrupled, and by 1996 it reached an estimated 701,000 (Census 1984, 1993b, 1997). The increase in immigration from Central America in the early 1990s resulted from the political violence in that area. The devastation caused by Hurricane Mitch in the fall of 1998

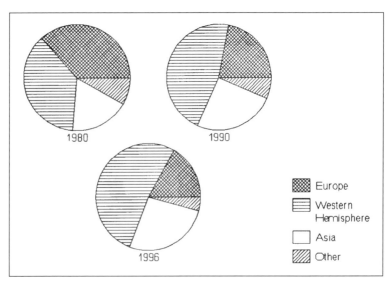

FIGURE 1.3. *Regions of birth of foreign-born populations, 1980, 1990, and 1996.*

may increase the numbers of immigrants from that region still more.

Most recent immigrants from the Western Hemisphere were born in Spanish-speaking countries. Their arrival has reinforced the Spanish-language minority in the United States, and it has added a diversity of national origins. To the extent that some immigrants from Western Hemisphere countries speak indigenous languages as their first languages, immigration from the Western Hemisphere has also added to linguistic diversity. The increase in immigration from Asian countries has brought speakers of languages previously nearly unknown here and has greatly increased cultural diversity.

As Table 1.2 shows, among Asian groups the populations of people from Southeast Asia increased the most. Many of these people, like many from Central America in the early 1990s, were refugees from war and political violence. The Vietnamese-born population increased by 135 percent between 1980 and 1990; it grew to about 740,000, or by 36 percent, between 1990 and 1996 (Census 1984, 1993b, 1997). Other Southeast Asian populations, such as those from Cambodia and Laos, grew even more during the 1980s: that of Cambodians from an estimated 20,000 to 119,000 and that of Laotians from 55,000 to 172,000 (Census 1984, 1993b). While not refugees, many immigrants arrived from India in the 1980s: the number of immigrants born in India more than doubled between 1980 and 1990 and reached about 757,000 by 1996, a growth of an additional 68 percent (Census 1984, 1993b, 1997).

Two traditional sources of the Asian population in the United States—the Philippines and China—have continued to provide newcomers: people born in the Philippines, about a half a million in 1980, numbered 1.2 million in 1996, and Chinese-born people, 286,000 in 1980, totaled 801,000 in 1996 (Census 1984, 1997).

Language-Minority People in the United States

Together with immigration, which brought many new language-minority people to the United States in the 1980s, the population living in households in which at least one person speaks a language other than English has also grown. There are now at least a third more such people than there were in 1980. In 1980 this population numbered 35.3 million; it grew to 47.1 million, or by 34 percent, throughout the 1980s, as shown in Table 1.3. The highest ten-year growth rate—50 percent—was that in the population of young children under five years of age, one or both of whose parents speak a language other than English at home. The number of school-age children who speak the home language increased by 38 percent, and in 1990 they constituted nearly two-thirds of all youngsters living in language-minority households (Census 1984, 1995a).

In all, there were 10 million language-minority children and youth of school age in 1990. There were 3.9 million children under age five in 1990 who became part of the school-age population in the 1990s (Census 1995a). Although information on possible difficulty speaking English is available only for those reported to speak the non-English language at home, and although no objective national information is available on English-language proficiency, including proficiency in reading and writing as well as speaking and understanding, all language-minority children and youth are potentially limited in English proficiency. They represent the population that may need special help to progress in school and achieve their full potential in U.S. society.

TABLE 1.3. Estimated Numbers of Language-Minority People in 1980 and 1990 and Ten-Year Growth Rates, by Age Group and Home Language, United States

Age group and home language usage	1980	1990	Growth rate
Total	35,306,000	47,122,000	33.5
Under 5	2,562,000	3,856,000	50.5
Aged 5 to 17	8,123,000	9,985,000	22.9
Speak English at home	3,555,000	3,662,000	3.0
Speak non-English language at home	4,568,000	6,323,000	38.4
Aged 18 and older	24,621,000	33,281,000	35.2
Speak English at home	6,130,000	7,759,000	26.6
Speak non-English language at home	18,492,000	25,522,000	38.0

NOTE: Percentages calculated on unrounded numbers.
SOURCES: U.S. Bureau of the Census, *1980 Census of Population, Detailed Population Characteristics, United States Summary*, Washington, D.C., U. S. Government Printing Office, 1984; 1990 Census of Population and Housing, Five Percent Public Use Microdata Sample, 1995.

More than half of all language-minority people live in households in which Spanish is spoken. In 1990 there were 24.8 million Spanish-language minority people, or 53 percent of the total, as shown in Table 1.4. Six other languages were spoken in households with at least a million people each in 1990: French, German, Italian, Chinese languages, Tagalog and Ilocano, and Polish (Census 1995a).

TABLE 1.4. Estimated Language-Minority Population, by Age Group, Language Spoken at Home, and Language Group: United States, 1990 (Numbers in thousands)

Language group	Total	Under 5	Aged 5-17 Total	Eng	Non-Eng	Aged 18 and older Total	Eng	Non-Eng
Total	47,122	3,856	9,985	3,662	6,323	33,281	7,759	25,522
American Indian/Alaska Native languages	538	62	145	72	74	331	73	258
Arabic	518	56	103	38	66	359	69	289
Armenian	181	11	30	5	25	141	15	125
Asian Indian languages	817	71	174	55	119	572	45	528
Chinese languages	1,580	106	271	52	219	1,203	103	1,100
Czech	139	3	14	9	5	122	34	88
Dutch	250	17	41	27	14	192	64	128
Farsi	263	24	49	13	36	191	25	166
French	3,391	197	688	420	269	2,506	1,065	1,441
German	2,922	167	496	313	183	2,259	894	1,365
Greek	537	29	83	32	51	426	88	338
Haitian Creole	263	27	64	20	44	172	28	144
Hebrew	222	23	52	19	33	148	36	111
Hmong	107	23	42	1	41	42	1	41
Hungarian	216	8	24	14	10	185	46	138
Italian	2,143	90	263	169	94	1,791	576	1,215
Japanese	664	38	96	46	49	531	153	378
Korean	833	64	171	55	116	599	88	510
Mon-Khmer	154	21	52	3	49	82	3	79
Norwegian	141	6	17	12	6	118	43	75
Polish	1,072	39	116	61	55	917	248	669
Portuguese	584	40	111	35	76	432	78	355
Russian	316	17	52	15	37	248	43	205
Serbo-Croatian	198	10	28	11	17	161	36	125
Slovak	128	3	10	7	3	115	38	77
Spanish	24,782	2,390	5,954	1,786	4,168	16,438	3,260	13,177
Swedish	135	6	18	11	7	111	41	70
Tagalog and Ilocano	1,328	103	275	173	102	951	168	782
Thai and Lao	275	24	75	19	57	175	26	149
Ukrainian	141	6	17	10	6	119	28	90
Vietnamese	622	52	159	25	135	412	39	372
West African languages	114	16	24	16	7	74	16	58
Yiddish	288	17	43	11	32	227	46	181
Other languages	1,258	94	229	109	121	935	242	693

NOTE: Detail may not add to total because of rounding.
SOURCE: 1990 Census of Population, Five Percent Public Use Microdata Sample, 1995.

Some states are more linguistically diverse than others, and the impact of the numbers of language-minority children and youth varies, as shown in Table 1.5. In 1990 a quarter of the total language-minority population, 11.7 million people, lived in California. Texas was home to 5.4 million and New York to 5.3 mil-

TABLE 1.5. Estimated Language-Minority Population and Language-Minority Population under Age 18 and Percentages of the Total Population, by State: United States, 1990

State	Total Number	Total Percentage	Under age 18 Number	Under age 18 Percentage
Total	47,122,000	18.9	13,840,000	21.8
Alabama	241,000	6.0	74,000	7.0
Alaska	103,000	18.6	35,000	20.4
Arizona	1,039,000	28.4	361,000	36.7
Arkansas	135,000	5.7	44,000	7.0
California	11,661,000	39.2	3,651,000	47.1
Colorado	537,000	16.3	158,000	18.3
Connecticut	689,000	21.0	171,000	22.8
Delaware	73,000	11.0	20,000	12.0
District of Columbia	106,000	17.5	22,000	18.5
Florida	2,863,000	22.1	719,000	25.1
Georgia	543,000	8.4	164,000	9.5
Hawaii	405,000	36.6	99,000	35.2
Idaho	111,000	11.0	40,000	12.9
Illinois	2,166,000	18.9	626,000	21.2
Indiana	465,000	8.4	141,000	9.7
Iowa	197,000	7.1	58,000	8.1
Kansas	234,000	9.5	72,000	10.9
Kentucky	192,000	5.2	60,000	6.3
Louisiana	709,000	16.8	193,000	15.8
Maine	179,000	14.6	41,000	13.2
Maryland	654,000	13.7	175,000	15.1
Massachusetts	1,240,000	20.6	307,000	22.7
Michigan	1,001,000	10.8	269,000	10.9
Minnesota	412,000	9.4	116,000	9.9
Mississippi	151,000	5.9	51,000	6.9
Missouri	355,000	6.9	103,000	7.8
Montana	70,000	8.8	21,000	9.5
Nebraska	134,000	8.5	38,000	9.0
Nevada	233,000	19.3	64,000	21.6
New Hampshire	156,000	14.1	35,000	12.7
New Jersey	1,972,000	25.5	508,000	28.2
New Mexico	712,000	47.0	240,000	53.7
New York	5,304,000	29.5	1,381,000	32.4
North Carolina	496,000	7.5	150,000	9.3
North Dakota	81,000	12.6	17,000	9.9
Ohio	997,000	9.2	278,000	9.9
Oklahoma	276,000	8.8	88,000	10.5
Oregon	326,000	11.5	99,000	13.6
Pennsylvania	1,359,000	11.4	342,000	12.2
Rhode Island	229,000	22.8	55,000	24.6
South Carolina	245,000	7.0	75,000	8.1
South Dakota	79,000	11.4	25,000	12.7
Tennessee	280,000	5.7	84,000	6.9
Texas	5,411,000	31.9	1,891,000	39.1

Table 1.5 continued

State	Total Number	Total Percentage	Under age 18 Number	Under age 18 Percentage
Utah	247,000	14.4	93,000	14.8
Vermont	57,000	10.1	13,000	9.3
Virginia	705,000	11.4	196,000	13.0
Washington	669,000	13.7	202,000	16.0
West Virginia	96,000	5.4	27,000	6.0
Wisconsin	478,000	9.8	136,000	11.0
Wyoming	47,000	10.4	16,000	11.4

SOURCE: 1990 Census of Population and Housing, Five Percent Public Use Microdata Sample, 1995.

lion. Three other states had at least half a million: Florida, Illinois, and New Jersey. In contrast, Wyoming had only an estimated 47,000 language-minority people.

In addition to leading in the overall numbers of language-minority people, California also leads in the number of language-minority children and youth under age eighteen. In 1990 there were 3.7 million school-age language-minority children living in California, and they constituted nearly half of all children and youth in the state. New Mexico leads the states in linguistic diversity: in 1990 54 percent of all its children and youth lived in households in which one or more people speak a language other than English. In Texas, 39 percent of children and youth lived in language-minority households; in Arizona, 37 percent; in Hawaii, 35 percent; and in New York, 32 percent. Moreover, in three other states, New Jersey, Florida, and Rhode Island, language-minority children and youth constituted at least a quarter of the population under eighteen in 1990 (Census 1995a).

Home Speakers of Languages Other Than English

The numbers of people who speak languages other than English at home increased by about 38 percent in the 1980s, or nearly as much as the numbers of the foreign-born population, as shown in Figure 1.2. The growth reflects the increase in the number of immigrants from Asian countries. In 1980 there were 23 million home speakers of non-English languages; in 1990 there were 31.8 million. Table 1.6 compares the ten-year growth rates in the

TABLE 1.6. Estimated Numbers of Home Speakers of Non-English Languages, Aged 5 and Older, in 1980 and 1990 and Ten-Year Growth Rates, by Selected Language, United States

Language	1980	1990	Growth rate
Total, all languages	23,060,000	31,845,000	38.1
American Indian/Alaska Native languages	333,000	332,000	-0.4
Arabic	218,000	355,000	63.3
Armenian	101,000	150,000	48.8
Asian Indian languages	243,000	644,000	164.8
Chinese languages	631,000	1,319,000	109.2
Czech	122,000	92,000	-24.4
Dutch	148,000	148,000	0.1
Farsi	107,000	202,000	88.7
Filipino languages	474,000	899,000	89.5
French	1,551,000	1,702,000	9.8
German	1,587,000	1,548,000	-2.4
Greek	401,000	388,000	-3.3
Hungarian	179,000	148,000	-17.4
Italian	1,618,000	1,309,000	-19.1
Japanese	336,000	428,000	27.2
Korean	266,000	626,000	135.3
Norwegian	112,000	81,000	-28.2
Polish	821,000	723,000	-11.8
Portuguese	352,000	430,000	22.4
Russian	173,000	243,000	39.6
Serbo-Croatian	150,000	142,000	-5.4
Spanish	11,116,000	17,340,000	56.0
Swedish	100,000	78,000	-22.5
Thai and Laotian	85,000	206,000	142.8
Ukrainian	121,000	97,000	-20.4
Vietnamese	195,000	507,000	160.6
Yiddish	316,000	213,000	-32.6

NOTE: Percentages calculated on unrounded numbers.
SOURCES: U.S. Bureau of the Census, *1980 Census of Population, Detailed Population Characteristics, United States Summary,* Washington, D.C., U.S. Government Printing Office, 1984; 1990 Census of Population and Housing, Five Percent Public Use Microdata Sample, 1995.

numbers of speakers of languages spoken by at least 50,000 people in 1990 for which comparable 1980 data are available. As shown, the largest increases were in the numbers of speakers of Asian Indian, Vietnamese, Thai and Laotian, Korean, and Chinese languages. Conversely, the numbers of speakers of languages such as Yiddish, Czech, Swedish, and Ukrainian declined, reflecting the gradual demise of the use of these languages among descendants of immigrants and the lack of significant new immigration from the countries in which the languages are spoken (Census 1984, 1995a).

The age distribution of home speakers of non-English languages also reflects the immigration history of the various groups. As shown in Figure 1.4, few of the speakers of languages of recent immigrant groups (Asian Indian languages, Vietnamese, and Korean) are sixty-five or older. The groups with relatively more

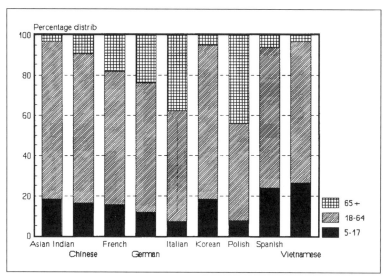

FIGURE 1.4. *Age distribution of home speakers of various non-English languages, 1990.*

older people and fewer school-age children (Polish, Italian, and German) are those which are not being fed by new immigration. Table 1.7 (see page 18) provides the estimated numbers of speakers of languages spoken by at least 50,000 people in 1990 in the various age groups (Census 1995b).

More than half of all people and two-thirds of school-age children and youth who speak non-English languages at home speak Spanish, but most Spanish speakers are not immigrants, despite the substantial immigration from Central America and the Caribbean in the 1980s. In 1990 there were about 17.3 million home speakers of Spanish, up from 11.1 million, or 56 percent more than in 1980. Nearly three out of five of them were born in this country (Census 1995a). The Spanish-speaking population, like the Hispanic American population which it overlaps, is younger than the population of home speakers of non-English languages in general. In 1990, nearly a quarter of Spanish speakers were of school age and only 6 percent were over sixty-four years of age. In comparison, among non-English home speakers in general, one in five was aged five to seventeen, and 12 percent were over sixty-four (Census 1995b).

TABLE 1.7. Estimated Numbers of Home Speakers of Non-English Languages, Aged 5 and Older, by Age Group and Language: United States, 1990

Language	Total	5-17	18-64	65+
Total, all languages	31,845,000	6,323,000	21,708,000	3,814,000
American Indian and Alaska Native	332,000	74,000	227,000	31,000
Arabic	355,000	66,000	263,000	26,000
Armenian	150,000	25,000	99,000	26,000
Asian Indian languages	646,000	119,000	508,000	20,000
Chinese languages	1,319,000	219,000	978,000	122,000
Czech	92,000	5,000	41,000	47,000
Dutch	143,000	14,000	94,000	34,000
Farsi	202,000	36,000	156,000	10,000
Finnish	54,000	3,000	24,000	28,000
French	1,709,000	269,000	1,131,000	309,000
German	1,548,000	183,000	995,000	370,000
Greek	388,000	51,000	270,000	67,000
Haitian Creole	188,000	44,000	134,000	9,000
Hebrew	144,000	33,000	99,000	13,000
Hmong	82,000	41,000	39,000	3,000
Hungarian	148,000	10,000	79,000	59,000
Italian	1,309,000	94,000	721,000	494,000
Japanese	428,000	49,000	308,000	70,000
Korean	626,000	116,000	478,000	32,000
Kwa	66,000	7,000	58,000	*
Lithuanian	56,000	3,000	23,000	30,000
Mon-Khmer	127,000	49,000	75,000	4,000
Norwegian	81,000	6,000	36,000	39,000
Pennsylvania Dutch	84,000	23,000	44,000	16,000
Polish	723,000	55,000	350,000	319,000
Portuguese	431,000	76,000	299,000	55,000
Romanian	65,000	12,000	43,000	11,000
Russian	242,000	37,000	151,000	55,000
Serbo-Croatian	142,000	17,000	87,000	38,000
Slovak	80,000	3,000	29,000	48,000
Spanish	17,345,000	4,168,000	12,121,000	1,057,000
Swedish	78,000	7,000	39,000	31,000
Tagalog and Ilocano	884,000	102,000	693,000	89,000
Thai and Laotian	206,000	57,000	145,000	5,000
Ukrainian	97,000	6,000	49,000	41,000
Vietnamese	507,000	135,000	357,000	15,000
Yiddish	213,000	32,000	67,000	114,000

*Fewer than an estimated 1,000 people.
NOTE: Detail may not add to total because of rounding.
SOURCE: U.S. Bureau of the Census, "Social and Economic Characteristics of Selected Language Groups for U.S. and States: 1990," CPH-L 159, Washington, D.C., U.S. Bureau of the Census, 1995.

Four other languages or language groups have at least a million speakers: French, German, Chinese languages, and Italian. More than three-quarters of 1990 French speakers, more than two-thirds of Italian speakers, and about two-thirds of German speakers were born in this country. Speakers of these languages are all older than home speakers of non-English languages in general. Chinese speakers are largely foreign born, reflecting 1980s immigration from Hong Kong, Taiwan, and mainland China. Three-quarters of all Chinese speakers are working age (Census 1995a, 1995b).

Of the 6.3 million school-age home speakers of non-English languages, 4.2 million spoke Spanish in 1990. Seven other languages or language groups claimed at least 100,000 speakers, aged five to seventeen, i.e., French, Chinese languages, German, Vietnamese, Asian Indian languages, Korean, and Tagalog and Ilocano (Census 1995b).

Populations with Difficulty in English

The population of home speakers of non-English languages who have difficulty speaking English—those reported in the census to speak English less than very well[3]—is not growing any faster than the population of non-English home speakers as a whole. On the other hand, the number of those in this group who do not speak English at all is increasing. Between 1980 and 1990, the population with English-speaking difficulty grew from an estimated 10.2 million to an estimated 14 million, a ten-year growth rate of about 37.3 percent. The population of non-English speakers grew from 1.2 million to 1.8 million, a growth rate of 51.5 percent, as pictured in Figure 1.2. The increase in the numbers of school-age children with difficulty speaking English as reported by household respondents was less. From 1980 to 1990, the growth rate of this group was only a little more than a quarter and, among those who did not speak English at all, it was 15 percent (Census 1984, 1995a). These data are shown in Table 1.8 (see page 20).

The language groups differ greatly in the likelihood of speakers to have difficulty speaking English. As shown in Figure 1.5 (see page 20), Vietnamese speakers are about two and a half times as likely as German speakers to experience English-speaking difficulty, the first group largely composed of newcomers and the second composed mostly of native-born people, with the remainder being long-time residents of this country.

About 43.9 percent of all home speakers of non-English languages in general reported in 1990 that they spoke English less than very well. Among school-age children, 37.8 percent had

TABLE 1.8. Estimated Numbers of Home Speakers of Non-English Languages, Aged 5 and Older, and Estimated Numbers, Aged 5 to 17, in 1980 and 1990 and Ten-Year Growth Rates, by Difficulty Speaking English, United States

Age group and English difficulty	1980	1990	Growth rate
Total, aged 5 and older	23,060,000	31,845,000	38.1
With difficulty speaking English	10,181,000	13,983,000	37.3
Non-English speaking	1,218,000	1,845,000	51.5
Aged 5 to 17	4,568,000	6,323,000	38.4
With difficulty speaking English	1,883,000	2,388,000	26.8
Non-English speaking	127,000	146,000	15.0

NOTE: Percentages calculated on unrounded numbers.
SOURCES: U.S. Bureau of the Census, *1980 Census of Population, Detailed Population Characteristics, United States Summary,* Washington, D.C., U. S. Government Printing Office, 1984; 1990 Census of Population and Housing, Five Percent Public Use Microdata Sample, 1995.

difficulty. The percentages of all speakers by language group ranged from more than seven in ten of Hmong and Mon-Khmer speakers and three in five of Vietnamese, Korean, and Chinese speakers, to only about 4 percent of the people who speak Dutch at home. Among school-age children, the range was from 72.7 percent of Hmong speakers to a fifth or less of speakers of

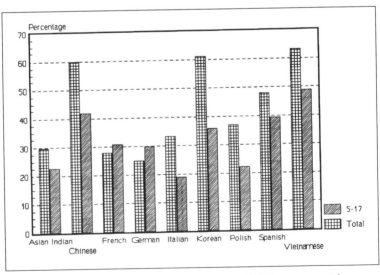

FIGURE 1.5. *Home speakers of various non-English languages with difficulty speaking English, 1990.*

European languages such as Serbo-Croatian, Lithuanian, Greek, Swedish, Italian, and Czech (Census 1995a). The estimated numbers of home speakers of the various non-English languages with difficulty speaking English are shown in Table 1.9. Since 1990 the number of school-age children who speak languages other than English at home has risen slightly, from 6.3

TABLE 1.9. Estimated Numbers of Home Speakers of Non-English Languages, Aged 5 and Older, and School-Age Home Speakers of Non-English Languages, by Difficulty in English and Language: United States, 1990

Language	Total, aged 5+			Aged 5-17	
	Total	With difficulty[1]	No English	Total	With difficulty[1]
Total, all languages	31,845,000	13,983,000	1,845,000	6,323,000	2,388,000
American Indian and Alaska Native	332,000	129,000	9,000	74,000	33,000
Arabic	355,000	120,000	6,000	66,000	17,000
Armenian	150,000	75,000	13,000	25,000	10,000
Asian Indian languages	646,000	192,000	12,000	119,000	27,000
Chinese languages	1,319,000	791,000	112,000	219,000	92,000
Czech	92,000	27,000	*	5,000	1,000
Dutch	143,000	6,000	*	14,000	5,000
Farsi	202,000	77,000	5,000	36,000	10,000
Finnish	54,000	13,000	*	3,000	1,000
French	1,709,000	478,000	8,000	269,000	83,000
German	1,548,000	386,000	4,000	183,000	55,000
Greek	388,000	122,000	5,000	51,000	8,000
Haitian Creole	188,000	99,000	6,000	44,000	16,000
Hebrew	144,000	34,000	1,000	33,000	7,000
Hmong	82,000	64,000	11,000	41,000	29,000
Hungarian	148,000	52,000	1,000	10,000	2,000
Italian	1,309,000	435,000	17,000	94,000	18,000
Japanese	428,000	224,000	8,000	49,000	24,000
Korean	626,000	384,000	34,000	116,000	41,000
Kwa	66,000	12,000	*	7,000	2,000
Lithuanian	56,000	17,000	*	3,000	*
Mon-Khmer	127,000	93,000	14,000	49,000	33,000
Norwegian	81,000	17,000	*	6,000	1,000
Pennsylvania Dutch	84,000	36,000	1,000	23,000	14,000
Polish	723,000	268,000	13,000	55,000	12,000
Portuguese	431,000	195,000	27,000	76,000	18,000
Romanian	65,000	32,000	2,000	12,000	4,000
Russian	242,000	131,000	15,000	37,000	17,000
Serbo-Croatian	142,000	52,000	2,000	17,000	3,000
Slovak	80,000	22,000	*	3,000	1,000
Spanish	17,345,000	8,310,000	1,460,000	4,168,000	1,637,000
Swedish	78,000	15,000	*	7,000	1,000
Tagalog and Ilocano	884,000	310,000	6,000	102,000	31,000
Thai and Laotian	206,000	128,000	10,000	57,000	28,000
Ukrainian	97,000	36,000	1,000	6,000	2,000
Vietnamese	507,000	321,000	25,000	135,000	66,000
Yiddish	213,000	62,000	2,000	32,000	14,000

[1]Including those who speak no English at all. *Fewer than an estimated 1,000 people.
SOURCES: U.S. Bureau of the Census, "Social and Economic Characteristics of Selected Language Groups for U.S. and States: 1990," CPH-L 159, Washington, D.C., Census,1995; 1980 Census of Population and Housing, Five Percent Public Use Microdata Sample, 1995.

million to 6.7 million, but their proportion of the total U.S. school-age population has remained about the same—13 percent. The number and proportion of school-age home speakers of non-English languages who have difficulty speaking English have not changed significantly (Census 1995a, U.S. Department of Education 1997). Data comparing the numbers and proportions for 1980, 1990, 1992, and 1995 are shown in Table 1.10.

Diversity in the Future

Whether or not the latest available estimates of the numbers of children and youth with difficulty speaking English indicate that the need for special help to acquire English proficiency is leveling off, it is clear that the minority populations are increasing and will continue to increase. The Bureau of the Census projects that majority Whites will represent only a little over half of the total U.S. population by the middle of the next century. In contrast, Hispanics/Latinos will have grown from 6 percent to a quarter of the population, Asians and Pacific Islanders from 2 percent to 8 percent, and African Americans from 12 percent to 14 percent if the Bureau's moderate assumptions for fertility, life expectancy, and net immigration prove accurate (Census 1996). Figure 1.6 illustrates the projected growth of minority populations as proportions of the total population.

TABLE 1.10. Estimated Numbers and Percentages of School-Age Home Speakers of Non-English Languages and of Those with Difficulty Speaking English, United States, 1980 to 1995

	1980	1990	1992	1995
Total population	47,494,000	45,342,000	47,113,000	50,747,000
Speak non-English language	4,568,000	6,323,000	6,440,000	6,669,000
% of total	9.6	13.9	13.7	13.1
Have English difficulty	1,883,000	2,388,000	2,179,000	2,431,000
% of non-English speakers	41.2	37.8	33.8	36.5

Sources: U.S. Bureau of the Census, *1980 Census of Population, Detailed population Characteristics, United States Summary,* Washington, D.C., U.S. Government Printing Office, 1984; 1990 Census of Population and Housing, Five Percent Public Use Microdata Sample, 1995; and special tabulations from the October 1992 and October 1995 Bureau of the Census current population surveys for the U.S. Department of Education, National Center for Education Statistics, *The Condition of Education, 1997,* Washington, D.C., U.S. Government Printing Office, 1997.

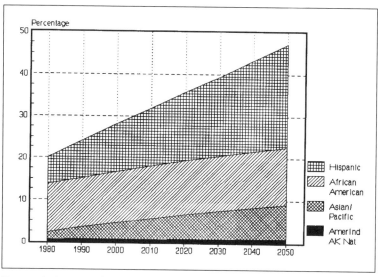

FIGURE 1.6. *Growth of racial/ethnic minorities as proportions of the total U.S. population, 1980 to 2050.*

The projections for the years 2000 to 2050 assume there will be a net immigration of 350,000 Hispanics/Latinos, including Hispanics from Puerto Rico; 226,000 Asians and Pacific Islanders; 186,000 non-Hispanic Whites; and 57,000 African Americans per year. These assumptions are necessarily imprecise because many unforeseen factors influence actual immigration: changing economic conditions, new restrictions on immigration and stricter enforcement of U.S. immigration laws, natural disasters, wars, and political turmoil abroad. Even without immigration, however, the minority proportion of the total population will continue to grow as the White population ages. The Bureau of the Census projects that natural increase (births minus deaths) will decrease among all segments of the population. Among non-Hispanic Whites, however, deaths will begin to exceed births by 2034, and by mid-century, Whites will have a negative natural increase of –1.8 percent per thousand people per year. The natural increase rate projected for Hispanics/Latinos by 2050 will be 18 percent; that for American Indians and Alaska Natives, 9 percent; that for Asians and Pacific Islanders, 8 percent; and that for African Americans, 7 percent (Census 1996).

The growth of minority populations does not necessarily mean that the number of people who speak languages other than English at home will grow at the same rate, much less the numbers with English-speaking difficulty and those who do not speak English at all. As suggested in the discussion of home speakers of languages other than English, without new immigration most languages tend to die out as their speakers age and fail to pass on the languages to their offspring. This does not appear to be happening with Spanish speakers. In 1990, as shown in Table 1.11, three out of five native-born Hispanic/Latino children and nearly seven out of ten native-born Hispanic/Latino adults spoke Spanish in their homes. Among native-born home speakers of non-English languages, Hispanics/Latinos constituted nearly half (Census 1993c). Since most Hispanics/Latinos are native born, even without immigration the proportion of home speakers of Spanish in the total population can only increase with the projected growth of the Hispanic/Latino population in the twenty-first century.

Table 1.11 also shows the proportions of native-born Asian Americans as a whole and of three of the largest Asian groups

TABLE 1.11. Estimated Numbers and Proportions of Native-Born Home Speakers of Non-English Languages and Those with Difficulty Speaking English, by Selected Racial/Ethnic Group and Age Group: United States, 1990

	Total, all groups	Hispanics	Asian Americans All Asian Americans	Chinese	Filipino	Asian Indian
Aged 5 to 17						
Number	43,511,000	4,405,000	851,000	168,000	207,000	104,000
Speak non-English language	4,729,000	2,723,000	397,000	111,000	47,000	56,000
% of total	10.9	61.8	46.6	66.0	22.9	53.9
Have English difficulty	1,567,000	959,000	135,000	36,000	12,000	11,000
% of non-English speakers	33.1	35.2	34.0	32.5	25.6	19.3
Aged 18 and older						
Number	167,428,000	7,471,000	1,029,000	238,000	202,000	32,000
Speak non-English language	11,686,000	5,155,000	306,000	103,000	51,000	14,000
% of total	7.0	69.0	29.7	43.4	25.1	44.8
Have English difficulty	3,255,000	1,642,000	95,000	25,000	14,000	3,000
% of non-English speakers	27.9	31.8	30.9	24.1	26.9	19.8

NOTE: Percentages calculated on unrounded numbers.
SOURCES: U.S. Bureau of the Census, *1990 Census of Population, Asians and Pacific Islanders in the United States*, Washington, D.C., U.S. Government Printing Office, 1993; U.S. Bureau of the Census, *1990 Census of Population, Persons of Hispanic Origin in the United States*, Washington, D.C., U.S. Government Printing Office, 1993.

that speak the Asian languages at home. Many of these people are the children of immigrants. Thus, although nearly half of all native-born Asian school-age children and three in ten native-born adults spoke their ethnic languages at home in 1990, the extent to which Asian Americans in general or Chinese people, Filipinos, or Asian Indians are maintaining their languages and passing them on cannot be determined. Not shown in the table because they are largely native born are African Americans, American Indians and Alaska Natives, and non-Hispanic Whites. In 1990, 6.2 percent of all African Americans, 23.8 percent of American Indians and Alaska Natives, and 5.7 percent of non-Hispanic Whites spoke languages other than English at home (Census 1993d, 1995b). With strenuous efforts on their part, Native Americans may preserve their languages in the future, but none of these groups will be the source of much growth in the population of home speakers of non-English languages in 2000 and beyond.

Among native-born non-English home speakers in general, a third of the children and nearly three in ten of the adults reported English-speaking difficulty in 1990, as shown in Table 1.11. There were 1.6 million children and 3.3 million adults. Three out of five of the children and half of the adults were Hispanics/Latinos. Fewer than 10 percent of the children and only 3 percent of the adults were Asians. The others were non-Hispanic Whites, American Indians and Alaska Natives, African Americans, and Pacific Islanders (Census 1993a, 1993c). These data suggest that many native-born home speakers are not acquiring English-speaking skills, much less proficiency in reading and writing. Whether the numbers of people with limited English proficiency increase depends largely on the extent to which we can develop better educational programs to meet their needs.

Diversity is a fact in our country. It will be even more so in the new century. We must work to make our educational system reflect this diversity, not just to provide better programs for the people who need to learn or improve their English-language skills in order to participate in our society, but to incorporate the linguistic and cultural strengths of all our population in everything we do.

Notes

1. Based on his analysis of decennial censuses since 1960, Jeffrey S. Passel (1996) attributes the growth of the American Indian population primarily to "changing patterns of racial self-identification on the part of people with only partial or distant American Indian ancestry" rather than to demographic factors. American Indians and Alaska Natives, however, have the second highest natural increase rate of all groups, as indicated in Passel's discussion on diversity in the future.

2. People born in Puerto Rico are native-born citizens of the United States. The census data used in this paper include only people living in the fifty states and the District of Columbia. In 1990, 3.5 million people lived in Puerto Rico (Census 1991). They and other Puerto Ricans move freely back and forth between the island and the mainland.

3. In the 1980 and 1990 censuses, respondents were asked to rate the English-speaking ability of household members who spoke languages other than English at home. The response categories were Very well, Well, Not well, and Not at all. The estimates of those with difficulty speaking English are the totals of all individuals except those reported to speak English very well. The count of home speakers of non-English languages who were reported not to speak English very well is a surrogate measure for the count of all language-minority people, including those now speaking only English at home, who would be found to be limited in English proficiency (i.e., limited in reading and writing as well as speaking and understanding English) if tested objectively. See U.S. Department of Education (1993, 3–5) for a discussion of measuring English ability to obtain national estimates of populations in need of special assistance.

Works Cited

Passel, Jeffrey S. 1996. "The Growing American Indian Population, 1960–1990: Beyond Demography." In G. D. Sandefur, R. R. Rindfuss, and B. Cohen, eds., *Changing Numbers, Changing Needs: American Indian Demography and Public Health*. Washington, D.C.: National Academy Press. 79–102.

U.S. Bureau of the Census. 1983. *1980 Census of Population: General Social and Economic Characteristics, United States Summary.* Washington, D.C.: U.S. Government Printing Office.

———. 1984. *1980 Census of Population: Detailed Population Characteristics, United States Summary.* Washington, D.C.: U.S. Government Printing Office.

————. 1991. Press release, Aug. 23.

————. 1992. *1990 Census of Population and Housing: Summary Population and Housing Characteristics, United States.* Washington, D.C.: U.S. Government Printing Office.

————. 1993a. *1990 Census of Population: Asians and Pacific Islanders in the United States.* Washington, D.C.: U.S. Government Printing Office.

————. 1993b. *1990 Census of Population: The Foreign-Born Population in the United States.* Washington, D.C.: U.S. Government Printing Office.

————. 1993c. *1990 Census of Population: Persons of Hispanic Origin in the United States.* Washington, D.C.: U.S. Government Printing Office.

————. 1993d. *1990 Census of Population: Social and Economic Characteristics, United States.* Washington, D.C.: U.S. Government Printing Office.

————. 1995a. *1990 Census of Population and Housing: Public Use Microdata Samples (Five Percent Sample).* Washington, D.C.: U.S. Department of Commerce.

————. 1995b. "Social and Economic Characteristics of Selected Language Groups for U.S. and States: 1990." CPH-L-159. Washington, D.C.: Bureau of the Census.

————. 1996. *Population Projections of the United States by Age, Sex, Race, and Hispanic Origin: 1995 to 2050,* by J. C. Day. Current Population Reports, P25-1130. Washington, D.C.: U.S. Government Printing Office.

————. 1997. *The Foreign-Born Population: 1996,* by K. A. Hansen and C. S. Faber. Current Population Reports, P20-494. Washington, D.C.: U.S. Department of Commerce.

U.S. Department of Education, National Center for Education Statistics. 1993. *Language Characteristics and Schooling in the United States, A Changing Picture: 1979 and 1989,* by Edith K. McArthur (NCES 93-699). Washington, D.C.: U.S. Government Printing Office.

————. 1997. *The Condition of Education, 1997,* by Thomas M. Smith et al. (NCES 97-388). Washington, D.C., U.S. Government Printing Office.

CHAPTER TWO

Proposition 227:
A New Phase of the English
Only Movement

JAMES CRAWFORD

Californians decisively rejected bilingual education on June 2, 1998, approving a mandate for English Only instruction known as Proposition 227. The vote was so one-sided—61 to 39 percent—that it is difficult to say what, if anything, could have altered the outcome. Since the election, two viewpoints have emerged. One is that anti-immigrant sentiment among voters made this ballot campaign, like other English Only initiatives before it, virtually unstoppable.[1] The other is that, armed with a different strategy, bilingual education advocates might have beaten back the assault.

In this disagreement, there is more at stake than a desire to apportion blame, or deny responsibility, for a disastrous defeat. The two viewpoints reflect conflicting analyses of why Proposition 227 passed, what it represents as a political phenomenon, and how advocates for language-minority students should respond. The implications of this argument extend well beyond California. A new wave of antibilingual activism is spreading to other states, school districts, and the U.S. Congress.

Few would dispute that issues of demographic change—immigration, race, ethnicity, and language—have preoccupied and often polarized Californians in the 1990s. Public schools have become a special point of concern. The enrollment of lim-

An earlier version of this essay was published in 1997 under the title "The Campaign against Proposition 227: A Post Mortem" (*Bilingual Research Journal* 21[1]: 1–29).

ited-English-proficient (LEP) children has more than doubled
over the past decade, to 1.4 million; English learners now represent one-quarter of California's K–12 students and one-third of
those entering the first grade (California Department of Education 1998). This remarkable growth is due not only to rising
immigration but also to higher birthrates in language-minority
communities. Between 1990 and 1996, as the state's population
increased by 2.6 million, nine out of ten of the new Californians
were Latinos or Asians. These groups expanded to 29 percent
and 11 percent of state residents, respectively, while African
Americans held steady at 7 percent, and non-Hispanic/Latino
Whites slipped to 53 percent (California Department of Finance
1998).[2] Approaching minority status for the first time since the
gold rush, many White Californians feel threatened by the
impending shift in political power and resentful about paying
taxes to benefit "other" people's children (Schrag 1998). Still, in
the June 1998 election, they accounted for 69 percent of the voters statewide, African Americans 14 percent, Latinos 12 percent,
and Asians 3 percent (*Los Angeles Times*-CNN Poll 1998).[3]

Laurie Olsen (1998), a leader of the "No on 227" campaign,
argues that ethnic factors were key to the initiative's victory. From
the outset, she reports, opinion research revealed "a reservoir of
anger, distrust, and even hate focused on bilingual education,
bilingual educators, and immigrants—particularly Spanish-speaking immigrants" (31). Proposition 227 successfully exploited "a
set of fears and beliefs of a voting California [that was] unrepre-
sentative of the state—whiter, older, only 15 percent with children
in public schools" (32). A majority of this electorate expressed
"the sense of Spanish ruining this country, the sense of our nation
in threat. The sense that upholding English as the language of this
nation is a stance of protecting a way of life—this outweighed
every argument we could wage to try to defeat 227. This is what
we were up against and still are" (8). Such minds were closed to
considering the case for bilingual education, Olsen concludes. "It's
not just that they don't understand it—they don't like it" (41).

Other opponents of Proposition 227 acknowledge the role of
nativist attitudes but question whether they motivated a majority
of Californians who voted in its favor. Jim Shultz (1998), director
of the Democracy Center in San Francisco, attributes its victory

primarily to mistakes by the No on 227 campaign. In particular, he cites:

♦ a decision to focus on "tangential issues" rather than on explaining bilingual education in terms the voters could understand

♦ a refusal to take seriously complaints about the quality of bilingual programs, which were poorly serving numerous LEP students

♦ an insistence on blocking compromise bills in the California legislature that might have taken the steam out of the "Yes on 227" campaign by giving local school districts greater flexibility in teaching English learners

♦ a failure to mobilize grassroots support in language-minority communities and especially among the parents of children in bilingual programs

To assess the validity of these conflicting analyses, it is necessary to examine the public debate over Proposition 227; the role of the news media; the political agenda behind the initiative; and the responses of bilingual educators, researchers, and advocates.

English for the Children

The ballot initiative was conceived, financed, and directed by Ron Unz, a multimillionaire software developer and former Republican candidate for governor. He entitled it "English for the Children," a brilliant stroke of packaging. Here was a goal that no one could dispute. Who wanted to "vote against" English—or against children? The label also established a false choice in voters' minds: *either* teach students the language of the country *or* give them bilingual education. Perhaps most important, it focused debate on practical issues of educational effectiveness, avoiding the inflammatory symbolism of other English Only campaigns and thereby broadening the initiative's appeal.

Unlike previous English Only advocates, Unz made special efforts to "decouple" opposition to bilingual education from "anti-immigrant and anti-Latino views" (English for the Children 1997a). He spurned the support of Governor Pete Wilson, the most visible backer of Proposition 187, California's crackdown on undocumented immigration enacted in 1994—a measure that Unz had actively opposed. He picked fights with nativist groups and provoked them into opposing the initiative.[4] He filled campaign posts with Latinos and Asians, including Jaime Escalante, the legendary math teacher of *Stand and Deliver* fame, and Gloria Matta Tuchman, a first-grade teacher and candidate for state superintendent of public instruction.[5] Rather than attack immigrants for speaking other languages, Unz campaigned in their communities for children's "right" to learn English. In short, he posed as their advocate against unresponsive schools.

Unz claimed that Proposition 227 was inspired by a 1996 protest against bilingual education at the Ninth Street Elementary School in downtown Los Angeles. He alleged:

> Immigrant parents were forced to begin a public boycott after the school administration refused to allow their children to be taught English. Enormous numbers of California schoolchildren today leave years of schooling with limited spoken English and almost no ability to read or write English. We believe that the unity and prosperity our of society is [sic] gravely threatened by government efforts to prevent young immigrant children from learning English. (English for the Children 1997b)

What actually happened at Ninth Street was more complicated. The protest was orchestrated by Alice Callaghan, an Episcopal priest and community activist, who ran a day care center on which the boycotting parents depended; whether all of them participated freely in the protest remains a matter of dispute. Before pulling their children out of school, none of the parents had ever requested transfers to all-English instruction—an option that would have spared the students two weeks of disrupted schooling (Crawford 1998a). Of course, if the matter had been resolved without a confrontation, it would have failed to generate the sensational headlines that the organizer had sought: "80 Students Stay Out of School in Latino Boycott . . . Bilingual Schooling Is Failing, Parents Say" (Pyle 1996a, 1996b). Callaghan went on to play a leadership role in English for the Children.

Unz and Callaghan's version of the Ninth Street story became a central myth of the campaign: that bilingual education was unpopular among the very groups it was intended to serve. This claim hardly seemed unreasonable when the first *Los Angeles Times* poll (1997) on Proposition 227 reported that 84 percent of Latinos favored the measure; similar findings appeared throughout the campaign. In fact, 63 percent of Latinos voted against it on election day (*Los Angeles Times*-CNN Poll 1998), but this revelation came too late to correct the voters' misimpression. It is likely that many Californians with no direct knowledge of bilingual education reasoned, "If the parents of children in these programs don't support them, why should I?"

Why indeed? Californians of all backgrounds were dissatisfied with the public schools following two decades of funding constraints that began with another ballot initiative, Proposition 13, a property-tax limitation adopted in 1978. From one of the most generous states in per-pupil spending, California had slumped to 41st place (Schrag 1998). By the mid-1990s, students' reading and mathematics scores were among the lowest in the nation[6]—a trend that produced feverish media coverage and back-to-basics nostrums such as phonics instruction, mandated by state law in 1997.

Unz exploited this general discontent as well as a special concern about immigrant students: Why were the schools so slow to teach them English? Why did it take English learners four or more years to enter the mainstream? Bilingual approaches are often counterintuitive, not only for members of the public but also for the parents of English learners. Yet these were questions that school officials had rarely addressed.

Meanwhile, the California Association for Bilingual Education (CABE) used its clout with Latino lawmakers to resist perennial calls for "reform." On several occasions, the state senate voted to give districts greater discretion in educating English learners, by relaxing a state mandate for native-language instruction, but each time these bipartisan bills met a roadblock in the assembly. In the 1970s, a prescriptive law had been necessary to induce California school districts to try bilingual education.[7] Now that many—if not all—districts had become supporters of the program, it is unclear whether lifting the mandate would have had a significant pedagogical impact. It is almost certain, however, that a compromise would have lessened the political pressure for more radical changes. It also would have clarified the threat of Proposition 227 to local control of the curriculum. Nevertheless, CABE held out for stronger accountability provisions in the bill—requiring schools to document student progress in nonbilingual programs—which the sponsors were unwilling to accept. So, in September 1997, CABE's allies again killed the proposal in the assembly Education Committee.[8]

Educators' failure to respond to legitimate concerns about bilingual programs, combined with their backroom deal making in Sacramento, contributed to an image of bureaucratic arrogance and intransigence—an easy target for Ron Unz. He modeled his campaign along the populist lines typical of most ballot initiatives: mad-as-hell voters versus a system "completely gridlocked" by special interests (English for the Children 1997a). In particular, Unz (1997) demonized bilingual educators as "profiteers" who were "financially rewarded for not teaching English" with "as much as $1 billion" in annual subsidies.[9]

Framing the Issues

Unz's attack strategy proved appealing to the news media, which gave massive coverage to Proposition 227 compared with other ballot initiatives and primary races. More than six hundred newspaper articles (not to mention countless radio and television broadcasts) appeared on the antibilingual initiative in the six months before election day.[10] Most of these reports featured inflammatory charges by Ron Unz, rarely accompanied by effective counterarguments. By and large, the press defined the debate as Unz did: not "How can programs for English learners be improved?" or "Do school districts need greater flexibility in teaching these students?" but "Should bilingual education be eliminated in favor of intensive English instruction?" This way of framing the issue—as a misleading either/or decision—clearly benefited the Yes on 227 campaign. Moreover, it cast opponents in an unfamiliar and uncomfortable role: defenders of the status quo.

Media bias is a complex phenomenon, reflecting various external influences, internal workings of the "news business," and the culture of journalism (Ryan 1991). All of these sources contributed to the distorted and unbalanced coverage of Proposition

227. While a thorough analysis is beyond the scope of this chapter,[11] several related factors deserve mention:

- *The power of narrative.* Journalists tend to seek out and report what readers find compelling: human dramas, characters, and situations. So much the better if these are counterintuitive, "man bites dog" stories. English for the Children made skillful use of the Ninth Street boycott, a ready-made narrative so sensational that it was retold by virtually every reporter who covered the campaign. (Yet almost none ventured any original reporting that might have spoiled the myth; see Crawford 1998c.) By contrast, success stories for bilingual education—more difficult to ferret out and describe in dramatic terms—received little or no attention from California's major media outlets.

- *Emphasis on personalities.* In the celebrity-driven journalism of the 1990s, leaders of the Proposition 227 campaign were seen as unusual characters and thus "good copy." Reporters profiled them in lavish and often flattering detail: Callaghan as a self-styled liberal going against the tide of "political correctness"; Escalante and Matta Tuchman as courageous Latino teachers defying their own ethnic leadership; and Unz himself as a "white knight" reformer who was willing to spend his own fortune to promote the cause. By contrast, the initiative's opponents—researchers, administrators, teachers, and civil-rights advocates—stimulated little interest among the press, except when stereotyped as "faceless bureaucrats" or worse.[12]

- *Reportage by "template."* Clichés are endemic to news reporting owing to deadline and peer pressures, not to mention the skepticism of editors toward new perspectives. Challenging the conventional wisdom can bring rewards, but it entails even greater risks. So, for the career-oriented journalist, it is generally prudent to stick with familiar story lines. Unz was effective in supplying them: "Well-Intentioned Social Program Fails to Work as Promised," "Government Funding Creates Perverse Incentives against Meeting Stated Goals," "Stubborn Bureaucrats Defend Narrow Self-Interest." Such exposés of official failure, incompetence, and malfeasance are the stock-in-trade of contemporary journalism. In covering Proposition 227, most media were eager to use these templates to organize whatever facts they happened to gather.[13] Opponents of the initiative had nothing comparable to offer. A story line about bilingual programs working as intended—e.g., "Students Make Slow but Steady Progress"—was seldom regarded as news.

◆ *Conventions of political reporting.* Bilingual education is a school story, a science story, and a social change story, in addition to a political story. But today's journalists tend to class it exclusively under the final rubric, which is governed by special rules. In political reporting, all viewpoints are presumed to be fundamentally subjective. Unlike, say, in science writing, there is no obligation to investigate the objective truth of contending claims—only to offer each "side" a fair hearing. Thus unsupported charges may be counterposed against research-backed conclusions without giving readers any guidance in sorting out facts from falsehoods. The news media's approach to Proposition 227 could be summed up as follows: Give equal credence to the political critics of bilingual education on the one hand and to the field's "vested interests"—i.e., researchers and practitioners—on the other. And let the best sound bite win.

◆ *Cultivating controversy.* By nature, journalism must simplify subject matter to make it meaningful to a wide audience. Often this means highlighting the sharpest points of conflict—in this case, language of instruction. Since Proposition 227 framed the debate in this way, the intensive media focus on bilingual education, pro or con, was hardly surprising. By neglecting other issues, however, it implied that language of instruction was the crucial variable—perhaps the only variable—in the success or failure of English learners. So it is likely that voters paid little heed to factors such as students' poverty and lack of access to reading materials, the shortage of trained teachers, and various resource constraints. No doubt many reasoned that if LEP students were faring poorly, and if "the current system [was] centered on use of native language instruction" (English for the Children 1997a), then a radical change was in order.

Making the Case

To indict the "current system," Unz seized on a misleading figure from the California Department of Education. Since the early 1990s, about 5 to 7 percent of LEP students had been "redesignated" as fluent in English each year. He dubbed this the "95 percent annual failure rate" (English for the Children 1997b)—a memorable sound bite that was circulated widely by journalists. Seldom was it noted that, owing to an estimated shortage of 27,000 bilingual teachers, less than 30 percent of California's English learners were enrolled in bilingual classrooms and only 20 percent were taught by fully certified instructors (Gold 1997;

California Department of Education 1998). If programs were indeed "failing," it was more logical to blame English Only methodologies.[14]

Nor did the news media ask many questions about Unz's one-year standard for English acquisition, despite its lack of scientific support. A considerable body of research shows that, on average, academic proficiency in a second language takes four to seven years to develop (Collier and Thomas 1989). In a longitudinal study comparing well-implemented program models, Ramírez, Yuen, and Ramey (1991) found that, after one year, only 4 percent of English learners in "structured immersion," 12 percent of those in "late-exit" bilingual education, and 13 percent of those in early-exit bilingual education had become fluent in English. Yet such findings were rarely cited in the public debate over Proposition 227.

Researchers' explanations of program effects were complex and often unsatisfying to journalists looking for bottom-line conclusions. A report by the National Research Council (August and Hakuta 1997) did little to clarify matters. It criticized the "extreme politicization" of evaluation studies in bilingual education and pronounced them inconclusive on which approach is most effective for LEP students (138). Several commentators took this to mean that all research in the field was "worthless" as a guide to policymaking (e.g., Rodríguez 1997). Meanwhile, the news media largely ignored a significant study that appeared during the campaign. In a meta-analysis of the research literature, Greene (1998) reported a small but significant edge for bilingual pedagogies. (If anything, this review underestimated their benefits; see Krashen 1998).

With characteristic pragmatism, journalists continued to ask, in effect: "If bilingual education works, why are so many Latinos faring poorly in school?" With limited scientific data on outcomes, it was a difficult question to answer. "Redesignation rates" remained, despite their flaws, the California Department of Education's only "objective" gauge for measuring the progress of English learners. School districts also lacked much hard evidence to counter the "95 percent failure rate." Certainly they had nothing so dramatic to support the effectiveness of bilingual programs. With some exceptions, such as San Francisco and

Calexico, districts offered little response to Unz's charges and rarely tried to showcase exemplary schools. The No on 227 campaign refused to discuss the pedagogical effectiveness issues at all. Left unchallenged, the "failure" of bilingual education thus became part of the conventional wisdom, espoused even by editorial writers and Democratic politicians who opposed Proposition 227 as overly extreme (e.g., *Sacramento Bee* 1998; Davis 1998).

Unz's remedy was indeed radical: a statewide mandate for "sheltered English immersion . . . not normally intended to exceed one year," after which LEP students would be transferred to mainstream classrooms. Parents could still request bilingual instruction, but for children under age ten, such "waivers" would be restricted to those with "special physical, emotional, psychological, or educational needs." Educators who "willfully and repeatedly" violated the law requiring them to teach "overwhelmingly in English" could be sued and "held personally liable" for financial damages. None of these provisions could be repealed or amended without a two-thirds vote of the legislature and the governor's signature, or another ballot initiative (*English Language* 1998). In sum, Proposition 227 would impose an unproven pedagogy, limit local flexibility, restrict parental choice, and punish educators who resisted. Barring a successful challenge in court, it would be virtually written in stone.[15]

Nevertheless, the pros and cons of bilingual education—not of the initiative itself—commanded center stage throughout the campaign. Because Unz avoided nativist appeals and targeted pedagogical issues, few commentators saw the initiative as an attack on ethnic minorities. Rather, they portrayed it as a choice between a "depressing status quo," "the dismal experiment known as bilingual education," and "a meat-ax, 'one-size-fits-all' approach to a complicated issue," "a blunt instrument" requiring schools to stress English (*New York Times* 1998; *Stockton Record* 1998; *San Francisco Chronicle* 1998, *Contra Costa Times* 1998). Most voters opted for the latter.

Deciphering the Vote

Californians were clearly expressing their frustration. But why? Were they mainly fed up with immigration and its social costs?

Or were they worried about the life chances of schoolchildren who failed to learn English? On the basis of limited evidence, many seemed willing to believe the worst about bilingual education and bilingual educators—which suggests at least a subliminal ethnic bias (Crawford 1998b). Yet media coverage of the campaign rarely offered much evidence to challenge such perceptions, denying voters the information they needed to make an unbiased decision (Crawford 1998c).

Few opinion surveys are helpful in sorting out supporters' motives. Pollsters generally characterized the initiative as an intensive approach to the teaching of English, while downplaying its extreme provisions; most surveys registered overwhelming support among all sectors of the electorate.[16] One exception was a *Los Angeles Times* poll (1998) that probed more deeply into attitudes toward bilingual education and the stated reasons for supporting or opposing Proposition 227. It reported that 72 percent of likely "yes" voters explained their preference by saying: "If you live in America you need to speak English." Of course, this statement is subject to various interpretations. It may convey either a resentment toward immigrants who speak other languages or a genuine concern for their social and economic advancement. Or both.

Like other ethnically charged issues, bilingual education can generate conflicting feelings. No doubt many Californians do feel threatened by the cultural transformation of their communities. For some, the pervasiveness of Spanish or Chinese has come to symbolize a range of unsettling changes brought on by immigration, leading them to support English Only measures (Crawford 1992). Such reactions may increase voters' impatience to teach English to LEP children, as well as skepticism toward approaches that seem to delay the process. Yet one need not resent language minorities to worry about their progress toward integration and self-sufficiency, or to wonder about school programs that segregate their children for extended periods. Immigrants also worry about questions of assimilation, and they do not always agree among themselves, as their history in this country attests (see, for instance, Kloss 1998 on German Americans).

No doubt some voters rejected bilingual education out of ethnic animus. Other than focus-group anecdotes, however, there is a dearth of evidence to support Olsen's (1998) contention that a majority of Californians did so. Unlike the debate over Proposition 187 four years earlier, the 1998 campaign rhetoric featured no direct assaults on immigrants. Significantly, only 12 percent of likely voters who opposed Proposition 227 perceived it as racist or believed that it "discriminates against non-English-speaking students" (*Los Angeles Times* Poll 1998).

Poll findings also suggest that many supporters of the initiative were ambivalent about its restrictions. Or perhaps they simply failed to read the fine print. A poll by Spanish-language media in Los Angeles found that 68 percent of Latino parents favored bilingual education, including 88 percent of those with children in bilingual programs; yet 43 percent also expressed support for Proposition 227 (Rivera 1998). Another survey found all voters evenly divided on whether to impose "one uniform standard in California for teaching children with limited English skills" or to give local districts "more flexibility to choose the method they think is best." Meanwhile, 61 percent favored at least "a year or two" of bilingual instruction (*Los Angeles Times* Poll 1998). Yet, on election day, 61 percent approved an initiative to override local option and dismantle bilingual programs.

If the voters were so perplexed or conflicted about the initiative and its likely impact, one might reasonably question the effectiveness of the No on 227 campaign. Before reviewing its strategy and organizing efforts, however, it is helpful to analyze what it was up against: a more sophisticated version of English Only politics than Californians had seen before.

Language Restrictionism of a New Type

Prior to Ron Unz, English Only advocates had hesitated to stage a frontal assault on bilingual education. Instead, they focused their legislative efforts on declaring English the official language of various states and the federal government. The group U.S. English (1991) had long complained about bilingual education in its advertising campaigns, funded academic critics of the program, and supported "local flexibility" in the education of LEP students. Yet its Official English proposals always exempted bilingual education from restrictions on the use of other languages.[17]

Congressional sponsors of H.R. 123, the so-called English Language Empowerment Act of 1996, also took pains to emphasize that it would have no effect on the teaching of languages. As passed by the House of Representatives, the bill declared English the sole official language of the U.S. government and banned most federal publications in other tongues, such as social security information, income tax forms, tourist brochures, and voting materials. Because of Senate inaction, the measure died in the 104th Congress. Had it become law, H.R. 123 would have impeded access to government for anyone whose English was limited, a chilling precedent for minority-language rights (Chen 1995). As a practical matter, however, the Government Printing Office already published 99.94 percent of its materials in English (U.S. General Accounting Office 1995). Thus the impact of H.R. 123 would have been minimal, affecting relatively few people who needed language assistance. It was the principle of language restrictionism that stimulated interest on both sides.

The English Only debate has been largely a symbolic one, a conflict over the impact of immigration and demographic diversity. The magnitude of public spending to accommodate non-English speakers—usually quite small—is rarely at issue. Rather, it is *the idea of such expenditures* that strikes English Only proponents as "un-American." Immigrants should be grateful to be here, the reasoning goes. They should show their respect for this country by adapting to our ways, rather than demanding that we adapt to theirs. Why should newcomers be able to file their tax returns or take a driver's test in their native language? What kind of "message" does that send about the responsibilities of citizenship? According to this mindset, offering bilingual services today seems terribly "unfair" to the memory of immigrant ancestors who struggled to learn English without special help.[18] In sum, the English Only movement is a classic case of "status anxieties" expressed through the politics of language (Fishman 1992). Enthusiasm for the cause waxes and wanes depending on social, political, and economic trends far removed from language itself.

With the rise of anti-immigrant fervor in the 1990s, English Only politics turned sharply partisan. House Republicans, who came to power on the same day that Californians adopted Proposition 187, sought to exploit the public mood. They portrayed "bilingualism" as a menace to national unity, arguing that English needed "legal protection" to preserve Americans' most important "common bond." Celebrating a marriage of convenience between English Only and "free-market" ideologies, they insisted that banning bilingual services would "empower" immigrants by motivating them to learn English, the "language of opportunity." For their part, Democrats condemned H.R. 123 as divisive, mean-spirited, and potentially unconstitutional in its restrictions on civil rights (*Congressional Record* 1996). The bill passed, 259 to 167, largely along party lines.

House Speaker Newt Gingrich took a special interest in the measure, asserting that English was "at the heart of our civilization," whereas language diversity could lead to its "decay" (*Congressional Record* 1996, H9768). More to the point, in closed meetings of the Republican caucus, he predicted that H.R. 123 would boost his party's chances in the 1996 election; the speaker urged colleagues to stress it in their campaigns. In most congressional races, however, the language issue appeared to generate limited interest, except to further alienate Latino and Asian voters already offended by Republicans' "get tough" proposals on immigration. The English Only fervor quickly cooled on Capitol Hill. Although H.R. 123 was reintroduced in the 105th Congress, Gingrich never scheduled a vote on the bill.

At first impression, the idea of Official English had seemed innocuous to most mainstream Americans. Within six months after Californians passed such a ballot initiative in 1986, similar legislation was considered by thirty-seven other states (Crawford 1987). Most of these bills appeared to be ceremonial gestures reaffirming the importance of English. Gradually, however, the public has learned there is more at stake. Although the proposed restrictions on other languages are often trivial in practice, they have come to symbolize nativist intolerance. English Only measures are deeply offensive to ethnic minorities—immigrant and otherwise—who feel their patriotism is being impugned and their culture denigrated. And to what end? Advocates have failed to make a convincing case that the dominance of English is "threatened" in the United States by a handful of transitional services conducted in other languages. Nor have they been able to explain how enacting gratuitous insults toward minority groups will somehow "unite" the country.

For these reasons, the heyday of the traditional English Only movement may have passed. Such organizations continue to raise millions each year, to promote their message widely, and to win occasional victories for Official English at the state level. Yet their program is increasingly irrelevant to the major currents of U.S. politics. As the antibilingual education campaign unfolded in California, U.S. English and English First focused their efforts in Congress, opposing legislation that might have some day created a Spanish-speaking state of Puerto Rico.[19] They played no role whatsoever in the passage of Proposition 227.

Ron Unz neither needed nor wanted help from the established English Only lobbies. With deep pockets of his own, he had no reason to share leadership with these forces in exchange for campaign funding. Privately he expressed disdain for their narrowness and amateurism. Most important, he strived to disassociate English for the Children from their nativist image.

Neoconservative Strategy

For John Tanton (1986), the founder of U.S. English, language restrictionism was a way to organize the backlash against ethnic diversity. Focusing on "bilingualism" served to highlight the "Latin onslaught" and its cultural impact, thereby advancing the cause of immigration restrictionism.[20] For Ron Unz (1994), the assault on bilingual education served a broader, neoconservative agenda. His ultimate objective was to "roll back our well-intentioned but failed welfare state" (38)—that is, to dismantle the social programs and civil rights reforms of the 1960s. Attacking native-language schooling also provided an opportunity to attack some favorite villains of the Right: ivory-tower academics, teachers' unions, civil rights advocates, ethnic politicians, and, of course, the dreaded "education establishment." As far as Unz was concerned, this was a campaign that Latinos were welcome to join; indeed, enlisting their support was among his strategic goals.

Following his loss to Governor Wilson in the 1994 Republican primary, Unz (1994) warned that certain members of the party (e.g., his rival) were exploiting nativism for "momentary political gain." By ignoring demographic trends, they were "sacrificing the long-term future of their party—and of America itself" (37). After all, it would be difficult to build a Republican majority while continuing to bash fast-growing minorities in key states. Latinos, for example, are projected to represent two out of five voters in California and Texas by the year 2025, one out of four in Florida, and one out of five in New York (Balz 1998). Unz (1994) argued that "most Hispanics are classic blue-collar Reagan Democrats" whose views on social issues such as abortion draw them toward conservatism, while Asians are a privileged stratum "much like Jews . . . but without the liberal guilt." He portrayed both groups as "natural constituencies" for Republicans. Thus the party should seek "to unite rather than divide conservative natives and immigrants" by stressing "core policies" such as free markets and limited government. Conversely, it should oppose "divisive" programs such as affirmative action and bilingual education in the name of "individual liberty, community spirit, and personal self-reliance." In other words, conservatives should be both "pro-immigrant" and pro-assimilation (35–38). Unz could therefore maintain ideological consistency while doing the following:

- ◆ actively opposing Proposition 187 in 1994, a measure that, among other things, would have turned California educators into agents of the Immigration and Naturalization Service, requiring them to hunt down and expel the children of "illegal aliens" from school

- ◆ actively supporting Proposition 209 in 1996, the state's ban on affirmative action programs, championing "meritocracy" over the values of diversity and equality

- ◆ sponsoring Proposition 227 in 1998, a measure that advertised itself as immigrants' ticket to "the American Dream of economic and social advancement" (*English Language* 1998)

Unz's initiative provided the first test of his ideas for conservative coalition building: Could the fears of English speakers be assuaged without alienating too many language minorities? Was opportunity-through-assimilation an idea that could be sold to immigrants and natives alike? Would it be credible to attack bilingual education on behalf of those it was designed to benefit? The results were mixed. Unz fell far short of the 80 to 90 percent support among Latinos that he predicted at the outset of his campaign (Humphrey 1997); in the June primary, they opposed the initiative by nearly two to one (*Los Angeles Times*-CNN Poll 1998). His dreams of a political realignment in California looked even more outlandish, as ethnic minorities turned out in record numbers to back Democratic candidates in November 1998. Clearly, immigrants and their descendants continued to associate the Republican party with the nativist elements it had courted in recent years.

Nevertheless, judging by the vote on Proposition 227, Unz's short-term strategy had a wide appeal among Californians. The initiative passed easily, despite a disproportionate turnout of liberal and Democratic voters, who defeated other conservative ballot measures.[21] Ethnic opposition was considerably weaker than it had been over Proposition 187 four years earlier: 37 percent of Latinos and 57 percent of Asians voted for the antibilingual initiative (*Los Angeles Times*-CNN Poll 1998),[22] versus 23 percent of Latinos and 47 percent of Asians for the anti-immigrant initiative (*Los Angeles Times* Poll 1994). In other words, attacking bilingual education did not result in the polarization that many had expected.

Evidence is fragmentary on which language-minority voters supported Proposition 227 and why. Opinion polls indicate, however, that its popularity among all voters was closely correlated with economic status. Respondents with annual household incomes over $60,000 were more than twice as likely to oppose bilingual education as those with incomes below $20,000 (Pinkerton 1998). Among Latinos, the vote was close in middle-class communities such as Montebello, while the initiative lost by nearly three to one in working-class Huntington Park (Pyle, McDonnell, and Tobar 1998). A poll of Chinese Americans in San Francisco—a less affluent Asian community, where most respondents preferred to be surveyed in Cantonese or Mandarin—found that 73 percent planned to vote no (Chao 1998).

Thus the available data suggest that recent immigrants with children in bilingual education were far more likely to oppose Proposition 227.

It appears that Unz's arguments had more resonance for higher-income, English-proficient Asians and Latinos. Letters to the editor during the campaign provide anecdotal evidence of the attitudes of immigrant professionals. Citing their own experiences, assimilated language minorities argued that being "forced to join the mainstream" and being required "to learn English as quickly as possible" were keys to success in the United States (Sanchez 1998; Yi 1998). For many, class tended to take precedence over ethnicity as a prism for viewing the issue. Having limited contact with current programs for English learners, they formed opinions largely on the basis of media accounts. In short, they seemed to approach Proposition 227 in a manner similar to that of affluent White Americans. And they rendered the same verdict on bilingual education: guilty as charged. The outcome might have been different, however, if the program's advocates had mounted a defense.

Conceding the Public Debate

By the time the initiative's opponents got organized in November 1997, they were trailing by more than four to one among registered voters (*Los Angeles Times* Poll 1997). Ron Unz had been circulating ballot petitions for more than four months, receiving extensive media coverage, and encountering no organized response from the advocates of bilingual education. Failing to answer such attacks was hardly a new phenomenon; nor was it limited to California. Years of inattention to the program's public image had left numerous misconceptions unchallenged. Journalists, echoing the conventional wisdom, were skeptical of research findings favorable to bilingual pedagogies (McQuillan and Tse 1996). Opinion surveys usually found that the idea of intensive English instruction was popular in immigrant communities. Latino politicians, impressed by the early polls on Proposition 227, were reluctant to speak out against it. Meanwhile, other Democrats expressed impatience with the California Association for Bilingual Education for opposing compromise legislation; they too remained largely silent about the initiative.[23]

Isolated and misunderstood, bilingual educators reached out to allies in California's education, civil rights, and immigrant-advocacy communities who recognized the extreme nature of Unz's proposal. These forces came together to form Citizens for an Educated America, the official No on 227 organization. With initial funding from the California Association for Bilingual Education (CABE) and the California Teachers Association (CTA), they conducted polls and focus groups while seeking professional advice from political and media consultants.

For No on 227, the immediate task was developing a strategy for the underdog campaign. Based on their analysis of the electorate, the consultants offered the following recommendations:

- ◆ In a state of 33 million people, reaching the electorate would mean relying heavily on broadcast media. Because of the expense of advertising—more than $1 million a week to saturate the major television markets—fund-raising would have to be a high priority for the No on 227 campaign.

- ◆ Traditional supporters of bilingual education—language minorities and progressives—were unlikely to turn out in large enough numbers to defeat Proposition 227. It would also be necessary to win over swing voters who had yet to form a strong opinion. Of these, the most promising demographic sector was determined to be "Republican women over 50."

- ◆ A winning message should highlight the initiative's extreme provisions rather than challenge the conventional wisdom about the "failure" of bilingual education. Opinion research suggested that, while Unz's solution could be discredited, there was too little time to change voters' minds about the problem. In short, the consultants advised: "*DO NOT* get into a discussion defending bilingual education" (Citizens for an Educated America 1998a; emphasis in original).

This last recommendation came as a shock to many bilingual educators and researchers. How could they fail to respond to falsehoods about their profession or stand by silently while ideologues maligned programs that benefited LEP children? Some advocates viewed the Proposition 227 debate as an excellent opportunity to educate the public about second-language acquisition (Stephen Krashen, personal communication, 1998). They also worried that refusing to challenge Unz's charges would be seen as conceding their validity.

Ultimately, however, the leaders of Citizens and its organizational sponsors accepted the consultants' advice.[24] They came to believe that not discussing bilingual education offered the best hope of saving it. The "Don't Defend" strategy was then sold to CABE members and to bilingual directors throughout the state, who were counseled not to respond to attacks on their programs. Activists, including those working in language-minority communities, were urged to highlight what was wrong with Proposition 227, not what was right with bilingual education. "Put aside your personal feelings," they were told in effect. "Trust the professionals to run this campaign." Many advocates did so; others worked independently of Citizens.[25] Grassroots efforts sprouted throughout the state, but they received limited support or coordination from the campaign apparatus except for those that involved fundraising (Campbell 1998).

To represent its views, No on 227 hired spokespersons with no background in bilingual education. Whenever the subject came up in public debates or media interviews, they sought to redirect the discussion, saying, "Bilingual education is *not* on the ballot in June. What is on the ballot is Ron Unz's very specific proposal for California's school children. . . . I'll be happy to discuss the merits of different bilingual education programs on June 3 [the day after the election]—assuming the Ron Unz Initiative fails and we can still have a meaningful conversation" (Citizens for an Educated America 1998b, 1; italics in original).

Based on its private polling, Citizens singled out various features of Proposition 227 for criticism. Initially, it stressed provisions that allowed children to be mixed by age and grade for English instruction, that restricted special help to 180 days, and that made teachers vulnerable to lawsuits and personal financial penalties for violating the English Only mandate. None of these issues seemed to capture the public's attention. So, in the campaign's late stages, a new target was selected: the initiative's $50 million annual appropriation to teach English to adults who would agree to tutor children in the language. Clearly, Unz had inserted this provision to bolster his "pro-immigrant" image; it was hardly the most promising way to serve LEP students. Nevertheless, it resembled the federal Family English Literacy program,[26] which bilingual educators had long supported. The proposed funding was relatively modest—about one-sixth of 1 percent of California's education budget—and it addressed a real need. Citizens determined, however, that diverting funds from K–12 schools to benefit adult immigrants was unpopular with many Californians. So attacking the idea became the centerpiece of its multi-million-dollar advertising blitz (Citizens for an Educated America 1998c). This position required an about-face for the coalition opposing Unz. Over the past decade, several of its members had lobbied to remedy the chronic shortage of adult English classes, exposing the hypocrisy of English Only advocates who declined to support additional funding. Now it was the No on 227 campaign that appeared hypocritical. Unz (1998) seized on the issue, accusing his opponents of betraying their own principles out of desperation.

Meanwhile, the news media did not stop reporting on the charges against bilingual education—only effective responses to those charges. Some journalists did seek to balance their accounts with the opinions of bilingual educators and researchers who acted independently of the No on 227 campaign. Parents and teachers sought to publicize local success stories for bilingual education, two-way—or dual immersion—programs in particular. Local organizers rallied supporters through demonstrations and candlelight marches. Yet these individual advocates spoke with many voices, delivering diverse messages. They had little success in discrediting the claims of Ron Unz and his allies, which continued to dominate the news.

Citizens for an Educated America had limited success in focusing attention on the initiative itself or in generating media coverage of any kind. Its attack on the $50-million adult English provision never became a central issue for voters, except perhaps for anti-immigrant extremists. Meanwhile, Californians who were skeptical about bilingual education had some principled reasons to oppose Proposition 227—notably, its severe restrictions on parental choice and local control in educating English learners. Yet No on 227 never stressed these features of the initiative, which in a different kind of campaign might have been decisive. No matter that Citizens outspent English for the Children by nearly five to one.[27] Yes on 227 had no need to run television ads because it received such favorable free media attention.

Naturally Unz (1998) cited the "Don't Defend" strategy as evidence that bilingual education was indefensible. It is hard to fault most Californians for believing him, because few heard the other side. No on 227 began with the premise that voters' minds were closed to considering the merits of bilingual programs. So, rather than engage them in discussion on the issue, the campaign sought to distract them with diversionary gimmicks. Instead of appealing to their sense of fairness, it pandered to their nativism and parsimony. When the strategy failed, many advocates concluded that the electorate was so bigoted that their cause had been hopeless from the start. With its defeatist approach, however, Citizens failed to put this hypothesis to any logical test. Whether Californians could have been convinced to support bilingual education—or at least resolve to "mend it, don't end it"—is impossible to say. No on 227 never tried.

Survival Strategies

The victory of Proposition 227 raises painful but inescapable questions for bilingual educators throughout the United States:

- How long can an unpopular pedagogy be sustained—especially one that depends on public funding and, in some cases, legal mandates for survival?

- Why are the opponents of bilingual education expanding their influence over voters and policymakers?

- What strategies offer hope for changing minds about the program before it is dismantled or restricted?

- Where will the political clout be found—i.e., which constituencies will provide the needed support—to block poorly considered "reform" legislation?

- Who will take the lead in organizing the defense of bilingual education?

Few advocates for language-minority students in the United States are any better prepared to answer these questions today than their colleagues were in California. Yet the questions are increasingly urgent. Shortly after passage of Proposition 227, the U.S. House of Representatives approved legislation that would have curtailed federal grants for bilingual education, turned the funding over to states, restricted enforcement of civil rights laws for LEP students, and limited all programs for English learners to two years.[28] Meanwhile, Ron Unz began to export his antibilingual ballot campaign to other states. Some bilingual education advocates—for example, in Arizona—have responded with serious organizing drives of their own. Yet such efforts remain the exception. Despite stereotypes to the contrary, many bilingual educators express an aversion to politics. Thus they rarely get around to discussing survival strategies in any systematic way.

What is to be done? One answer is offered by an expert panel of the National Research Council (NRC) (August and Hakuta 1997), which argues for *depoliticizing* the discussion of how to serve English learners. It accuses advocates on both sides of polarizing matters by slanting research findings and focusing narrowly on language of instruction, to the exclusion of other variables. Both bilingual and English Only approaches have proved beneficial, the NRC's review of the literature concludes, so "there is little value" in continuing to debate their relative merits. "The key issue is not finding a program that works for all children and all localities, but rather finding a set of program components that works for the children in the community of interest, given that community's goals, demographics, and resources" (138). In effect, the report calls for a cease-fire in the political battles over bilingual education, freeing researchers and practitioners to make decisions strictly on their pedagogical merits.

This solution has understandable appeal for professionals who would like to shield their work from politics—and from charges of political influence. It fails, however, to address the reality of politicization: a concerted assault on bilingual education, originating in the English Only movement of the 1980s and intensifying under the leadership of neoconservatives in the 1990s. Ideological rather than pedagogical concerns have driven the opposition, which helps to explain why the policy debate has become so polarized.

Blaming "both sides" for this state of affairs portrays a false symmetry, to say the least. However stubbornly they may champion their favorite programs, bilingual educators and researchers have no political agenda (hidden or otherwise) to advance outside the schools. Nor do they receive financial support from those who do. Rarely do they make inflammatory statements for the news media or write polemics for mass-circulation magazines. To the extent they have participated in politics, they have almost invariably acted out of professional, not ideological, commitments.

By contrast, the academic critics of bilingual education seem to have few qualms about political activism or close ties to English Only lobbies. The READ Institute, founded by Keith Baker and now directed by Rosalie Porter, has received large research grants from U.S. English and its benefactors (Crawford 1999). Christine Rossell serves, along with Ron Unz, as an adviser to the so-called Center for Equal Opportunity, a group formed by Linda Chavez to combat affirmative action and multiculturalism. This organization sued the Albuquerque Public Schools in 1998, demanding an end to native-language instruction, enlisting Porter and Rossell as "expert witnesses." During the Proposition 227 campaign, Rossell launched *ad hominem* attacks on researchers who support bilingual education as "opportunists" in pursuit of "big money." In a media interview, she stated: "It is my belief that Krashen and Cummins came up with their theory of language acquisition to justify a practice that was spreading like wildfire through the schools" (Stewart 1998).[29] Like similar charges against individuals—which are meant to discredit the field as a whole—Rossell's politicking went unchallenged by other researchers.

Moreover, the critics enjoy generous support from Right-leaning foundations and political figures seeking to influence public opinion on language-minority education. In 1998 their views were highlighted in national publications, including *Reader's Digest, Atlantic Monthly, Wall Street Journal, New Republic,* and *Phi Delta Kappan.* The READ Institute's analysis of the NRC report (Glenn 1997) was sent to every school superintendent and principal in Massachusetts by John Silber, chair of the state board of education. Rarely are the arguments of bilingual education advocates articulated so widely or so well—outside the pages of academic journals. A less "politicized" approach would render them virtually invisible.

This is not to say that advocates should make unscientific claims or exaggerate the case for bilingual pedagogies or stoop to character assassination. Nor should they tolerate a single-minded focus on language of instruction, which has made for a polarized and unproductive debate, as the NRC panel notes (August and Hakuta 1997). At the same time, however, it is important to recognize that the public's obsession with this issue is unlikely to subside on its own. The controversy will continue until bilingual education is better understood as an effective means to acquire English—or until it is repudiated, marginalized, and dismantled. Researchers have a vital role to play in the outcome. If they fail to explain second-language acquisition in an accessible way, the vacuum will be filled by Ron Unz et al. If their evaluation studies deemphasize comparisons of bilingual and nonbilingual approaches, as the NRC recommends, policymakers will likely favor the latter, which are more popular and more intuitive to voters. Excessive caution and evenhandedness in presenting scientific evidence will surely work to the advantage of partisan critics.

It is understandable that researchers and practitioners would prefer to avoid political distractions. Yet, for professionals in language-minority education today, they are inescapable. To influence decisions that are crucial to LEP students, educators must learn to participate more effectively in the policy debate: not by distorting research evidence or by denouncing their opponents as racists, but by explaining bilingual pedagogies in a credible way—that is, in a *political context* that members of the public can understand and endorse. In the 1960s, that context was the war on poverty; in the 1970s, equal educational opportunity. Earlier in our history, it was parents' right to pass on their cultural heritage (Crawford 1998d). Today another rationale might be more appropriate. Whatever the strategy, to be successful it must be determined—very soon—by the field and its supporters. Let the discussion begin.

Notes

1. Six states have adopted official English legislation by ballot initiative, beginning with California in 1986; followed by Arizona, Colorado, and Florida in 1988; Alabama in 1990; and Alaska in 1998. No such initiative has been defeated at the polls, and all but one passed easily. The exception was Arizona's Proposition 106, an especially restrictive measure that was later ruled unconstitutional by state and federal courts. An additional seventeen states have declared English their official language by other means, for a total of twenty-two such laws currently in force (see Crawford 1999).

2. Native Americans increased slightly, to 0.6 percent.

3. In addition, June 1998 voters were disproportionately affluent and elderly; nearly half had family incomes exceeding $60,000 and more than half were at least fifty years of age. By comparison, California's median household income was $37,009 in 1995; residents over fifty represented approximately one-third of its voting-age population (U.S. Bureau of the Census 1998).

4. One provision of Unz's initiative that worried immigration restrictionists was a statement that "the government and the public schools of California have a moral obligation and a constitutional duty to provide all of California's children, regardless of their ethnicity or national origins, with the skills necessary to become productive members of our society." (*English Language* 1998). Proposition 187 had sought to deny schooling to the children of undocumented immigrants, a provision whose constitutionality was still being decided by the courts. Nativist groups also objected to a provision appropriating $500 million over ten years to fund adult English classes (Garcia 1998).

5. Matta Tuchman won enough votes to force a runoff election and nearly unseated the incumbent, Delaine Eastin, in November 1998.

6. Proponents of systematic phonics instruction have blamed whole language approaches, which began to be adopted in 1987, for a precipitous decline in literacy. McQuillan (1998) has shown, however, that reading scores have remained fairly constant since 1984—albeit low relative to the rest of the United States.

7. The comprehensive Chacón-Moscone Bilingual-Bicultural Education Act had been allowed to "sunset" in 1987; Governors Deukmejian and Wilson vetoed several attempts to extend it. Yet other requirements for native-language instruction, where appropriate to serve English learners, continued to be enforced by the California Department of Education.

8. The bipartisan bill, sponsored by Senator Dede Alpert, a Democrat, and Assemblyman Brooks Firestone, a Republican, finally passed the legislature—over CABE's continuing objections—on April 20, 1998. Governor Wilson vetoed the measure, calling it "too little, too late," and threw his support behind Proposition 227 (Ingram 1998).

9. In fact, according to the California Department of Education, state categorical funding to defray districts' expenses in educating English learners totaled $319 million in 1995–96—that is, 1.2 percent of K–12 spending statewide, or a supplemental cost of $241 for each LEP student. About 30 percent of this amount—$98 million—flowed directly to bilingual classrooms. The federal Title VII program also provided $55 million and the Title I program an unspecified amount for various programs serving LEP students.

10. An archive of news coverage on the English for the Children Web site includes 675 articles, mostly from California print media; see http://www.onenation.org/news.html.

11. For additional press criticism, see Crawford 1998c; Media Alliance 1998.

12. Stephen Krashen, one of the few bilingual education advocates to be profiled in the press, was the target of an extended and highly personal assault by Stewart (1998).

13. For example, the *Los Angeles Times* embraced Unz's theme of bilingual education as a vested interest (Anderson and Pyle 1998). As support, it cited per capita subsidies for LEP students as a disincentive to redesignating them as English proficient and noted the numerous publishers who exhibited Spanish-language materials at the conference of the California Association for Bilingual Education. More balanced reporting would have uncovered contradictory evidence: First, administrators' evaluations and promotions in numerous districts, including Los Angeles Unified, are based in part on how *rapidly* they redesignate LEP students (Forrest Ross, LAUSD Language Acquisition and Bilingual Development Branch, personal communication). Second, Spanish materials are a loss leader for textbook publishers seeking adoption of their English materials. Thus they stood to gain financially from passage of Proposition 227; none of the large publishers contributed to the No on 227 campaign.

14. Even Unz acknowledged that the "95 percent failure rate" was based on shaky statistics. But he found the sound bite too effective to abandon. Challenged on this point at a legislative hearing, he said, "I have no claim that the numbers are realistic or accurate. . . . But they

are the only numbers available, and I have to work with them" (Anderson 1997).

15. Litigation to overturn Proposition 227 on civil rights grounds continues, but a federal judge declined to issue a preliminary injunction blocking the initiative. So it took effect as scheduled on August 2, 1998, sixty days after the vote.

16. The highly influential *Los Angeles Times* Poll (1997) failed to mention the initiative's restrictive provisions. It posed its question as follows:

> There is a new initiative trying to qualify for the June primary ballot that would require all public school instruction to be conducted in English and for students not fluent in English to be placed in a short-term English immersion program. If the June 1998 primary election were being held today, would you vote for or against this measure?

When Proposition 227 was described in more detail, responses differed dramatically. Krashen, Crawford, and Kim (1998) conducted a comparative poll, using the following modified question:

> There is a new initiative trying to qualify for the June primary ballot that would severely restrict the use of the child's native language in school. This initiative would limit special help in English to one year (180 school days). After this time, limited English proficient children would be expected to know enough English to do school work at the same level as native speakers of English their age. The initiative would dismantle many current programs that have been demonstrated to be successful in helping children acquire English, and would hold teachers financially responsible if they violate this policy. If passed, schools would have 60 days to conform to the new policy. If the June 1998 primary election were being held today, would you vote for or against this policy?

When asked the *Los Angeles Times* Poll question, 57 percent of respondents supported Proposition 227; when asked the modified question, only 15 percent did so.

17. An exception is English First, a more radical group, which did target the Bilingual Education Act for elimination in some versions of Official English legislation. Yet its influence has been limited to extreme right-wing factions in Congress.

18. In fact, earlier arrivals were generally slower to learn English than today's newcomers (Veltman 1983), while bilingual accommodations were commonplace until the early twentieth century. In 1900 at least 4 percent of the U.S. elementary school population received part or all of its instruction in the German language (Kloss 1998), probably a larger

proportion than all language groups enrolled in bilingual education today. But none of these realities has diminished the power of melting pot mythology.

19. The House narrowly passed the bill, H.R. 856, authorizing a plebiscite on the island's political status. In the process, it rejected an amendment that would have imposed requirements for English Only government if Puerto Ricans opted for statehood. The Senate did not act on the bill in the 105th Congress.

20. Tanton resigned as chairman of U.S. English in October 1988 amid the furor following public disclosure of this memorandum (Crawford 1992). He continues to promote language-restrictionist goals as head of a smaller organization, English Language Advocates.

21. For example, voters turned thumbs down on Proposition 226, which would have limited unions' ability to spend their members' dues on political campaigns. In exit polls, 48 percent of voters identified themselves as Democrats and 20 percent as liberals, versus 40 percent and 17 percent, respectively, in the November 1994 election when Proposition 187 was adopted (*Los Angeles Times* Poll 1994, 1998).

22. The "black xenophobia" Unz (1994) had warned about failed to materialize, as African Americans voted against Proposition 227, 48 to 52 percent. Non-Hispanic/Latino Whites voted in favor, 67 to 33 percent (*Los Angeles Times*-CNN Poll 1998).

23. Mike Honda, a first-year member of the assembly from San Jose, was the notable exception.

24. Like most campaigns, Citizens was neither a formal coalition nor a membership organization; there was no structure for democratic decision making or regular communication with volunteers. The No on 227 steering committee was beholden to its sponsoring groups, in particular those supplying the financial resources. Most day-to-day operations were delegated to Richie Ross, a Sacramento political consultant.

25. I belonged to this latter camp, helping to organize an effort to influence media coverage known as UnzWatch.

26. This program was funded through the Bilingual Education Act from 1984 to 1994.

27. Citizens for an Educated America raised and spent $4,754,157. English for the Children raised $1,289,815 but spent only $976,632. Ron Unz personally contributed $752,738 (California Secretary of State 1998).

28. H.R. 3892, sponsored by Representative Frank Riggs (R-Calif.), passed the House, 221-189, largely along party lines. It never came to a vote in the Senate during the 105th Congress.

29. Rossell is no stranger to "big money" herself. In 1988, when the Berkeley (Calif.) Unified School District was sued by parents demanding stronger bilingual programs, Rossell served as an expert witness for the defense. She took home $129,049 in fees and expenses for her consulting work. Baker and Porter were paid $40,950 and $12,937, respectively (BUSD associate superintendent Anton Jungherr, personal communication).

Works Cited

Anderson, Nick. 1997. "Bilingual Debate Comes to L.A." *Los Angeles Times,* Dec. 3.

Anderson, Nick, and Amy Pyle. 1998. "Bilingual Classes a Knotty Issue." Los Angeles Times, May 18.

August, Diane, and Kenji Hakuta, eds. 1997. *Improving Schooling for Language-Minority Children: A Research Agenda.* Washington, D.C.: National Academy Press/U.S. Department of Education.

Balz, Dan. 1998. "GOP Analysts Buff Up Nov. 3 Results." *Washington Post,* Nov. 20.

California Department of Education, Educational Demographics Unit. 1998. *Language Census, 1997–98* [Online]: http://www.cde.ca.gov/demographics/reports/.

California Secretary of State, Political Reform Division. 1998. *Financing California's Statewide Ballot Measures: Campaign Receipts and Expenditures through June 30, 1998* [Online]: http://www.ss.ca.gov/prd/bmprimary98_2/prop227-2.htm.

Campbell, Duane. 1998. "Draft Analysis of the No on 227 Campaign." *Our Struggle/Nuestra Lucha* 16(2): 1.

Chao, Julie. 1998. "Bilingual Poll: S.F. Chinese Back Fong, Oppose Prop. 227." *San Francisco Examiner,* May 27.

Chen, Edward. M. 1995. *Civil liberties implications of "Official English" Legislation before the United States House of Representatives Committee on Economic and Educational Opportunities, Subcommittee on Early Childhood, Youth, and Families.* Nov. 1 [Online]: http://www.aclu.org/congress/chen.html.

Citizens for an Educated America. 1998a. *Sample Letter-to-the-Editor Points*. Press release, February.

———. 1998b. *Q & A: What's in Unz?* Press release, February.

———. 1998c. *Talking Points against 227*. Press release, February.

Collier, Virginia P., and Wayne P. Thomas. 1989. "How Quickly Can Immigrants Become Proficient in School English?" *Journal of Educational Issues of Language Minority Students* 5: 26–39.

Congressional Record. 1996. Debate on H.R. 123. Vol. 142, No. 116, Pt. II, H9738-72.

Contra Costa Times. 1998. "Vote Yes on Prop. 227." May 29.

Crawford, James. 1987. "37 States Consider 'English Only' Bills, with Mixed Results." *Education Week,* June 17.

———. 1992. *Hold Your Tongue: Bilingualism and the Politics of "English Only."* Reading, MA: Addison-Wesley.

———. 1998a. "The Ninth Street Myth: Who Speaks for Latino Parents?" *Hispanic Link News Service* [Online], May 25. http://ourworld.compuserve.com/homepages/jwcrawford/HL3.htm.

———. 1998b. "Quality of Debate Suffers from Distortions, Stereotypes." *San Jose Mercury News* [Online], May 31. http://ourworld.compuserve.com/homepages/jwcrawford/SJMN27.htm.

———. 1998c. *The Bilingual Education Story: Why Can't the News Media Get It Right?* [Online]. Speech to the National Association of Hispanic Journalists, Miami, FL, June 26. http://ourworld.compuserve.com/homepages/jwcrawford/NAHJ.htm.

———. 1998d. "Language Politics in the U.S.A.: The Paradox of Bilingual Education" [Online]. *Social Justice* 25: 50–69. http://ourworld.compuserve.com/homepages/jwcrawford/paradox.htm.

———. 1999. *Bilingual Education: History, Politics, Theory, and Practice.* 4th ed. Los Angeles: Bilingual Educational Services.

Davis, G. 1998. *California Gubernatorial Candidates' Forum: Unanimous Opposition to Prop. 227* [Online]: Los Angeles, May 13. http://ourworld.compuserve.com/homepages/jwcrawford/govforum.html/.

English for the Children. 1997a. *The 1998 California "English for the Children" Initiative* [Online]: http://www.onenation.org/facts.html.

———. 1997b. *Proposition 227: The 1998 California "English for the Children" Initiative* [Online]: http://www.onenation.org/index.html.

English Language in Public Schools. 1998. Initiative Statute (Proposition 227) [Online]: http://Primary98.ss.ca.gov/VoterGuide/Propositions/ 227.htm.

Fishman, Joshua A. 1992. "The Displaced Anxieties of Anglo-Americans." In James Crawford, ed., *Language Loyalties: A Source Book on the Official English Controversy.* Chicago: University of Chicago Press. 165–70.

Garcia, Phil. 1998."Unz's Bilingual Measure Assailed from Right." *Sacramento Bee,* Feb. 1.

Glenn, Charles L. 1997. Review of the National Research Council study *Improving Schooling for Language-Minority Students: A Research Agenda.* READ Abstracts [Online]: May. http://www. doe.mass.edu/doedocs/NRCINT~2.html.

Gold, Norman C. 1997. *Teachers for LEP Students: Demand, Supply, and Shortage.* Sacramento: California Department of Education, Complaints Management and Bilingual Compliance Unit.

Greene, Jay. 1998. *A Meta-Analysis of the Effectiveness of Bilingual Education* [Online]. Claremont, CA: Tomás Rivera Policy Institute. http://ourworld.compuserve.com/homepages/jwcrawford/greene.htm.

Humphrey, Lisa. 1997. "Pollsters Skeptical of Anti-Bilingual Findings." *North County Times,* Nov. 9.

Ingram, Carl. 1998. "Wilson Backs Ballot Measure to Ban Bilingual Education." *Los Angeles Times,* May 19.

Kloss, Heinz. 1998. *The American Bilingual Tradition.* 2nd ed. Washington, D.C.: ERIC Clearinghouse on Languages and Linguistics.

Krashen, Stephen. 1998. "A Note on Greene's 'A Meta-Analysis of the Effectiveness of Bilingual Education'" [Online]: http://ourworld. compuserve.com/homepages/jwcrawford/Krashen2.htm.

Krashen, Stephen, James Crawford, and Haeyong Kim. 1998. "Bias in Polls on Bilingual Education: A Demonstration" [Online]: http:// ourworld.compuserve.com/homepages/jwcrawford/USCpoll.htm.

Los Angeles Times—CNN Poll. 1998. "Exit Poll: Profile of the Electorate" [Online]. June 4. http://www.latimes.com/HOME/NEWS/ POLLS/exitpollsuper.htm.

Los Angeles Times Poll. 1994. "A Look at the Electorate" [Online]. *Los Angeles Times,* Nov. 10. http://www.latimes.com/news/timespoll.

———. 1997. *Study #400* [Online]. Oct.15. http://www.latimes.com/ HOME/NEWS/POLLS/400pa4da.pdf.

————. 1998. *Study #410* [Online]. April 13. http://www.latimes.com/ HOME/NEWS/POLLS/PDF/410pa2da.pdf.

McQuillan, Jeff. 1998. *The Literacy Crisis: False Claims, Real Solutions.* Portsmouth, NH: Heinemann.

McQuillan, Jeff, and Lucy Tse. 1996. "Does Research Matter? An Analysis of Media Opinion on Bilingual Education, 1984–1994." *Bilingual Research Journal* 20: 1–27.

Media Alliance. 1998. *New Study Finds Omissions in California Media Coverage of Proposition 227* [Online]. http://ourworld.compuserve. com/homepages/jwcrawford/mediall.htm.

New York Times. 1998. "A Cramped Approach to Bilingualism." April 30.

Olsen, Laurie. 1999. "Reflections on the Key Role of Two-Way Bilingual Immersion Programs in This Proposition 227 Era." *Multilingual Educator* (February): 30–43.

Pinkerton, Sharon. 1998. "California's Public School Education Gets Lukewarm Review from California Parents." *Los Angeles Times,* May 19.

Pyle, Amy. 1996a. "Bilingual Schooling is Failing, Parents Say." *Los Angeles Times,* Jan. 16.

————. 1996b. "80 Students Stay Out of School in Latino Boycott." *Los Angeles Times,* Feb. 14.

Pyle, Amy, Patrick J. McDonnell, and Hector Tobar. 1998. "Latino Voter Participation Doubled Since '94 Primary." *Los Angeles Times,* June 4.

Ramírez, J. David, Sandra Yuen, and Dena Ramey. 1991. *Final Report: Longitudinal Study of Structured Immersion Strategy, Early-Exit, and Late-Exit Transitional Bilingual Education Programs for Language-Minority Children. Executive Summary.* San Mateo, CA: Aguirre International.

Rivera, Carla. 1998. "Bilingual Classes Get Support in Poll." *Los Angeles Times,* Feb. 10.

Rodríguez, Gregory. 1997. "An Opportunity for Latino Lawmakers to Take the Lead." *Washington Post,* Nov. 30.

Ryan, Charlotte. 1991. *Prime Time Activism: Media Strategies for Grassroots Organizing.* Boston: South End Press.

Sacramento Bee. 1998. "No on Prop. 227: Bilingual Initiative Is a Dangerous Experiment with Kids." May 14.

Sanchez, Miguel. 1998. "Learning English in Silicon Valley." *San Jose Mercury News,* Feb. 7.

San Francisco Chronicle. 1998. "A Good Bilingual Alternative." April 23.

Schrag, Peter. 1998. *Paradise Lost: California's Experience, America's Future.* New York: New Press.

Shultz, Jim. 1998. "Lessons of 227." *San Jose Mercury News,* June 5.

State of California Department of Finance, Demographic Research Unit. 1998. *Race/Ethnic Population Estimates: Components of Change for California Counties, April 1990 to July 1998* [Online]: http://www.dof.ca.gov/html/Demograp/race-eth.htm.

Stewart, J. 1998. "Krashen Burn." *New Times LA,* May 29.

Stockton Record. 1998. "227 Wrong Fix for What Ails Bilingual Ed." May 20.

Tanton, John. 1986. Memorandum to WITAN IV Attendees. Oct. 10.

Unz, Ron K. 1994. "Immigration or the Welfare State: Which Is Our Real Enemy?" *Policy Review* 70: 33–38.

———. 1997. "Bilingual Is a Damaging Myth." *Los Angeles Times,* Oct. 19.

———. 1998. Debate with James Crawford at the Sonoma County Office of Education, Santa Rosa, CA, Mar. 31.

U.S. Bureau of the Census. 1998. *State Profile: California* [Online]: http://www.census.gov/statab/www/states/ca.txt.

U.S. English. 1991. U.S. English Education Program Fact Sheet. Washington, DC: Author.

U.S. General Accounting Office. 1995. *Federal Foreign Language Documents.* Report #D-95-253R. Washington, D.C.: U.S. Government Printing Office.

Veltman, Calvin. 1983. *Language Shift in the United States.* Berlin: Mouton.

Yi, Joseph. 1998. "An Immigrant's Advice: Learn English." *Los Angeles Times,* April 11.

CHAPTER THREE

The Politics of English Only in the United States: Historical, Social, and Legal Aspects

CAROL SCHMID
Guilford Technical Community College

In Noam Chomsky's words, "questions of language are basically questions of power" (1979, 191). This chapter is concerned with the process by which non-English languages were and are devalued, conquered, assimilated, and partially accommodated. The founding fathers and later policymakers held ambivalent attitudes toward languages other than English, ranging from pragmatic acceptance to deliberate policies of forced extermination and assimilation.

The first section of this chapter explores the relationship between language movements and high levels of immigrants in the early and late twentieth century. High levels of immigration in the United States have typically led to two trends: an increase in various strains of xenophobia and a crusade to "Americanize" the new immigrants. As Higham (1967) observes, "When neither a preventative nativism nor the natural health of a free society seemed sufficient to cope with disunity, a conscious drive to hasten the assimilative process, to heat and stir the melting pot, emerged" (235). Both the post-1965 era and the period of Americanization campaigns, defined as the decades between the 1890s and the 1920s aimed at the "new immigration" from southern and eastern Europe, shared a significant upsurge of newcomers who were thought to be significantly different from the older native-born population and incapable of being assimilated into American culture (Graham and Koed 1993). High immigration is also an important factor in the emergence of political movements to abolish bilingual services, such as the recent initiatives in California.

The second section examines Official English legislation and recent legal cases, focusing on English Only laws and Proposition 227, which effectively eliminates bilingual education in California. Despite its obvious importance, there has been relatively little scholarly attention directed toward the issue of language rights in the United States. The last section analyzes the issues raised by English Only rules. The imposition of English in the United States has not been uniform across different language groups. Of particular interest is the divergent treatment of linguistic groups and the ideological aims on the part of the dominant groups.

Language Restriction, High Immigration, and the Politics of Exclusion

Early-Twentieth-Century Language Conflict

The first English-language requirement for naturalization was adopted with the explicit purpose of limiting the entrance into the United States of southern and eastern Europeans. During World War I, the idea of expulsion as an alternative to assimilation was frequently discussed. In 1916 the National Americanization Committee, which worked closely with the Federal Bureau of Education, sponsored a bill in Congress to deport all aliens who would not apply for citizenship within three years. The U.S. Congress in the Revenue Act of 1918 doubled income tax rates on "nonresident" aliens—an ill-defined term, but one clearly intended to increase the rate of naturalization. In 1919 fifteen states decreed English as the sole language of instruction. An Oregon law required foreign-language newspapers to publish English translations, and a California law mandated that foreigners pay a special poll tax of $10.20 (Graham and Koed 1993; Higham 1967).

The late nineteenth century through World War I was a time of high immigration and a crusade to "Americanize" the new immigrants. In 1911 a federal commission issued a forty-two-volume study of the foreign-born population alleging that the "new immigrants" were less skilled and educated, more clannish, slower to learn English, and generally less desirable as citizens than the "old immigrants" (Handlin 1957). A 1919 article in the *American Journal of Sociology* also echoed this theme, observing that "unlike the earlier immigrants, many of the late-comers manifested no intention of making America a permanent home and no desire of becoming Americans" (Hill 1919, 611).

The "new immigrants" came from those regions of Europe— the Russian Empire, Austria-Hungary, Italy, and the Balkans— which were comparatively poor and had a less democratic tradition compared to the "old immigrants" from the British Isles, Germany, Holland, and other sections of northwestern Europe. This first wave of newcomers came from those regions of Europe which had a common fund of social mores and practices, and a somewhat similar socioeconomic and political experience. In addition, most of the first wave of immigrants was Protestant, while the second wave tended to be Catholic or Jewish. The new immigrant groups began to migrate to the United States in significant numbers as early as 1875, when approximately 10 percent of the total number of immigrants came from eastern and southern Europe. Each year thereafter the percentage increased; by 1896 it reached 57 percent, and by 1902, it was over 76 percent. From 1873 to 1910, it has been estimated that approximately 9,306,000 immigrants from southern and eastern Europe migrated to the United States (Hartmann 1948). At the turn of the century, the nation's already high immigration increased dramatically, doubling between 1902 and 1907 (Landes, Cessna, and Foster 1993).

Even western European immigrants have come under attack when their numbers increased or political events called special attention to the group. Before World War I, German Americans, as the largest language minority in the United States, came under immediate suspicion. The large increase in German speakers in all likelihood made the population more visible. Between 1850 and 1880, the number of foreign-born Germans whose mother tongue was German increased from 15 to 60 percent, largely as a result of immigration (Kloss 1977, 13). After the United States entered World War I, measures were taken in many states against the German population. The war, according to Wittke (1936), "precipitated a violent, concerted movement to eradicate everything German from American civilization" (163).

In 1917 an amendment to the Espionage Act was submitted to Congress requiring every foreign-language paper to submit precise English translations of all articles containing news on the war. The primary purpose of the amendment was to provide effective censorship of the foreign-language press, most notably of papers in the German language. Although there was some protest, the law went into effect on October 15, 1917. The law had a dampening effect on German-language newspapers in the United States. By 1920, ten papers which had previously been printed in German appeared exclusively in English. Although there were few arrests, several editors were interned as alien enemies. The editor of the *Cleveland Echo,* a socialist paper, was arrested for not filing a translation of an article attacking the American Protective League (Wittke 1936).

German schools had enjoyed a privileged position in the curricula of some school systems. The hysteria of the war, however, changed this situation. Petitions were circulated to eliminate German from the curriculum. Almost immediately the number of students taking German in the schools dropped significantly. For example, in Cincinnati high schools in the fall of 1918, less than thirty students elected to take German. On April 1, 1919, Governor James Cox urged the adoption of a law to abolish the teaching and use of German in the public, private, and parochial elementary schools of Ohio as "a distinct menace to Americanization, and a part of a plot formed by the German government to make the school children loyal to it" (Wittke 1936, 181). By 1923 thirty-four states adopted laws banning instruction in students' native languages, and some states also banned foreign-language teaching in the early grades (Leibowitz 1971).

Through immigration and nationality laws, the federal government ranked populations into hierarchies of assimilability, in which some groups were regarded as more likely to "fit in" than others (Carter, Green, and Halpern 1996). Attempts to exclude foreign-born immigrants deemed "racially" undesirable became apparent when Congress passed an act to suspend Chinese immigration in 1882. Fundamental to the opposition of the Chinese and other undesirable groups was the antagonism of race, reinforced by economic competition (Sandmeyer 1939). The reconstitution of national identity was articulated through concepts of race, language, country of origin, and religion. The debate over immigration policy helped to expose the extent of anxiety over who was to be included in the nation. This started a process by which the federal government codified in immigration law racist and nationalist discourse. Over the next two decades, the principle of exclusion by race was extended to several groups which were thought to be unassimilable. The exclusion of Japanese workers was accomplished by the Gentleman's Agreement of 1907. Immigrants from southern and eastern Europe were also racialized.

Immigration restrictionists were motivated by a variety of factors, which included ideological commitments to white supremacy, acceptance of social Darwinistic thinking, vote-getting demagoguery, and the belief that the increase in immigration that took place from the 1890s onwards, particularly from southern and eastern Europe, would threaten the nation's ability to absorb and Americanize the newcomers (Carter, Green, and Halpern 1996). Wartime intolerance of German Americans, coupled with language, ethnic, and racial antagonism, combined to create an atmosphere conducive to the revision of the United States' once liberal immigration policy.

Bilingualism came directly under attack beginning in the 1920s, bolstered by new psychometric tests. The majority of studies by psychologists consistently reported evidence that bilingual children suffered from a language handicap. In comparison with monolingual children, bilingual youth were found to be inferior in intelligence test scores and on a range of verbal and nonverbal linguistic abilities. Nature rather than nurture was cited as cause of the low IQ among bilingual immigrant schoolchildren (Portes and Rumbaut 1996). Collectively, these findings supported attempts to vastly reduce the number of newcomers.

The decades of the Americanization movement culminated in legislation in 1921 and 1924 creating the national origins quota system, effectively closing the gates to mass immigration. The 1921 Immigration Act limited admissions from each European country to 3 percent of each foreign-born nationality in

1910, with an annual maximum of 350,000 entrants. The consequence was that northern Europeans were favored at the expense of southern and eastern Europeans. Higham observed that the 1921 act

> proved in the long-run to be the most important turning point in American immigration policy. It imposed the first sharp and absolute numerical limits on European immigration. It established a nationality quota system based on the pre-existing composition of the American population—an idea which has survived in one form or another through all subsequent legislation. (Higham 1967, 311)

Large-scale evasion of the quotas quickly began, with estimates of illegal entrants ranging from 100,000 a year to 1,000 a day (Keller 1994, 229). In 1924 the Johnson Act superseded the 1921 legislation. It was even more extreme in reducing the number of immigrants by using the 1890 census as a benchmark and reducing quotas from 3 percent to 2 percent. The 1924 act also excluded immigrants ineligible for citizenship, that is, Chinese and Japanese. Furthermore, it provided for an examination of prospective immigrants overseas, and put the burden of proof of admissibility on the would-be immigrants (Hutchinson 1981). Immigration restriction marked the conclusion of an era of nationalistic and nativistic legislation in the mid-1920s. Language and immigration issues then lay largely dormant as a public issue for the next half a century.

Late-Twentieth-Century Language Conflict

Today's "new era"[1] immigration waves represent a significant departure from the past. This stems in part from the change in immigrants' national origins, with most of the newcomers arriving from Latin America and Asia rather than from Europe. Half of the newcomers between 1955 and 1964 came from Europe, with most of the remainder arriving from North America, primarily Mexico, the Caribbean, and Central America. By the decade from 1965 to 1974, the proportion arriving from Europe had dropped to barely 30 percent, while the percentage arriving from Asia increased dramatically to 22 percent, and the percentage coming from Mexico and Central America increased by 40 percent (Landes, Cessna, and Foster 1993). Immigration increased dramatically around 1965 after a lull of almost four decades. The rate of increase in the immigrant population was nearly twice as fast in the 1980s as in the 1970s. Much of the surge was among Hispanics/Latinos, who comprised 48 percent of immigrants during the 1980s. In 1991 newcomers from Mexico comprised almost 52 percent of the total immigrant population (U.S. Immigration Service 1997).

Much like the immigrants who came before them, the most recent wave of newcomers are highly concentrated among a few states and metropolitan areas. California, New York, Florida, Texas, Illinois, and New Jersey contain nearly three-fourths of the foreign residents counted in the 1990 census. California, a traditional destination for immigrants from Asia as well as Latin America, contained one-third of the U.S. foreign-born population in 1990. Although many immigrants are from rural backgrounds, 90 percent live in metropolitan areas, many of which are experiencing economic decline. Nearly five million Hispanic Americans live in the Los Angeles consolidated metropolitan statistical area (CMSA), while nearly three million live in New York. Close to a million Hispanics/Latinos live in the CMSAs of Miami, San Francisco, and Chicago (U.S. Bureau of the Census 1993).

The context in which immigration occurs today differs from that of earlier immigrants. Newcomers in the early part of the twentieth century were more likely to find an expanding economy that needed unskilled labor. Recent immigrants enter an economy that is growing more slowly. Current skill and education levels required by the marketplace are very different from those of the past, with an increased need for skilled individuals and a limited market for unskilled labor. The changes in the economy threaten the mobility of unskilled immigrant and citizen populations. Furthermore, the new era immigration is more global in its impact, with the flow and composition of immigrants determined by recent global and national economic and political transformations (Abelmann and Lie 1995; Ong, Bonacich, and Cheng 1994).

Language rights and antiforeigner sentiment have emerged as important issues in the second half of the twentieth century. The massive wave of immigration from Latin America and Asia that began in the 1960s fueled demands that government provide education, election ballots, emergency services, and other information in languages other than English.

Other factors have also contributed to the recent emergence of language as a source of conflict in the political arena. These include immigration reform, limited government recognition of bilingualism, and a heightened sense of nationalism and patriotism. The new national-origins system increased the number of immigrants allowed into the United States and gave priority to applicants who already had family members in the country. Settlement patterns exacerbated the language conflict since the growth of the Hispanic/Latino and Asian communities are heavily concentrated in five states, with almost 40 percent in California. The recent entry of so many immigrants who speak languages other than English makes them more visible and distorts perceptions of how well immigrants are learning English and adapting to the United States. Both English-language ability and incomes tend to increase with time spent in the country (Fix and Passel 1994).

Another important factor is the limited legal recognition of languages other than English. The Bilingual Education Act reversed our two-hundred-year-old tradition of a laissez-faire attitude toward language. It seemed to contradict ingrained assumptions about the role of second languages and the melting pot in U.S. society. The goals of the act were unclear, so it was variously interpreted as a remedial effort, enrichment program, and opportunity to maintain one's own language and culture through the public schools (Crawford 1989).

Finally, unstable economic conditions and current events seem to have fueled a new search for a national identity. According to Fishman, the English Only movement represents middle-class mainstream American fears and anxieties manifested by the creation of "mythical and simplistic and stereotyped scapegoats" (Fishman 1988, 132). As Donald Horowitz (1985) observes, language is an especially salient symbolic issue because it links political claims with psychological feelings of group worth. As in the early decades of the twentieth century, contemporary nativists blame many problems on the new immigrants. They find convenient scapegoats for the crisis in public institutions, including schools, health care, and welfare, as well as for high crime rates in poor immigrant quarters and the trend toward higher taxes.

Complaints about a breakdown in the process of assimilation are especially prevalent during periods of high immigration, economic restructuring, and job insecurity, providing fertile soil for the growth of nativism and a negative nationalism. This trend has not abated even though the new immigrants do not directly affect the vast majority of U.S. workers. The newcomers do not directly threaten most of their jobs. Several studies indicate that objective self-interests or economic conditions seem to be less important in shaping popular attitudes than the intensity of feelings toward a group or political symbol (Tatalovich 1995).

U.S. English is the largest, most aggressive, and most successful of the political groups promoting English as the official language in the United States. It has grown rapidly, from 300 members in 1983 to 400,000 nationwide as of 1990, with about half of these members in California (Schmid 1992). Currently, U.S. English reports 620,000 contributors (Tatalovich 1997). The activities of U.S. English include lobbying for a federal constitutional amendment making English the official language of the United States, restricting government funding for bilingual education to short-term transitional programs, and supporting state Official English statutes (Schmid 1992). So far voters or legislators have enacted English Only legislation in twenty-one states, and nowhere has such an initiative been defeated at the polls. In 1986 California voters, by a margin of 73-27 percent, adopted a constitutional amendment declaring English the state's official language. In November 1988, voters in the states of Arizona, Colorado, and Florida passed English Only amendments to their state constitutions by 51 percent in Arizona, 61 percent in Colorado, and 84 percent in Florida.

An important factor that sparks anti-immigrant sentiment in the United States and provides support for U.S. English and other restrictionist groups is the perception that new immigrants are unwilling or unable to learn English as readily as earlier immigrants. The lack of English proficiency has been blamed for numerous economic, social, and health problems encountered by immigrants and in society as a whole. Economists argue that English proficiency is a form of human capital and that limited knowledge is associated with lower earnings, less schooling for adolescents, and communication barriers with health care providers (Espenhade and Fu 1997).

Not since the beginning of this century has language received as much attention in the United States. Language battles in the 1980s and 1990s, like their counterparts in the 1900s, appeal to patriotism and unity, often casting language minorities in the role of outsiders who deliberately choose not to learn English. Unlike the earlier period, when these issues tended to be more localized, the last decade and a half has seen a campaign orchestrated at the national level. While the stated goal of U.S. English is to establish English as the official language in the United States, its connections to immigration restriction groups suggest a more far-reaching agenda.

The Federation for American Immigration Reform (FAIR) and U.S. English possess many common roots. Dr. John Tanton, a Michigan ophthalmologist, environmentalist, and population-control activist, launched FAIR in the late 1970s. FAIR is a Washington, D.C.–based lobby that advocates tighter restrictions on immigration. FAIR has proposed reducing the current level of about one million legal immigrants per year to 300,000 or fewer (Seper 1995). Prior to organizing FAIR, Tanton served as president of Zero Population Growth. Former Senator S. I. Hayakawa and Tanton organized U.S. English in 1983 as an offshoot of FAIR. By highlighting the cultural impact of immigration, U.S. English was able to bolster FAIR's demands for stricter control of the nation's borders. Until mid-1988, according to federal tax returns, U.S. English was a project of US Inc., a tax-exempt corporation that also channels large grants to FAIR, Americans for Border Control, Californians for Population Stabilization, and other immigration restrictionist groups. While FAIR did not hesitate to target Hispanic/Latino newcomers, in particular undocumented Mexicans, U.S. English focused on language while avoiding immigration issues (Crawford 1992, 153). Both organizations supported Proposition 187 (which restricted almost all social services, including education, of undocumented workers) in California. In this way, the two sister organizations were able to increase their social and economic influence.

Most attempts to protect English, although ostensibly neutral, have targeted Spanish speakers (Liebowicz 1985, 522). Spanish is the largest single non-English language spoken in the United States and comprises the largest group of limited-English-proficient (LEP) students. U.S. English has recently depicted Spanish-speaking communities in the United States as having unprecedented rates of language and cultural maintenance. Tanton, in a memo leaked to the press, warned of a Hispanic "political takeover" through immigration, language maintenance, high birthrates, and cultural maintenance.

The focus on language differences and opposition to bilingualism is seen by many political and social scientists as thinly veiled hostility and resentment toward Hispanics/Latinos and other minority-language groups (Alatis 1986; Heath and Krasner 1986; Judd 1987; Marshall 1986). The loss of a common language is an often repeated theme of U.S. English (de la Peña 1991). There is little evidence, however, to support this claim. Many myths surround language proficiency and the speed at which new immigrants and their children are learning English.

Despite widespread belief that immigrants are less likely to learn English than older waves of newcomers and their children, current studies do not support this commonly held opinion. In 1990, 14 percent of the nation's population spoke a language other than English in the home, but less than 3 percent did not speak English well or at all. In one of the best-designed studies looking at language shift, drawing on the 1976 Survey of Income and Education, Veltman (1988) concluded that data "certainly do not indicate that hispanophone immigrants resist the learning of English; in fact, the data indicate very rapid movement to English on the part of Spanish immigrants" (44). He found that more than three-fourths of any given age group of immigrants will come to speak English on a regular basis after approximately fifteen years of residence. Even more important, approximately 70 percent of the youngest immigrants and 40 percent of those aged ten to fourteen at the time of arrival will make English their primary language. According to a detailed 1989 study, despite significant differences according to age, education, nationality group, year of immigration, and English knowledge prior to immigration, most immigrants' English-language skills improve with added years of experience in the United States. New immigrants, especially those from Asian and Latin American countries, may encounter initial problems with the English language during their first few years. Based on the evidence of the study, however, "fears that America's newcomers are failing to learn English appear to be greatly exaggerated" (Espenshade and Fu 1997, 302).

In the late twentieth century, the English language has taken its place beside the American flag as a symbol of what it means to be an American. Countersymbols that challenge the melting pot theory, such as the legitimacy of speaking and perhaps even maintaining a language in addition to English, add to the current social conflict. One could vividly see this clash in Proposition 227 in California. The California measure passed 61 percent to 39 percent in June 1998. Proposition 227 significantly changes the way that LEP students are taught in California. Specifically, it requires that "all children in California public schools shall be taught English by being taught in English." In most cases, this would eliminate bilingual classes—programs that provide students with academic instruction in their primary language while they learn English. LEP students are entitled to "be taught English . . . as effectively as possible." The initiative, however, shortens the time most LEP students would stay in special classes, prescribing programs of "sheltered English immersion during a temporary transition period not normally intended to exceed one year" (*English Language Education* 1998, Ch. 3, §300).

The reception of bilingual education is not equally negative in all parts of the country. Perceived economic incentives, especially in the business community, and a sense that bilingual education is "enrichment" rather than "remedial" education are two important variables explaining why bilingual education is better received in some states. In Florida a new push for bilingual education is coming from the Miami business community. A 1995 survey of businesses in Miami and surrounding Dade County found that more than half of the businesses worked at least 25 percent in Spanish. In addition, 95 percent of the businesses surveyed agreed on the importance of a bilingual workforce. A University of Miami study found that bilingual Hispanics/Latinos who are fluent in both English and Spanish earned about $3,000 a year more on average than unilingual English speakers. These conditions contrast sharply with those in California, where bilingual education has become equated with remedial education rather than an enrichment program. Businesses in California have been slow to recognize the advantage of bilingual employees (Anderson 1988).

Despite significant opposition to bilingual education in California, most LEP students do not study in bilingual classes. There are simply not enough classes to accommodate the rapidly growing numbers. California's public schools serve 5.6 million students in kindergarten through twelfth grades. In the 1996–97 school year, schools identified 1.4 million LEP students. These are students insufficiently proficient in English to keep up with their grade level in school. Only 30 percent of California students with limited English ability are taught in bilingual classes. These students receive some or all of their academic subjects in their home languages. Opposition to bilingual education was at the heart of the Unz initiative,[2] even though a majority of Hispanics/Latinos are not in bilingual classes. About 40 percent of all LEP students are taught their academic subjects in English with specially designed materials for students who lack fluency in English. The remaining 30 percent of LEP students do not receive special help in their academic subjects, either because they do not need it or because the school does not provide it (*English Language in Public Schools* 1998). Unfortunately, the question of what is the best method to teach children English, especially children from less privileged backgrounds, was lost in the noise of the campaign.

California is particularly ripe for conflict over bilingual education since the number of students labeled "limited English proficient" has more than doubled in the past ten years. They comprise nearly a quarter of the state's public school students and roughly 50 percent of all LEP students in the nation. Approximately 80 percent of LEP students speak Spanish as their mother tongue (*Plaintiff Legal Brief* 1998).

Race and ethnicity played a significant role in support or rejection of Proposition 227. African American support for the initiative fell below 50 percent, according to a *Los Angeles Times*-CNN exit poll, with just under half (48 percent) supporting the measure. Fewer than four in ten (37 percent) Hispanic/Latino voters backed the initiative. For many Hispanics/Latinos, an attack on bilingual education became synonymous with prejudice toward the large California Mexican American community of new immigrants. The proposition failed in two dozen precincts where Hispanics/Latinos accounted for at least half of the registered voters. Latino presence at the polls grew to 12 percent of all California voters in 1994 (Pyle, McDonnell, and Tobar 1998). Even though they are the state's fastest growing population, the Hispanic electorate is much smaller (12 percent in 1998) than the group's 29.4 percent share of the California population.[3] Non-Hispanic/Latino Whites, on the other hand, overwhelmingly supported the Unz measure. Almost seven in ten Whites (67 percent) supported Proposition 227. Endorsement of the initiative was particularly strong among Republicans, who provided the major support (77 percent) (*Los Angeles Times* Poll 1998).

The June 2, 1998, outcome appeared to follow other elections in California in which Latinos were in a minority and went against the tide on measures that were more likely to affect them personally: the anti–legal immigrant Proposition 187, and the anti–affirmative action Proposition 209. Latinos opposed both measures passed by state voters. Proposition 227 was the third racially divisive ballot measure in as many election years in California.

Immediately after Proposition 227 was passed, the Mexican American Legal Defense and Educational Fund, the American Civil Liberties Foundation, and other concerned civil rights organizations requested a preliminary injunction. A federal judge refused to block its enforcement. The following section analyzes language rights and the legal status of English Only laws. Is there a legal right to receive governmental services in languages other than English? To what extent is bilingual education guaranteed in the law?

Language Rights and the Legal Status of English Only Laws

The Constitutional Issue Avoided: Lau and Title VI

Almost twenty-five years ago in *Lau v. Nichols,* the Supreme Court held that placing non-English-speaking students in a classroom with no special assistance and providing them with instruction that was not comprehensible to them violated Title VI of the federal Civil Rights Act of 1964. In *Lau,* a class of approximately 1,800 non-English-speaking Chinese students in the San Francisco schools raised an equal-protection claim and a claim under Title VI. Title VI prohibits discrimination based on the grounds of race, color, or national origin in any program or activity receiving federal financial assistance.

In its analysis, the Supreme Court observed the importance of the English language in the California educational scheme. English fluency was a prerequisite for high school graduation. School attendance was compulsory. Furthermore, English as the basic language of instruction was mandated by the state. Given these state imposed standards, "there is no equality of treatment merely by providing students with the same facilities, textbooks, teachers, and curriculum; for students who do not understand English are effectively foreclosed from any meaningful education" (*Lau v. Nichols* 1974, 566).

In addition to Title VI, the *Lau* court relied on the guidelines promulgated by the Department of Health, Education and Welfare (HEW) in reaching this conclusion. The guidelines required that school districts take affirmative steps to address the language needs of minority-language children. Failure to rectify language deficiencies constitutes discrimination on the basis of national origin, even if it is not deliberate. The Court did not resolve the question of whether the failure to provide educational assistance to non-English-speaking students violated the constitution. The *Lau* decision did not order a specific remedy since none was requested by the plaintiffs, although it did identify bilingual education and English as a second language (ESL) instruction as options.

In *Serna v. Portales,* the Tenth Circuit Court closely followed the reasoning in *Lau,* and also ruled on Title VI rather than constitutional grounds. The *Serna* court noted that the children were required to attend schools in which classes were conducted in English. Since it failed to provide remedial measures to meet the needs of Mexican American students, the Portales school curriculum was discriminatory and in violation of Title VI and the HEW regulations (*Serna v. Portales* 1974).

As the only Supreme Court case on the issue of the right of language-minority children to an equal education, the *Lau* case established guidelines for similar cases. Courts tended to avoid the constitutional issue, rely on the discriminatory-effect rationalization of Title VI, choose a remedy on a case-by-case basis, and take into account the number of students involved (McFadden 1983). While there appears to be a limited right to rectify language deficiencies where school policies have had the effect of discriminating against national-origin minorities under Title VI, there is not an absolute right to bilingual education. In school districts with both language and racial minorities, conflicting remedies present difficult problems. With the future of *Lau* remedies increasingly uncertain, there has been more reliance on the Equal Educational Opportunity Act (EEOA) of 1974. Shortly after the *Lau* decision, Congress in effect codified the Supreme Court's holding.

The Equal Educational Opportunities Act

Section 1703(f) of the Equal Educational Opportunities Act requires school districts to "take appropriate action to overcome language barriers that impede equal participation by its students in its instructional programs." For the first time, Congress recognized the right of language-minority students to seek redress for a school system's inequity, whether or not it received subsidies from the federal government. Soon after the passage of section 1703(f), the Fifth Circuit Court held that a violation of this act requires no discriminatory intent on the part of school authorities, simply a failure to take appropriate action (*Morales v. Shannon* 1975).

The courts have been split, however, on the form this "appropriate" action must take. In 1978 the district court for the Eastern District of New York, in *Cintron v. Brentwood Union Free School District* (1978), held that where a bilingual program is implemented under section 1703(f), it must include instruction in the child's native language in most subjects. The Ninth Circuit Court, on the other hand, in *Guadalupe Organization, Inc. v. Tempe Elementary School* (1978), concluded that appropriate action under 1703(f) need not be bilingual-bicultural education staffed with bilingual instructors. The ESL program proposed for the Arizona school district qualified as an appropriate program for English-deficient children.

The interpretation of 1703(f) was clarified in the 1981 Fifth Circuit Court case of *Castaneda v. Pickard* (1981). Agreeing with Cintron, the court held that it was not necessary for a school district to discriminate intentionally in order for 1703(f) to be invoked. It also determined that the type of appropriate compensatory language programs should be left up to the state and local educational authorities. The Fifth Circuit Court of Appeals formulated a set of basic standards to determine a school district's compliance with EEOA. The *Castaneda* test included three major criteria: (1) the school must pursue a program based on an educational theory recognized as sound or, at least, as a legitimate experimental strategy; (2) the school must actually implement the program with instructional practices, resources, and personnel necessary to transfer theory into reality; and (3) the school must not persist in a program that fails to produce results. Therefore the court specified that at a minimum, schools must have a program predicated on and "reasonably calculated" to implement a "sound" educational theory and must be adequate in actually overcoming the students' language barriers (*Castaneda v. Pickard* 1981, 1010–1019). The influence of *Castaneda* has extended beyond the Fifth Circuit Court, making it one of the most significant cases affecting language-minority students after *Lau.*

While Section 1703(f) of the Equal Education Opportunity Act provides some protection for language minorities, like the *Lau* decision and Title VI, there is not a right to bilingual-bicultural education. The EEOA did, however, recognize a duty on behalf of educational agencies to ensure access to instructional programs for LEP students. In addition, it provided aggrieved individuals with a private right of action to compel such relief, and it allowed the attorney general of the United States to sue on behalf of those individuals.

On July 15, 1998, a federal court district judge rejected a move to block Proposition 227. Judge Charles Legge held, "Since there is no constitutional right to bilingual education, the voters of California were free to reject bilingual education." The plaintiffs argued that the initiative's "one-size-fits-all" program overrides choices of local schools and school districts and deprives them of the individualized flexibility to address the specific needs of the diverse composition of LEP students. "It reverses the State's proper role as a supervisor and guarantor of compliance, converting it into an enforcer of an arbitrary ceiling on educational services that impedes, rather than facilitates, compliance with the EEOA" (*Plaintiff Legal Brief* 1998, 23). The civil rights organizations argued that the initiative would cause "irreparable harm" by forcing schools to teach many students in a language they barely understand.

Opposing this view, attorneys for the state argued that the initiative simply favors an educational policy of language "immersion" that is followed elsewhere in the country. They observed that the initiative statute allows parents to apply for waivers to enable children to continue to receive bilingual teaching under limited circumstances. Judge Legge agreed that opponents had "terribly overstated" the restrictions and agreed with the state that the initiative allows educational agencies significant flexibility in catering to LEP students (Anderson and Sahagun 1998). The ruling is likely to be appealed to the United States Court of Appeals for the Ninth Circuit. The appellate courts are generally reluctant to stay a voter-approved law such as Proposition 227, particularly when a trial judge already has found no compelling reason to provide an injunction.

The Application of the Equal Protection Clause and Language Rights

Another argument put forth by the plaintiffs was that Proposition 227 "violates the Equal Protection Clause of the Fourteenth Amendment and is subject to strict scrutiny because it forecloses minorities' options in the area of equal educational opportunity, and restructures the political process to embed its single anointed option of 'immersion' to the preclusion of all others" (*Plaintiff*

Legal Brief 1998, 34). The Supreme Court applies a "strict scrutiny" standard of review to classifications that infringe on rights considered "fundamental," or classifications that single out "suspect classes." Strict scrutiny has been interpreted as applying not only to discrimination on the basis of race, but also to discrimination based on national origin. When strict scrutiny is applied, statutes generally fail unless they serve a compelling state interest. Classifications that do not implicate either specially protected rights or specially protected persons are granted broad deference by the courts on the "rational basis" standard. The courts will uphold the law so long as it has a rational or reasonable basis (Tribe 1978).

The Supreme Court has not resolved the question of whether language-based discrimination constitutes a "suspect" class. A number of legal scholars have argued that language-based discrimination should be afforded strict scrutiny or at least intermediate level scrutiny (Moran 1981; Califa 1989). They have emphasized the need for strict scrutiny because of the close relationship to national-origin discrimination. Like racial minorities, non-English speakers have suffered a history of discrimination (including voting and access to political power), been stigmatized by government action, and suffered economic and social disadvantage.

In general, the courts have rejected an equal-protection challenge to language minorities unless the case involves a close relationship to national-origin discrimination or involves rights considered fundamental. More common is the reasoning in *Soberal-Perez v. Heckler,* a Second Circuit Court case, which rejected an equal-protection challenge for the failure to provide information in Spanish to Social Security recipients and applicants, holding that "[l]anguage, by itself, does not identify members of a suspect class" (*Soberal-Perez v. Heckler* 1983, 41). In addition to the Second Circuit Court, the Sixth and Ninth Circuit Courts, employing similar reasoning, have continued to hold that language is not synonymous with nationality (*Frontera v. Sindell* 1975; *Carmona v. Sheffield* 1973). The standard of judicial review under the Equal Protection Clause will continue to be a major issue in the area of language rights. The current interpretation of the equal-protection analysis does not recognize language discrimination as a subset of national-origin discrimination.

Therefore, English Only laws for which language, as opposed to national origin, is at issue are rarely deemed "suspect."

Protection of Language Rights under the First Amendment

Very few cases have challenged Official English laws or governmental restraints on the use of foreign languages. Thus far courts have ruled that most state English Only laws are mainly of symbolic value. One important exception is the Arizona constitutional amendment, which is the most restrictive Official English statute. In 1988 the citizens of Arizona, by a 51 percent majority, amended their state constitution to require that all governmental employees and officials during working hours "shall act in English and no other language" (Arizona Constitution article 28 § 3[1][a]).

Maria-Kelley Yñiguez, a state employee, challenged the constitutionality of the amendment, arguing that it violated her free speech rights under the First Amendment. The district court agreed, holding that the amendment was unconstitutionally overbroad. When the state of Arizona chose not to appeal the decision, Arizonans for Official English, a group supported by U.S. English (which proposed the amendment) sought permission to do so. The Ninth Circuit Court of Appeals eventually granted that permission and heard the appeal. Prior to the Court of Appeals rule, Yñiguez resigned her position. The Court of Appeals, en banc, voted 6-5 to affirm the district court's decision. The case was appealed to the United States Supreme Court. Because of procedural problems, however, the Supreme Court case was not decided on the merits. The Court held that the actual controversy in the case ended when Yñiguez resigned her position and was no longer subject to the English Only amendment, so the case was ordered to be dismissed as moot (*Arizonans for Official English v. Arizona* 1997).

The constitutional amendment finally went to the Arizona Supreme Court. In an April 28, 1998, decision, the state supreme court held that the law violates the First Amendment because it interferes with the ability of non-English-speaking people to obtain government information, and hinders communication by public officials and employees (*Ruiz v. Hull* 1998). The law has limited application, applying only to Arizona, and does not affect other English Only state laws.

Conclusion

The English Only movement, like the Americanization movement before it in the 1920s, has prompted a resurgence of antiforeigner sentiment. Fueled by high rates of immigration from Latin American and Asian countries, English Only forces have attempted to limit bilingual services and encourage English Only laws in the public and private sectors. They seek to limit bilingual education and bilingual services. In California the passage of Proposition 227 will vastly curtail the use of native-language instruction in the classroom.

Many troubling aspects of the English Only movement and the official English laws remain. The laws have not increased the proficiency of individuals with a limited knowledge of English. Rather than promote national unity and tolerance of Hispanic/Latino and Asian newcomers, these laws have promoted an antiforeigner attitude among the population. Immigrants are perceived as refusing to assimilate and to learn the English language, even though studies show that most language minorities lose their mother tongues by the second or at most the third generation. Unless there are proper safeguards for language minorities, nativist groups will be able to promote a hidden agenda that has little to do with language.

Notes

1. This term is borrowed from Meissner, Hormats, Walker, and Ogata (1993), whose book is entitled *International Migration Challenges in a New Era*. The term "new era immigration" is used in this chapter to differentiate the post-1965 waves of immigration from the "new immigration" which took place from the 1890s through the 1920s.

2. Ron Unz is the wealthy Silicon Valley businessman who sponsored Proposition 227. He is a conservative Republican and former gubernatorial candidate. Unz has no educational background and, according to newspaper reports, has never set foot in a bilingual class (Terry 1998).

3. At parents' request, "waivers" of the English Only rule may be allowed for older LEP students and those with "special needs." These waivers are subject to many restrictions, however. Teachers, administrators, and school board members who failed to provide English Only instruction may be held personally liable for financial damages (*English for the Children* 1998, §§311, 320).

Works Cited

Abelmann, Nancy, and John Lie. 1995. *Blue Dreams: Korean Americans and the Los Angeles Riots.* Cambridge: Harvard University Press.

Alatis, James E. 1986. "Comment: The Question of Language Policy." *International Journal of the Sociology of Language* 60: 197–200.

Anderson, Nick. 1988. "A Boomtown of Bilingual Education." *Los Angeles Times,* 25 May [Online]: http://ourworld.compuserve.com/homepages/jwcrawford/LAT86.htm.

Anderson, Nick, and Louis Sahagun. 1998. "Judge Refuses to Stand in Way of Prop. 227" [Online]: *Los Angeles Times,* 16 July. http://ourworld.compuserve.com/homepages/jwcrawford/LAT111.htm.

Califa, Antonio J. 1989. "Declaring English the Official Language: Prejudice Spoken Here." *Harvard Civil Rights-Civil Liberties Law Review* 24: 293–348.

Carter, Bob, Marci Green, and Rick Halpern. 1996. "Immigration Policy and the Racialization of Migrant Labour: The Construction of National Identities in the USA and Britain." *Ethnic and Racial Studies* 19: 135–57.

Chomsky, Noam. 1979. *Language and Responsibility.* Sussex, Eng.: Harvester Press.

Crawford, James. 1989. *Bilingual Education: History, Politics, Theory and Practice.* Trenton: Crane.

———. 1992. *Hold Your Tongue: Bilingualism and the Politics of "English Only."* Reading, MA: Addison-Wesley.

English Language Education for Immigrant Children. 1998. California Education Code, Chapter 3, Section 300 [Online]: http://primary98.ss.ca.gov/VoterGuide/Propositions/227text.htm.

English Language in Public Schools. 1998. Initiative Statute [Online]. California Secretary of State Analysis. http://primary98.ss.ca.gov/VoterGuide/Propositions/227analysis.htm.

Espenhade, Thomas J., and Haishau Fu. 1997. "An Analysis of English-Language Proficiency Among US Immigrants." *American Sociological Review* 62: 288–305.

Fishman, Joshua. 1988. "English Only: Its Ghosts, Myths and Dangers." *International Journal of Sociology of Language* 74: 124–42.

Fix, Michael, and Jeffrey S. Passel. 1994. *Immigration and Immigrants : Setting the Record Straight.* Washington, D.C.: The Urban Institute.

Graham, Otis L. Jr., and Elizabeth Koed. 1993. "Americanizing of the Immigrant, Past and Future: History and Implications of a Social Movement." *The Public Historian* 15: 24–45.

Handlin, Oscar. 1957. *Race and Nationality in American Life.* Boston: Little Brown.

Hartmann, Edward George. 1948. *The Movement to Americanize the Immigrant.* New York: Columbia University Press.

Heath, Shirley Brice, and Lawrence Krasner. 1986. "Comment." *International Journal of the Sociology of Language* 60: 157–62.

Higham, John. 1967. *Strangers in the Land.* New York: Atheneum.

Hill, Howard C. 1919. "The Americanization Movement." *American Journal of Sociology* 24: 609–42.

Horowitz, Donald L. 1985. *Ethnic Groups in Conflict.* Berkeley: University of California Press.

Hutchinson, E. P. 1981. *Legislative History of American Immigration Policy, 1798–1965.* Philadelphia: University of Pennsylvania Press.

Judd, Elliot L. 1987. "The English Language Amendment: A Case Study on Language and Politics." *TESOL Quarterly* 21: 113–33.

Keller, Morton. 1994. *Regulating a New Society.* Cambridge: Harvard University Press.

Kloss, Heinz. 1977. *The American Tradition.* Rowley: Newbury House.

Landes, Alison, Cornelia B. Cessna, and Carol D. Foster. 1993. *Immigration and Illegal Aliens.* Wylie: Information Plus.

Leibowitz, Arnold. 1971. "Educational Policy and Political Acceptance: The Imposition of English as the Language of Instruction in America's Schools." Washington D.C.: Center for Applied Linguistics.

Leibowicz, Joseph. 1985. "The Proposed English Language Amendment: Shield or Sword?" *Yale Law and Policy Review* 3: 519–50.

Los Angeles Times-CNN Poll. 1998. "Profile of the California Electorate—Ballot Propositions." 4 June [Online]. http://www.latimes.com/HOME/NEWS/POLLS/exitpollsuper.htm.

Marshall, David F. 1986. "The Question of an Official Language: Language Rights and the English Language Amendment." *International Journal of the Sociology of Language* 60: 7–75.

McFadden, Bernard J. 1983. "Bilingual Education and the Law," *Journal of Law and Education* 12: 1–27.

Meissner, Doris, Robert D. Hormats, Antonio Garrigues Walker, and Shijuro Ogata. 1993. *International Migration Challenges in a New Era*. New York: The Trilateral Commission.

Moran, Rachel F. 1981. "Quasi-Suspect Classes and Proof of Discriminatory Intent: A New Model." *Yale Law Journal* 90: 912–31.

Ong, Paul, Edna Bonacich, and Lucie Cheng, eds. 1994. *The New Asian Immigration in Los Angeles and Global Restructuring*. Philadelphia: Temple Press.

de la Peña, Fernando. 1991. *Democracy or Babel? The Case for Official English*. Washington, D.C.: U.S. English.

Plaintiff Legal Brief, Proposition 227. 1998. Plaintiffs' Legal Brief Requesting a Preliminary Injunction. U.S. District Court, San Francisco. June.

Portes, Alejandro, and Rubén G. Rumbaut. 1996. *Immigrant America*. Berkeley: University of California Press.

Pyle, Amy, Patrick J. McDonnell, and Hector Tobar. 1998. "Latino Voter Participation Doubled since '94 Primary." *Los Angeles Times*, June 4.

Sandmeyer, Elmer Clarence. 1939. *The Anti-Chinese Movement in California*. Urbana: University of Illinois Press.

Schmid, Carol. 1992. "Language Rights and the Legal Status of English Only Laws in the Public and Private Sector." *North Carolina Central Law Journal* 36: 903–8.

Seper, Jerry. 1995. "Group's 10-Point Plan Offers Hill Standard for Immigration Reform." *Washington Times*, March 10.

Tatalovich, Raymond. 1995. *Nativism Reborn?* Lexington: University of Kentucky Press.

———. 1997. "Official English as Nativist Backlash." In Juan F. Perea, ed., *Immigrants Out*. New York: New York University Press.

Terry, Don. 1998. "Bilingual Education Faces Major Test in California." *New York Times*, March 10 [Online]. http://www.nytimes.com/yr/mo/day/news/national/calif-bilingual-edu.html.

Tribe, Lawrence. 1978. *American Constitutional Law*. Mineola, NY: Foundation Press.

U.S. Bureau of the Census. 1993. *The Foreign-Born Population of the United States*, CP-3-1. Washington, D.C.: U.S. Government Printing Office.

U.S. Immigration Service. 1997. *Statistical Yearbook of the Immigration and Naturalization Service, 1995*. Washington, D.C.: U.S. Government Printing Office.

Veltman, Calvin. 1988. *The Future of the Spanish Language in the United States*. New York: Hispanic Policy Development Project.

Wittke, Carl. 1936. *German-Americans and the World War*. Columbus: The Ohio State Archeological and Historical Society.

Court Cases Cited

Arizonans for Official English v. Arizona. 1997. 117 S. Ct. 1055.

Carmona v. Sheffield, 475 F.2d 738 (9th Cir.), 1973.

Castaneda v. Pickard, 648 F.2d 989 (5th Cir.), 1981.

Cintron v. Brentwood Union Free School District. 455 F. Supp. 56 (E.D.N.Y.), 1978.

Frontera v. Sindell, 522 F.2d 1215, 1975.

Guadalupe Organization, Inc. v. Tempe Elementary School, 587 F.2d 1022 (9th Cir.), 1978.

Lau v. Nichols, 414 US 563, 1974.

Morales v. Shannon, 516 F.2d 411 (5th Cir.), 1975.

Ruiz v. Hull, CV-96-0493-PR, 1998.

Serna v. Portales, 499 F.2d 1147 (10th Cir.), 1974.

Soberal-Perez v. Heckler, 717 F.2d 36 (2nd Cir.), 1983.

——————— II ———————

RESEARCH AND POLITICS

The chapters in this section illustrate different aspects of the troubled relationship between research and politics regarding the education of language-minority children. Eugene E. García approaches the instructional challenge of minority students in the United States from a uniquely diverse perspective. García has worked in research and participated in policymaking and thus has played a significant role in shaping pedagogy. In addition, growing up in a large Hispanic/Latino family has taught him to turn diversity into an asset. As director of the Office of Bilingual Education and Minority Language Affairs, García found a common pattern in the diverse principles applied by successful schools: no matter how much these schools vary in method or approach, they all share two overarching assumptions—that diversity is a positive force in education and that difference is a source of learning, not an obstacle to it. In view of this research, García can safely conclude that English Only policy is at odds with what are known to be components of successful educational programs at the turn of the twenty-first century.

Thomas Scovel addresses the conflict between politics and research from a different perspective, placing popular but mistaken assumptions about language learning under a microscope. Scovel uses the term "myth" to express his reservations about the dubious epistemological status of some commonsense assumptions about language that are often fostered by the "junk science" spread in the media. But as Scovel also reckons, myths are not simply the antonyms of facts; they are based on claims that are "at least half true." The epistemological conflict between "myth" and "sound knowledge," or between "half truth" and "truth" is further aggravated by the contrast between the public's search for general answers to general questions and the scientist's reluctance to deal with such "unanswerable generalities." As Scovel notes, linguists prefer "breaking down their inquiry into smaller queries until a manageable research question emerges." For example, Scovel turns the plain question, "Are children better language learners than adults?" into a series of equally complex inquiries, such as who is considered a child and who an adult, or what exactly better language learning consists of. While Scovel meticulously analyzes and addresses some of these questions based on available research, he is also aware of what he calls "sociocultural pressures . . . to pursue myths." Yet he argues that professionals should not give up the hope that they can raise some public consciousness about the complexity of these issues, and they should not cease to warn the public about the precarious consequences of anchoring educational or political decisions in fallacious but popular myths.

Bilingual education has been the most recent target of English Only advocates, and it is probably one of the most misunderstood and misrepresented instructional programs in the history of U.S. education. Moreover, bilingual education is also a good example of the huge gap between research and politics. One problem is that according to popular belief, bilingual education promotes first language use and delays English proficiency. In fact, as Stephen D. Krashen's chapter argues, the majority of the bilingual education programs in the United States are designed to maintain academic development until the students' English proficiency is sound enough to give them a fair chance of keeping up with the content of their classes in English. Schools do not teach "English only"; schools teach math, science, arts, social studies, and literature. But, as Krashen points out, the political advocates of English Only often overlook what is an obvious pursuit of educational institutions. Namely, the main responsibility of schools is not restricted to teaching English; it involves making these various content areas meaningful and available for all students, including those whose English is not up to the required level of proficiency. Krashen reviews several important research projects, concluding that bilingual education, when properly implemented by the school and strongly supported by the community, can help bilingual children flourish both academically and linguistically. Therefore, Krashen assumes that those who oppose these programs not only ignore evidence from research, but they also deny the importance of these more general goals in education.

CHAPTER FOUR

Treating Linguistic and Cultural Diversity as a Resource: The Research Response to the Challenges Inherent in the Improving America's Schools Act and California's Proposition 227

EUGENE E. GARCÍA

University of California, Berkeley

A s typical teachers look at the students in their classroom, they see a picture much different from the classroom of their childhood. Today, one in three children nationwide is from an ethnic or racial minority group, one in seven speaks a language other than English at home, and one in fifteen is born outside the United States. By the year 2015, one in ten new students in U.S. schools will be of immigrant background, while in states such as Texas, California, New York, Florida, and Arizona, one in five new students will be immigrants (García 1998). The linguistic and cultural diversity of America's school population has increased dramatically during the past decade and is expected to increase even more in the future. Educating children from linguistically and culturally diverse families is a major concern of school systems across the country. For many of these children, U.S. education has not been and continues not to be a successful experience. While one-tenth of non-Hispanic/Latino White students leave school without a diploma, one-fourth of African Americans, one-third of Hispanic Americans, one-half of Native Americans, and two-thirds of immigrant students drop out of school.

Confronted with this dismal reality, administrators, teachers, parents, and policymakers urge each other to do something different—change teaching methods, adopt new curricula, allocate more funding. Such actions may well be needed, but they will not be meaningful unless we begin to think differently about these students. In order to educate them, we must first educate ourselves about who they are and what they need in order to succeed. Thinking differently involves viewing these students in new ways that may contradict conventional notions and may lead to a new set of realizations.

During my recent assignment in Washington, D.C. as director of the Office of Bilingual Education and Minority Languages Affairs (OBEMLA) in the U.S. Department of Education, I attempted to apply my professional experience and expertise as an educational researcher, and I also relied on my personal cultural and linguistic experiences in addressing the challenging tasks of national educational policy (García and Gonzales 1995). The professional in me was and continues to be nurtured in some of the best educational institutions of this country. The nonprofessional in me was and continues to live in a large, rural, Mexican American family—all speaking Spanish as our native language, all born in the United States like our parents, grandparents, and great-grandparents. I am one of ten children, one of five who graduated from high school, and the only one who graduated from college. I found bringing these *personas* (the Spanish term for "persons") together not as difficult as I might have expected. I even came to the conclusion that this intersection of cultures within me was quite helpful in addressing my colleagues and the wide variety of audiences with whom I interacted in this national role. In fact, I found that, by bringing together these *personas,* I was able to communicate to individuals in ways that would not have been possible if I spoke with only one or separate voices.

This chapter is my attempt to put into writing these intersecting but distinct voices and to help further our understanding of living in a diverse society. Moreover, I emphasize the role of educational institutions that strive to serve a linguistic and culturally diverse population today and that will need to serve them better in the future. For there is no doubt that the historical pattern of the education of these populations in the United States is a continuous story of underachievement. It need not be that way in the future. In fact, the new federal policy based on the Improving America's Schools Act (IASA) can reverse this pattern for linguistically and culturally diverse students.

In the footsteps of hopeful federal activity, however, we often see policy on the state or local levels that does not reflect an understanding of issues of diversity. For example, Proposition 227, the California state initiative passed in 1998, is one of the most recent actions to restrict the use of a language other than English in the delivery of educational services to non-English-speaking children. The ballot measure identified as English for the Children and passed by 61 percent of the vote on June 2, 1998, proposes to:

1. require that all children be placed in English-language classrooms, and that English-language learners be educated through a prescribed methodology identified as "structured English immersion"

2. prescribe methodology that will be provided during a temporary transition period, normally not to exceed one year

3. allow instruction in the child's native language only in situations in which a waiver is granted in writing, which requires yearly renewal and a school visit by parents

4. prohibit native-language instruction unless the student already has mastered English and is over ten years of age, and such instruction is approved by the principal and the teacher

Taken together, these provisions are the most restrictive measures yet proposed for serving language-minority students either nationally or within any state by means of legislation or the courts. Moreover, such legislation is a far cry from the key principles declared in the Improving America's Schools Act (passed in 1994), which include upholding high standards for all children; flexibility to stimulate local initiatives for school reform and accountability; and fostering connections among schools, parents, and communities.

As this country and the world shrink communicatively, and as economic, social, and intellectual exchanges across the global community become more common, our diversity becomes more visible and harder to hide. In fact, diversity has been and will always be there, but our social institutions need to address its growing prevalence better than they have done in the past. Specifically, it is extremely important to put into operation a plan to address how our educational institutions will meet the challenge of diversity successfully. At the core of addressing this challenge are two presuppositions: (1) to honor diversity is to honor the social complexity in which we live and to grant every individual integrity and language equally; (2) unity is absolutely necessary, but to insist on it without embracing diversity is to destroy the essence of the very thing that will allow us to unite—individual and collective dignity. The rest of this chapter presents the outcome of educational research that not only supports these principles but that also can help educators of the future overcome old notions and develop new ones that can better address the needs of a diverse student population.

One Size Does Not Fit All

Students from linguistically and culturally diverse families are often defined by the characteristics they share—a lack of English fluency (Cummins 1986; Crawford 1989). But such a definition masks their diversity and underestimates the challenge facing schools. Schools serve students who are new immigrants, ignorant of American life beyond what they have seen in movies, as well as African Americans, Mexican Americans, Asian Americans, Native Americans, and European American students, whose families have lived here for generations. Students representing dozens of native languages may attend a single school; in some school districts, more than 125 languages are spoken. In many schools, a majority of the students come from immigrant or ethnic minority families. Some schools face a mobility problem; student turnover is high and the ethnic mix shifts radically from year to year (Barona and García 1990).

Along with linguistic diversity comes diversity in culture, religion, and academic preparation. Some students visit their home country frequently, while others lack that opportunity. Some immigrant students have had excellent schooling in their home country before coming to the United States; others have had their schooling interrupted by war, and still others have never attended school. Some are illiterate in their own language, and some speak languages that were only oral until recently; others come from cultures with long literary traditions.

The differences between these students will affect their academic success much more than their common lack of English. These differences include their age and entry into the U.S. school, the quality of their prior schooling, their own and their parents'/family's/community's native language, the number of native-language compatriots in their class, their parents' education and English-language skills, and their family history and current circumstances. Since all these differences matter as much as if not more than proficiency in English, a policy such as English Only that does not consider all these factors, or narrowly focuses on these students' English-language proficiency, is not likely to guarantee the academic success of this diverse student population.

Educational Practices That Meet the Challenge

Recent research findings have redefined the nature of the educational vulnerability of linguistically and culturally diverse students (Cole 1995; García 1995, 1997). This research has destroyed common stereotypes and myths and laid a foundation on which to reconceptualize present educational practices and from which to launch new initiatives. This foundation recognizes both the homogeneity and heterogeneity within and between diverse student populations, and presumes that no exclusive set of descriptions or prescriptions will suffice. A set of commonalties found at different levels and on various sites of schooling, however, emerged from the most recent research. The common elements in these successful programs deserve particular attention.

California Tomorrow (1995), in a study of early childhood care in California, concluded that the following set of principles guided quality child care across a variety of care settings which serve a growing community of linguistically and culturally diverse families. Successful child care must

1. support development of ethnic identity and antiracist attitudes among children

2. build on the cultures of families and promote cross-cultural understanding among children

3. foster the preservation of the children's home language and encourage bilingualism among all children

4. engage in ongoing reflection and dialogue (California Tomorrow 1995, 8)

Cohen and Pompa (1994) interviewed experts in the early childhood field and conducted a formative literature review of research on multicultural early childhood approaches. They came to the same conclusion, noting in particular that universal notions of "developmentally appropriate" approaches must recognize the more specific issues of "culturally appropriate development."

Berman (1992), in a state-mandated study of exemplary schools serving California's linguistically and culturally diverse students, indicated that several key attributes were common in those exemplary schools serving these students. These included characteristics such as flexibility—adapting to the diversity of languages, social mobility, and special nonschool needs of these students and their families; coordination—utilizing sometimes scarce and diverse resources from federal, state, and local community organizations in combination to achieve academic goals more effectively; cultural validation—validating students' cultural identity by incorporating materials and discussions that build on the linguistic and cultural aspects of the community; and a shared vision—developing a coherent sense of who the students are and what they hope to accomplish led by a school's principal, staff, instructional aides, parents, and community.

Three slightly more recent "effective-exemplary" analyses of schools that serve high percentages of linguistically and culturally diverse students nationally are worthy of mention. Collier (1995) reports a series of studies in five urban and suburban school districts in various regions of the United States. These studies focus on the length of time students need to be academically successful in a second language, and they outline the student, program, and instructional variables that influence language-minority academic success. Studies included some 42,000 student records per school year and from eight to twelve years of data for each school district. The three key factors reported as significant in producing academic success for students in the schools studied are the following:

1. cognitively complex academic instruction in the students' first language for as long as possible, and in the second language for part of the school day

2. use of current approaches to teaching academic curriculum in both the students' first and second language through active discovery and cognitively complex learning

3. changes in the sociocultural context of schooling including the integration of English speakers, the implementation of additive bilingual instructional goals, and the transformation of minority/majority relations to a positive plane (Thomas and Collier 1997)

McLeod (1996) also surveys a series of case studies of exemplary schools throughout the United States serving highly diverse and poor student populations. In these studies, selected schools with demonstrated academic success records were subjected to intensive site-by-site study with the goal of identifying specific attributes at each site related to the functioning of the school. As part of a more ambitious effort, common attributes across the sites were also identified. Schools in various states (Texas, Illinois, California, Massachusetts) were found to be particularly successful in achieving high academic outcomes with a diverse set of students. All the successful schools were reported to set some or all of the following goals for ensuring high quality teaching:

1. *Foster English acquisition through the development of mature literacy.* Schools utilized students' native-language abilities to develop their literacy expertise, which was transferred to English-literacy development. Programs in these schools were more interested in this mature development than in transitioning students

quickly into English-language instruction. This approach paid off both in the students' literacy and English-language development.

2. *Deliver grade-level content.* Providing challenging work in the academic disciplines was concomitant with pursuing the goals of English-language learning. Teachers organized lessons to deliver grade-level instruction through a variety of native-language, sheltered-English, and ESL activities.

3. *Organize instruction in innovative ways.* Examples of such innovations included developing "schools-within-schools" programs to deal more responsively with the diverse language needs of the students. These programs included the creation of "families" of students who stayed together for major parts of a middle school day, and "continuum classes," in which teachers remained with their students for two to three years and the assisting teachers became more familiar with and responsive to the diversity of their students. Finally, students in such programs were grouped more flexibly and on a continuous basis to meet the changing needs of their native- and second-language development.

4. *Protect and extend instructional time.* Schools utilized after-school programs, supportive computer-based instruction, voluntary Saturday schools, and summer academies designed to multiply the students' exposure to academic material. Regular teachers or trained tutors were employed to extend learning time. Not surprisingly, a majority of students took advantage of these voluntary extensions. At the same time, the available daily instructional time was carefully protected, and the teachers' auxiliary responsibilities were not allowed to take valuable time away from instruction.

5. *Expand teachers' roles and responsibilities.* Teachers were given a much greater role in instructional and curricular decision making. This decision making was collective in nature to ensure cross-grade articulation and coordination. Teachers in these schools became full co-partners. They devised their own "authentic" forms of assessment, used various tools and rubrics to assess

development in writing and math, and developed a scoring system which could effectively inform instruction.

6. *Address students' social and emotional needs.* Some of the schools were located in low-income neighborhoods serving poor families, and these schools adopted a proactive stance with regard to issues associated with these communities. For example, family-oriented after-school activities were organized to help deal with issues of alcohol and drug abuse or family violence. The schools actively participated in addressing their student communities' health care and related social service needs. These activities brought the school staff together with social service agencies at one school site. Similar examples of actual family counseling and direct medical care were arranged at other sites.

7. *Involve parents in their children's education.* Some of the schools studied were magnet schools. Since parents had chosen to send their students to these schools in the first place, parent involvement was part of the magnet school contract. This involvement included participation on school committees and assistance with school festivals, celebrations, or other extracurricular programs, field trips, and so forth. But parent-outreach services were an integral part of the successful schools' operation in nonmagnet schools, too. In all cases, communication with families on a regular basis and in the various languages used in the students' homes was accomplished. Parent participation in school governance was a common attribute, although the rate of actual participation by parents was highly variable (McLeod 1996).

In a more intensive case study of two elementary schools and one middle school, Miramontes, Nadeau, and Commins (1997) describe in detail the development of exemplary-school attributes with an emphasis on linking decision making to effective programs. These schools, over a period of several years, earned local, state, and national recognition for their academic success with linguistically and culturally diverse student bodies. In some of the exemplary schools of the case study, as many as five languages were represented in significant proportions. Yet these schools managed to produce outstanding academic work and effective programs.

In a similar vein, researchers have described linguistically and culturally responsive learning environments that will be essential in developing effective schooling (August and Hakuta 1997; García 1998) and high performance learning communities (Berman 1996). The social, cultural, and linguistic diversity represented by students in today's public schools challenges us to reconsider the theoretical and practical aspects of educational success. That is, high-performing learning communities must necessarily address issues of diversity in order to maximize their potential and to sustain educational improvement over time.

Embedded in this research is the understanding that language, culture, and their accompanying values are acquired in the home and community environments; that children come to school with some knowledge about what language is, how it works, and what it is used for; that children learn higher-level metacognitive and metalinguistic skills as they engage in socially meaningful activities; and that children's development and learning are best understood if conceptualized as the interaction between linguistic, sociocultural, and cognitive experiences. One important practical outcome of such a conceptualization is that the native language of students who do not speak English is perceived as a resource instead of a problem. In general theoretical terms, this research suggests moving away from a needs-assessment and diversity-as-a-problem approach to an asset-inventory and diversity-as-a-resource approach.

A more appropriate perspective on learning, then, is one which recognizes that learning is enhanced when it occurs in contexts that are both socioculturally and linguistically meaningful for the learner. Such meaningful events, however, are not generally accessible to linguistically diverse children. Those schooling practices which contribute to the academic vulnerability of this student population and which tend to dramatize the lack of fit between the student and the school experience are reflected in the monolithic culture transmitted by schools in the forms of pedagogy, curricula, instruction, classroom configuration, and language. Such practices include the systematic exclusion of the students' histories, language, experience, and values from classroom curricula and activities; "tracking," which limits access to academic courses and learning environments and does not foster the student's self-perception as a competent learner and language user; and limited opportunities to engage in developmentally and culturally appropriate learning beyond teacher-led instruction.

The implications of rethinking the students' and their family's language and culture as a resource have profound effects on the teaching and learning enterprise. The result is a *responsive pedagogy*, which redefines the classroom as a community of learners, a community in which speakers, readers, and writers come together to negotiate the meaning of the academic experience. It argues for the respect and integration of the students' values, beliefs, histories, and experiences, and recognizes the active role that students must play in the learning process. In addition, this responsive pedagogy expands the students' knowledge beyond their own immediate experiences by using those experiences as a sound foundation for appropriating new knowledge. Furthermore, a responsive pedagogy for academic learning requires a redefinition of the instructor's role. Instructors must become familiar with the cognitive, social, and cultural dimensions of learning, and they need to recognize the ways in which diversity of instruction, assessment, and evaluation affect learning. They should become more aware of the classroom curriculum, its purported purpose, and the degree of its implementation. The configuration of the classroom environment and the nature of interaction between students and teacher and between students and other students are just as significant as other, less dynamic factors of education. Moreover, instructors must recognize that the acquisition of academic content requires helping students display their knowledge in ways that suggest their competence as learners and language users. *Students need to maximize their use of language in acquiring learning, not only in learning language.* This approach places an emphasis on using language as a learning tool instead of focusing on learning language as a goal in itself.

Finally, this approach requires that teachers let go of their unfounded assumptions about decontextualized learning processes and underprepared students. In particular, teachers must reexamine the myths about those who come from lower socioeconomic households or from homes in which English is not the primary language. To embrace the new concept of responsive pedagogy, high academic expectations and educational horizons are a must.

The research focusing on classroom teachers, principals, and parents (García 1998) revealed an interesting set of perspectives regarding the education of students in successful schools. Classroom teachers were highly committed to the educational success of their students; perceived themselves as instructional innovators utilizing "new" learning theories and instructional philosophies to guide their practice; continued to be involved in professional development activities including participation in small-group support networks; had a strong, demonstrated commitment to student-home communication (several teachers were implementing a weekly parent-interaction format); and felt they had the autonomy to create or change the instruction and curriculum in their classrooms, even if they did not comply completely with the district guidelines. Significantly, these instructors "adopted" their students. They had high academic expectations for all their students ("everyone will learn to read in my classroom") and also served as advocates for their students. They rejected any conclusion that their students were intellectually or academically disadvantaged.

Principals tended to be highly articulate about the curriculum and instructional strategies undertaken in their schools. They were also highly supportive of their instructional staff and took pride in their accomplishments. These principals reported support for teacher autonomy although they were quite aware of the potential problems regarding the pressure to strictly conform to district policies. Parents expressed a high level of satisfaction in and appreciation for their children's education experience in these schools. Both Anglo-American and Hispanic/Latino parents were quite involved in the schools' formal parent-support activities. Anglo-American parents' attitudes, however, were much more aligned with a "child advocacy" perspective, somewhat distrustful of the schools' specific interest in doing what was right for their child. Conversely, Hispanic/Latino parents expressed a high level of trust for the teaching and administrative staff.

This recent research does address some significant questions regarding effective academic environments for linguistically and culturally diverse students. Four of these questions are summarized here:

1. What role did native-language instruction play?

   These "effective" schools considered native-language instruction key, particularly in the early grades (K–3). They implemented an articulated native-language and literacy effort which recognized language as a tool for learning and not as a learning objective.

2. Was there one best curriculum?

   No common curriculum was identified. But a well-trained instructional staff implementing an integrated student-centered curriculum with literacy pervasive in all aspects of instruction was consistently observed across grade levels. High expectations were the rule for all students, not just the exception for a few students.

3. What instructional strategies were effective?

   Consistently, teachers organized instruction so as to ensure small collaborative academic activities requiring a high degree of heterogeneous, grouped student-to-student interaction.

4. Who were the key players in this effective schooling drama?

   School administrators and parents played important roles. Teachers, however, were the key players. They achieved the educational confidence of their peers and supervisors; worked to organize instruction, create new instructional environments, assess effectiveness, and advocate for their students; and were proud of their students, academically reassuring but consistently demanding. They rejected any notion of their students' academic, linguistic, cultural, or intellectual inferiority; they were student advocates (see August and Hakuta 1997 and García 1998 for details regarding these findings).

New National Education Policy

From this broader context, specific changes in policy were developed in the 1994 Improving America's Schools Act. Typical rationales for changes in national policy are often related to crisis intervention: there is a problem and it must be addressed quickly, usually with more political and philosophical rhetoric than action. The past national policy for serving linguistically and culturally diverse students and their families was driven to a large extent by the "crisis" rationale. Accordingly, crisis policies in this arena have been shortsighted, inflexible, and minimally cohesive and integrated; they are not always informed by a strong knowledge base that includes conceptual, empirical, or simply practical wisdom. Past articulations of Title I and Title VII of the Elementary and Secondary Education Act (ESEA), both prime examples of the crisis intervention approach related to providing services to Hispanic/Latino language-minority students, have suffered from these disadvantages.

New policies under the 1994 reauthorization of ESEA, while recognizing the acute need to serve this student population, also recognized the following in developing new policy:

1. The new knowledge base, both conceptual and empirical, must be central to any proposed changes.

2. High standards for all children are essential.

3. Flexibility in adaptation to particular circumstances in the field is critical so as to capitalize on the wisdom of current policy, administration, curriculum, and instructional practice that work under specific sets of challenges. Accountability in the form of benchmarks tied to standards and instruction must be in place.

4. Policies and programs must be cohesive in order to effectively integrate services provided. This cohesiveness must reflect the partnership and collaboration at local school sites as well as between national, state, and local educational policies and programs.

5. The demographic and budgetary realities that are present today and will continue to influence new directions throughout this decade must be acknowledged. There will be few "new" resources to meet even greater numbers of students; therefore, resources must be targeted and efficient.

6. Instructional change will be dependent on teachers who are primarily responsible for constructing teaching/learning environments.

These articulated policy directions have attempted to view the provisions of the services to students in a comprehensive and integrated manner. Through the introduction of new legislation in Goals 2000, the U.S. Department of Education has set the stage for the state-by-state development of standards. Then, with the passage of the Improving America's Schools Act and the reauthorization of the Elementary and Secondary Educational Act (ESEA), an alignment of the goals and standards with specific resource allocation policies was accomplished. This alignment recognizes that the integration of federal, state, and local government efforts must occur in order to enhance effectiveness and efficiency. Moreover, the federal role must allow flexibility at the state and local levels while requiring that all children achieve at the highest levels.

Title VII services to limited-English-proficient (LEP) students as a component of ESEA are not seen as yet another intervention aimed at meeting an educational crisis in U.S. education. Instead, these services are key components of the integrated effort to address effectively the educational needs of students. Specifically, Title VII will continue to provide for leadership and national, state, and local capacity building of educational services, professional development, and research related to linguistically and culturally diverse populations. Other programs, however, particularly Title I, are important and will more directly increase the services needed by all students living in poverty, including those with limited English proficiency.

A review of the research on what works in schools shows that a variety of factors contribute to success; however, no empirical case studies or comparative research support any one type of mandated intervention for English-language learning or general academic achievement. This knowledge, or lack thereof, however, does not always inform policy on a local level. For example, in California, 85 percent of language-minority students are not served by appropriately staffed native-language programs; therefore, the conclusion that these native-language programs do not work is unfounded and based only on general data of poor academic performance by these students. In fact, recent data from Los Angeles and San Francisco indicate that participation in a bilingual program for between three and four years results in bilingual education students outscoring English Only language-minority students in fifth grade on measures of English achievement in reading and mathematics.

By restricting native-language instruction, Proposition 227 not only reproduces crisis-driven policy, but it also runs counter to our present theoretical understanding of how children learn from past learning. There has been no theoretical debate about the significance of the use of native language in learning English (National Research Council 1997; NCTE/IRA 1996). A policy that follows the argument of Proposition 227 ignores both large-scale quantitative data and the more specific qualitative case-study data quoted in this chapter. All of the data support the use of native-language instruction in effective academic and English development at elementary, middle school, and high school levels (August and Hakuta 1997; García 1998). Even more significant is the real possibility that forcing young children to learn to read and perform at high levels in academic content areas in a non-native language can produce delayed English-language, literacy, and academic development, placing children at risk for later failure in school.

Any proposition that stresses the English Only approach in addressing diversity of language and culture in schools instead of supporting what works and eliminating what does not work is simply a public referendum based on a public theory which places children at risk. It mandates an instructional intervention state-wide, thwarts local control and flexibility, and purports a "one-size-fits-all" methodology without any provision for holding schools accountable for the English-language development or academic achievement of their students. A policy that stresses more English as a panacea for all the problems that cause lack of success for linguistically and culturally diverse students is simply an input control mechanism without any provision for results. In other words, it controls the amount and type of instruction without stipulating what results can be expected or how they can be measured.

Future Research

Numerous research and evaluation studies have been funded by Title VII/OBEMLA during the past twenty-nine years; however, limited theoretical, practical, or policy research has been conducted. One of the inherent and persistent problems in demographic and descriptive studies (let alone evaluative and comparative research) is the diversity of the various populations we educators call "language minority" and "limited English proficient."

During this early period of Title VII research at the Office of Bilingual Education and Minority Languages Affairs, three main areas emerged that were to become the focus of the committee's research and evaluation studies:

1. A description of language-minority populations and an assessment of their levels of English-language proficiency
2. The reevaluation of methods used to measure program effectiveness
3. The development of new instructional and curricular methodologies

These three "categories" of research and evaluation studies set out in 1979 have continued to be the focus of study up to the present time. Consequently, demographic studies—the *who* of Title VII's focus—and evaluation—the *what works* of Title VII programs—have characterized the funded research at OBEMLA.

In Title VII's broad goal, however, little priority has been given to promoting the child's sociocultural competence. Sociocultural competence can be defined as the child's everyday effectiveness in dealing with both present environment and responsibilities in school and life. Sociocultural competence takes into account the interrelatedness of cognitive and intellectual development and a broad range of physical and mental factors that enable a child to function optimally. These factors were not given high priority in the research that informed Title VII. Likewise, little attention has been devoted to parent and family outcomes, or to the schools' impact on other institutions and relationships within the community. These are all critical questions for future research.

Two Critical Questions for a New Research Agenda

In light of what we now know and how federal resources are distributed in support of services to linguistically and culturally diverse populations, a new research agenda needs to be delineated. The presence of California's Proposition 227 also warrants a new research agenda to inform future policy more effectively. We propose that the research focus on two questions: "What works best for whom, and why?" and "How can favorable effects be maintained?" These two issues are addressed more specifically in the following critical questions that are recommended as the basis of organizing future research and evaluation planning:

1. Which bilingual education practices maximize benefits for children and families with different characteristics under what types of circumstances? Why?

2. Are gains sustained for children and families after the bilingual education experience?

The focus here is on producing a knowledge base that can provide a foundation for ongoing program improvement and upgrading quality within Title VII and among other educational program partners (such as Title I, Indian Education, Migrant Education). It is the lack of answers to these critical questions that places bilingual education and educational services to language-minority students in jeopardy of haphazard and highly politicized policy initiatives such as California's Proposition 227.

The first question acknowledges the diversity and flexibility of such programs. Average outcomes of average programs, which were the aim of an earlier generation of studies, pose the risk of misleading findings and fail to provide the information needed to tailor services to identifiable subgroups of children and families. In moving toward universal educational reform, strategies must be developed that respond to the multidimensional information needs so that quality improvements and societal benefits can be achieved. Put simply, what works in El Paso may not work in Los Angeles, New York City, or Miami. We need not only "effective" or generic "best practices," but also rich contextual information about the interventions and about the students served by those interventions. The question "Why?" implicates the need for an intellectual/theoretical foundation for the research as that research intersects with practices in the field. We need a set of theories or constructs that help us understand better why some interventions work and others do not for the diverse populations that are served. Such theories or constructs allow us more readily to adapt new interventions that are different from those we have studied.

The second question reflects issues that have come to the forefront in the policy and research communities as a result of findings of socially meaningful, lasting gains for children who have participated in educational programs. For example, Fillmore (1991) found that English-emphasis programs for language-minority students generated significant intergenerational communication gaps that negatively affected children, parents, and grandparents. Attention to this type of social consequence has been sorely absent. Moreover, attention directed to issues related to lasting effects should not be interpreted as implying that the bilingual education experience by itself would necessarily be responsible for producing long-term outcomes. On the contrary, the most plausible scenario is that the long-term outcomes are a product of the combined influences of the schooling experience, family dynamics, and follow-up actions of other community agencies that serve to extend or attenuate the effects of Title VII efforts.

Even keeping in mind these critical questions and the importance of addressing them in new research with language-minority students, it is important to realize that policy-related research does require clarity in causal inference. In such research, it is the impact of policies and practices that is examined: did this or that intervention work? Reforms, revisions, and add-ons to federal policy are implemented to make a difference. While much of social science can avoid the troubled issues of direction of causal effects, "reforms"—or "ameliorative programs"—cannot. Policy research, and program evaluation in particular, has a commitment to causal inference and a need to optimize the clarity of the inference. Description is not enough.

Unfortunately, there is a general perception that most government program evaluations are low-quality products of dubious value (August and Hakuta 1997). This perception is shared by those applied scientists in the universities who attempt to use this research in cumulative scholarship and by those federal administrators whose policy choices are supposed to be guided by it.

These criticisms have been leveled at "research/policy" reviews published in the mid-1990s, in particular the work by Rossell and Baker (1996). Instead, as in the physical sciences, policy advice should come from the community of mutually critical applied social scientists who make use of all the relevant research and who have access to the methodological details and criticisms of that research. A major goal of bilingual education research should be to implement its research program in a way that fosters such an applied science community. Having said this, the policy of mandated federal program evaluations still suffers from the following three misconceptions:

1. that useful causal inference relevant to policy change can be obtained from any setting

2. that one study by one qualified scientist produces valid applied science

3. that a specific study should inform a particular policy decision

Finally, honesty and integrity in reporting results must be directly reinforced. Just as the ancient tyrant executed the messenger who brought bad news, at every level of the research process the present system is biased against negative data. At the level of the local program, participant and staff evaluations should be totally separate from refunding. In particular, it should be made clear that reporting on failures and imperfections will not jeopardize future funding. Policy-relevant research instruments should not be mixed with report forms used for managerial control, where "bias" is impossible to avoid. Researchers and program-alternative implementers should not be punished (nor should their receipt of future contracts and grants be jeopardized) for honest reporting of failed implementations, lack of effects, and other undesirable factors. In other words, federal policy should be guided by a myriad of quantitative and qualitative research with varied populations in varied places, all linked through the process of learning from both successes and failures. This is not how the policy world currently operates, particularly not with policies related to language-minority students.

Conclusion

In general, bilingual education programs now in place are already performing valuable services for their communities. Individual programs are exploring local variations designed to improve their effectiveness. While I recognize and applaud the resulting diversity of programs, this diversity is underutilized as a source of new alternatives that educational and community institutions might want to borrow and/or cross-validate. In addition, bilingual education and federal research in general must take the lead in developing, assessing, and "moving" the field. New ideas, methodologies, and articulated conceptualizations regarding the education of culturally and linguistically diverse children must be nurtured and directly supported. We are now more than ever challenged by political agendas such as California's Proposition 227 that place language-minority students at risk. The following suggestions form part of such a research agenda that is responsive to these new challenges:

1. Bilingual education researchers must expand the shared knowledge base of educational programs for linguistically and culturally diverse students, evidence of their effectiveness, and estimates of cost and staffing. Such efforts will invite reports on diverse exemplary programs, including those that do and those that do not claim to be innovative.

2. More bilingual education research requires interdisciplinary demonstration of field studies, encouraging recruitment of local practitioners and researchers.

3. Bilingual education experts need to be encouraged to develop the proposals that break new ground theoretically.

4. Bilingual education researchers need to become informed by diverse sets of practitioners and researchers to enhance the theoretical and methodological soundness of their research and evaluation activities.

5. New bilingual education research should be committed to developing a framework for government (U.S. Department of Education, NSF, NIH, etc.) and public-private (foundation) collaboration to ensure nonduplication and efficient collaboration on research on linguistically and culturally diverse populations.

In summary, new federal and state policies recognize that any attempt to address the needs of linguistically and culturally diverse students in a deficit or "subtractive" mode is counterproductive. Instead, the new knowledge base recognizes, conceptually, that educators must take an "additive" approach to these students. In other words, we must be responsive to the rich lore of intellectual, linguistic, academic, and cultural skills these students bring to the classroom, and regard these as added resources rather than as deficits. In the same way, new and old streams of resources from federal, state, and local entities must flow into the schools to enhance effective schooling efforts that allow *all* students to achieve at high levels. Gone are the days of low expectations, segmented "pots" of resources, and compensatory education. Here are the days of serious collaboration within and between previously segmented educational endeavors. With each act of collaboration built on respect for diversity comes a need for rethinking our research agenda in bilingual education.

Works Cited

August, Diane, and Kenji Hakuta, eds. 1997. *Improving Schooling for Language-Minority Children: A Research Agenda*. Washington, D.C.: National Academy Press, U.S. Department of Education.

Barona, Andrés, and Eugene E. Garcia, eds. 1990. *Children at Risk: Poverty, Minority Status and Other Issues in Educational Equity*. Washington, D.C.: National Association of School Psychologists.

Berman, Paul. 1992. *Meeting the Challenge of Language Diversity: An Evaluation of California Programs for Pupils with Limited Proficiency in English*. Presented at the American Educational Research Association, New York City, April 7.

————. 1996. *High Performance Learning Communities: Proposal to the U.S. Department of Education*. Emeryville, CA: Research, Policy, and Practice Associates.

California Tomorrow. 1994. *The Unfinished Journey: Restructuring Schools in a Diverse Society*. San Francisco: Author.

Cohen, Nancy E., and Delia Pompa. 1994. *Multicultural Perspectives on Quality in Early Care and Education: Culturally Specific Practices and Universal Outcomes*. New Haven: Yale University Press.

Cole, Robert W., ed. 1995. *Educating Everybody's Children: Diverse Teaching Strategies for Diverse Learners: What Research and Practice Say about Improving Achievement.* Alexandria, VA: Association for Supervision and Curriculum Development.

Collier, Virginia P. 1995. "Acquiring a Second Language for School" [Online]. *Directions in Language and Education* 1(4). National Clearinghouse for Bilingual Education, Washington, D.C.: http://www.ncbe.gwu.edu/.

Crawford, James. 1989. *Bilingual Education: History, Politics, Theory, and Practice.* Trenton, NJ: Crane.

Cummins, Jim. 1986. "Empowering Minority Students: A Framework for Intervention." *Harvard Educational Review* 56(1): 18–36.

Fillmore, Lily Wong. 1991. "When Learning a Second Language Means Losing a First." *Early Childhood Research Quarterly* 6(3): 323–47.

García, Eugene. 1995. "Educating Mexican American Students: Past Treatment and Recent Developments in Theory, Research, Policy, and Practice." In J. Banks and C. A. McGee Banks, eds., *Handbook of Research on Multicultural Education.* New York: Macmillan. 372–84.

———. 1997. "The Education of Hispanics in Early Childhood: Of Roots and Wings." *Young Children* 52(3): 5–14.

———. 1998. "Promoting the Contributions of Multicultural Students in the Work Force of the 21st Century." In S. H. Fradd and O. Lee, eds., *Educational Policies and Practices for Students Learning English as a New Language.* Tallahassee: University of Florida and the Florida Department of Education. VII1–VII13.

García, Eugene, and Rene Gonzalez. 1995. "Issues in Systemic Reform for Culturally and Linguistically Diverse Students." *College Record* 96(3): 418–31.

McLeod, Beverly. 1996. *School Reform and Student Diversity: Exemplary Schooling for Language Minority Students.* Washington, D.C.: George Washington University, Institute for the Study of Language and Education.

Miramontes, Ofelia, Adel Nadeau, and Nancy Commins. 1997. *Restructuring Schools for Linguistic Diversity: Linking Decision Making to Effective Programs.* New York: Teachers College Press.

National Research Council. 1997. *The New Americans: Economic, Demographic, and Fiscal Effects of Immigration.* Washington, D.C.: National Academy Press.

National Council of Teachers of English and International Reading Association. 1996. *Standards for the English Language Arts.* Urbana, IL, and Newark, DE: Authors.

Rossell, Christine, and Keith Baker. 1996. "The Educational Effectiveness of Bilingual Education." *Research in the Teaching of English* 30(1): 7–74.

Thomas, Wayne P., and Virginia P. Collier. 1997. *School Effectiveness for Language Minority Students.* Washington, D.C.: National Clearinghouse on Bilingual Education.

CHAPTER FIVE

"The Younger, the Better" Myth and Bilingual Education

THOMAS SCOVEL
San Francisco State University

One of the frustrating consequences of living in an age when both scientific knowledge and mass communication have grown exponentially is the fact that it has become increasingly more difficult to report on academic research to the general public in an accurate and balanced manner. On the one hand, because of the massive expansion of academic and scientific scholarship in recent decades, there are complex and elaborate developments in subfields of science and technology which cannot be completely understood even by some of the experts in these fields. On the other hand, there has been such an enormous proliferation of sources of information (magazines, talk radio, the Internet, etc.) that almost anyone can get ideas about anything from anywhere at any time. When we couple these two developments within a social atmosphere where superficial deference is paid to science and technology, the situation is ripe for research to be misinterpreted, misunderstood, and misappropriated. We should not be so surprised then to find our media and our popular sources of information filled with "junk" or pseudoscience. Those of us who are applied linguists or language educators are inadequately trained to do anything to correct this misinformation in such fields as nutrition, alternative medicine, or neuropsychology, although it is hoped that the academic rigor and critical thinking we have learned to apply in our own disciplines can spill over into the way we appraise claims and "findings" in these other fields as they are interpreted for us by the media. Because of the expertise and discipline we have accumulated in our own narrow field of science, however, it is not only our right but also our *obligation* to interpret language learning and teaching to the public at large in as fair and accurate a manner as possible.

One example from the field of linguistics of the "junk science" I am talking about is an illustration of the strong version of the Whorfian hypothesis which has relentlessly pervaded any public discussion of how language might influence thought. "Everyone knows," so the claim goes, that the Eskimo have many different words for snow but that most other languages are like English and have only one. This myth itself has had packaged into it so many presuppositions that a linguist confronting it feels very much like a mosquito encountering a nudist camp—you hardly know where to begin! There is no single language called "Eskimo"; many languages have different words for types of snow; it turns out that languages spoken in northeastern Canada such as Inuit do *not* have a disproportionately large number of words for this cold white stuff, etcetera, etcetera. Despite witty and trenchant attempts by linguists to set the record straight (Pullum 1991; Steinberg 1993; Pinker 1994), this myth not only refuses to die, but because of the proliferation of sources of information already mentioned, it actually may have gained strength over the years.

Although issues relating to the Whorfian hypothesis bear portent for bilingual education and research on bilingualism, I have not chosen it as a topic for this anthology, partly because I have written about it elsewhere (Scovel 1993), partly because many psycholinguists have questioned the validity of the theory (Steinberg 1993; Pinker 1994), and partly because it is an exceedingly difficult hypothesis to understand, even for those who would promulgate it (Lee 1996). In contrast, I think that the topic of age constraints on language acquisition relates much more directly to bilingual education, and furthermore, unlike the Whorfian hypothesis, this is a subject upon which I have devoted a substantial portion of my own professional research. Nonetheless, I would like to use this topic to examine the larger issue of public perceptions of scientific knowledge, for essentially I am interested in the ways that science, especially the field of linguistics, has been misunderstood by the public. At times, this misperception has resulted from the misinterpretation of linguistic research by proponents of political viewpoints (e.g., as in the 1998 Unz-Tuchman ballot initiative in California), so it is all the more vital for anyone interested in bilingual education, as well as for the general public, to have a clearer understanding of current research in applied linguistics.

The Myth Defined

One dictionary definition of *myth* is "one of the fictions or half-truths forming part of the ideology of a society" (*American Heritage Dictionary* 1969). To begin with, I think it is helpful to balance the negative meaning usually associated with this particular usage of the word with a more neutral connotation. A "myth" is not the antonym of a fact, at least not in the sense I am emphasizing here; rather, it is a piece of information that is based, as the definition suggests, on a claim which is at least partially true. Viewing the word in this sense, we can have a greater appreciation of why myths occupy such a prominent place in the social psyche. If myths were complete fabrications (i.e., a synonym for *lie*), they would die quickly, as soon as they were exposed. But because they germinate in truth, it is hard to separate which half is fact and which is fiction once they have sprouted full-blown into the public's consciousness. No one can deny, to return to the Whorfian myth about the Eskimo, that languages differ and that different people think differently; nor can they refute the claim that the indigenous people of northern Canada spend a lot more time in and with snow than people from most other cultures. Thus it is easy to allow these facts to mushroom into the belief that the Eskimo must have many words to describe the cold stuff that surrounds them, and furthermore, that these words, in which they have been immersed since infancy, influence how they perceive or conceive of their snowy world. The myth that emerges, then, is that it is not the snow but the *words* for snow that influence Eskimo thought.

Turning to "the younger, the better" myth of language acquisition, again it is patently clear that most children all over the globe become fluent in at least one language. Contrast this to other, infinitely easier, socially acquired abilities. Virtually all children grow up in societies surrounded by music, and yet a large number of people, perhaps more than half the world's population, cannot sing on pitch. Conversely, in most situations, once children have matured to adulthood, they become relatively unsuccessful language learners, even though, in contrast, many can learn to sing on pitch as adults, given sufficient opportunity and training. Coupled with this general perception about the apparent ubiquity of language acquisition among children is the observation that in most cultures, precocity among infants is both praised and exaggerated. When a two-year-old abruptly says she wants to "go potty," we are tickled and enamored, but if a twenty-year-old blurts out the same thing, we are unimpressed and perhaps even affronted. Put all of this together and it starts to become clear why most people believe "the younger, the better" myth, and also why they enjoy entertaining such a notion. Just as it is important for linguists to help educate the public about misperceptions about vocabulary limitations among the world's languages, it is equally their responsibility to help people become aware of the conflicting evidence about child language learning. And when these "mythological" beliefs become codified into public statements about bilingual education, it is especially vital for linguists to step in with disciplinary evidence. This clear need to educate the general public about language learning and bilingual education in particular is the motivation behind this chapter. I begin with three illustrations of how this myth influences public perceptions and policy about second-language education: the first deals with bilingual education in the United States; the second with foreign-language education, also in the United States; and the third with the teaching of English in foreign countries, especially in Asia.

The Myth Promoted

The first example is taken from the campaign for the Unz-Tuchman initiative (Proposition 227) for the California primary election of June 2, 1998. In essence, this proposition was designed to replace all bilingual education programs in the state with a one-year "immersion" English class, and after a great deal of campaign debate and publicity, the initiative was passed by a substantial majority of the voters. Although I am not a sociolinguist and have no direct association with bilingual education programs, I became involved with the issues surrounding this initiative because our local newspaper, *The Contra Costa Times*, asked me to assist them as an impartial consultant for a series of feature stories they had decided to run. I also was asked to cochair a televised debate on the proposition between Ron Unz, the guiding force behind Proposition 227, and a spokesperson for the opposition. I felt that the coverage provided by *The Contra Costa Times* was detailed, fair, and informative, and I heard unofficial reports from both factions that the newspaper did a more thorough job of covering this story than any other paper in the state of California. My point here is not to debate this proposition or to discuss its consequences; this has been done much more competently and eloquently in this volume and elsewhere than I could ever accomplish. Rather, the relevant concern for me is the way proponents and opponents of this initiative dealt with "the younger, the better" myth.

In the *California Voter Information Guide* for this primary election, the promoters of Proposition 227 were very clear about where they stood, as can be seen from the following claim they affirmed in Section 1, Article 1 of the text for the proposition:

> (e) Whereas, young immigrant children can easily acquire full fluency in a new language, such as English, if they are heavily exposed to that language in the classroom at an early age. (f) Therefore, it is resolved that: all children in California public schools shall be taught English as rapidly and effectively as possible. (*California Voter Information Guide* 1998, 75)

This claim was made again in the section of the same voter guide where arguments for and against propositions were listed. The proponents of Proposition 227 go on to state as the first item in their list entitled "Common Sense about Learning English" that "Learning a new language is easier the younger the age of the child" (*California Voter Information Guide* 1998, 34).

Although the majority of the campaign literature directed against the Unz-Tuchman initiative never questioned this presupposition about age and acquisition, a few opponents of the measure did seem to criticize this point. For example, in an article published by *TESOL Matters,* Crawford (1998) lists an article-by-article critique of Proposition 227 and speaks directly against "the younger, the better" claim quoted above.

> This is the most pervasive myth about second-language learning. What appears "so obvious" to laypersons, however, is unsupported by science. Children do tend to "pick up" oral communication skills at a young age, often without the anxiety and self-consciousness that can impede adult learners. But research on bilingualism has repeatedly shown that it takes them considerably longer—typically 5 to 7 years—to acquire the complex, decontextualized academic language needed for success in the classroom. (20)

But although Crawford is attempting to argue against the proposition's contention that immigrant children "can easily" gain "full fluency" in a new language, he is *not* objecting to "the younger, the better" premise upon which this contention is based. In fact, he explicitly endorses this premise with the assertion that children do indeed acquire "oral skills at a young age, often without the anxiety and self-consciousness that can impede adult learners." Granted, there are several components to Crawford's argument. For example, he claims that children experience less negative interference from anxiety and self-consciousness than adults, although this is another myth that has garnered mixed support from applied linguists (Scovel 1978; Horwitz and Young 1991). Implicit in Crawford's position, however, is the idea that children are indeed better than adults at acquiring everyday personal conversation, what Cummins (1994) has called "basic interpersonal communicative skills (BICS)," but when it comes to the language of schooling, what Cummins terms "cognitive academic language proficiency (CALP)," children are not so successful and take much longer to acquire it. Notice from Cummins's quote that even a vociferous opponent of the Unz-Tuchman measure supports, at least in part (e.g., for BICS but not for CALP), the premise that younger language learners are superior to adult language learners.

A second illustration of how this myth infuses public decisions about language learning is the support the U.S. Department of Education gives to foreign-language learning for young children through the Title VI grants for Foreign Languages in Elementary Schools (FLES). Again, I would like to make clear that I am not taking a stance for or against this policy. One could cogently argue, for example, that relative to the department's overall budget, and certainly compared to the annual budget of the federal government, these Title VI funds amount to a few pennies, so my remarks should not be misinterpreted as criticism that the funding is misdirected. Instead, my only interest here is the way in which people's belief that children make the best language learners gets interpreted into public decisions about education. For many years, the Department of Education has promoted the teaching of languages other than English (LOTE) to schoolchildren, including those languages that have been less commonly taught in the United States (e.g., Chinese, Japanese, and Russian). States' interest in applying for this Title VI funding has varied, but Washington is an example of a state which has become more heavily involved in this effort. In a report surveying the effects of FLES funding on LOTE in Washington, Parks (1998) records that out of 162 elementary schools in the state which responded to her questionnaire, the majority taught Spanish (104), but along with the more typically taught European languages such as French and Spanish, several schools also had FLES classes in Japanese, Chinese, Russian, Arabic, and Korean. Relevant to the discussion here is the way this report endorses a fundamental concept of all FLES programs by making explicit claims about the reputed foreign-language precocity of younger learners. Characteristic of this endorsement are claims like, "A growing number of studies suggests that the optimal time to begin learning a second language is before the age of ten." Or, "Most importantly, children's capacity to learn languages best beginning at the elementary level must not be wasted" (Parks 1998, 9).

Further support for FLES programs and their "the younger, the better" premise comes from public documents which are readily accessible to teachers, parents, and school districts (e.g., Curtain 1993). One example of these is the brochure, "Why, How, and When Should My Child Learn a Second Language?" which is available from ERIC. "Studies have shown—and experience has supported—that children who learn a language before the onset of adolescence are much more likely to have native-like pronunciation. A number of experts attribute this proficiency to physiological changes that occur in the maturing brain as a child enters puberty" (Marcos 1997). I find this series of statements particularly intriguing because much of my own research has been involved with age constraints of nativelike pronunciation and with the possibility that these limitations have a neurological etiology (e.g., Chapter 5, "Neurological Explanations of a Critical Period" in Scovel 1988). The assumption that young children potentially make the best foreign-language learners is not confined to the United States, of course, and for a third illustration of how this myth becomes translated into public policy, I turn to the teaching of English in other countries, specifically those in Asia with which I have some direct familiarity.

Ever since the conclusion of World War II, nations around the globe have promoted the teaching of English, and this process has accelerated over the past several decades with the evolution of English into the major language of international communication (Crystal 1990). I have witnessed the direct consequence of this evolution in the proliferation of English teaching programs in both the public and private sectors in Asia, where I have had ample experience for many years living and teaching, and in my work there as an English-language teaching consultant. The quest to acquire English has had such a significant impact that in the world's most populous nation, China, there are likely more people learning English than there are native speakers in the entire United States (Scovel 1995). Although this zeal for English abounds in virtually every nation in this region of the world, there are differences among these countries in the motivations, methods, and policies surrounding foreign-language learning. For example, in most of the postcolonial, "outer circle" (Kachru 1985) nations of south Asia (e.g., Pakistan, India, Sri Lanka, and Singapore), English not only is vital for international trade and communication, but it serves as a language of national unity as well. Conversely, in "expanding circle" countries such as Vietnam, Korea, and Mongolia, English plays no significant role as a national language, but it is vital to their present and future commerce. So despite the differences in terms of national function and planning, English is extremely important in the education policies of all these nations, and for this reason, their respective Ministries of Education are heavily involved in dictating how and when English is to be taught. In most of these Asian countries, there is an implicit faith that younger learners are better language learners, and coupled with the aforementioned conviction that the knowledge of English is vital to educational success and economic prosperity, this mythic belief in "the younger, the better" fuels both the private and public resolve to introduce the study of the world's language at younger and younger ages.

In the private sphere, parents in urban areas are especially keen to enroll their children in nursery schools or kindergartens which commit a substantial amount of time and resources to English-language instruction. In several instances, these programs pledge to provide the young learners with total immersion in the language. In countries such as Japan, where sociocultural factors limit the number of children in a family, or in China, where the government stringently limits families to a single child (at least in urban areas), parents, who believe that much of the future success of their child is vitally tied to the early acquisition of English, are anxious to enroll their child in these private, commercial institutions. All of this has resulted in a proliferation of English-language nurseries and programs (e.g., the "Ladder Schools" in Taiwan and China) which adopt "Sesame Street"–type activities but which, in general, are more commercially than pedagogically successful. In the public sector, the Ministries of Education of countries such as Thailand and Japan, where English-language instruction was originally begun only at the junior or senior high school levels, have now introduced English in the fourth grade, based largely on the premise that younger learners are much better language learners. An added advantage of this policy, as viewed by these countries, is that by starting English-language instruction in a lower grade, students will be exposed to English two to four years longer than in the past, and this increase in time on task will help improve the pupils' foreign-language competence. By and large, the governments which have made these far-reaching educational decisions have not carefully weighed their belief in the efficacy of "the younger, the better" approach against other factors. In all of these places, for example, the English competence of most middle school teachers is relatively limited, so it is quite evident that involving many more teachers in English-language instruction will not only attenuate the personnel and resources presently available but also invariably ensure that a greater amount of incompetence is diffused among a much larger number of young learners. Countries such as Korea and Japan have tried to counterbalance this constraint by hiring thousands of native speakers of English and sprinkling them through the nation's school systems (e.g., the Japanese JET program), but the linguistic benefits of these programs on English-language teaching are unsubstantiated.

From these international examples we can see that "the younger, the better" myth is so powerful that it can encourage both parents and governments to make major pedagogical decisions about the language education of their youth that entail costly and not necessarily beneficial consequences for the long-term pedagogical development of a nation's young people. Obviously, there are innumerable differences between these illustrations of English foreign-language policy in Asia and the course of bilingual education in the United States. One of the many points of contrast is that in the former, "the younger, the better" myth is coupled with other pedagogical beliefs such as "the more, the better." For example, the gates to the language institute in China where my wife and I taught for one year in 1979 were emblazoned with the exhortation, *xuexi, xuexi, zai xuexi!* ("Study, study, and study again!"). In the United States, however, time on task is not so highly valued and can be superseded by other beliefs about language learning (e.g., by limiting English-language instruction to just one school year, Proposition 227 undervalues the amount of time involved for competent second-language learning and appears to endorse a "sink or swim" approach).

The Myth Examined

Let us turn now to examine this "the younger, the better" myth from the perspective of applied linguists who have been investigating this notion over the years. First, to return to the problem with which this chapter was introduced, science does not deal well with generalities, but because the media and the general public have neither the training, patience, nor interest in detailed studies of minutiae, junk science fills the gap with attempts to answer such broad-reaching and unanswerable questions like: "Does being a vegetarian ensure longevity?"; "Can acupuncture cure disease?"; or "Are women's brains different from those of men?" When applied linguists confront such a far-ranging issue as "Are children better language learners than adults?," like all scientists they begin by breaking down this inquiry into smaller and smaller queries until a manageable research question emerges.

A large part of this process involves definitions and comparisons. At what age does a "child" become an adult: six, twelve, eighteen? By "better" do we mean better at speaking, better at grammar, or better at writing? And "better" compared to what? Very often, for example, a child's assumed precocity at first-language acquisition is contrasted to an adult's attempt to master a second language after a semester or two of study. Is it fair to compare the thousands of hours of mother-tongue exposure a child experiences during the first decade or so of life with the few hundred hours a college student gets in a typical two-semester foreign-language class? Brown (1994) emphasizes this point by means of a two-by-two matrix in which the child and adult columns are juxtaposed against two rows—one for the first language and one for the second. This yields four cells: child-first language, child-second language, adult-first language, and adult-second language (see Figure 5.1).

Some may wonder, incidentally, if there can be such a category as "adult-first language," but if we base our motivation on linguistic criteria and define "adults" as anyone over about the

	Child	Adult
First Language	C1	A1
Second Language	C2	A2

FIGURE 5.1. *Contrasting child and adult bilingualism.*
Source: Adapted from *Principles of Language Learning and Teaching,* 2nd edition, by H. Douglas Brown (Englewood Cliffs: NJ: Prentice, 1994).

age of ten, there are several well-documented cases of feral children who tried to learn their first and only language as young "adults" (Candland 1993). Brown (1994) makes the sage observation that too often (as in the myth under discussion here) a double comparison is made, contrasting kids learning their mother tongue with adults attempting to acquire a second language (i.e., C1 vs. A2). One of the reasons this is an unreasonable contrast is that adults aren't children. A fairer contrast, according to Brown, is to compare children learning a second language with adults trying to do the same: in other words, to cite one example, contrast kids in a bilingual program with college students taking foreign-language classes. For applied linguists, then, issues such as definitions and comparisons immediately begin to cloud what appears to be a transparent picture to the lay public, and, more significantly, they create the opportunity for a range of responses regarding the relationship between age and acquisition. Some writers who have not been directly involved in research on the issue have carefully hedged their arguments and are relatively neutral about the topic (Bialystok and Hakuta 1994; Cook 1996), but the majority of scholars who have been directly involved with investigating "the younger, the better" hypothesis have committed themselves to one of two positions: (1) the myth has it all backward—older learners are actually the better learners, and (2) the myth is validated in at least some aspects of second-language acquisition.

Evidence against the myth is strong and diverse. First of all, not even the most ardent proponents of the second position deny the supremacy of adults when it comes to the learning of certain linguistic skills. Certainly the strongest example of these is literacy, where in all cultures, in contrast to speaking and listening skills, the ability to read and write comes later on in childhood and is invariably learned in formal settings. For second-language learning, adults therefore can bring the literacy skills they have already acquired in their first language to bear on their acquisition of a second. They have long become acculturated to a preliteracy environment and have already developed scanning skills, recognized the appropriate contexts and contents of literacy, and so forth. They have learned how to make the relevant phoneme-to-grapheme correspondences for

the language(s) they are exposed to, they have developed awareness of different discourse patterns which appear in print, and
they have a vast range of schematic knowledge which they can
apply to new material they are about to read (or write). Finally,
they have had so much experience reading (and writing) that for
most adults these complex skills have become heavily automa-
tized and routinized. Even when the mother-tongue orthogra-
phy is markedly different from that of the second language (e.g.,
Korean to English, or much more dramatically, Japanese to English), many of the literacy abilities in the first language still
transfer over in a positive manner. Given all of this, no one
would argue that after a week's exposure to the writing system
of a second language, a six-year-old would be a better reader
and writer than a sixteen- or a sixty-year-old. Right away, it is
obvious that "the younger, the better" myth tacitly excludes the
ability to become literate in a new language.

But virtually everyone is in agreement that adults are superior
in the acquisition of several other linguistic skills as well. Unar-
guably, the single most useful aspect to acquire in any language is
its vocabulary, and a growing number of applied linguists have
recently contended that, because lexical knowledge involves a
huge number of phrases and collocations, the acquisition of
vocabulary also assures the learning of a substantial portion of
what is traditionally considered grammar (Lewis 1993). Because
adults are able to exploit cognates and employ word-decoding
skills, they acquire new words more rapidly, especially when the
second language is historically and/or typologically related to the
mother tongue. As an illustration, because they possess such large
vocabularies with so many cognates, Spanish-speaking adults can
comprehend and produce more words in English than Spanish-
speaking children attempting to acquire the same tongue.
Another area in which adults enjoy an advantage is pragmatics.
Young children learn only rudimentary aspects of pragmatics,
and not until early adolescence do most learners acquire full pragmatic competence in their mother tongue (e.g., they have learned
to use declarative sentences to initiate requests—"I don't seem to
have a pen"—or they have grasped how, when, and to whom to
use the morphological politeness levels which are socially appropriate in languages such as Japanese). Again, this pragmatic

knowledge is of great benefit to adults when they start to learn a foreign language, even when the pragmatics of the target language differs from that of their mother tongue. Bilingual children are often unaware that they are violating pragmatic constraints even in their own language, let alone in a second tongue. Finally, because of their cognitive and experiential maturity, adults have a much more expansive schematic knowledge to apply to second-language learning contexts than do young children, and this assists them especially in comprehending a new language. Ask very young children what the word *transportation* means and, if they can guess its meaning, they will come up with a synonym like "choo choo train" or make a zooming noise as they fly their hands like an imaginary airplane. Because adults have the concept of a "transportation schema," they can use this schematic knowledge to decode and remember the new words and phrases in a second language that deal with transportation. They are therefore able to deploy this semantic networking to predict destinations, routes, costs, and carriers, and it is exactly this kind of schematic knowledge that helps adults understand novel conversations and texts in a foreign language and also helps them select appropriate expressions whenever they attempt to speak or write. From all of this, we can readily see that in many areas of second-language acquisition, there can be no disagreement that it is "the older," not "the younger," that is "the better."

When we move from these broad arguments in favor of adult learners to the more narrow claims of second-language acquisition research, it is of course more difficult to come up with definitive evidence. An oft-cited study by Snow and Hoefnagel-Hohle (1977) demonstrated that even for pronunciation, older second-language learners (in this case adolescents) were more accurate than their younger counterparts. These results were unusual but suggestive. The few investigations of phonological acquisition which go against "the younger, the better" hypothesis do not so much "prove" that adults are better second-language speakers; rather, they show that some adults can replicate the ability of many children to learn to speak a new language without a foreign accent. There are at least two experiments in this vein which purport to show that there is no critical period for the acquisition of pronunciation and that given the right conditions, older learners can gain the same nativelike fluency in a foreign tongue as many bilingual children. Neufeld (1977) and Bongaerts, van Summeren, Planken, and Schils (1997) developed experiments involving different groups of languages that apparently showed that under optimal circumstances, adult learners of a second language who tape-recorded short segments of their speech could trick judges who were native speakers of those target languages into thinking that they were actually native speakers of the languages. There is a great deal of published discussion over the validity of these studies and their relevance to the relationship between age and acquisition (cf. Singleton and Lengyel 1995), but some researchers have pointed out that limitations in the research design of these two sets of experiments vitiate their claims against the critical-period hypothesis (Long 1990; Scovel 1997). Be that as it may, even without the clear-cut support of research, it is apparent that if we broaden the scope of "the younger, the better" myth to encompass every aspect of language acquisition, in such areas as literacy and vocabulary acquisition the myth remains unsubstantiated, and in some cases the reverse appears to be more valid.

Turning to the second-language-acquisition (SLA) researchers who have been able to muster some supporting evidence for "the younger, the better" hypothesis, they express a fairly wide range of opinions, which has led to substantial disagreement over which linguistic skills purportedly give younger learners an advantage. Summarizing the studies that several others have published, and based on my own research, I have contended for many years that young learners do indeed enjoy an advantage over older second-language learners but that this linguistic precocity is confined to a solitary skill—being able to sound like a native speaker (Scovel 1988). In essence, the "strong version" of the critical-period hypothesis claims that given all the right opportunities, learners younger than the age of ten can pick up a new language so well that they will sound like a native. Given these opportunities, bilingual children will have the added advantage of growing up sounding like native speakers in two languages. I think it is crucial to recognize that even though my own research appears to document the fact that children can be better language learners than adults, this claim is restricted to one very narrow linguistic skill—nativelike pronunciation. Because this ability is such an insignificant component among the wide panoply of skills needed to become fully bilingual, I do not view my own research as supportive of "the younger, the better" hypothesis and see no contradiction between this work and the contention I have been trying to make here that overall, adults are more effective learners.

Some researchers have apparently demonstrated that younger learners are better than adults in a very different linguistic ability. They have argued that irrespective of whether there is a critical period for developing accentless speech, there does seem to be evidence of a critical period for developing syntax. A recent study by Spadaro (1998) concludes that there may even be age constraints on the acquisition of second-language vocabulary. Patkowski (1980) and Slavoff and Johnson (1995) are among several investigators who appear to have shown that before puberty, second-language learners seem to have acquired native-speaker competence in syntax, but if they acquire a second language after about the age of thirteen, they seem to exhibit limited competence in their grammatical knowledge, especially of more complex structures. For example, Johnson and Newport (1989) have shown that young learners of English as a second language (ESL) were just as good as native speakers in grammatical judgments about English sentences, but ESL learners who were in their teens or older made a significant number of errors. These researchers controlled for the overall number of years of exposure to the second language, so the advantage the younger learners held was not simply a consequence of their having spent many more years learning the language. Many SLA researchers find this evidence for critical-period constraints convincing, but I remain somewhat skeptical. For one thing, grammatical judgments seem to me to be based more on *meta*-linguistic than linguistic ability. For another, some linguists have questioned the empirical validity of using these judgments as a foundation for evidence of linguistic competence (Schütze 1996). Be that as it may, several prominent scholars in the field have embraced both the phonological and the syntactic evidence for critical-period constraints and hold that for at least these two areas of language acquisition, younger learners have an advantage (Ellis 1994; Skehan 1998). Nevertheless, not even the most enthusiastic proponents of the critical-period hypothesis have gone so far as to use this evidence to counterbalance all the other factors which must be taken into account and gone on to promote the notion that whenever possible we should initiate second-language instruction as early in schooling as possible.

The Myth and Bilingual Education

What is the relevance of this discussion concerning "the younger, the better" myth to bilingual education, especially as it is practiced in the United States? The first and certainly most important conclusion to draw, based on the way I have presented the evidence here, is that all of the promoters, practitioners, and policy-makers of bilingual education—indeed, even its critics, such as the promulgators of the Unz-Tuchman initiative in California in 1998—should think critically and seriously about basing any of their arguments or principles on the notion that the youngest language learners are the best learners. Counterarguments in abundance have already been cited, but they can be aptly encapsulated in the following illustration. Take any individual acquiring his or her mother tongue: pushed to its extreme, "the younger, the better" argument would contend that neonates are better learners than infants, infants better than toddlers, toddlers better than preschoolers, and so on. Although there has been a great deal of fascinating research on language acquisition in the crib over the past few decades (Jusczyk 1997), it is clear that first-language acquisition does not begin to flower until after the first year, and if we are to look at all aspects of linguistic learning (i.e., grammar, pragmatics, vocabulary, literacy, sociolinguistic appropriateness, discourse awareness, etc.), children do not gain full fluency in any language until early adolescence.

As early as 1979, Krashen, Long, and Scarcella put forward the idea that although older learners were *initially* more successful in learning a new language, under "naturalistic" conditions, child learners would eventually end up with greater competence in the second language. This proposal seemed to account for some of the conflicting data gleaned in "the younger, the better" research, and Krashen has used it in his support of bilingual education over the years (Krashen 1996). Many of Krashen's premises, however, have been strongly criticized (e.g., for a single collection of essays, see Barasch and James 1994), and although most SLA scholars might not go as far as Spolsky (1989), who has posited seventy-four variables which can affect the course of language acquisition, the majority believe there are many factors affecting language learning which can override or at least mitigate the effects of age. To cite just one—the quantity, quality, and consistency of second-language input varies enormously among language learners of any age and do not fit neatly into such dualistic categories as "learning vs. acquisition" or "CALP vs. BICS" (see Chapter 7, "Input and Interaction and Second Language Acquisition," Ellis 1994).

A second application of all this evidence is directly pertinent to the aforementioned Proposition 227, passed by the voters of California in 1998. Because I was unofficially involved as a media consultant during the debate over the Unz-Tuchman initiative, I collected samples of advertisements and other campaign materials both for and against the proposition. Given the fact that this proposition explicitly propounded "the younger, the better" hypothesis, it was not surprising that the initiative proposed to replace most of the bilingual education programs it sought to dismantle with a one-year "immersion" program in English. Opposition to Proposition 227 during the campaign was vigorous and spirited, but virtually no one opposing the initiative publicly criticized "the younger, the better" principle on which it was founded and which formed the justification for its English-in-one-year solution. Many opponents of the measure pointed out in the media and in campaign literature that one year was not long enough for any child to acquire cognitive academic language proficiency in a second language, the kind of linguistic competence necessary for scholastic success, but there was no criticism that I can recall of the underlying premise that young children are the best language learners. Even more extraordinary, despite the fact that the largest group of language teachers in the state, California Teachers of English to Speakers of Other Languages (CATESOL), and the largest group internationally, Teachers of English to Speakers of Other Languages (TESOL), both threw their support against the passage of Proposition 227, linguists in these two organizations did not single out the manner in which this measure was so heavily predicated on "the younger, the better" myth. Even with the gift of hindsight, it is exceedingly difficult to determine why certain initiatives fail and why others pass so easily, but I believe that a great many voters supported this proposition because they felt that "everyone knows" that children are good language learners and that most children could easily pick up a new language such as English within a year. Had the opponents of Proposition 227 chosen to show the public how spurious this myth actually is, it is conceivable that Californians would have voted against the measure, or at least supported it with a much slimmer majority.

The prevalence of "the younger, the better" myth in our views about bilingual education in this country might explain the degree to which so much of the emphasis is skewed toward younger learners. At least in the United States, bilingual education evokes images of children, pupils, and schools. Neither implicitly nor explicitly does the term call to mind images of adult immigrants acquiring English, and even less, images of American businesspeople studying Portuguese by means of cassettes in anticipation of a new assignment to Brazil. And yet it is worth remembering that as many adults as children are becoming bilingual (if not more). Bilingual education in this country is also often equated with the learning of *English* as the additional language, yet despite the fact that English is clearly the global language, many native speakers of English in the United States attempt to become bilingual in a new tongue. Reflecting on "the younger, the better" myth prompts a broader perspective on bilingual education: that it is not confined to children nor restricted to the acquisition of English as the second tongue.

A fourth and final insight we can gain from examining "the younger, the better" hypothesis concerns the way students of a second language are often and unfairly viewed as limited learners. Individuals attempting to acquire a new tongue, whether child or adult, are frequently perceived as linguistically *limited*, but as Cook (1993) has so aptly observed, whatever their degree of proficiency in a new language, bilinguals are not limited but *multicompetent*. In other words, because they are fully fluent in their mother tongue, any amount of second-language competence they are able to achieve only augments their overall linguistic abilities. Too often we measure bilinguals in terms of their "limitations" in the new language and forget to add their second-language knowledge on to the native competence the learners already possess in the first language. Multicompetence can occur at any age, of course, but adults, not children, are the best examples of multicompetence. Very young learners are not completely fluent even in their mother tongue, so they are not as multicompetent as older learners. Furthermore, if we look at polyglots, people with proficiency in more than two languages, they are much more likely to be adults; therefore, using multicompetence as a measure of linguistic ability, once again adult learners prove to be superior to children.

Returning to the theme with which this chapter began, in today's complex world, sociocultural pressures inevitably encourage the general populace to pursue myths, and because of these forces, I am not sanguine that even concerted efforts among applied linguists and language educators can convince people that "the younger, the better" belief is more spurious than real. But, if we in the academy do not follow our conscience and attempt to educate the public about our particular domain of inquiry, who will? Pseudoscientific speculations have garnered enough press and media attention. For those of us who harbor special appreciation for competence in more than one language, it is all the more essential to continue to contribute our professional knowledge to raising public consciousness on these vital issues and policies.

Works Cited

American Heritage Dictionary of the English Language, The. 1969. Boston: American Heritage Publishing Company.

Barasch, Ronald, and C. Vaughan James, eds. 1994. *Beyond the Monitor Model: Comments on Current Theory and Practice in Second Language Acquisition.* Boston: Heinle and Heinle.

Bialystok, Ellen, and Kenji Hakuta. 1994. *In Other Words: The Science and Psychology of Second-Language Acquisition.* New York: Basic Books.

Bongaerts, Theo, Chantal van Summeren, Brigette Planken, and Erik Schils. 1997. "Age and Ultimate Attainment in the Pronunciation of a Foreign Language." *Studies in Second Language Acquisition* 19: 447–65.

Brown, H. Douglas. 1994. *Principles of Language Learning and Teaching*, 3rd ed. Englewood Cliffs, NJ: Prentice-Hall Regents.

California Voter Information Guide: Primary Election June 2, 1998. Sacramento, CA: Secretary of State.

Candland, Douglas. 1993. *Feral Children and Clever Animals: Reflections on Human Nature.* New York: Oxford University Press.

Cook, Vivian. 1993. *Linguistics and Second Language Acquisition.* New York: St. Martin's Press.

———. 1996. *Second Language Learning and Language Teaching.* 2nd ed. London: Arnold.

Crawford, James. 1998. "English Only for the Children?" *TESOL Matters* 8(2): 20–21.

Crystal, David. 1990. *The English Language.* London: Penguin Books.

Cummins, James. 1994. "Primary Language Instruction and the Education of Language Minority Students." In C. Leybad, ed., *Schooling and Language Minority Students: A Theoretical Framework.* 2nd ed. Sacramento: California State Department of Education. 3–46.

Curtain, Helena. 1993. *An Early Start: A Resource Book for Elementary School Foreign Language.* Washington, D.C.: Center for Applied Linguistics.

Ellis, Rod. 1994. *The Study of Second Language Acquisition.* Oxford: Oxford University Press.

Horwitz, Elaine, and Dolly Young, eds. 1991. *Language Anxiety: From Theory and Research to Classroom Implications.* Englewood Cliffs, NJ: Prentice-Hall.

Johnson, Jacqueline, and Elissa Newport. 1989. "Critical Period Effects in Second Language Learning: The Influence of Maturational State on the Acquisition of English as a Second Language." *Cognitive Psychology* 21: 60–99.

Jusczyk, Peter. 1997. *The Discovery of Spoken Language.* Cambridge, MA: MIT Press.

Kachru, Braj. 1985. "Standards, Codifiction and Sociolinguistic Realism: The English Language in the Outer Circle." In Randolph Quirk and Henry Widdowson, eds., *English in the World: Teaching and Learning the Language and Literatures*. Cambridge: Cambridge University Press. 11–30.

Krashen, Stephen. 1996. *Under Attack: The Case against Bilingual Education*. Culver City, CA: Language Education Associates.

Krashen, Stephen, Michael Long, and Robin Scarcella. 1979. "Age, Rate, and Eventual Attainment in Second Language Acquisition." *TESOL Quarterly* 13(4): 573–82.

Lee, Penny. 1996. *The Whorf Theory Complex: A Critical Reconstruction*. Amsterdam: John Benjamins.

Lewis, Michael. 1993. *The Lexical Approach: The State of ELT and a Way Forward*. Hove, Eng.: Language Teaching Publications.

Long, Michael. 1990. "Maturational Constraints on Language Development." *Studies in Second Language Acquisition* 12: 251–85.

Marcos, Kathleen. 1997. *Why, How, and When Should My Child Learn a Second Language?* Washington, D.C.: ERIC.

Neufeld, Gerald. 1977. "Language Learning Ability in Adults: A Study of the Acquisition of Prosodic and Articulatory Features." *Working Papers in Bilingualism* (Toronto: OISE) 12: 45–60.

Parks, Deborah. 1998. "Capacity for Starting Elementary Foreign Language Programs in the Public Schools of Washington State." *PNCFL Newsletter* 21: 6–9.

Patkowski, Mark. 1980. "The Sensitive Period for the Acquisition of Syntax in a Second Language." *Language Learning* 30: 449–72.

Pinker, Stephen. 1994. *The Language Instinct*. New York: Harper-Perennial.

Pullum, Geoffrey. 1991. *The Great Eskimo Vocabulary Hoax, and Other Irreverent Essays on the Study of Language*. Chicago: University of Chicago Press.

Schütze, Carson. 1996. *The Empirical Base of Linguistics: Grammaticality Judgments and Linguistic Methodology*. Chicago: University of Chicago Press.

Scovel, Thomas. 1978. "The Effect of Affect: A Review of the Anxiety Literature." *Language Learning* 28: 129–42.

————. 1988. *A Time to Speak: A Psycholinguistic Inquiry into the Critical Period for Human Speech*. New York: Newbury House.

————. 1993. "Why Languages Do Not Shape Cognition: Psycho- and Neurolinguistic Evidence." *JALT Journal* 13: 43–56.

————. 1995. *English Teaching in China*. Unpublished report for the United States Information Agency, Washington, D.C.

————. 1997. "Review of David Singleton and Zsolt Lengyel, 'The Age Factor in Second Language Acquisition.'" *Modern Language Journal* 81: 118–19.

Singleton, David, and Zsolt Lengyel, eds. 1995. *The Age Factor in Second Language Acquisition: A Critical Look at the Critical Theory Hypothesis*. Clevedon, Eng.: Multilingual Matters.

Skehan, Peter. 1998. *A Cognitive Approach to Language Learning*. Oxford.: Oxford University Press.

Slavoff, Georgina, and Jacqueline Johnson. 1995. "The Effects of Age on the Rate of Learning a Second Language." *Studies in Second Language Acquisition* 17: 1–16.

Snow, Catherine, and M. Hoefnagel-Hohle. 1977. "The Critical Period for Language Acquisition: Evidence from Second Language Learning." *Child Development* 49: 1114–28.

Spadaro, Katherine. 1998. *Maturational Constraints on Lexical Acquisition in a Second Language*. Unpublished doctoral dissertation, University of Western Australia, Nedlands.

Spolsky, Bernard. 1989. *Conditions for Second Language Learning: Introduction to a General Theory* Oxford.: Oxford University Press.

Steinberg, Danny. 1993. *An Introduction to Psycholinguistics*. London: Longman.

CHAPTER SIX

Bilingual Education:
The Debate Continues

STEPHEN D. KRASHEN
University of Southern California

In this chapter, I discuss several recent as well as ongoing issues in bilingual education:

- How bilingual education is defined: I attempt to define bilingual education in terms of its components, which rest solidly on theory of language acquisition, and I provide one example of how these components are actualized in a program. It is crucial to do this because critics of bilingual education define bilingual education very differently.

- How bilingual education should be evaluated: One of the major critics of bilingual education, Christine Rossell, insists that evaluations of bilingual education follow strict scientific guidelines. I argue that many critics of bilingual education frequently violate Rossell's guidelines.

- Claims that bilingual education and bilingualism result in fewer earnings: I argue that careful inspection of the data shows that these claims are not well-founded.

- Whether one year of intensive English instruction can provide enough English competence for mainstream success: California's Proposition 227 allows only one year of intensive English; because Proposition 227 passed in California, this idea may spread elsewhere, and it is therefore essential to examine the data. I argue that research from all sides—supporters and critics—converges: one year is nowhere near enough time.

Defining Bilingual Education

To avoid confusion about what is and what is not bilingual education, it may be helpful to attempt a definition. Full bilingual education programs have these characteristics:

1. They teach subject matter in the primary language.

2. They develop literacy in the primary language.

3. They provide comprehensible input in the second language in the form of English as a second language (ESL) classes and "sheltered" subject matter teaching.

All three of these characteristics promote second-language acquisition, a major goal of bilingual education. The third characteristic promotes second-language acquisition obviously and directly. The first two do so indirectly but powerfully. Students who have a solid knowledge of subject matter, thanks to instruction in their first language, will understand more when subject matter is taught in the second language and will thus acquire more of the second language. Also, developing literacy in the primary language is a shortcut to second-language literacy. It is much easier to learn to read in a language you understand, and once you can read, this ability transfers rapidly to other languages, even if the alphabets are different (Krashen 1996).[1]

These three characteristics can be considered characteristics of "early" bilingual education (although they could be used in programs for older students who are in early stages of second-language acquisition). They help children attain the important and central goal of second-language development, which in the United States means English-language development. In addition, for cognitive, affective, and practical reasons it is desirable to provide for continuing first-language development even after students are mainstreamed (Krashen, Tse, and McQuillan 1998).

An Example: The Gradual-Exit Program

The central goal of the gradual-exit plan is to introduce children to subject matter teaching in English as soon as it can be made comprehensible. The program contains the three components listed previously, combining ESL instruction, sheltered subject matter teaching, and teaching in the primary language.

The idea behind sheltered subject matter teaching comes from Canadian immersion programs, and the term refers to teaching subject matter to second-language acquirers in a comprehensible way. It was pioneered at the University of Ottawa with literate, educated, adult second-language acquirers (Edwards, Wesche, Krashen, Clement, and Krudinier 1984). That study and numerous others have confirmed that students in sheltered classes learn subject matter and acquire impressive amounts of the second language (Krashen 1991). In the gradual-exit program, sheltered subject matter serves as a bridge between education in the primary language and in mainstream classes.

In the initial stage of the gradual-exit program, non-English-speaking children receive core subject matter instruction in the primary language, along with ESL instruction. As soon as possible, they receive sheltered subject matter instruction in those subjects that are the easiest to make comprehensible in English—math and science, which at this level do not demand a great deal of abstract language use. Note that a child in sheltered math at this stage has already had some ESL instruction and some instruction in math in the primary language: both help make the sheltered class more comprehensible. Sheltered classes are thus for intermediate learners, not beginners. In later stages, math and science are studied in mainstream classes, and other subjects, such as social studies, are taught in sheltered classes in English. Eventually, all subjects are taught in mainstream classes (see Table 6.1 on page 140).

Once full mainstreaming is complete, advanced first-language development is available. This kind of plan avoids problems associated with exiting children too early from first-language instruction (before the English they encounter is comprehensible) and provides instruction in the first language where it is most needed. These plans also allow children to have the advantages of advanced first-language development (Krashen, Tse, and McQuillan 1998).

TABLE 6.1. The Gradual-Exit Model

	Mainstream	ESL/sheltered	First language
Beginning	art, music, PE	ESL	all core subjects
Intermediate	art, music, PE	ESL, math, science	social studies, language arts
Advanced	art, music, PE, math, science	ESL, social studies	language arts
Mainstream development	all subjects		heritage-language

Other Definitions of Bilingual Education

Critics define bilingual education somewhat differently than I do. Rossell (1998, 2 §6) maintains that transitional bilingual education contains the following "essential elements":

◆ LEP children learn to read and write in their native tongue.

◆ LEP children learn subject matter (math, science, social studies, etc.) in their native tongue.

◆ LEP children are taught English for some portion of the day.

◆ When the child is literate in his or her native tongue and proficient in English, he or she is transitioned to all-English instruction.

The first three elements accurately describe the first stage of the gradual-exit plan, but they describe *only* the first stage. In the gradual-exit program, children study in English long before full proficiency is achieved in English and long before full literacy is developed in the first language. Rossell has maintained (at the CEO conference in Washington on bilingual education, September 18, 1995, and on a radio debate, June 1, 1998, KCRW, Los Angeles) that bilingual educators insist on full literacy in the first language and full proficiency in English before any study of subject matter in English takes place. This is not true.

Porter (1996) presents a similar description of bilingual education: "Bilingual programs assign children to a separate track of schooling for three to seven years, teach all school subjects including reading and writing in the native language for several years, and delay the teaching of English literacy for three or four years" (3, §7). This certainly does not happen in the gradual-exit program.

The Research and Scientific Method

In the typical research study evaluating the effects of bilingual education, an experimental group participates in some kind of bilingual program, and a comparison group is exposed to a program that is conducted primarily in the second language. Rossell (e.g., Rossell and Baker 1996; Rossell 1998) recommends that we apply the scientific method when we discuss research. According to Rossell, this means accepting the results of experiments only when a treatment and comparison group are used and when there is some control for differences that existed in subjects before the treatment began (Rossell 1998, §17).

There are good reasons for following this strategy. Without a control group, a group that had experiences similar to that of the experimental group but without the experimental treatment, we don't know if changes in the experimental group were due to the treatment or to some other factor, such as maturation or another event that occurred during the treatment (Campbell and Stanley 1966). If, for example, a group of children in a bilingual program improve in English over a two-year time span, we cannot conclude that bilingual education is more effective than other approaches. Students will normally make some progress in English over two years if they live in the United States and get any comprehensible input at all. If there had been a comparison group of students with similar backgrounds who did not receive bilingual education, one could compare the gains and see which treatment produced more growth in English.

Studies lacking comparison groups are far from useless, however. If students do not make any progress acquiring English using bilingual education, bilingual education would be in deep trouble whether or not a comparison group is used. While demonstrated growth in English without a comparison group may not provide convincing supporting evidence for the effectiveness of bilingual education, lack of growth would be damaging.

Studies without comparison groups thus provide a test that a hypothesis must pass. Studies without comparison groups can also be useful when they use other bases for comparisons. Instead of a control group that underwent a different or no treatment at the same time as the experimental group, the comparison group could be last year's students in the same school who were at the same age a year ago, a previous "cohort."

Another option is to apply established norms, to examine expected growth for students of the same age over the same time period. This is, of course, only valid when the students examined have similar backgrounds and other conditions are the same. One can argue that using norms is not as valid as using a "genuine" control group because the comparison will be less exact, but when the groups on which the norms are based are similar to the experimental group, and when results of these comparisons are consistent (robust), the results should be taken seriously. We appealed to such alternative control groups in Krashen and Biber (1988), using district norms, city norms, and previous cohorts when their scores were based on students who had backgrounds similar to the experimental subjects (in one case, we compared English-language acquirers to native speakers of English, a comparison group that would be expected to do much better on tests of English reading). Our results were consistent and favorable to bilingual education.

Rossell also recommends that studies control for differences that existed before the experiment began. The preferred method involves randomly assigning subjects to experimental and control groups, equalizing subjects on all characteristics, including those the researchers may not be aware of. A second method is to statistically control for initial differences, using statistical tools such as analysis of covariance. This is less preferred because it only controls for those variables that experimenters are aware of.

Rossell excludes several studies from consideration that do not employ one of these methods of controlling for initial differences. But some of these studies can be useful. I have argued (Krashen 1996) that the results of some post-test-only designs that compare bilingual education and all-English approaches can be used to evaluate the efficacy of bilingual education when there is no reason to suspect that comparison and experimental subjects differed in important ways before the study began. Also, when the same result turns up in many different "uncontrolled" studies, done under slightly different conditions, we have a built-in form of randomization. Large numbers of post-test-only studies for which there is no reason to think there were initial differences among subjects are informative when they provide consistent results.

I therefore agree with Rossell that we should use the scientific method, although I advocate a somewhat more relaxed standard. I do not exclude all studies without control groups and without standard controls for initial differences if these flaws do not present threats to validity. But there are limits to relaxing standards. In some cases, writers draw conclusions from studies that are completely uncontrolled and that present serious threats to validity.

The 5 Percent Argument

A striking example of overly relaxed standards is the well-known claim that bilingual education has failed in California because only about 5 percent of limited-English-proficient children "learn English every year" ("English for the Children" 1997). (A similar argument has been used in Arizona.) This accusation has been made by an individual who claims to be scientifically trained—Ron Unz. Unz dismisses all experimental research in bilingual education as low quality but frequently appeals to this kind of completely unscientific data. Let us apply Rossell's criteria to Unz's "study." The 5 percent figure refers to all LEP children in California, whether or not they were in bilingual programs. If most were in bilingual education, one could consider this observation to be a study without a control group. But only 30 percent of the LEP children in California are in bilingual programs. Without knowing the reclassification rates of those in bilingual education and those in other programs, we can conclude nothing about the effectiveness of bilingual education from these data. This is thus a study without an experimental group *and* without a control group.

One could claim that the 5 percent figure is too low and condemn all programs for LEP children. But "reclassification" represents a very high level of competence in academic English. Many children operate comfortably in English long before they are reclassified, doing most of their schoolwork in English and even participating in mainstream instruction. In some districts, to be reclassified, a student must place in the upper two-thirds of all students on reading comprehension tests normed on native speakers; by definition, one-third of native speakers would not achieve this. The finding that 5 percent of LEP students are reclassified does not mean that only 5 percent "learn English each year." It means that about 5 percent achieve a very high standard in English-language competency.

Bilingual Education in Leiden

Glenn (1998a, 1998b) also dismisses experimental studies but puts a great deal of faith in unscientific observation. He notes that studies comparing alternative methods are "inconclusive as a basis for policy decisions" (1998a, 3 §9). He specifically discounts studies conducted in Leiden and Enschede in the Netherlands, noting that "they have not been replicated because the results have not convinced policy-makers that this was in the best interests of [language-minority] children" (4.1 §12). Glenn provides no other discussion or data, but some readers might be curious to examine these results, which appear to be quite encouraging.

The Leiden study is described in Appel (1984) (see also Altena and Appel 1982; Appel 1988) and involved twenty-six Turkish and thirty-one Moroccan children ages 7.0 to 12.6 who were placed in either bilingual or "regular" classes in Leiden. Appel reported no initial differences between the groups in type of neighborhood lived in, TV watching habits, socioeconomic situation, nonverbal intelligence, or educational level reached by parents in country of origin: "we tried to match the two groups on certain background variables as much as possible" (35). The mean age of those in the bilingual program was 9.4, and for students in the regular program, it was 9.6.

While both groups received special instruction in Dutch for 20 percent of the school day, for the bilingual group, all subjects were taught in the primary language for the first year; but "as soon as the immigrant children were able to understand and speak some Dutch, they joined Dutch children for a few hours a week in activities (gymnastics, music, and crafts) which were meant to encourage their integration into Dutch life" (Appel 1984, 30). In the second year, the program was 50 percent primary language and 50 percent Dutch, and in year three all instruction was in Dutch. Table 6.2 presents typical test scores for Dutch-language development.

Appel (1984) noted that

[i]n general, it can be concluded that the amount of time on minority-language teaching in the transitional bilingual school . . . did not harm or hinder the second language acquisition of the Turkish and Moroccan immigrant workers' children. At

TABLE 6.2. Bilingual versus Nonbilingual Education Students

	After 2 Years		Follow-up One Year Later	
	bilingual	regular	bilingual	regular
Oral Language				
Mean length utterance	4.1	3.8	4.9	4.4
Number of different words produced (measure of vocabulary)	168.1	157.1	213.1	205.9
Picture Test (oral)				
Morphology (e.g., plurals)	33.2	34.1	65.9	58.2
Imitation (form sentence from words presented in vertical column)	57.5	50.0	71.5	57.7
Written Language				
Cloze test	52.1	51.5	64.3	50.9 (sig, $p < .05$)

Source: Figures taken from Appel 1984, 49, Table 2.3.

the end of the research period, these children were even somewhat ahead in oral and written second-language proficiency as
compared to children who were instructed entirely or almost
entirely in Dutch. (50)

The impact of bilingual education was apparently not limited to
language: "In the first three school years the mean percentage of
'problem children' in the [regular] group was nearly twice as high
as in the [bilingual] group (24% vs. 13%). Social-emotional
problems were exhibited in aggressive behavior, apathy" (57).

Much less information is available on the bilingual program
in Enschede. Appel (1988) presents a preliminary report of the
progress of Turkish and Moroccan children who had a full bilingual program (56 percent primary language the first year, 44 percent the second [Glenn 1996, 460]) compared with those who
had only a few hours of first-language instruction per week.
Appel reported that bilingual students outperformed comparison-
group students in Dutch reading, and that the Turkish bilingual
children approached native-speaker norms in reading and even
performed above this level two years after leaving the program.
Citing Eldering (1983), Glenn (1996), however, notes that in one
evaluation, nine out of fourteen Moroccan children (but only one
out of seventeen Turkish children) who had participated in the
Enschede program had to repeat grade 3, this time in mainstream
instruction (460). We are not told how this compares to the performance of similar children who did not get bilingual education.

The Delaware-Massachusetts Argument

Glenn (1998b) claims that we can investigate the effects of bilingual education with a "natural experiment," comparing English-
language development in states that mandate bilingual education
with English-language development in states that prohibit it:
"Massachusetts mandates bilingual education, for example,
Delaware prohibits it, but Hispanic achievement is not notably
higher in one state than in the other; indeed, the gap between Hispanic and non-Hispanic white scores on the National Assessment
of Education Progress was substantially larger in Massachusetts
than it was in Delaware" (6).

Everything is wrong with this argument. Recall that, according to Rossell, there needs to be some kind of control for preexisting differences between groups. The Hispanic/Latino populations in the two states may differ in ways that could influence school achievement, such as socioeconomic status and recency of immigration. Jim Crawford pointed out to me in a personal conversation that the two states were certainly different in the percentage of LEP students. The following data are from 1996 to 1997:

	Number of Hispanic/Latino students	Hispanic/Latino LEP
Massachusetts	62,271	27,076 (43%)
Delaware	4,346	1,299 (30%)

Source: Massachusetts data provided by Tom Louie, who obtained them from the Web sites of the Massachusetts Department of Education and the Delaware Department of Public Instruction.

Clearly, Delaware has a lower percentage of LEP Hispanic/Latino students, which certainly could influence English reading scores and which suggests that the groups differ in other important ways.

Second, it is not clear that Massachusetts's Hispanics/Latinos are more involved in bilingual education than are Delaware's Hispanics/Latinos. Even though bilingual education is officially banned in Delaware, this ban is not enforced (see Crawford 1995, 42). Jim Crawford pointed out to me that while only one district in Delaware actually implements bilingual education, it is a significant district: Red Clay Consolidated. In the 1996–1997 school year, 795 out of Delaware's 1,725 LEP children and 762 of the 1,299 Hispanic/Latino LEP children were enrolled in Red Clay. There appears to be plenty of bilingual education in Delaware.

Finally, a look at the actual data (see Table 6.3 on page 148) shows that Hispanics/Latinos in Massachusetts actually scored higher than Hispanics/Latinos in Delaware, in both 1994 (a small difference, not "notable," as Glenn [1998b] points out) and 1992 (a larger difference, one that is quite notable). In 1992 the difference between non-Hispanic/Latino Whites and Hispanics/Latinos

TABLE 6.3. Comparison of Two States: NAEP Fourth-Grade Reading

1994	White	Hispanic/Latino	difference
Massachusetts	231	194	37
Delaware	215	190	25
1992	White	Hispanic/Latino	difference
Massachusetts	231	201	30
Delaware	222	187	35

Source: Data from Williams et al. 1995, Table D.2.

was larger in Delaware than in Massachusetts. Thus, even if we accepted the Massachusetts-Delaware comparison as a true experiment—which it is not—the data do not consistently support Glenn's assertions.

The Delaware-Massachusetts argument fails in every way: (1) the groups compared may have differed in important ways that could influence school performance, (2) it has not been established that Delaware actually provides less bilingual education for its Hispanic/Latino students, and (3) the NAEP scores do not, in fact, show that Massachusetts's Hispanics/Latinos do better than Delaware's.

Bilingualism, Bilingual Education, and Earnings

Lopez and Mora (1998) claim that Hispanics who participated in bilingual education programs earn significantly less in their late twenties than comparison subjects who did not participate in bilingual education. In a recent paper, Jeffrey McQuillan and I argue that this conclusion is incorrect (Krashen and McQuillan 1998). Lopez and Mora obtained their data from the High School and Beyond study, which consists of interviews with high school sophomores and seniors, as well as follow-up interviews. In the data set used by Lopez and Mora, subjects were sophomores in high school in 1980; they were interviewed again in 1992, when they were twenty-eight years old. Twelve percent of the sample said they had had ESL classes, and 27.5 percent said they had been in bilingual education.

Table 6.4 from Lopez and Mora provides the crucial statistics, presenting earnings for those who had ESL instruction (without bilingual education), those who had bilingual education, and members of the comparison group (no bilingual education and no ESL instruction), adjusted for differences among schools (e.g., public/private, teacher-student ratio, and so forth).

Lopez and Mora claim that (1) while there is no difference among the groups for the overall sample, first- and second-generation comparison students (neither ESL nor bilingual education) earn significantly more than those who participated in bilingual education; (2) first- and second-generation subjects who had bilingual education earn less than those who had ESL instruction only.

There are many things wrong with these conclusions.

1. *The comparison group.* Those interviewed in the High School and Beyond survey were asked the following questions:

    a. What is the first language you spoke?

    b. What other first language [sic] did you speak?

    c. What language is spoken in your home today?

    d. What other language is spoken in your home today?

    e. What language do you speak most often today?

TABLE 6.4. Earnings and Bilingual Education

	Generation			
	full sample	first	second	third or more
ESL	17,212	19,674	21,712	14,012
Transitional bilingual education	17,041	17,664	18,227	19,462
Neither ESL nor bilingual education	17,040	24,200	23,513	17,516
Number of observations	1,298	216	253	645

Source: Lopez and Mora 1998, Table 3.

If a language other than English was reported in response to *any* of these questions, and the respondent had not been in ESL or bilingual education, he or she was assigned to Lopez and Mora's comparison group. This procedure allows subjects into the comparison group who grew up in a home in which another language was spoken. But this could easily include those who speak English very well, those who speak English much better than the family language, and even those who speak only English! It is quite likely that a significant number of subjects in Lopez and Mora's comparison group are competent English speakers who never needed either ESL or bilingual education.

2. *The ESL-bilingual education difference.* Lopez and Mora note in their Table 3, and again on page 46 of their article, that the differences between first- and second-generation former ESL and bilingual education students *were not statistically significant.* Nor were there any major differences. Lopez and Mora claim that the lack of statistical significance found was due to the small sample size for ESL students. They do not tell us, however, how many of the sample were in ESL and how many were in bilingual education.

3. *The third generation mystery.* For third-generation subjects, those who had bilingual education did better than those who only had ESL and also did better than the comparison group. But we wonder why third-generation students would be in ESL or bilingual education. By the third generation, the dominance of English is firmly established; language shift, in fact, has often taken place by the second generation, for Hispanics/Latinos as well as other language groups (Krashen 1996). Thirty-eight percent of the entire sample studied were considered third generation. Lopez and Mora do not tell us how many of this group were in ESL and/or bilingual education.

4. *Incomplete information.* We also have no information on how bilingual education was conducted and are dependent on the memories of high school sophomores for evidence of participation. It is not even clear whether "bilingual education" included ESL as a component.

Jim Crawford has pointed out to me that Lopez and Mora's students would have been participants in bilingual education in the early 1970s, a time when bilingual education programs were quite rare. A 1969 survey covering states in which bilingual programs were the most prevalent—California, Arizona, Colorado, and Texas—found that only 6.5 percent of the schools surveyed had bilingual education, and these programs reached only 2.7 percent of the Mexican American population. Recall that Lopez and Mora reported that 27.5 percent of their sample participants said they had been in bilingual education.

Bilingual education was not up and running until well after Lopez and Mora's subjects were in junior high school: it was mandated in Massachusetts in 1971, in Illinois and Colorado in 1973, and in Michigan and California in 1976, and compliance took a long time to achieve. In general, LEP children got little attention in those days: only 5.5 percent of Mexican American children in the Southwest received ESL instruction (Crawford 1995).

To summarize:

♦ Lopez and Mora's comparison group included, most likely, a substantial number of subjects who were never limited English proficient.

♦ The differences in earnings between former ESL and bilingual education students were not statistically significant.

♦ The existence of third- (and second-) generation subjects who participated in ESL or bilingual education is contrary to what is known about language shift.

♦ Self-report of high school sophomores concerning the programs they were in years ago may not be reliable. While 27.5 percent said they were in bilingual education, bilingual education was not widespread during the years Lopez and Mora's subjects would have been eligible for it.

Chiswick and Miller (1998) claim that bilingualism itself leads to lower earnings. On the basis of an analysis of data from the 1990 census, they claim that of males aged twenty-five to sixty-four born in the United States,

1. those who spoke only English earned more in 1989 than those who reported that another language was spoken in their home, even when they controlled for factors such as schooling, years

in the labor market, amount worked, marital status, and differences between urban and rural settings. Overall, those who spoke only English earned about 8 percent more.

2. even those bilinguals who reported that they spoke English "very well" earned less than those who spoke only English.

Chiswick and Miller conclude that there is "no statistical support for the proposition that bilingualism, as measured in this study, enhances earning in the United States. It does provide support for the proposition that whatever detracts from full proficiency in English has an adverse effect on earnings" (15).

Other studies, however, show no ill effects and even show economic advantages for bilingualism (Krashen 1998). The problem here is that Chiswick and Miller's definition of bilingualism did not consider how well the heritage language was spoken. Studies showing a positive effect of bilingualism on academic performance and occupational status report that it is *full bilingualism* that produces positive effects. Subjects in these studies developed their heritage language to high levels in addition to acquiring English.

Most of those who speak another language at home probably do not develop it to high levels, for a variety of factors. Language shift is powerful. Most of Chiswick and Miller's subjects were most likely weak heritage-language speakers. Their data are therefore consistent with the hypothesis that full development of the heritage language is positive, and that weak development of the heritage language is a disadvantage. A reasonable conclusion one can draw from their data, seen in the context of other studies, is that heritage languages should be developed.

The One-Year Issue

California's Proposition 227 allows one year of "sheltered immersion" before students are placed in mainstream classrooms. The results of several studies provide clear evidence that this amount of time is nowhere near enough to develop sufficient academic language—that is, to be able to solve story problems, learn about history and science, and write with an acceptable control of spelling, punctuation, and grammar.

Ramirez (1992) conducted a massive study of different ways of educating non-English-speaking children. One of the conditions was "immersion," which looked very much like the instruction Proposition 227 called for. In immersion programs, English was used 94 to 99 percent of the time, it was used to teach content, and children were mainstreamed as soon as possible. In addition, in the immersion programs Ramirez studied, most of the children (70 percent) knew some English when they entered school. After one year, the children were not even close to being ready for the mainstream classroom, nor were they ready after two, three, or even four years. Table 6.5 presents the percentage of children "redesignated" after each year—that is, considered "fluent English proficient"—and the percentage of children actually placed in the mainstream classroom:

In a recent evaluation of LEP children in the Santa Ana school district (Mitchell, Destino, and Karam 1997), students with low intermediate proficiency in English on entering school (2.18 on a 1 to 5 scale, where 4 = sufficient proficiency to survive in the mainstream) were placed in an immersion program, similar to that which Proposition 227 requires. After one year, students showed some growth in English but were nowhere near the level required to do academic work in the mainstream classroom: They moved from 2.18 to 2.84 in English, on a five-point scale. Even after a second year of immersion, their mean English rating was only 3.24.

Kreuger and Townshend (1997) describe a program for LEP first graders in Quebec who were given a great deal of help in English literacy: small-group work (three to four students per

TABLE 6.5. Redesignation and Mainstreaming of Immersion Students

	Percent redesignated	Percent mainstreamed
End of kindergarten	3.9	1.3
End of grade 1	21.2	10.7
End of grade 2	37.9	19.4
End of grade 3	66.7	25.6

Source: Ramirez 1992.

group) for two hours daily devoted exclusively to literacy development. Nineteen of the twenty-three students went on to grade 2, but the students were still well behind native speakers of English, scoring at the middle of grade 1 in reading at the end of the year, "still well below the class average" (127). These students also had already had a full year of kindergarten entirely in English in a semisheltered situation: 75 percent of the class consisted of second-language acquirers. Thus two years of the equivalent of sheltered immersion did not do the job. Even those who are opposed to or who are critical of bilingual education note that it takes more than one year to acquire academic language, the kind of English-language competence children need to succeed in school.

Goldberg (1997, 1998) described an all-English program for LEP students in the Bethlehem school district in Pennsylvania in which kindergartners "receive a language-rich curriculum [in English] based on thematic units" (Goldberg 1997, 64). The program is all-English but is probably not all comprehensible English; in other words, it is not sheltered subject matter teaching. Beginners receive seventy-five minutes a day of intensive ESL instruction and are exposed to English the rest of the day in their classes, which is probably not comprehensible for many students. Goldberg (1998) reported that those who arrive at the beginner level require three to three and a half years until they reach the advanced level, the lowest level in which children are able to "understand main ideas appropriate to grade level" (68), even with additional ESL support.

While 90 percent of the beginning-level students showed some growth in English in one year, most still scored in the beginner range on a test of oral proficiency in English, clearly not ready for a full academic program in English. Goldberg (1997) presents the following case "to illustrate typical student growth":

> Jesennia was evaluated initially before kindergarten entrance in April 1993 and, under the guidelines of the old program, would have been placed into a Spanish-speaking kindergarten. After a year in the English-speaking kindergarten (May, 1994), the tester wrote that Jesennia could now understand simple directions, identify simple nouns, and distinguish correct adjectives. Her expressive skills were still quite limited. (72)

The Little Hoover Commission report on bilingual education, published in 1993, is highly critical of bilingual education. It notes that "some experts believe that English can be academically comprehensible for children in *as little as two years*, while others believe that six or more years of assistance is necessary"(36; italic added). The minimum estimate is two years, twice the amount of time that Proposition 227 allows.

One year will not be enough for older students either. In a letter published on Ron Unz's Web site (www.onenation.org), ESL teacher Johanna Haver, a supporter of Proposition 227, noted that her high school ESL students "claimed that it had taken them about six months to understand English and another six months to be able to respond in English. Of course, reading and writing was taking much longer." This is considerably longer than the 180-day limit imposed by Proposition 227.

It could be argued that after one year, children will know enough English to do mainstream work with support. It appears to be the case that Proposition 227 does not forbid additional ESL teaching after one year. Goldberg (1998), in fact, points out that ESL support was "designed to pre-teach and re-teach the content of the regular classroom" (76) to make regular instruction more comprehensible. The evidence provided here, however, shows that a great deal of such support will be necessary for a child with only one year of exposure to English. The gradual-exit program makes this much less necessary.

Rossell (1998) does not consider these studies but presents three arguments to support her contention that students are better off in mainstream rather than sheltered classrooms after one year.

1. *French immersion:* "The studies of French immersion programs in Canada indicate that the students were able to understand what the teacher said to them sometime during the first semester of the first year" (23, par. 58). But French immersion classes are sheltered, not mainstream, classes, and are designed to be comprehensible to second-language acquirers. Native speakers of French do not participate in these classes. This point confirms the value of sheltered subject matter teaching.

2. *Newcomer centers:* The length of time students spend in newcomer centers, according to Rossell, is about six months to one year. In addition, "there are one year immersion programs for

kindergarten students all over California and the U.S." (24). But in no case does Rossell ever provide data showing that this length of time is sufficient for success in the mainstream classroom. McDonnell and Hill (1993), one of the sources Rossell uses in her discussion of newcomer schools, suggest that one year is not enough: "several factors prevent them [newcomer programs] from being declared an unqualified success. . . . [T]hey only serve a minority of immigrants and for only a short period (one year in most cases, six months in San Francisco). The reason for their limited availability is cost" (97).

3. *Informal survey:* "Over the years I have asked LEP students in ESL and structured immersion classes, as well as formerly LEP students in my classes at Boston University, 'How long was it after you started school before you were understanding what your teacher was saying in English in your regular classroom?' The most common answer I have received is three months" (24 §61). This is an amazing conclusion. We do not know how many students were interviewed; what level of understanding was achieved; whether everything the teacher said was comprehensible or whether only some topics were; the background of the students; the age of the students when they entered the school system; how much English was available outside of school, i.e., in the neighborhood; and how much variability there was around this "average" figure. It is surprising that a scientist such as Professor Rossell, one whose career has been based on criticism of the experimental designs of others, would present such data as evidence.

Conclusion

Those familiar with the continuing controversy over bilingual education know that the issues discussed here are only some of many. Critics have also accused bilingual education of being the cause of dropouts, claimed that bilingual education is conducted only in the United States, asserted that immersion is a better option, claimed that children languish in bilingual programs for years and never acquire English, claimed that immigrants typically succeed without bilingual education, and so on. I have argued, in several other publications, that these accusations are false (Krashen 1996, 1999). These issues have been brought up by opponents of bilingual education. But in all cases, investigation of the research leads to the conclusion that bilingual education is an effective educational tool, and instead of undermining bilingual education, the research provides more support for it.

Note

1. Rossell (1998) maintains that bilingual education theorists only promote reading in the first language when a Roman alphabet is used in both languages. There is, however, extensive data supporting the existence of transfer of literacy across languages with different orthographies, evidence showing that the underlying psycholinguistic processes of reading in languages with different alphabets are similar, evidence showing that the process of the development of literacy in these languages is similar, and evidence showing positive correlations between literacy development in the first and second languages, when the study controls for length of residence in the country where the second language is spoken (Krashen 1996). This evidence is available for a wide variety of languages, including Chinese, Vietnamese, Turkish, Japanese, and Yiddish. Rossell does not attempt to refute these findings. In fact, Rossell even claims that this evidence does not exist: "The bilingual education theory is absolutely silent on the non-applicability of its theory to non-Roman alphabet languages" (5 §11).

Instead of dealing with the published research, she gives these two arguments. The first is this: "I can read fluently in English, but I cannot read in Russian, Arabic, Hebrew, Chinese, Japanese, Hindi or any other non-Roman alphabet language. I can only read in Roman alphabet languages" (4 §11). This is not the point at all. The point is that someone who is literate in his or her first language will find *learning to read* in another language easier than someone not literate in the first language. A literate speaker of Chinese will have an easier time learning to read English than an illiterate speaker of Chinese but will not be able to read English the first time he or she encounters an English text.

Rossell's second argument is that she has not personally observed first-language literacy instruction in bilingual classrooms: "Indeed, in the decade I have been observing bilingual classrooms throughout the U.S., I have never seen one taught in Chinese according to the theory—that is students learning to read and write in their native tongue—and I have seen only one school where the teacher even used a Chinese dialect [sic] in instruction. Children are not taught to read and write Chinese because there are no teachers in the U.S. so crazy as to think that the skill of learning to read and write in Chinese, an ideographic language that bears no resemblance to English, is transferable to English" (4 §10).

There certainly are teachers "crazy enough" to think that literacy development in Chinese is a good idea. Tse, Wong, and Cook (1995) asked 116 Chinese bilingual teachers (105 Cantonese, 11 Mandarin) if they felt it was important to be literate in Chinese to be a good bilingual teacher. Seventy-one percent of the sample felt Chinese literacy was "very necessary" or "somewhat necessary." Those who reported being proficient in reading and writing Chinese felt more strongly about the importance of Chinese literacy in teaching: 84 percent of those who reported that they read Chinese "very well" felt Chinese literacy was important in teaching, but 47 percent of those who said they read Chinese "not well" felt this way, still a substantial percentage. Hoover (1982) reported a positive relationship between literacy developed in the first language for Cantonese speakers and the development of English literacy when literacy was "substantially" developed in the first language. This occurred when children had literacy development in their home country. For those who had small amounts of Cantonese literacy development in the United States, there was no relationship between first- and second-language literacy. Hoover concludes that "although such instruction represents time spent away from direct English literacy instruction, it does not show the detrimental effects some hypotheses would predict" (4). These results suggest that more literacy instruction in Chinese as part of a bilingual program would be a good thing.

Works Cited

Altena, Nelleke, and René Appel. 1982. "Mother Tongue Teaching and the Acquisition of Dutch by Turkish and Morrocan Immigrant Workers' Children." *Journal of Multilingual and Multicultural Development* 3(4): 315–32.

Appel, René. 1984. *Immigrant Children Learning Dutch: Sociolinguistic and Psycholinguistic Aspects of Second-Language Acquisition.* Dordrecht, The Netherlands: Foris.

———. 1988. "The Language Education of Immigrant Workers' Children in The Netherlands." In Tove Skutnabb-Kangas and Jim Cummins, eds., *Minority Education: From Shame to Struggle.* Clevedon, Eng.: Multilingual Matters. 57–78.

Campbell, Donald, and Julian Stanley. 1966. *Experimental and Quasi-Experimental Designs for Research.* Chicago: Rand McNally.

Chiswick, Barry, and Paul Miller. 1998. *The Economic Cost to Native-Born Americans of Limited English Language Proficiency.* Report prepared for the Center for Equal Opportunity. August.

Crawford, Jim. 1995. *Bilingual Education: History, Politics, Theory and Practice.* 3rd ed. Los Angeles: Bilingual Educational Services.

Edwards, Henry, Marjorie Wesche, Stephen Krashen, Richard Clement, and Bastain Kruidenier. 1984. "Second Language Acquisition through Subject-Matter Learning: A Study of Sheltered Psychology Classes at the University of Ottawa." *Canadian Modern Language Review* 41: 268–82.

"English for the Children." 1997. http://www.onenation.org.

Glenn, Charles. 1996. *Educating Immigrant Children: Schools and Language Minorities in Twelve Nations.* New York: Garland.

———. 1998a. *Declaration.* United States District Court, Northern District of California. July 15, 1998, Case No. C98-2252.

———. 1998b. "Rethinking Bilingual Education: Changes for Massachusetts." *READ Abstracts, Research and Policy Review,* August.

Goldberg, Ann. 1997. "Follow-up Study on the Bethlehem, Pa. School District's English Acquisition Program." *READ Perspectives* 4:59–94.

———. 1998. "Four Year Longitudinal Report for the English Acquisition Program in the Bethlehem Area School District." *READ Perspectives* 5(2): 65–80.

Hoover, Wesley A. 1982. *Language and Literacy Learning in Bilingual Instruction: Cantonese Site Analytic Study.* Austin: Southwest Educational Development Laboratory.

Krashen, Stephen. 1991. "Sheltered Subject Matter Teaching." *Cross Currents* 18: 183–88. Reprinted in John Oller, ed., *Methods That Work.* Boston: Heinle and Heinle. 143–48.

———. 1996. *Under Attack: The Case against Bilingual Education.* Culver City, CA: Language Education Associates.

———. 1998. "Heritage Language Development: Some Practical Arguments." In Stephen Krashen, Lucy Tse, and Jeffrey McQuillan, eds., *Heritage Language Development.* Culver City, CA: Language Education Associates. 3–13.

———. 1999. *Condemned without a Trial: Bogus Arguments against Bilingual Education.* Portsmouth, NH: Heinemann.

Krashen, Stephen, and Douglas Biber. 1988. *On Course: Bilingual Education's Success in California.* Los Angeles: California Association for Bilingual Education.

Krashen, Stephen, and Jeffrey McQuillan. 1998. "Do Graduates of Bilingual Programs Really Earn Less? A Response to Lopez and Mora." *NABE News* 22(3): 506.

Krashen, Stephen, Lucy Tse, and Jeffrey McQuillan, eds. 1998. *Heritage Language Development.* Culver City, CA: Language Education Associates.

Kreuger, Elizabeth, and Nancy Townshend. 1997. "Reading Clubs Boost Second-Language First Graders' Reading Achievement." *The Reading Teacher* 51: 122–27.

Little Hoover Commission. 1993. *A Chance to Succeed: Providing English Learners with Supportive Education.* Sacramento, CA: Commission on California State Government and Economy.

Lopez, Mark, and Marie Mora. 1998. "The Labor Market Effects of Bilingual Education among Hispanic Workers." *READ Perspectives* 5(2): 33–54.

McDonnell, Lorraine, and Paul Thomas Hill. 1993. *Newcomers in American Schools: Meeting the Educational Needs of Immigrant Youth.* Santa Monica: Rand Corporation.

Mitchell, Douglas, Tom Destino, and Rita Karam. 1997. *Evaluation of English Language Development Programs in the Santa Ana Unified School District.* Riverside, CA: California Educational Research Cooperative, University of California, Riverside.

Porter, Rosalie. 1996. *Forked Tongue: The Politics of Bilingual Education.* 2nd edition. New Brunswick, NJ: Transaction.

Ramirez, David. 1992. "Executive Summary of the Final Report: Longitudinal Study of Structured English Immersion Strategy, Early-Exit and Late-Exit Transitional Bilingual Education Program for Language-Minority Children." *Bilingual Research Journal* 16(1-2): 1–62.

Rossell, Christine. 1998. *Declaration.* United States District Court, Northern District of California. July 15, 1998, Case No. C98-2252.

Rossell, Christine, and Keith Baker. 1996. "The Educational Effectiveness of Bilingual Education." *Research in the Teaching of English* 30(1): 7–74.

Tse, Lucy, Gae Wong, and Thomas Cook. 1995. "The Relationship between Chinese Literacy and Bilingual Teacher Attitudes." *NABE News* 18(8): 33–34.

Williams, Paul, Clyde Reese, Jay Campbell, John Mazzeo, and Gary Phillips. 1995. *NAEP 1994 Reading: A First Look.* Washington D.C.: U.S. Dept of Education. NCES 95-748.

III

POLITICS, ECONOMY, AND THE CLASSROOM

The most recent English Only slogan, "English for the Children," is not only simplistic, emotional, and hard to resist on rational grounds, but it also ignores that a large percentage of low-proficiency English speakers are adults at various stages of their struggle for a better life for themselves and the families they may support. The three chapters in this section provide important insight into the educational and economic prospects of this adult ESL learner population. Elliot L. Judd reveals a host of serious contradictions between the perception and the reality of the ESL adult education scenario. Judd points out that adults who do not speak English proficiently in the United States are frequently "blamed for not learning English, yet are not provided with opportunities to do so." Moreover, since many of these U.S. residents are not voting members of the political community, their needs and aspirations are grossly underrepresented in the political arena. Judd reminds us that, just as in the case of bilingual education, English Only proponents generalize from a few less successful and seriously underfunded ESL programs to claim that all ESL programs, or, for that matter, all English-language instruction in this country, are useless and inefficient. These assumptions hurt the ESL and bilingual education profession as much as they contribute to a hostile anti-immigrant environment. Consequently, it is unlikely that the legislation English Only supporters advocate would "cause non-English speakers to learn English."

Elsa Roberts Auerbach's study stresses the ideological components of Official English and demonstrates how the logic of hegemonic ideologies of language makes its way into the adult education language classes by spreading the pedagogically unfounded myth that English can best be learned through English Only instruction. Auerbach reveals that English only has been a policy in many ESL classrooms despite the fact that, at least for the past thirty years, all experts in the teaching of language have advocated methods that respect diversity and value a supportive learning environment. Yet somehow there is a lingering and recurrent assumption that English can best be taught when the learner's first language is completely excluded from the process. Auerbach's work with adult ESL and community literacy classes proves, however, that such myths do not stand the test of empirical inquiry. In fact, these learners thrive and learn more in an environment that respects their home literacy and allows them to utilize their home language as a source of learning and self-expression. The classroom narratives of Auerbach's adult learners testify that learning a new language becomes more meaningful and efficient when the learner's first language is looked upon as a rich resource from which new knowledge of language and culture can be generated, and not as an obstacle that needs to be eradicated.

Finally, Arturo Gonzalez's empirical research examines the economic value of English-language skills for ESL learners. His survey of a select immigrant group of adults reveals the strong economic and social incentives this group confronts in the process of improving its position in the labor market. All evidence in Gonzalez's survey shows that the labor market values English-language skills, and this value can be expressed in increased percentages of earned wages. Not all language skills are valued equally, however, and not all immigrants learn equally, no matter how strong the overall economic incentives to acquire English. The findings of this survey can be interpreted in many ways; nevertheless, it is obvious that English Only legislation would not positively affect either the efficiency of language acquisition or the already evident relationship between language skills and labor market positions.

Chapter Seven

English Only and ESL Instruction: Will It Make a Difference?

Elliot L. Judd
University of Illinois at Chicago

O ne often-stated justification for those who advance English Only legislation is that enacting such bills will cause non-English speakers to learn English (Judd 1987; Baron 1990; Crawford 1992a; Wiley and Lukes 1996; McGroarty 1997; Ricento 1998). It is argued that those who come to the United States in recent years have failed to learn English, in marked contrast to earlier immigrant groups. Further, advocates of English Only measures claim that since existing legislation, such as bilingual education and bilingual ballots, only serves to discourage non-English speakers from learning English, such legislation must be abandoned. This chapter focuses on one major question: will enactment of English Only measures lead to increased mastery of English by those who have little or no mastery of the language? I attempt to show that in fact such proposals will have absolutely no effect on English-language mastery. Additionally, such legislation will prove harmful to both teachers and learners of English as a second language (ESL) since they falsely raise expectations that can never be realistically achieved, resulting in heightened negative reactions against those who are trying to learn ESL and those who are providing instruction to ESL students.

Dispelling Folk Beliefs

Many Americans believe that the number of non-English speakers is on the rise in this country. Proponents of English Only legislation capitalize on this folk belief because they want people to believe that the dominance of English in the United States is being threatened by non-English languages, especially Spanish (McGroarty 1997). Despite the persistence of this myth, however, English is alive and healthy. Its power is not being eroded. English is still the dominant language of the economic, political, and social life of our country. In fact, there is no solid evidence supporting claims of the demise of English in the United States.

Equally important is the mistaken belief, also held by many people and overtly or covertly articulated by English Only advocates, that new immigrants are not learning English. This position is often voiced in what may be labeled the "grandfather myth"; that is, "My grandfather came to this country and learned English quickly and without any special help. Why can't these new immigrants do the same?" Existing data suggest otherwise. New immigrants are following exactly the same patterns as those of previous generations of newcomers to the United States. Within three generations or fewer, the immigrants' language has been lost and replaced by English. There is no evidence to support the contention that this process can be speeded up, nor that immigrants who arrived in previous generations instantly learned English and abandoned their native languages. Historical documentation provides ample proof that languages other than English flourished throughout the United States in numerous immigrant communities, both urban and rural (Fishman 1966; Kloss 1977; Baron 1990).

Learning a Second Language

Learning a second language is a complex process requiring time, effort, and motivation. Rather than review the detailed literature on second-language acquisition, let us proceed from common sense. Most native English speakers have attempted to learn another language as part of their secondary or university education. How many of them attain fluency? Can they truly function in that other language? Could they live their normal lives using that language? Could they even apply and be interviewed for, let alone hold, a decent job in which they had to perform in that language? Could they read technical and nontechnical material or write information on forms and in technical reports in that language? The answer is obvious. Most would fail miserably and be terrified at the prospect of having to undertake any complex communication in a language other than English. If we were to pass a law making Icelandic the language of the United States, would the populace immediately begin speaking Icelandic? Obviously not; merely passing a law does not induce or increase language learning (Baron 1990). Other conditions are necessary for second-language proficiency.

Three important factors, among many, are relevant to our discussion of second-language acquisition: motivation, need, and time. Clearly, personal motivation is necessary for learning another language; if you have no desire to learn the language, you will not do so. There also has to be an obvious need to learn any language. For most learners, purely aesthetic reasons are insufficient; they must have a reason to learn, such as getting a job or wanting to live in another country or communicate with those who speak that language. Certainly these two factors can explain the dismal record of most Americans endeavoring to learn another language in school—they see no reason to learn the language and thus have no strong desire to do so (beyond perhaps fulfilling a high school or college requirement, which is a relatively weak reason). In contrast, for those arriving in the United States, both the need for and motivation to learn English are strong. Immigrants are not ignorant or blind; they readily see the need to learn English, for without it their lives and the opportunities for their children are limited. Further, when given a chance, they readily attend classes to learn English. Anyone who teaches ESL or is familiar with such programs is aware of the great desire such students show for learning. Classes are often oversubscribed, with waiting lists to get into the programs (especially when the classes are priced within the limited budgets of these ESL learners). Within non-English-speaking communities, there may be debate over the need to maintain the native language; there is no serious discussion about the need to learn English when living in the United States. Even among those who are unable to attend ESL classes, often due to the need to obtain immediate employment to provide a livelihood or to tend to their families, there is no evidence of a lack of motivation or a failure to realize the need for learning English. To claim otherwise is to perpetuate a harmful, destructive myth.

The third factor relevant to second-language acquisition is time. Learning a second language does not occur overnight; no one can wave a magic wand and immediately produce a speaker of another language. Becoming a fluent user of a language, one who is able to function fully in our society at a level commensurate with native English speakers, is an arduous task. The more complex the language expectations, the longer fluency takes. What this means in concrete terms is that we should expect children who are studying ESL to become fully functional in aspects of school language—not merely socially skilled in orally communicating with their peers, but also able to speak, comprehend, read, and write in the complex academic language required for the study of mathematics, science, social studies, and language arts at the appropriate age/grade level of their native-English-speaking peers. This process can take many years (Cummins 1981, 1986; Collier 1989). For adults, especially if we desire that they obtain higher-level jobs and advance socially and economically in our society, the English-language expectations are equally daunting—full communicative abilities (in oral and written language) at a cognitive level equal to that of their English-speaking peers. In light of these expectations, we can clearly see that adequate second-language learning, which is needed for advanced communicative abilities, is a time-consuming process. How many monolingual English speakers could immediately go to another country and assume a comparable job while functioning in another language? Could they communicate in another language at the intellectual and social level of their peers? Could they read complex articles, or even daily newspapers, in that language, or write competent works in that language? Could their children be immediately plunged into the school system and continue to learn at grade level in another language? Could the politicians, commentators, and scholars who rail against immigrants and champion English Only legislation function in another language and issue their diatribes in that language?

One other factor which can facilitate English-language mastery also needs to be mentioned: quality ESL instruction. Certainly it is possible to master another language without formal instruction. Yet, if we desire mastery of English in all four language skills—listening, speaking, reading, and writing—it is better to have quality language instruction taught by those who are trained in ESL and who employ current methodology, materials, and curricula that are grounded in valid research. We cannot have quality medical care without qualified personnel, and we cannot have quality ESL instruction without trained ESL professionals. Let us now turn to a discussion of the state of ESL instruction in the United States today. Without an understanding of the present situation, it is impossible to discuss the future accurately.

Educating Non-English Speakers in the United States

In order to provide an overview of the current educational situation of ESL in the United States, it is necessary to divide the discussion into two categories: elementary/secondary ESL and adult education. Excluded from the discussion are ESL programs for foreign students who are studying at universities, because their visa status is for temporary residence in the United States, and many will not permanently reside in this country when they complete their studies; also excluded are those who come on business assignments and will be returning to their native countries.

School-age children who are not proficient in English clearly need some sort of specialized education in order to survive and succeed in our English-dominant school system. This not only makes common sense, but it is also a legal requirement under the Supreme Court's ruling in *Lau v. Nichols* (1974). There are numerous models for such ESL instructional programs. Some children are enrolled in federally supported bilingual education programs. In reality, and despite public claims to the contrary, these only affect a minority of all ESL children (Lyons 1990). For those studying in such programs, the majority are in so-called "transitional" programs, in which children receive native-language instruction and ESL only until sufficient English is mastered and the children are mainstreamed into regular classes. Other ESL students are in non-federally-funded bilingual programs (again the majority are transitional); in ESL classes without native-language instruction, including "sheltered English" programs; or in some sort of ESL "pull-out" tutorials in small groups or on an individual basis. Perhaps the smallest category includes those in experimental long-term bilingual programs lasting five years or more. Research on which type of program leads to the highest success rates for ESL students is contradictory, although current findings suggest that long-term programs are the most successful (Collier 1989; Crawford 1992a; Ricento 1998). No doubt one reason for researchers' inability to assess quality in ESL programs is the difficulty in isolating ESL instruction from other factors. Programs vary widely, not only in terms of instructional design but also in terms of the quality of educational programs and instructors. Many ESL programs of all kinds suffer from the lack of current, valid materials and curricula. Further, many who teach ESL to children are untrained and unqualified to do so—be they bilingual or nonbilingual teachers. The assessment problem is compounded by the fact that many ESL children live in the poorest neighborhoods with the highest crime rates, lowest standards of living, worst schools, and a myriad other factors that make it difficult to isolate ESL instruction from other educational and noneducational factors. What can be said with some degree of certainty is that non-English-speaking children often have great difficulties in school, often drop out before finishing, suffer from poor instruction and poor educational materials, and in general perform below national norms. It should be remembered, however, that this profile is not limited to ESL children; poor urban and rural non-ESL children suffer equally. Further, not all non- and limited-English-speaking children fail in our educational system. The point is that we need to look at the *typical* ESL child and remember that the "Horatio Alger" cases are deviations from the norm.

The current situation in adult ESL is even more chaotic. A variety of programs exist—some publicly funded, others private; some for-profit, some not-for-profit; some with specific content (vocational, literacy, academic, etc.), some unspecified; some directed toward one specific language group, others serving a multilingual ESL population. There are no standard curricula or materials, nor is there any standard teaching methodology. In some programs, the curricula are outdated (even to the extent of following the now discredited grammar-translation or audiolingual methods), while others implement specific designs that have been created to meet students' needs. In some programs, the texts used (if they are used at all) are outdated and discredited; in others, current materials are used or are specifically developed. The key characteristic shared by the vast majority of programs is that they employ untrained ESL teachers on a part-time, no-benefits basis. In fact, no standards exist at all for opening and maintaining adult ESL programs—any individual, group, corporation, or institution can simply announce that it has an adult ESL program and begin operation (Kaplan 1997). Since the demand for ESL in immigrant communities is huge (contrary to what some English Only proponents want us to believe), these programs are filled. Yet the question of the quality of education that students receive remains. Since most of the programs employ untrained teachers, the quality of many is suspect, and since there are no supervising agencies or professional associations overseeing these programs, no accurate figures exist to assess how successful the programs are.

Why are some programs staffed by untrained teachers? The answer is both economic and political. The proprietors of private language programs realize that there is a huge demand for ESL instruction and that there is money to be made. Obviously, the cost of employing professionally trained ESL teachers would cut into profit margins; it is much cheaper to employ untrained teachers and to hire them on a part-time and/or hourly basis, thereby eliminating the need to pay benefits. In the public or not-for-profit sector, the number of untrained, part-time staff is also huge since the students are generally poor and there is little governmental funding for adult education. Consequently, economics again affect quality of staffing. A further explanation for this phenomenon is that many well-trained ESL teachers will not work in these substandard programs owing to poor wages, lack of benefits, lack of quality materials and curricula, and so on. For political reasons, adult ESL programs do not attract government funds because they cater to a disenfranchised population; many politicians are not eager to fund these programs for little or no political payback. The point is that while these programs are providing some ESL instruction, they are generally not providing quality learning, thus frustrating the needs and aspirations of the very students who enter the programs seeking to improve their English. No one in our country who can avoid it goes to an untrained doctor for a medical need or to an untrained lawyer for a legal need. Even within the educational institutions in our country, we would never consider hiring science or mathematics instructors who are not trained in their specialties. In ESL programs, however, untrained, unqualified teachers regularly dispense their services, and society's overwhelming reaction is one of supreme unconcern.

The Likelihood of Improved English Mastery

In light of what we know about how second languages are mastered, the documented record of current immigrant groups learning English, and the current state of affairs in ESL instruction in the United States, we can return to the original question: will English Only measures lead to increased mastery of English? The answer is simply no. Both adults and children are already learning English, and no piece of legislation can speed up the natural process of second-language acquisition. Equally important is the fact that the proposals being advanced make no mention of improving the quality of formal ESL instruction. Since many of the advocates of such legislation also favor limiting bilingual educational to a minimal transitional level or abolishing bilingual education altogether, the prospects for increased English proficiency appear to be diminishing rather than improving. Additionally, since the proponents of English Only legislation are notably silent on increased funding for adult ESL education, it is unlikely that there will be any marked improvement in English proficiency for those many adult immigrants who have actively demonstrated an interest in improving their English.

Finally, since English Only supporters on the federal, state, and local levels seem totally unconcerned about improving the quality of existing programs and uninterested in creating standards or monitoring the professional quality of such programs, the quality of instruction within such programs is also unlikely to improve, owing to the economic and political conditions discussed.

The Danger of English Only for ESL

Since English Only legislation will not improve ESL learning, is there any potential harm to ESL learners or instructors when such bills are legislated? The answer is yes for both groups. ESL learners will be harmed because programs providing quality bilingual education, which aims for long-term mastery of both the cognitive and social functions of English, will be eliminated in favor of programs that will mainstream unprepared students into native-English-speaker classes, where they will not be ready to handle the linguistic rigors of the English-dominant educational system. Rather than having developed the cognitive and academic skills necessary for successful academic performance, the vast majority of these students, having been prematurely exited from bilingual and other specially designed programs and lacking the basics of English, will encounter failure and either receive a substandard education or drop out of the system entirely. These students, who would normally have been gaining academic knowledge while mastering English as a second language, will be forced into quick-fix ESL programs which cannot hope to prepare students for the academic rigors of a monolingual English system. The results will be both permanent deficiencies in English and failure in academic subjects, which will handicap these students throughout their lifetime and prevent them from advancing up the educational and economic ladders of success. Such a scenario is not hypothetical. In California, under Proposition 227, students are only allowed one year of ESL instruction before being mainstreamed into the monolingual English classroom. In such a situation, it is impossible for students to master all the social and cognitive skills in all academic areas necessary to compete with native speakers of English. A permanent underclass of ESL students, unprepared and ill-equipped for monolingual instruction, is being created through the implementation of an unsound educational policy.

For adult ESL learners, the situation will be equally dismal. Those who have little or no knowledge of English will encounter economic, social, and, perhaps, legal discrimination (Piatt 1990). Yet there will not be enough ESL classes to accommodate the need, since there is little likelihood that those who support English Only will also provide for improved adult ESL education. Again, this scenario is not merely hypothetical. This very situation occurred in California following the passage of Proposition 63, an English Only measure, in 1986. There were simply not enough classroom programs to keep up with the demand of those seeking adult ESL programs, which were already underfunded and under-staffed. The fact is that those who champion English Only in the United States Congress also oppose increased federal aid to both adult and elementary/secondary education (Judd 1998).

What are the results? On the one hand, both adults and chil-dren are being told by English Only supporters to abandon their native languages and adopt English. On the other hand, little funding is being provided to expand quality ESL programs, and even those programs already deemed educationally viable are not supported. Thus those who are encouraged to learn English are not provided with viable programs in which to do so and are forced to enter programs that will not help them succeed. They will be blamed for not learning English, yet they will not have been provided with opportunities to do so.

Further, as noted earlier, the professional qualifications of those who teach ESL classes—at all levels and in both public and private programs—are suspect. How can programs be effective when they are not staffed by trained practitioners? Again, stu-dents will be faulted for their poor English when the blame should be cast on those who are hiring untrained professionals to deliver these ESL classes.

Of course, not all ESL programs are of poor quality, nor are all ESL instructors professionally inept. Many people do not understand this, however, and those who are anti-immigrant tend to view the world monolithically. If programs are not working, *all* programs must not be working. If teachers are unqualified, *all* teachers are failures. Thus serious professionals who teach in suc-cessful programs face the same accusations as those who are abusing ESL as a profession: that ESL programs do not train stu-dents to learn English, that they are a waste of money, that they are unnecessary. It is much easier to blame the victims, both qual-ified ESL teachers and serious ESL learners, than to address the root causes of the problems—quick-fix educational "solutions" that are not supported by educational wisdom (for example, see Collier 1989) delivered by teachers who are not professionally trained. English Only proponents capitalize on this ignorance and fail to propose serious solutions, offering instead the simplistic pronouncement that everyone should speak English.

What Are the Real Motives?

If English Only legislation will not affect either the rate at which non-English users learn English or the quality of ESL instruction in the United States, despite pronouncements to the contrary, why are these measures being proposed? As many writers have suggested, English Only legislation is not based on sound rationales for learning English because its proponents are not actually motivated by a desire to help non-English speakers learn English. Instead, this legislation is directed against those who do not speak English (Judd 1987; Baron 1990; Daniels 1990; Piatt 1990; Crawford 1992a, 1992b; Tatalovich 1995). Simply stated, there is a strong anti-immigrant underpinning to these bills. Proponents of English Only are capitalizing on many Americans' xenophobia, with special attention directed to Hispanics/Latinos and Asians whose skin color and culture differ from earlier generations of European immigrants. Further, English Only serves to divert attention from difficult issues facing U.S. politicians, such as loss of jobs, uncertainty in the economic system, crime, lower educational performance, etc., and turns the blame for these issues onto immigrants. It is certainly far easier and cheaper to blame immigrants and non-English speakers than to propose serious legislation to deal with these problems. In short, the issue of teaching English to non-English and limited-English speakers is a smoke screen behind which certain politicians can hide and make proposals that sound virtuous but accomplish little. The reality is that none of society's problems will be solved even if English Only legislation were the law of the land.

Proposals for Meaningful ESL Teaching

Rather than engage in meaningless polemics which only distort reality and hinder meaningful English instruction for those who need to improve their English skills, I offer the following proposals and invite English Only advocates and others to join in supporting them.

1. Support research and disseminate the results of studies on immigrants' mastery of English. These investigations should systematically gather information on whether immigrant groups are learning English or resisting the process. If people are indeed mastering English, let us stop making assertions to the contrary.

2. Encourage the creation and maintenance of programs that teach ESL to children in our elementary and secondary schools. Determine which programs are most effective and which are ineffective in preparing students for the academic and social demands of English-dominant schools. Do not rule out bilingual programs, even if they are long term, if they achieve this educational goal.

3. Enact and fund legislation that creates meaningful and productive ESL classes for adults. Ensure that these classes produce users of English who have not only a rudimentary knowledge of English but also sophisticated skills in English that will allow them to advance educationally, economically, and socially in our society.

4. Mandate that those who teach ESL at any level be professionally trained to do so. Censure and remove funding from programs that do not follow accepted professional standards or that employ unqualified teachers. If English learning is important in our society, those who provide instruction must be qualified. We do not allow nonprofessionals to practice law or medicine, nor do we allow unqualified teachers to teach subjects such as mathematics, science, or English for native speakers; we must not allow this to occur in ESL instruction.

5. Acknowledge that non-English languages and cultures have always been part of the rich heritage of the United States and that new immigrant groups are part of the American mosaic; encourage programs that honestly discuss the contributions made by immigrants to our society. At the same time, disavow those who demean or slander newer immigrants with false accusations that they are disloyal or un-American. Educate monolingual Americans about the fact that it is possible for individuals to speak a language other than English and yet also speak English.

If we can all support these proposals, then we may progress to the point at which ESL learning becomes effective and the goal of having immigrants participate meaningfully in our society can be achieved—without distortions, lies, or innuendos.

Works Cited

Baron, Dennis E. 1990. *The English-Only Question: An Official Language for Americans?* New Haven: Yale University Press.

Collier, Virginia P. 1989. "How Long? A Synthesis of Research on Academic Achievement in a Second Language." *TESOL Quarterly* 23: 509–31.

Crawford, James. 1992a. *Hold Your Tongue: Bilingualism and the Politics of "English Only."* Reading, MA: Addison-Wesley.

———, ed. 1992b. *Language Loyalties: A Source Book on the Official English Controversy.* Chicago: University of Chicago Press.

Cummins, Jim. 1981. "The Role of Primary Language Development in Promoting Educational Success for Language Minority Children." In Office of Bilingual Bicultural Education, *Schooling and Language Minority Children: A Theoretical Framework*. Los Angeles: California State University Evaluation, Dissemination and Assessment Center. 3–49.

———. 1986. "Empowering Minority Children: A Framework for Intervention." *Harvard Educational Review* 56: 18–36.

Daniels, Harvey A. 1990. *Not Only English: Affirming America's Multilingual Heritage.* Urbana, IL: National Council of Teachers of English.

Fishman Joshua, ed. 1966. *Language Loyalty in the United States.* The Hague, Netherlands: Mouton.

Judd, Elliot L. 1987. "The English Language Amendment: A Case Study on Language and Politics." *TESOL Quarterly* 21: 113–35.

———. 1998. "The U.S. Congress and Current Language Policy." Paper delivered at the Annual TESOL Conference, Seattle.

Kaplan, Robert B. 1997. "Foreword: Palmat Qui Meruit Ferat." In William Eggington and Helen Wren, eds., *Language Policy: Dominant English, Pluralist Challenges*. Amsterdam: John Benjamins. xi–xxiii.

Kloss, Heinz. 1997. *The American Bilingual Tradition*. Rowley, MA: Newbury House.

Lau v. Nichols. 1974. 94S. Ct. 486. 414 U.S. 563; 39L. Ed. 2d I.

Lyons, James J. 1990. "The Past and Future Directions of Federal Bilingual-Education Policy." *Annals of the American Academy of Political and Social Science* 508: 66–80.

McGroarty, Mary. 1997. "Language Policy in the USA: National Values, Local Loyalties, Pragmatic Pressures." In William Eggington and Helen Wren, eds., *Language Policy: Dominant English, Pluralist Challenges*. Amsterdam: John Benjamins. 67–90.

Piatt, Bill. 1990. *Only English? Law and Language Policy in the United States*. Albuquerque: University of New Mexico Press.

Ricento, Thomas. 1998. "Partitioning by Language: Whose Rights Are Threatened?" In Thomas Ricento and Barbara Burnaby, eds., *Language and Politics in the United States and Canada: Myths and Realities*. Mahwah, NJ: Lawrence Erlbaum. 317–30.

Tatalovich, Raymond. 1995. *Nativism Reborn? The Official English Language Movement and the American States*. Lexington, KY: University Press of Kentucky.

Wiley, Terrence G., and Marguerite Lukes. 1996. "English-Only and Standard English Ideologies in the United States." *TESOL Quarterly* 30: 511–35.

CHAPTER EIGHT

When Pedagogy Meets Politics: Challenging English Only in Adult Education

ELSA ROBERTS AUERBACH
University of Massachusetts Boston

While many of the chapters in this book examine the politics of U.S. language policy and planning on a macro level, the central argument of this chapter is that what happens on a micro level behind the closed doors of a classroom is no less politically charged. But because language instruction is often conceived of as a neutral transfer of skills, knowledge, or competencies, the ways in which it is implicated in larger struggles about voice and power are obscured. This chapter focuses on the ideological nature of pedagogical practices in the domain of language and literacy instruction for adult immigrants and refugees in the United States.

In the current political climate of English Only and "welfare reform," policy initiatives push for fast English for Speakers of Other Languages (ESOL) instruction, the goal of which is ostensibly to move newcomers as quickly as possible into minimum wage jobs which reduce their "dependence" on government subsidies. Most ESOL educators vehemently oppose these policies as politically reactionary and educationally unsound; they are often at the forefront of the struggle to uphold language rights and oppose linguistic repression. The Teachers of English to Speakers of Other Languages and of Standard English as a Second Dialect (TESOL) organization itself has passed a language rights resolution supporting "measures which protect the right of all individuals to preserve and foster their linguistic and cultural origins; . . . [and opposing] all measures declaring English the official language of the United States of America" (*TESOL Resolution* 1987).

At the same time, however, many of those who oppose English Only on a policy level have embraced the commonsense perspective that English is the only acceptable medium of instruction once students enter the door of the classroom. They insist on English on *pedagogical* grounds, arguing that excluding the first language is in the students' best interests. The common rationale is that total immersion in English is the quickest route to English acquisition; there is no function for the first language in the United States, so there is no role for it in education; and students will rely on their first language (L1) if they are permitted to use it. These views have become almost axiomatic: teachers devise elaborate games, signals, and penalty systems to enforce the use of English Only. Even an official TESOL publication ran an article boasting of *fining* students for committing the "crime" of using their first language in an ESOL class; the teacher told students, "This is an 'English Only' classroom. If you speak Spanish or Cantonese or Mandarin or Vietnamese or Thai or Russian or Farsi, you pay me 25 cents. I can be rich" (Weinberg 1990, 5). The dogma underlying these practices seems to be: We hold this truth to be self-evident that English and English only shall be used in the ESOL classroom. The single route to English is all English and nothing but English.

I argue in this chapter that these taken-for-granted beliefs in adult education regarding the inclusion or exclusion of learners' native languages are as much political choices as pedagogical ones: although they may appear to be informed by apolitical professional considerations, they are grounded in invisible but powerful ideological assumptions which need to be reexamined and problematized. I am not suggesting that one prescription or axiom be replaced by another, or that the issue of language use be reduced to an either/or question (either it's always fine to use the native language or it's always bad). Rather, I am suggesting that seemingly pedagogical choices be examined in terms of their political underpinnings and implications. As Paulo Freire (1970) has argued, the way we address the question of language use in adult education is both a mirror of and a rehearsal for relations of power in the broader society.

Situating Commonsense Practices in an Ideological Framework

In order to understand how classroom practices can reinforce or challenge power relations, the first question we must ask is: what is power and how does it manifest itself through language use? Fairclough (1989) argues that dominant classes exercise power in two basic ways: through coercion and through consent—either by forcing others to go along with them or by convincing them that it is in their best interest. Consent, however, is not necessarily the result of conscious choice, but rather an unconscious acceptance of institutional practices, and institutional practices which people draw on without thinking often embody assumptions which directly or indirectly legitimize existing power relations. Practices can often be shown to originate in the dominant class or the dominant bloc and to have become naturalized. In other words, practices which are unconsciously accepted as the natural and inevitable way of doing things may in fact be inherently political, serving to maintain the relative position of participants vis-á-vis each other. These everyday, taken-for-granted practices constitute what Fairclough calls "ideological power," one of the central mechanisms of ensuring control by consent. He argues that discourse plays a particularly important role in exercising this control: authority and power are manifested in and perpetuated by institutional practices around the ways language is used and the purposes for which it is used.

That educational institutions in general, and literacy education in particular, are among the primary mechanisms for promulgating ideological power is by no means a new argument. An enormous body of literature (too large to cite here) documents the role of education in socializing learners for particular life roles, not just on the level of policy and planning but through differential content and processes of educational interactions. To the extent that it is the knowledge, life experience, language, and discourse of the dominant class which are valued in educational institutions, it is their power which is perpetuated. Brian Street (1984) extends this analysis to conceptions about literacy, arguing that it is no accident that traditionally literacy has been seen as a set of universal, decontextualized cognitive skills which exist independently of how, where, why, and by whom they are used: it is a way of privileging one group's literacy and discourse practices over others', and as such it is a mechanism for perpetuating the status quo. Elevating one culture-specific set of literacy practices (namely, those of the mainstream, dominant culture) to "universal" status privileges those from that culture. Instructional approaches which claim that knowledge, language use, and literacy practices are neutral "tend to verify, legitimize and reinforce the language and literacy related experiences . . . and the cultural capital of the white (mostly male), English speaking middle class," with the result that "class, racial/ethnic and gender stratifications are exacerbated"; thus, while literacy is touted as a key to access, access to literacy development is limited by unequal power relations (Walsh 1994, 9). Within this framework, classrooms can be seen as sites of struggle about whose knowledge, experiences, literacy and discourse practices, and ways of using language count.

While the mechanisms of ideological control exercised through language policy have been examined extensively on a global level (e.g., Tollefson 1991; Phillipson 1992; Skutnabb-Kangas 1988), they have been less fully explored on the level of day-to-day interactions between teachers and learners. What I want to show in this chapter is that the insistence on using only English in the classroom represents precisely the kind of taken-for-granted and naturalized everyday practice that Fairclough (1989) discusses: while English Only instruction has come to be justified in pedagogical terms, it rests on unexamined assumptions, originates in the political agenda of the dominant classes, and serves to reinforce existing relations. Precisely because its mechanisms are hidden, it is a prime example of Fairclough's notion of covert ideological control.

Historical Roots of English Only Instruction

Other chapters in this volume address the historical context of language policy in the United States. Although this is not the place to look in detail at how language pedagogy fits into this history, two historical points are relevant to my argument. First, accounts of language education in the United States reveal that monolingual approaches to the teaching of English have by no means always been the norm (Baron 1990; Crawford 1991; Daniels 1990). Second, the cyclical fluctuations in language-education policy have often been determined by political rather than pedagogical factors. In the nineteenth century, for example, the decentralized and locally controlled nature of public schooling allowed for bilingual education in accordance with the political power of particular ethnic groups. It was the resurgence of nativism and antiforeign political sentiment in the late nineteenth century that triggered the decline of bilingual education. The advent of World War I, the increase in immigration from southern and eastern Europe, and the growing role of immigrants in the labor movement contributed to an increasing xenophobic atmosphere in the early twentieth century; "foreign influence" was blamed for the nation's political and economic problems, and the Americanization movement was promoted as a means of countering this influence. According to Baron (1990), the spread of ESOL instruction in the first quarter of the twentieth century was a direct outcome of the Americanization movement. It was during this period that direct methods stressing oral English gained favor over methods which allowed the use of the students' native language, and English Only became the norm in the ESOL classes. ESOL instruction became a vehicle to enhance loyalty to both the country and the company (Crawford 1991, 22). English was associated with patriotism—speaking "good" English was equated with being a "good" American (Baron 1990, 155). Thus we see that practices which have come to be viewed as natural and that we take for granted as pedagogically grounded have antecedents in overtly ideological tendencies.

Research on Monolingual versus Bilingual Adult Education

"It was simply not a topic in the research."

Although policymakers, funders, and often educators believe that English Only in the classroom is the "best practice" in adult education, there is little research to support this belief. The abundant research supporting bilingual education for children is rarely examined in terms of its relevance for adults. Even teachers who fully support bilingual education often embrace English Only for adult ESOL as an uncritical reaction to the discredited grammar-translation approach, justifying their practices with reference (either implicit or explicit) to studies of immersion programs. It is not clear, however, that the immersion research applies to adult immigrant and refugee students. Research clearly indicates that immersion programs are effective for learners from dominant language groups whose first language (L1) is valued and supported both at home and in the broader society, while bilingual instruction is more effective for language-minority students whose language has less social status (Cummins 1981). Further, there is evidence that strong L1 literacy and schooling are key factors in successful second-language (L2) acquisition (Cummins 1981; Snow 1990; Klassen 1991; Robson 1982). A growing percentage of students in adult ESOL classes come from precisely the groups shown to benefit most from bilingual approaches, namely, subordinated minority-language groups and those with limited L1 literacy/schooling backgrounds. Therefore this research suggests that relations of power and their affective consequences are implicated in language acquisition: acquiring a second language is to some extent contingent on the societally determined value attributed to the L1. This in turn suggests that prohibiting the native language within the context of ESOL instruction may impede language acquisition precisely because it mirrors disempowering relations.

Implications of these findings for adult education have until quite recently been virtually ignored. In fact, research on the relative effects of monolingual ESOL versus bilingual or native-language literacy approaches to adult ESOL have been minimal. A National Clearinghouse for Literacy Education (NCLE) survey was able to identify only two research studies (Robson 1982; Burtoff 1985) investigating the effectiveness of initial native-language literacy for adult students (Gillespie 1994). Both of these studies point to the beneficial effects of initial literacy in the native language on subsequent development of oral and written English-language proficiency. Despite this evidence, the NCLE found that only 68 of the almost 600 adult education programs surveyed offer classes in learners' native languages; of these, all but ten were established after 1980 (Gillespie 1994). Taken together, these findings suggest that the commonly accepted practice of enforcing monolingual ESOL instruction for adult learners is based on questionable assumptions and a lack of research evidence.

Within the last decade, however, researchers looking at ESOL practice have increasingly begun to challenge the enforcement of the English Only provision for adult learners (Wrigley and Guth 1992; Gillespie 1994; Rivera 1988). Practitioners have in many cases taken matters into their own hands when confronted with the lack of research on monolingual ESOL and native-language literacy. Lisa Earl, one of the practitioners who embarked on her own research to examine the effects of L1 literacy (or lack thereof) in ESOL acquisition, wrote:

> I was a teacher by trade, not a researcher, but I had found myself more and more concerned with how to address the needs of students [with minimal L1 literacy proficiency]. But it was simply not a topic in the research on second language learning, which either dealt with children or with literate adults. . . . Where teaching literacy to adults was addressed at all, no distinction was made between primary literacy for learners not literate in any language, and second language literacy for those already literate in their native tongue. Low-literate students' needs were rarely addressed in ESOL teaching practice either. Here the prevailing techniques were either to ignore such students completely or to assume that they would benefit from rote copying tasks, whether or not they understood them. (Earl 1994, 14)

A growing body of practitioner accounts like Earl's provides evidence for the debate about the role of native languages in adult education. These accounts come from a range of contexts: those in which students who are not literate in their native language are forced to learn English monolingually; those in which native-language literacy is taught as a precursor to ESOL; and those in which English is taught bilingually. In the next section, I look at five arguments drawn largely from practitioner research that provide counterevidence to the English Only pedagogical argument.

Without Literacy, Progress in English Is Difficult

"I am always lost. I waste my time."

Perhaps the strongest evidence against monolingual adult ESOL comes from examining what actually happens when this approach is enforced in the ESOL classroom. Very often, English and literacy skills are not differentiated in assessment and placement: literacy is equated with English literacy and English proficiency is equated with oral English proficiency. The result is that students with little L1 literacy background are grouped with those who are literate in their first language but have beginning oral ESOL proficiency. For those with little L1 literacy background and schooling, the effect is often to completely preclude participation and progress, causing the "revolving door syndrome" in which students start a course, fail, start again, and eventually give up (Strei 1992). Community-based programs such as Casa Azatlan in Chicago report that the majority of students who drop out of ESOL classes are those who are unable to read and write in their first language (Gillespie 1994). Minimally literate students in monolingual ESOL classes often told their bilingual tutors in the UMass/Boston Student Literacy Corps that they had no idea what was going on in class: "I am always lost. I waste my time" (Auerbach 1993, 17).

Similarly, Klassen's ethnographic study in Toronto's Hispanic/Latino community found that monolingual ESOL classes were virtually incomprehensible to the low-literate Hispanics/Latinos. Despite their lack of Spanish literacy, the people he interviewed were able to manage most domains of their lives *except the ESOL classroom;* there, they reported becoming completely silenced, making no progress, or dropping out:

> Angela . . . said that she had never gone back to an ESOL class she once started because the teacher embarrassed her by asking her about things she had never learned before. Maria and Doña Lucia described spending their time in class "drawing" letters and words they could not understand while everyone else read the words and learned. Maria said she left class knowing no more than when she first came. (Klassen 1991, 52)

Moreover, the people Klassen interviewed reported a strong sense of exclusion in their English classes. Two of them "experienced the classroom as a place where teachers isolated them from other students" (Klassen 1991, 53). Their response was perhaps based on the teachers' own frustration at being unable to communicate effectively using a lesson content that was reduced to the most elementary, childlike uses of language. The students' sense of exclusion within the class was compounded by the fact that it led to exclusion in the outside world as well: the lack of Spanish literacy was an obstacle to participating in the higher-level ESOL courses required for entry into job training programs, which in turn limited their employment possibilities.

Lisa Earl's study, which was based on information from nearly three hundred students, found that students' scores on measures of oral English proficiency correlated most closely with number of years of primary schooling rather than with factors such as age on arrival, previous study of English, or length of residence in the United States (Earl 1994, 16–17). Earl describes the effects of ESOL instruction on one student who had minimal schooling:

> Mercedes was in the ESOL program for four years. She was a very dynamic lady, an entertaining storyteller in Spanish, but her progress in English, especially written work, well, it was a major achievement when she finally copied something from the blackboard. She felt that she couldn't learn, described herself as stupid. But she had only been to first grade! I saw her as a talented, intelligent woman who came every day and sat there, tried so hard, and kept saying, "I want to learn English." But she was held at a standstill because of her lack of schooling. . . . To ask people to sit in an ESOL classroom year after year without giving them access to basic skills is a way of reinforcing failure. (18–19)

Based on her quantitative data, as well as on interviews with students and teachers, Earl concludes that "there is a definite link between native language literacy, in this case Spanish, and the subsequent acquisition of oral English proficiency. The fact is that students with limited schooling simply have a much harder time learning English whether in or out of class" (Earl 1994, 19).

L1 Literacy Instruction Attracts Previously Unserved Population

"I'm finally learning. I didn't know I could."

On the flip side, when the native language *is* used, practitioners, researchers, and learners consistently report positive results. Rivera outlines various models for incorporating the first language into instruction, including initial literacy in the L1 (with or without simultaneous but separate ESOL classes) and bilingual instruction (in which both languages are utilized within one class). One benefit of such programs at the beginning levels is that they attract previously unserved students who had given up trying to learn English because of limited first-language literacy and schooling. They often enable the same students who had dropped out of ESOL programs or become stuck in a cycle of failure to return to learning with a renewed sense of possibility and confidence in their own ability to learn. Lisa Earl, for example, quotes the teacher of Mercedes as saying, "now she's finally had a success. She's in a Spanish literacy class; it took her four years of waiting to get in, but now she tells me, 'I'm finally learning. I didn't know I could'" (Earl 1994, 18–19). Likewise, Heide Spruck Wrigley reported that when she interviewed learners around the country who were participating in L1 literacy classes, they talked about changes in their sense of possibility: "Learners kept saying to us, 'We know we're not really literate yet; we cannot do all the things that we want to do, but now we feel that we can'" (qtd. in Gillespie 1994, 19).

When British researchers Monica Lucerno and Jan Thompson (1994) interviewed students in bilingual ESOL classes about why they had not learned English before, or why they had abandoned previous attempts to learn English, their responses were: "Because I felt as a child"; "I felt ridiculous"; "I could not give opinions" (27–28). Lucerno and Thompson (1994) reported, however, that once these individuals were in classes in which the teacher shared their mother tongue, the use of the mother tongue helped to break down communication barriers and develop a sense of solidarity among the students (28).

L1 Literacy Enhances Retention and Progress in English Classes

"I can't say this in English, but I really want to say it."

Contrary to the claim that use of the L1 will slow the transition to and impede progress in English, numerous accounts suggest that the opposite may be true. For example, Strei (1992) reported that a pilot native-language literacy program for Haitians in Palm Beach County resulted in the dramatic increase of their retention rate once they enrolled in ESOL classes: the dropout rate decreased from 85 percent prior to the program to only 10 percent after it was started. In a study designed to investigate the effectiveness of using "pedagogically unsophisticated" bilingual tutors to teach nonliterate Cambodians, D'Annunzio (1991) found that the students made rapid gains in ESOL. Despite a relatively short total instructional time, highly significant results were attained in speaking, reading, and vocabulary as indicated by pre- and posttest scores on a number of standardized tests, portfolio analysis, and ongoing informal assessment. Similarly, Hemmindinger (1987) discovered that a bilingual problem–posing approach to initial ESOL for nonliterate and nonschooled Hmong refugees was more effective than a monolingual approach; while students made almost no progress in two to three years of monolingual ESOL classes, once a bilingual approach was introduced, progress was rapid. Hemmindinger attributed this in part to the fact that the bilingual approach alleviated language and culture shock. Lucerno and Thompson (1994) likewise suggest that bilingual approaches enhance learning:

> [T]he advantages of using bilingual approaches to develop English literacy skills were clearly demonstrated by the speed with which students moved from basic to high level literacy skills (this was most notable in the Arabic group, where even students illiterate in the mother tongue made tangible progress), which enabled them to make choices about employment or further study. (33)

Others report that L1 usage may actually pave the way for ESOL acquisition. Shamash (1990), for example, describes an approach to teaching ESOL used at the Invergarry Learning Center near Vancouver that might be considered heretical by some: students start by writing about their lives in their L1 or a mixture of their L1 and English; this text is then translated into English with the help of bilingual tutors or learners, providing "a natural bridge for overcoming problems of vocabulary, sentence structure and language confidence" (Shamash 1990, 72). At a certain point in the learning process, according to Shamash, the learner is willing to experiment and take risks with English. Thus starting with the L1 provides a sense of security and validates the learners' lived experiences, allowing them to express themselves "while at the same time providing meaningful written material to work with" (Shamash 1990, 75).

Similarly, teachers at Centro Presente in Cambridge, Massachusetts, report that use of the L1 naturally gives way to increasing use of English (Auerbach 1993, 19). Their students often say, "I can't say this in English, but I really want to say it"; once they have expressed their ideas in Spanish, the group helps them express them in English. Centro Presente teachers argue that since students do not start by thinking in the L2, allowing for the exploration of ideas in the L1 supports a gradual, developmental process in which use of the L1 drops off naturally as it becomes less necessary (Auerbach 1993, 20). One of my graduate students wrote the following journal entry about a story one of her classmates had told:

> The student, who taught ESOL to a variety of older immigrants, sensed in her classroom one day a great deal of frustration in her students. They were having a really difficult time with some English lesson, so the teacher called a time out. Normally, she said, she insisted on English only. But that day she asked each of her students to say something in his/her native language and then explain it to the others. There was a palpable sense of relief as each student spoke. When they returned to the difficult lesson, they seemed to have an easier time. The teacher felt that having them speak, however briefly, in their native languages reminded them of their competency in those languages and that they were then able to bring that renewed belief in themselves and their ability to learn English back to the lesson.

L1 Literacy Facilitates Communicative, Learner-Centered Instruction

"They used language to help solve problems."

These findings concerning use of the L1 are congruent with current theories of second-language acquisition which advocate meaning-centered and responsive pedagogies. As many of the section-opening quotes indicate, utilizing the L1 as a learning tool can enhance the affective environment for learning and reduce learners' anxiety; it can enable teachers to incorporate learners' life experiences and allow for participatory curriculum development. Most important, it constructs language as a meaning-making tool and allows language learning to become a means of communicating ideas and shaping life outside the classroom rather than an end in itself. As Piasecka (1988) says:

> Teaching bilingually does not mean a return to the Grammar Translation method, but rather a standpoint which accepts that the thinking, feeling, and artistic life of a person is very much rooted in their mother tongue. If the communicative approach is to live up to its name, then there are many occasions in which the original impulse to speak can only be found in the mother tongue. At the initial stages of learning a new language, the students' repertoire is limited to those few utterances already learnt, and they must constantly think before speaking. When having a conversation, we often become fully aware of what we actually mean only after speaking. We need to speak in order to sort out our ideas, and when learning a new language, this is often best done through the mother tongue. (97)

Clearly, however, in order to maximize these benefits, a certain kind of pedagogy is necessary—a pedagogy that draws on the learners' strengths and linguistic resources; a pedagogy that connects their oral language proficiency to the written code and respects their ability to think critically even if they don't have basic skills; a pedagogy that encourages them to use their life experiences as a way into literacy, and literacy as a way to make sense of their life experiences; a pedagogy that engages them as adults who have lived through challenging circumstances and who struggle every day with the realities of being in a new culture.

Because the question of language choice is so closely tied to issues of power both inside and outside the classroom, many native-language and bilingual adult educators have been inspired by Paulo Freire's pedagogical approach in which curriculum content is drawn from participants' experiences and invites reflection on these experiences. Goals are often framed in terms of challenging and changing oppressive conditions in learners' lives; as Rivera says, "The role of education in this approach is to empower learners to use their native language actively in order to generate their own curriculum, and, therefore, their own knowledge" (Rivera 1988, 2).

The classes studied by Lucerno and Thompson (1994) exemplify this approach. In these classes, use of the mother tongue enabled students from different social and educational backgrounds and with different life experiences to find common ground: teachers could identify learning needs, "generative themes" about immigrant life, and issues of cultural transition. L1 use also facilitated negotiating learning content with students (28). Teaching materials were based on content provided by students: topics which emerged from L1 discussions were transformed into items for language learning, and "language was quickly absorbed as the linguistic material had direct relevance to students" (30). Because they felt free to use their own language, the students lost their fear of taking risks and gained a greater sense of control of their own learning. Lucerno and Thompson (1994) concluded:

> The most immediate benefits could be seen in the way that students were able, through discussion in the mother tongue, to set their own agenda and contribute to the construction of a curriculum which reflected the complexities of their experiences. . . . The use of the mother tongue provided a framework for all that went on in the classroom and was a means of establishing a sense of solidarity within each group. (31)

> The combination of the radical pedagogies of critical literacy theory, involving discussion and problematisation, with more formal teacher centered approaches seems to have provided a rigorous framework which allowed students to develop their literacy skills from a soundly grounded basis, through a process of critical analysis, and to take control of their learning. (33)

Likewise, Hemmindinger's (1987) study of a bilingual problem–posing approach to initial ESOL identified use of the first language as critical in implementing an empowering approach to ESOL: it allowed students to discuss vital issues in their lives which they were then able to address in English. As she says, "The class members thus still learned the new language they needed, but more important, they used that language to attempt to solve problems, such as in [a work-related] incident where they were cheated" (20). The important point here is that this pedagogy clearly posits and develops the connection between language acquisition and the ability to address the problems learners face in their lives outside the classroom; it recognizes that use of the first language reflects an ideological stance about learners' positioning in the outside world.

L1 Literacy Supports Maintenance of the Home Culture and Children's Achievement

"We must learn and keep Hmong literacy before our culture disappears."

Many people, including refugees and immigrants themselves, would argue that a key benefit of native-language literacy instruction is that it supports maintenance of the home culture, providing a bridge between the old and the new cultures, which in turn becomes a bridge between generations. Strong evidence for this benefit comes from the Hmong Literacy Project in Fresno, California, a project initiated at the request of Hmong community members (Kang, Kuehn, and Herrell 1996). The refugees who participated in that native-language family literacy project said that one of the main reasons for attending classes was to maintain their own history and culture in order to pass it on to their children. They were afraid that their language and culture would be lost and saw L1 literacy as a way to preserve it for future generations:

We must learn and keep Hmong literacy before our culture disappears. It's very important to teach our children how to

read, write, and speak Hmong so that we have a way of preserving our culture. We want to write down beautiful stories
about our culture, things that happen in our country, in
Hmong, for our children. . . . I want to write down what it
was like in my country so we can leave our children something about our culture, like folktales, stories, history. If we
don't write them down, they will disappear when our generation dies, and our children won't remember them. (Kang,
Kuehn, and Herrell 1996, 25)

Kang et al. (1996) saw the parents' role in shaping the curriculum
as critical in this process:

Experiences and information from this project underscore the
importance of parents' role and choice in their own and their
children's education. Allowing parents to make choices concerning the curriculum not only made the content relevant but
also helped the parents perform an important task of record-
ing and adding to their own history and culture. (30)

Thus this project not only supported first- and second-language
and literacy development, but it also helped the parents transmit
their culture, communicate their values, and develop stronger
bonds with their children.

A related benefit of L1 adult literacy instruction, as the
Hmong project shows, is that it supports the academic development of the next generation. There is a great deal of evidence that
fostering children's sense of cultural identity and creating a solid
basis in the first language are important for their achievement;
clearly, parents' ability to support their children's literacy development will be shaped by their own first-language literacy proficiency. Cummins (1981) reviews literature which shows that,
contrary to commonsense views (especially those often held by
mainstream teachers), parents who use the first language rather
than English in the home do not impede their children's success in
school. He argues that it is the quality of parent-child interaction
rather than the language in which it takes place that shapes
achievement:

Viewed from this perspective, encouraging minority parents
to communicate in English with their children in the home
can have very detrimental consequences. If parents are not

comfortable in English, the quality of their interaction with their children in English is likely to be less than in the first language. (33)

Further, a study of the literacy practices in Indochinese refugee families by Caplan, Choy, and Whitmore (1992) found that the parents' lack of English proficiency had very little effect on their children's school performance and, interestingly, that the parents' support for cultural maintenance enhanced academic achievement. They concluded, "Rather than adopting American ways and assimilating into the melting pot, the most successful Indochinese families appear to retain their own traditions and values" (41). Communication and literacy in the L1 are central to this process.

Beyond the Beginning

"They feel freer to express themselves and let me know what they want."

Even those who acknowledge the usefulness of a bilingual approach to beginning ESOL acquisition often view it as counterproductive beyond the beginning stages, arguing that overreliance on the L1 will interfere with ESOL acquisition. Evidence from both research and practice, however, again suggests that the first language may be a potential resource rather than an obstacle. On the research side, for example, a study by Osburne and Harss-Covaleski (1991) suggests that the widely frowned on practice of writing first in the L1 and then translating into the L2 is not detrimental to the quality of the written product. The conventional wisdom is that students should be discouraged from translating, as this will "cause them to make more errors, result in rhetorically inappropriate texts, and distract them from thinking in English—and that all these factors would negatively affect the quality of their writing" (5). To investigate the validity of this claim, Osburne and Harss-Covaleski compared ESOL compositions written directly in English with others written first in the L1 and then translated into English; the results indicated no significant difference in the quality or quantity of the written products. They conclude, "It seems then that there is no need for teachers to become overly anxious if students choose to employ translation as a composing strategy at times" (1991, 15).

While practitioners rarely advocate indiscriminate use of the L1, they do report finding selective and targeted integration of the L1 useful; accounts from practice identify a multiplicity of clearly delineated functions for such use. Piasecka (1988), for example, includes the following in her list of possible uses of the mother tongue: negotiating the syllabus and the lesson; profiling and record keeping; managing the classroom; setting the scene; analyzing language; covering rules governing grammar, phonology, morphology, and spelling; dealing with cross-cultural issues; instructing or prompting; explaining errors; and assessing comprehension. Collingham (1988) concurs with many of these uses, adding the following: developing ideas as a precursor to expressing them in the L2; reducing inhibitions or affective blocks to L2 production; eliciting language and discourse strategies for particular situations; providing explanations of grammar and language functions; and teaching vocabulary. Atkinson (1987) argues that there are several advantages to the "judicious" use of the mother tongue: eliciting language, checking comprehension, giving instructions, fostering cooperation among learners, discussing classroom methodology, checking for sense, and developing learning strategies. He goes on to list the dangers of overuse and stresses the point that context is key in determining whether mother-tongue use is productive (242). Brucker (1992) describes using the L1 as a tool for startup assessment to identify student needs and goals. She writes:

> I encouraged the students to answer this evaluation in Spanish. Although I don't read Spanish well, I can always find a staff person or another teacher to translate for me. This extra step is worth my time because students can give me "true," that is to say, more accurate and more complete answers, using their first language. They feel freer to express themselves and let me know what they want. It also gives me a sense of the students' native language competency. This is important in order for me to understand where students are starting. (37)

Thus, one of the primary advantages of teaching bilingually is that it enhances metacognitive awareness in language learning. As Lucerno and Thompson (1994) remark:

> The use of the mother tongue in the classroom unlocked the learning process by giving students access to knowledge about language and literacy; they were able to discuss grammatical categories, to label parts of speech and to discuss tenses in a way which is not possible in an ESOL class with an English [teacher]. (33)

Classroom Realities

"You want to keep us ignorant."

However persuasive these arguments in favor of native-language literacy or bilingual approaches to ESOL may sound, the reality of trying to implement them in the classroom is that they are often met with resistance from both teachers and learners. Teachers respond with a litany of concerns: "How can I possibly incorporate my students' first languages when half of them want me to enforce only English? They come from twenty different language backgrounds, and I don't speak their languages anyway." Students, too, may resist learning through the L1. In many cases, the pervasive English Only discourse translates into a sense that their own language is inferior; students may have internalized the socially constructed stigma against their own L1. For example, Haitian students in Boston who were placed in a Creole literacy class reacted initially by saying, "You people are educated; you want us to learn Creole because you want to keep us ignorant" (Auerbach et al. 1996). In mixed ESOL classes in which students come from a variety of language backgrounds, L1 use can be a source of classroom tension, with some students feeling that it wastes time or creates bad feelings, and others seeing it as a necessary support. And teachers who believe that L1 or bilingual approaches will benefit their students and also adhere to a learner-centered philosophy face an additional dilemma if students resist L1 use; they may feel, "If we truly advocate respecting students as adults who should participate in decision making processes, what should we do if they don't want L1 literacy? Do we follow their lead? Or do we impose L1 literacy because we think we know what's best for them?"

These questions have no easy answers. Because the underlying issue is not just a pedagogical one but an ideological one as well, I would argue that what is critical in addressing them is not so much the decision that ultimately gets made, but rather the process for making the decision. The issue of language choice is really part of the broader question of teacher and student roles, which in turn is a question of power—who gets to decide what should happen in the classroom? Traditionally, the teacher determines what is best for the students based on his or her status and expertise. As Freire (1970) argues, however, central to acquiring the skills and confidence for claiming more power outside the classroom is a shift of power inside the classroom. Students must be involved in the decision-making process.

But asking students their opinion is not enough; this does nothing to extend their capacity to understand the issues. The key here is providing them with the tools and contexts for making informed and critical decisions. What this means, I think, is that the arguments (both for and against L1 use) which have been addressed in this chapter need to be addressed *with* learners. Rather than the teacher making choices about language use for the students, the issue itself can become content for language and literacy work; the teacher can pose the issues to students for reflection and dialogue. In the various native-language and bilingual adult education projects I have worked with (Auerbach et al. 1996), teachers developed the following range of strategies for addressing these questions:

◆ discussing the relationship between L1 literacy and ESOL acquisition with students

◆ situating the issue in its broader historical and political context (discussing why people were unable to go to school in their home countries, why their first language was devalued, and/or how literacy was used as a tool for social stratification)

◆ inviting students to express and explore their attitudes toward L1 literacy, and making space for their resistance to it

- giving students choice about placements: inviting them to try L1 literacy class for a limited time or to try a beginning ESOL class and then decide

- discussing the issue of L1 literacy with the whole center in order to legitimate it and prevent marginalization of the L1 classes

- enhancing teachers' understanding of the history of, rationale for, and approaches to L1 instruction

- incorporating specific, limited time for ESOL instruction within L1 literacy classes to show how L1 literacy can facilitate ESOL acquisition

- posing the question of the advantages and disadvantages of L1 versus L2 use to students, and analyzing the functions of each in different contexts for different purposes with them

Through this kind of analysis and reflection, students can arrive at their own rules for language use in the classroom. Certainly teachers can contribute their own knowledge and opinions in these exchanges, but what is important is a shift toward shared authority. The teacher moves from being a problem solver or arbiter of tensions to a problem poser or facilitator of critical reflection. The tools that students develop for thinking critically, exploring alternatives, and making choices prepare them for addressing the issues they confront in everyday life.

Of course, for beginning ESOL classes, this kind of discussion can best take place in the L1; yet even reflecting on the ways that both languages are used to conduct this discussion can yield insights into the use of each language for various functions in other contexts. The pedagogical bonus is that students develop metacognitive awareness of language-learning strategies. The classroom management bonus is that it takes the teacher off the hot seat; students develop empathy for each others' perspectives, and tensions are relieved. Most important, students gain a greater sense of control over their own learning.

Reenvisioning Expertise

"I can help here. You need me."

The issue of the teacher not knowing the students' first language and thus being unable to use it as a resource in the classroom is the tip of another ideological iceberg—namely, the question of who should teach and what counts as qualifications. The taken-for-granted assumption in the field is that ESOL teachers do not need to know students' languages since all the teaching will be done in English anyway. The assumption is that native English speakers with TESOL degrees have the requisite qualifications by virtue of their linguistic background and advanced study: what counts is knowledge of English and second-language theories, research, approaches, and methods.

Of course, professionals in the field widely agree that it is wrong to assume that just because one speaks English, one can teach it—specialized training is required. Phillipson (1992), however, claims that many of those qualities which are seen to make native speakers intrinsically better qualified as English teachers (e.g., their fluency, appropriate usage, and knowledge of cultural connotations of the language) can be acquired or instilled through training. Moreover, he argues, non-native speakers possess certain qualifications which native speakers may not: they have gone through "the laborious process of acquiring English as a second language and . . . have insight into the linguistic and cultural needs of their learners" (195).

I would go further to argue that, in the case of ESOL instruction (as opposed to English as a foreign language [EFL]), in which English is taught to immigrants and refugees transplanted to an English-speaking country, it is not just experience as a language learner but the experience of sharing the struggles as a newcomer that is critical. If a central tenet of current second-language and literacy theory is the importance of contextualizing instruction around real, meaningful usage centered on content that is significant in learners' lives, who is better qualified to draw out, understand, and utilize learners' experiences than those who have had similar experiences? There is something about having actually lived these realities from the inside out that enables immigrant teachers to make connections that are otherwise not possible. While non-native speakers of English with nontraditional educational backgrounds can be trained in literacy/ESOL pedagogy, it is not clear that the obverse is true—that the understandings that come through shared life experience and cultural background can be imparted through training. Lucerno and Thompson (1994), for example, say that in their program, "The value of the [teacher] sharing mother tongue with students quickly became evident. It provided the team of [teachers] with in depth knowledge about the students and their educational needs" (27).

Others have likewise attributed the success of their programs to the expertise of non-Anglophone teachers. D'Annunzio (1991), for example, argues that his program was successful largely because of "the use of bilingual tutors who shared the students' experiences" (52). He says that, with a short training period, "pedagogically unsophisticated" bilinguals (who in the case of his program were "only high school graduates") can become effective tutors and trainers of other tutors; this model "may break the chain of reliance on heavy professional intervention" (52). Hornberger and Hardman's (1994) study of instructional practices in a Cambodian adult ESOL class and a Puerto Rican GED class corroborates the importance of shared background between teachers and learners. In the case of the Cambodian class, they found that although the teacher (who had finished just two years of college and a vocational program) tried to speak English exclusively, the students used Khmer to respond to her questions and help each other; in addition, the teacher and students shared assumptions about the learning paradigm, and classroom activities were intimately connected with learners' other life activities and cultural practices. Likewise, in the GED class instructional activities were embedded in a cultural and institutional context that integrated and validated learners' Puerto Rican identity.

Even in mixed ESOL sites where students come from many different language groups, non-native English-speaking teachers who do not speak the learners' languages can be an asset. Adult learners, seeing their peers in the role of teacher, may assume more responsibility for the learning of others. In one case, a student who had never spoken in class began to participate actively after being paired with a more advanced student; the advanced student then asked to remain in the class (even though he was ready for a higher level) because, as he said, "'I can help here. You need me'" (Auerbach 1993, 28).

Two Sides of the Same Coin

I hope to have demonstrated that the commonly accepted classroom practice of insisting on English Only in the classroom, far from being neutral and natural, has ideological origins and consequences for relations of power both inside and outside the classroom. It is a practice whose roots can be traced to the political and economic interests of the dominant classes in the same way that the English Only movement has been. The rationale and research used to justify English Only instruction are questionable, and there is increasing evidence that L1 and/or bilingual options are not only effective but necessary for adult ESOL students with limited L1 and schooling backgrounds.

On the one hand, it is clear from the accumulated body of research and practice that the result of monolingual ESOL instruction for students with minimal first-language literacy and schooling is often that, whether or not they drop out, their self-esteem suffers; their sense of powerlessness is reinforced, either because they are de facto excluded from the classroom or because their life experiences and language resources are excluded. This in turn has consequences for their lives outside the classroom, limiting job possibilities and reproducing a stratum of people who can only do the least skilled and least language- and/or literacy-dependent jobs (Spener 1988; Skutnabb-Kangas 1988). On the other hand, when students are given the opportunity to become literate in their first language or to learn English bilingually, the results are often dramatically different. There are advantages in terms of retention, progress, quality, and relevance of language acquisition; cultural maintenance; intergenerational communication; and access to jobs and further education, as well as the possibility of addressing problems in the social context. Thus, as Collingham (1988) says, what happens inside and outside the classroom are two sides of the same coin:

> To treat adult learners as if they know nothing of language is to accept the imbalance of power and so ultimately to collude with institutional racism; to adopt a bilingual approach and

to value the knowledge that learners already have is to begin to challenge that unequal power relationship and, one hopes, thereby enable learners to acquire the skills and confidence they need to claim back more power for themselves in the world beyond the classroom. (85)

The evidence presented suggests a strong correlation between L1 literacy and progress in English. This literacy and progress are in turn necessary for access to job training, suggesting that monolingual ESOL instruction virtually assures that low-literate language-minority adults will be excluded from access to both English and all but the most menial jobs. As such, English Only instruction undermines the possibilities for self-sufficiency, economic independence, and competitiveness in the workplace, the very goals it is ostensibly designed to support. Given these realities and the fact that funding for bilingual and native-language models is so limited, one has to wonder whether a skilled and literate English-speaking workforce really is the aim of these adult education policies. An alternative explanation might be that, in fact, the underlying policy agenda is "functional *illiteracy*": perhaps there are structural economic reasons to maintain a class of unskilled, non-English-speaking workers who are marginally literate and thus willing to take minimum wage jobs which others are unwilling to accept. To the extent that English Only instruction may feed into this dynamic, the importance of challenging it is all the more critical.

Respecting and incorporating learners' languages into adult education is vital because of the powerful social implications: valuing participants' linguistic resources in teaching is a measure of our willingness to address basic inequities in the broader society. As the field of adult education lets go of the need to enforce only English in the classroom and opens its ranks to community expertise, students will gain greater control of their own learning and greater strength in challenging the inequities they face outside the classroom. As Fairclough (1989) would suggest, unveiling the ways in which English Only functions on a pedagogical level is one step toward undermining the power that the dominant classes exert through institutional practices.

Works Cited

Atkinson, David. 1987. "The Mother Tongue in the Classroom: A Neglected Resource?" *ELT Journal* 41: 241–47.

Auerbach, Elsa. 1993. "Reexamining English Only in the ESL Classroom." *TESOL Quarterly* 27(1):9–32.

Auerbach, Elsa, with Byron Barahona, Julio Midy, Felipe Vaquerano, Ana Zambrano, and Joanne Arnaud. 1996. *From the Community to the Community: A Guidebook for Participatory Literacy Training.* Mahwah, NJ: Lawrence Erlbaum.

Baron, Dennis E. 1990. *The English Only Question: An Official Language for Americans?* New Haven: Yale University Press.

Brucker, Kathy. 1992. "When Asking Isn't Enough." *Adventures in Assessment* 2: 37–40. Massachusetts System for Adult Basic Education.

Burtoff, Michele. 1985. *Haitian Creole Literacy Evaluation Study: Final Report.* Washington, D.C.: Center for Applied Linguistics.

Caplan, Nathan, Marcella Choy, and John Whitmore. 1992. "Indochinese Refugee Families and Academic Achievement." *Scientific American* 266: 18–24.

Collingham, Monica. 1988. "Making Use of Students' Linguistic Resources." In Sandra Nicholls and Elizabeth Hoadley-Maidment, eds., *Current Issues in Teaching English as a Second Language to Adults.* London: Edward Arnold. 81–85.

Crawford, James. 1991. *Bilingual Education: History, Politics, Theory, and Practice.* 2nd edition. Los Angeles: Bilingual Educational Services.

Cummins, James. 1981. "The Role of Primary Language Development in Promoting Educational Success for Language Minority Students." In Office of Bilingual Bicultural Education, ed., *Schooling and Language Minority Students: A Theoretical Framework.* Los Angeles: Evaluation, Dissemination, and Assessment Center, California State University. 3–49.

Daniels, Harvey A., ed. 1990. *Not Only English: Affirming America's Multilingual Heritage.* Urbana, IL: National Council of Teachers of English.

D'Annunzio, Anthony. 1991. "Using Bilingual Tutors and Non-Directive Approaches in ESOL: A Follow-up Report." *Connections: A Journal of Adult Literacy* 4:51–52.

Earl, Lisa. 1994. "Necesitamos Aprender Bien El Español: The Effect of Literacy in Spanish on Latino Students' Acquisition of English." *Literacy Harvest: The Journal of the Literacy Assistance Center* 3(1):14–20.

Fairclough, Norman. 1989. *Language and Power*. London: Longman.

Freire, Paulo. 1970. *Pedagogy of the Oppressed*. New York: Seabury Press.

Gillespie, Marilyn. 1994. *Adult Native Language Literacy Instruction for Adults: Patterns, Issues and Promises*. Washington, D.C.: National Clearinghouse for ESOL Literacy Education.

Hemmindinger, Anna. 1987. *Two Models for Using Problem-Posing and Cultural Sharing in Teaching the Hmong English as a Second Language and First Language Literacy*. Unpublished master's thesis, St. Francis Xavier University, Antigonish, Nova Scotia, Canada.

Hornberger, Nancy H., and Joel Hardman. 1994. "Literacy as Cultural Practice and Cognitive Skill: Biliteracy in an ESL and a GED Program." In David Spener, ed., *Adult Biliteracy in the United States*. Washington, D.C.: Center for Applied Linguistics/Delta Systems. 147–69.

Kang, Hee-Won, Phyllis Kuehn, and Adrienne Herrell. 1996. "The Hmong Literacy Project: Parents Working to Preserve the Past and Ensure the Future." *The Journal of Educational Issues of Language Minority Students* 16:17–30.

Klassen, Cecil. 1991. "Bilingual Written Language Use by Low-Education Latin American Newcomers." In David Barton and Roz Ivanic, eds., *Writing in the Community*. London: Sage. 38–57.

Lucerno, Monica, and Jan Thompson. 1994. "Teaching English Literacy Using Bilingual Approaches." *RaPAL Bulletin* 25: 26–33.

Osburne, Andrea, and Sandra Harss-Covaleski. 1991. "Translation in the ESOL Composition Class." Unpublished paper. Central Connecticut State University.

Phillipson, Robert. 1992. *Linguistic Imperialism*. Oxford: Oxford University Press.

Piasecka, Krystna. 1988. "The Bilingual Teacher in the ESOL Classroom." In S. Nicholls and E. Hoadley-Maidment, eds., *Current Issues in Teaching English as a Second Language to Adults*. London: Edward Arnold. 97–103.

Rivera, Klaudia. 1988. "Not Either/Or but And: Literacy for Non-English Speakers." *Focus on Basics* 1: 1–3.

Robson, Barbara. 1982. "Hmong Literacy, Formal Education and their Effects on Performance in an ESL Class." In B. Downing and O. Douglas, eds., *The Hmong in the West*. Minneapolis: Center for Urban and Regional Affairs, University of Minnesota. 201–15.

Shamash, Yom. 1990. "Learning in Translation: Beyond Language Experience in ESOL." *Voices* 2(2): 71–75.

Skutnabb-Kangas, Tove. 1988. "Multilingualism and the Education of Minority Children." In Tove Skutnabb-Kangas and James Cummins, eds., *Minority Education: From Struggle to Shame*. Clevedon, Eng.: Multilingual Matters.

Snow, Catherine. 1990. "Rationales for Native Language Instruction: Evidence from Research." In Amada Padilla Halford Fairchild, and Concepcion Valadez, eds., *Bilingual Education: Issues and Strategies*. Newbury Park, CA: Sage Publications. 60–74.

Spener, David. 1988. "Transitional Bilingual Education and the Socialization of Immigrants." *Harvard Educational Review* 58(2): 133–53.

Street, Brian. 1984. *Literacy in Theory and Practice*. Cambridge: Cambridge University Press.

Strei, Gerry. 1992. "Advantages of Native Language Literacy Programs: Pilot Project." *TESOL Refugee Concerns Newsletter* 7: 7–8.

TESOL Resolution XX. Language Rights. 1987. TESOL Convention, Miami Beach, FL: TESOL.

Tollefson, James. 1991. *Planning Language, Planning Inequality: Language Policy in the Community*. London: Longman.

Walsh, Catherine. 1994. "Engaging Students in Learning: Literacy, Language and Knowledge Production with Latino Adolescents." In David Spener, ed., *Adult Biliteracy in the United States*. Washington, D.C.: Center for Applied Linguistics/Delta Systems. 211–37.

Weinberg, Joan. 1990. "Pennies from He Vinh." *TESOL Newsletter* 24(3): 5.

Wrigley, Heide S., and Gloria Guth. 1992. *Bringing Literacy to Life: Issues and Options in Adult ESL Literacy*. San Mateo: Aguirre International.

CHAPTER NINE

Which English Skills Matter to Immigrants? The Acquisition and Value of Four English Skills

ARTURO GONZALEZ

University of Arizona

The passage of Proposition 227 in California and the five bills considered by the 105th Congress that would have made English the official language of the United States (H.J.Res. 37, H.R. 622, S. 323, H.R.123, and H.R. 1005) have placed the English-speaking ability of immigrants once again center stage in the ongoing immigration debate. One of the beliefs driving these and past efforts is that immigrants are not learning English and therefore are less likely to become "integrated" into the American mainstream. For example, by making English the official language of the U.S. government, the Bill Emerson English Language Empowerment Act of 1996 (H.R.123) claims it would "help immigrants better assimilate and take full advantage of economic and occupational opportunities in the United States." While Mexican immigrants prefer to reside in neighborhoods with high concentrations of Mexicans because of the positive cultural benefits found only in such areas, this choice of neighborhood fosters anxiety about balkanization in certain segments of the population. This anxiety is clear in the Language of Government Act of 1997 (S.323), which states that "in order to preserve unity in diversity, and to prevent division along linguistic lines, the United States should maintain a language common to all people."

Those who would promote English Only initiatives as a way to increase the English ability of immigrants, however, overlook the economic and social incentives already confronting immigrants. While it is unclear what effect English Only legislation would have on the English proficiency of immigrants, a more effective mechanism encouraging the acquisition of English-language skills already exists—the labor market. Many of the economic studies that examine the relationship between earnings and English-language ability generally find that immigrants proficient at *speaking* English earn more than other immigrants with equal characteristics, such as education, age, and marital status. For example, Hispanic/Latino immigrants who report not being able to speak English earn 17 percent less than immigrants who speak English (Borjas 1994). Furthermore, the acquisition of English over time in the United States partly explains the convergence of native and immigrant wages (Funkhouser 1996; Carliner 1995).

This chapter informs the current English Only debate by examining the factors affecting the English proficiency of immigrants using a unique data set that for the first time allows us to investigate simultaneously four English skills: speaking, understanding, reading, and writing. Furthermore, investigating the factors related to proficiency in these skills makes it possible to analyze whether the English-proficiency rates of immigrants are stagnant. There is much evidence that English acquisition is dynamic not only among immigrants but also across generations. Veltman (1983), for example, notes the shift away from Spanish and into English among second and higher generation Hispanic Americans. Similarly, the present data set reveals a shift toward English proficiency among *first*-generation immigrants.

This study also examines the labor market rewards associated with English proficiency. This relationship is important for practical and philosophical reasons. While many English-instruction courses are justified on the grounds that immigrants become better citizens and participants in the United States by learning English, immigrants also benefit economically from these courses. While it is difficult to construct a metric for the civic and social reasons for learning English, it is possible to discover the economic benefit of these classes. The study examines the "returns" associated with proficiency in the four English-language skills, constituting another unique contribution to the literature.

The majority of studies conclude that English-language ability is a skill which is rewarded in the labor market; therefore, a certain level of English-language ability is required to achieve economic mobility in the United States. As recent immigrants reportedly have lower English-language skills than previous immigrants (Borjas 1994), research over their economic well-being must examine the acquisition of English among all immigrants. The literature on English-language ability of immigrants is extensive, but the majority of studies rely on data from the Census and Current Population Survey that contain only self-reported English *speaking* ability (Funkhouser 1996; Carliner 1995; McManus, Gould, and Welch 1983). Researchers such as McManus (1985), Chiswick (1991), Chiswick and Miller (1995, 1996), Rivera-Batiz (1990), and Espinosa and Massey (1997) forego the scope of the large national data sets in exchange for more detailed language information, such as self-reported and test-based measures of various English-language skills.

But while Chiswick (1991) and Espinosa and Massey (1997) examine several dimensions of English-language ability, their results are not applicable to the whole immigrant population because their data do not consist of a random sample of immigrants. Using information gathered from apprehended illegal immigrants, Chiswick (1991) finds that years in the United States especially affect speaking proficiency, while education plays a major role in determining reading proficiency. Espinosa and Massey (1997) consider the determinants of joint proficiency in speaking and understanding English for immigrants from over twenty Mexican American communities, and find that education and having children enrolled in U.S. schools increase the odds of proficiency. This study extends the work of these authors by examining four dimensions of English proficiency and at the same time utilizing a representative sample of the nation's immigrants.

The current study uses data from the 1992 National Adult Literacy Survey (NALS) (U.S. Dept. of Education 1997), a data set which contains information on four self-reported measures of English ability. This study also extends the literature by examining the relationship between immigrant earnings and the four

English-language skills. The NALS data make it possible to compare speaking ability with three other English-language skills to establish the validity of previous studies. Determining which English-language skills are more valuable also has important policy implications. Knowing the economic value of a particular English-language skill, for example, helps adult English courses base their curriculum on the skills that provide the greatest monetary benefit to immigrants.

The National Adult Literacy Survey

Survey Description

The demographic and labor market information in this study is derived from the National Adult Literacy Survey (NALS). The NALS was carried out during the first eight months of 1992 and consists of information on 24,944 persons, of which 1,205 are identified as male immigrants. To guarantee that a sufficient number of minorities were included in the survey, geographical areas with at least 25 percent Black or Hispanic/Latino adults were sampled at a rate up to three times that of other areas. The background variables are taken from a questionnaire given in either English or Spanish. As a consequence, more Spanish-speaking persons with low English-language skills are included in the data than similarly skilled persons who neither speak Spanish nor English.

Information about understanding, speaking, reading, and writing English comes from the question, "In regards to the English language, how well do you

1. understand it when it is spoken to you?"
2. speak it?"
3. read it?"
4. write it?"

Persons rate their ability from very well, well, not well, to not at all. Using such self-reported measures is a standard practice in social science research, and they are judged to be reasonable measures of English-speaking ability (Kominski 1989).

Sample Selection

From the full NALS sample, this study extracted male immigrants earning at least $40 per week who were sixteen to sixty-four years of age and not enrolled in school. Persons with missing information on certain variables were dropped from the sample because it is not possible to make the desired inference without sufficient information. However, those who stated that they attended grades 1–8 or 9–11 but who did not specify the exact highest grade were assigned grades 5 and 10, respectively, which is the respective average grade level for the 1–8 and 9–11 education categories. Only twenty-three such cases arose.

Immigrants from the following predominantly English-speaking countries were excluded: Australia, Bahamas, Bermuda, Canada, England, India, Ireland, Jamaica, New Zealand, Puerto Rico, and Scotland. Although South Africa and Nigeria are not on this list, only 8 immigrants from these countries (7 from Nigeria and 1 from South Africa) were included in the final sample. Immigrants with missing demographic or language information were also dropped from the sample. With these restrictions, the sample size was 601 immigrants. The use of sample weights makes it possible to draw inferences about the national immigrant population from the 601 immigrants examined in this study. For example, if one of every 100 Asian immigrants is sampled by the NALS, then the sample weight is 100, and each Asian is said to represent 100 other Asian immigrants.

Women were not included in this study (nor in those previously cited) because they present a unique challenge in any statistical analysis of labor market performance. Because a great percentage of women are not in the labor force and hence do not earn any work income, using the sample employed results in "sample selection bias" (Greene 1993, 739–47). To correct for this bias, a more complicated statistical procedure is needed. As a consequence, many studies in this area focus solely on male workers. In order for the analysis of language acquisition to be relevant to the labor market results, the same sample was used in both sections of this study.

Following the practice in previous studies, immigrants were classified as proficient (where proficiency refers to self-reported English-language ability) in any of the four skills if they answered "well" or "very well." As stated earlier, the NALS questionnaire was given in both Spanish and English, and this has implications for average proficiency rates. Since Spanish speakers with low levels of English were more likely to participate in the NALS than speakers of other languages with equal levels of English, Spanish speakers with lower English-language skills are overrepresented in the sample. This is a consequence of sample design, but it does not invalidate the NALS data. Special attention is given to how it affects the results.

Average Proficiency Rates

The NALS data reveal that adult immigrants have varying levels of English proficiency, depending on both the ethnicity of immigrants and the particular English-language ability examined. Since Hispanics, and Mexicans in particular, can be of any race and represent one of the largest growing immigrant populations, I collapsed the self-reported ethnic/racial (ethnic for simplicity) identifier into six mutually exclusive ethnic classifications: Black, Mexican, other Hispanic (non-Mexican Hispanics), Asian, White, and other race (for persons not stating a racial identity and those not in one of the other five categories). The ethnic distribution among the 601 respondents is approximately 6 percent Black, 40 percent Mexican, 23 percent other Hispanic, 12 percent Asian, 16 percent White, and 3 percent other race.

Table 9.1 lists the percentage of immigrants who reported proficiency in each the four English-language skills. Generally across all ethnic groups, speaking and understanding (oral) proficiency was more prevalent than proficiency in reading and writing (literacy) skills. White adult immigrants were the most English-proficient group, with the exception of speaking ability. While 96 percent of White immigrants reported proficiency in speaking English, 100 percent of Black immigrants reported proficiency. This finding among Black immigrants is surprising and is

TABLE 9.1. Self-Reported English-Proficiency Rates of Immigrants[a]

Ethnicity	English Skill			
	Understands	Speaks	Reads	Writes
Black	1.00	0.85	0.60	0.55
Mexican	0.42	0.34	0.26	0.14
Other Hispanic	0.57	0.51	0.47	0.42
Asian	0.78	0.81	0.79	0.74
White	0.96	0.93	0.84	0.78
Other Race	0.83	0.69	0.80	0.69

[a] Total sample size is 601. Sample weights are used.
Source: U.S. Department of Education 1992.

not explained by country of origin: nearly one-third (10 out of 33) come from Haiti, a French-speaking country, and another one-third (12 out of 33) come from "other countries" not listed by the NALS. Only 7 Black immigrants (or about 21 percent of all Blacks) are known to come from a country—Nigeria—where English is the official language.

Mexican immigrants were the least proficient of all immigrant groups. But, in accordance with the general finding for other ethnic groups, Mexican immigrants were more likely to be proficient in oral than literacy English-language skills. While less than 50 percent of Mexicans could not speak or understand English proficiently, their proficiency in reading and writing averaged about 20 percent. In contrast, other Hispanics, the next least speaking-proficient ethnic group, were over 15 percent more likely to be proficient in oral skills.

Comparing Hispanics with non-Hispanics is likely to result in a negative bias against Hispanics because more Spanish speakers with low English-speaking ability are represented in the sample, due to the fact that the NALS questionnaire was available in Spanish. Therefore, policymakers should be cautioned about making inferences from these interethnic English differences. Mexicans can only be compared to other Hispanics, and vice versa.

Table 9.2 presents the correlation between the four English-language skills. The correlation is greater within the oral and literacy skills than between these skills. In most instances, the correlation between speaking and understanding English is near 70 percent, while the correlation between understanding (speaking) and reading, and understanding (speaking) and writing is always less. For example, among Asians the correlation between understanding and speaking is 0.77, but the correlation between understanding and reading English is only 0.51.

Table 9.2 reveals a dichotomy in English-language skills. In particular, proficiency in understanding is generally associated with speaking proficiency but not necessarily with reading or writing proficiency. In other words, although four measures of English are reported, it may be possible to collapse English into two distinct dimensions: oral skills and literacy skills. The next sections further analyze this possibility.

English Acquisition

The outcomes described in Table 9.1 are the result of various socioeconomic factors, such as age, length of residence in the United States, and education. Table 9.1 also shows that the odds of English proficiency are higher in some English-language skills and lower in others even within ethnic groups. In other words, "English ability" is not a unidimensional characteristic, but rather encompasses several dimensions. As a consequence, it is also possible that the same background variables, such as education, may affect each English-language skill differently.

In this study, the factors examined are age, number of years spent in the United States since migration, language of origin and education, ethnicity, whether an English as a second language (ESL) course was taken (for spoken language or literacy), and whether the course for that ability was completed. In essence, Table 9.3 (see page 214) shows the change in probability of proficiency for each English-language ability associated with each of these factors. Technically, the figures in Table 9.3 are the "marginal effects" from four probit regressions (one for each English-language skill), estimated at the

TABLE 9.2. Correlation of English Proficiency by Ethnicity[a]

Black		Understands	Speaks	Reads	Writes
	Understands	—			
	Speaks	—	1.00		
	Reads	—	0.47	1.00	
	Writes	—	0.43	0.90	1.00
Mexican		**Understands**	**Speaks**	**Reads**	**Writes**
	Understands	1.00			
	Speaks	0.73	1.00		
	Reads	0.67	0.70	1.00	
	Writes	0.47	0.50	0.69	1.00
Hispanic		**Understands**	**Speaks**	**Reads**	**Writes**
	Understands	1.00			
	Speaks	0.85	1.00		
	Reads	0.73	0.80	1.00	
	Writes	0.70	0.82	0.90	1.00
Asian		**Understands**	**Speaks**	**Reads**	**Writes**
	Understands	1.00			
	Speaks	0.77	1.00		
	Reads	0.51	0.42	1.00	
	Writes	0.63	0.56	0.88	1.00
White		**Understands**	**Speaks**	**Reads**	**Writes**
	Understands	1.00			
	Speaks	0.65	1.00		
	Reads	0.40	0.49	1.00	
	Writes	0.40	0.26	0.72	1.00
Other Race		**Understands**	**Speaks**	**Reads**	**Writes**
	Understands	1.00			
	Speaks	0.68	1.00		
	Reads	0.39	0.16	1.00	
	Writes	0.67	0.35	0.76	1.00

[a]Sample weights are used.

TABLE 9.3. Change in Probability in English Proficiency Associated with Demographic Characteristics[a]

	English Skill			
	Understands	Speaks	Reads	Writes
Age	−0.012*	−0.013*	−0.009*	−0.014*
Years in U.S.: 6–10	0.192*	0.177*	0.105	0.131
Years in U.S.: 11–15	0.247*	0.251*	0.196*	0.228*
Years in U.S.: 16–20	0.279*	0.380*	0.286*	0.367*
Years in U.S.: 21–30	0.301*	0.346*	0.382*	0.512*
Years in U.S.: 31–40	0.305*	0.389*	0.444*	0.567*
Years in U.S.: over 40	0.233*	0.320*	0.353*	0.509*
ED×Spanish Language	0.039*	0.041*	0.067*	0.075*
ED×European Language	0.022	0.024	0.095*	0.083*
ED×Asian Language	0.036*	0.022*	0.102*	0.096*
ED×Other Language	0.033*	0.025*	0.096*	0.085*
Mexican	−0.604*	−0.612*	0.098	−0.211
Other Hispanic	−0.601*	−0.534*	0.138	−0.014
Asian	−0.502*	−0.116	−0.144	−0.083
Black	—[b]	0.100	0.018	0.083
Other Race	−0.287	−0.230	0.256	0.166
Taken Course to Learn English	−0.153*	−0.134*	−0.238*	−0.238*
Completed Course to Learn English	0.296*	0.335*	0.325*	0.371*
Observed proficiency	0.64	0.60	0.53	0.46
Predicted proficiency at means of variables	0.77	0.70	0.59	0.42
N	568	601	601	601
log likelihood	−213.2	−230.3	−222.9	−209.0

[a] Dependent variable is a 0–1 indicator of proficiency, where proficiency is defined as "well" or "very well." Sample weights are used. The marginal effect of dummy variables is for a change from 0 to 1.

[b] Blacks are dropped due to lack of variation in the dependent variable—all report proficiency.

* Underlying coefficient estimate is statistically significant at the 5 percent level.

mean of the sample of immigrants. A probit regression enables one to attain the relative probability of proficiency in any one English-language skill by assuming that proficiency follows a normal distribution. This is done by classifying proficient immigrants as "1" and nonproficient immigrants as "0." For example, Asians are about 50 percent less likely (–0.502) to be proficient in understanding English than White immigrants with equal demographic characteristics.

The results in Table 9.3 highlight several important factors associated with proficiency. In general, the background factors affect oral proficiency (understanding and speaking) differently than literacy (reading and writing) proficiency. Both oral skills, however, are affected similarly by the socioeconomic variables; the same is true for literacy skills. It is not surprising, however, that years in the United States, type of education, and ethnicity are particularly important factors related to proficiency in all four English-language skills.

Given the findings of Borjas (1994) that post-1965 immigrants are less "skilled" than earlier cohorts, one can only compare in Table 9.3 the *differential effect* of years in the United States on English-language ability. For example, it is possible to discover by how many percentage points X years in the United States makes reading more likely than writing, but not how many percentage points X years in the United States affects the odds of reading (or any other skill). Carliner (1995) is able to infer the *direct effect* of years in the United States because he uses the 1980 and 1990 censuses to create a longitudinal data set, which is what is required.

Nevertheless, time in the United States is associated with a higher probability of proficiency, but this effect differs for oral and literacy skills. During the initial twenty years in the United States, immigrants are more likely to be proficient in oral than in literacy skills. For example, the differential effect of years in the United States implies that immigrants who have been in the country for six to ten years are 5 to 9 percent more likely to be proficient in oral skills than in reading and writing skills (0.105 for Reads compared to 0.192 for Understands, for example) than newly arrived immigrants.

After twenty-one to thirty years in the United States, however, proficiency in reading and writing is generally more likely. For instance, living in the United States for thirty-one to forty years implies that the probability of proficiency in literacy is about 15 percent greater than the probability of oral proficiency. In general, the first two decades in the United States are associated with greater investments in oral skills, but the acquisition of literacy skills improves dramatically after this time.

Next, the effect of schooling on English proficiency is allowed to vary with the native language of immigrants, making it possible to differentiate between the home education systems of immigrants. Regardless of which country-of-origin education is examined, however, each additional year of schooling increases the probability of literacy more than the probability of oral proficiency. For example, a Spanish-speaking immigrant with eight years of education is about 16 percent less likely to be proficient in oral skills than another Spanish-speaking immigrant with a high school diploma. The same additional four years of schooling, however, increases the probability of literacy by approximately 28 percent.

Similarly, education is a significant variable explaining speaking, reading, and writing proficiency for Asian and "other" immigrants. Since the estimated education coefficients are statistically insignificant in the two oral specifications for Europeans, this implies that further education does not affect their English oral skills. The results for the literacy regressions, however, show that education does positively affect literacy. Since reading and writing English are more sophisticated abilities, schooling is more important for literacy skills than for understanding or speaking skills. This effect may explain why recent immigrants, who have lower levels of education than earlier immigrants, are less literate than earlier immigrants (Borjas 1994). This suggests that in order to increase the literacy among recent immigrants, basic educational skills may be necessary in adult ESL courses. As a consequence, immigrants without these basic skills may fail to reach full English proficiency.

The effect of ethnicity is not statistically significant in the literacy specifications but is significant in the oral specifications. In the understanding and speaking regressions, those of Hispanic descent are over 54 to 60 percent less likely than Whites to self-report either speaking or understanding proficiently. In contrast, Blacks and "others" do not differ from Whites in speaking and understanding proficiency. Only in the "Understands" variable are Asians more likely to report being less proficient than Whites. Ethnic-specific differences among the literacy variables in Table 9.1, however, disappear after factoring in demographic characteristics. In other words, age, education, years in the United States, and English-language courses explain ethnic English-literacy differences.

Since the NALS was given only in Spanish and English, it is not surprising to find that Spanish speakers are more likely to report being less proficient. In fact, regression analysis is supposed to eliminate this aspect of the sample design by including the ethnicity variable. The various regression results clearly indicate that the odds of proficiency in literacy skills do not vary across ethnic groups.

Consequently, politicians and others who proclaim that linguistic differences are preventing the development of English as the unifying language are wrong. Rather than espousing English Only to remedy this perceived ethnic disunity, Americans should embrace the English Plus Resolution, which proclaims that "multilingualism, or the ability to speak languages in addition to English, is a tremendous resource to the United States because . . . [it] promotes greater cross-cultural understanding between different racial and ethnic groups" (H.Cong.Res. 4).

Immigrants who take and complete a course to learn English are markedly more likely to be proficient than other immigrants. Those immigrants who *complete* a course to learn English are about 9 to 13 percent more likely to be proficient at reading and writing, and about 14 to 20 percent more likely to be proficient at understanding and speaking English than immigrants who never enrolled in English-language classes. Those who enroll but do not complete an ESL course, however, report lower proficiency rates than those who never enrolled. The 13 to 24 percent lower probability may result from the fact that those who drop out are harsher critics of their own English-language ability after failing to complete a course than others who complete the course and increase their English ability. Furthermore, those who never enroll in ESL courses may lack an understanding of the difficulties and challenges of English-language acquisition, and may therefore overestimate their English-language proficiency.

In sum, however, it is difficult to discern why immigrants who drop out of English classes are more likely to report lower proficiency in all four English-language abilities. Although education should not be a factor in these results, my tabulations show that persons who complete these courses average nearly fourteen years of schooling, while those who drop out average only ten years.

Policymakers interested in increasing English proficiency among immigrants must focus on the needs of less educated immigrants. Since it is possible that more educated immigrants took a course to learn English as part of their education in their home countries and will therefore succeed more often, less educated immigrants will struggle not only with English but also with the rudimentary skills such as reading and writing needed to master the new language.

Unfortunately, the possibility exists that policymakers interested in looking effective by reporting high proficiency rates among the "graduates" will limit not only availability of the course to those who are more likely to succeed but also the length of these courses. Given these and the education results discussed previously, quite the opposite is recommended. Specifically, as a high percentage of persons who enroll drop out, adult ESL courses should include methods that emphasize completion of the course.

While no curriculum recommendations are possible from these results, English teachers should note that the less educated students in their classrooms are at higher risk of dropping out. They should therefore focus part of class time on making sure these students do not feel lost or frustrated compared to their more educated classmates. One suggestion might be to group several less educated students with the more educated students and encourage group members to help each other. Furthermore, given the demands of attending ESL courses, plus the need to provide for a family by working one or more jobs at or near minimum wage, it is necessary to structure courses which are flexible enough to meet the needs of immigrants. This approach would go a long way in promoting success in ESL courses and reducing the dropout rate.

The Monetary Value of English Skills

The previous section demonstrated that the correlation of English-language skills is lowest between literacy and oral variables. Since most national surveys contain information only on speaking ability, it is important also to consider the relative monetary rewards of literacy as well as oral skills. The existence of such variables in the NALS makes it possible to evaluate the productivity value of these skills. This section adds to the research of Chiswick (1991), McManus (1990), Rivera-Batiz (1990, 1991), and others who recognize the limitations of a single English variable in earnings regressions.

To determine the monetary rewards associated with proficiency in each English-language skill, Table 9.4 presents the

TABLE 9.4. Predicted Weekly Earnings by English Proficiency[a]

English Proficiency	Not Proficient	Proficient
Understands	$377	$440
	(8.4)	(9.9)
Speaks	$379	$444
	(8.4)	(9.8)
Reads	$393	$441
	(8.8)	(9.9)
Writes	$396	$446
	(8.9)	(10.0)

[a] The values are from log weekly wage regressions. Standard errors in parentheses.

average predicted weekly wages from ordinary least-squares regressions of the logarithm of actual weekly earnings on demographic variables, plus each English-language skill. The demographic variables are age, age-squared, education, marital status, ethnicity, years in the United States, and census region of residence. As four English-language skills were considered, four different sets of predicted earnings were estimated.

Table 9.4 shows that predicted earnings are lower when there is a lack of oral proficiency than when there is a lack of literacy. For example, the first row indicates that immigrants who are not proficient at speaking English earn an average of $379 per week, but those who do speak English proficiently earn $444 per week. Those who become proficient in speaking or understanding English increase their earnings by about 17 percent. However, the percentage increase in earnings resulting from proficiency in either reading or writing is only about 12 percent.

The association between oral skills found in this study is identical to that reported by Borjas (1994) for speaking proficiency. The lower percent increase in earnings resulting from literacy skills, however, reveals a dichotomy in the rewards of English proficiency. Earnings increase from 12 to 17 percent when immigrants become proficient in a particular skill. Relying on speaking ability to estimate the monetary rewards of English proficiency results in an estimate that is at the upper limit of the rewards range. Given the earlier findings that oral proficiency is more likely than literacy proficiency during the initial years after immigration, immigrants reap the highest rewards possible by learning to understand and speak English. Once they attain proficiency in literacy skills, earnings increase by a smaller percentage.

Summary and Discussion

This chapter used data from the National Adult Literacy Survey (U.S. Dept. of Education 1997) to investigate the determinants of the proficiency of immigrants in four English-language skills: understanding, speaking, reading, and writing. The NALS provides a large representative sample of immigrants to examine these skills simultaneously, an advantage over past studies.

Table 9.1 showed that immigrants have a greater mastery of English oral skills than literacy skills. The most important variables explaining part of this difference are years in the United States, education, and the possible higher labor market returns to oral skills. During the initial years in the United States, oral skills are learned much more quickly than literacy skills, but literacy skills improve significantly after more than twenty years in the United States. Formal education aids English acquisition, especially for immigrants from Spanish-speaking and Asian countries, but it increases the probability of literacy more than the probability of oral skills.

The study also found that background variables affect oral fluency (speaking and understanding) differently than literacy (reading and writing). Finally, attending only part of an English-language course does not result in proficiency. Immigrants who complete these courses are more likely to be proficient. Policymakers interested in increasing the English skills of immigrants must also be prepared to provide ESL courses with basic-skills content.

Just as oral and literacy skills respond differently to the independent factors, earnings are affected differently by oral and literacy skills. Oral fluency, whether proficiency in speaking or understanding English, is associated with greater earnings than proficiency in either writing or reading English.

These results indicate that proficiency in oral skills results in greater income gains than proficiency in literacy. On the other hand, if immigrants have limited labor market opportunities and are employed in jobs that do not require extensive reading and writing skills, then proficiency in literacy skills does not pay. Furthermore, oral skills are easier to acquire than literacy skills, and immigrants may be maximizing short-term income by acquiring these skills. After some time in the United States, immigrants acquire literacy skills but do not see large increases in income. As the acquisition of these skills takes place at the same time that a decline in income is observed among workers (usually after the age of forty-five), it is not necessarily a surprise that such a small increase in wages accompanies literacy.

Table 9.1 showed that immigrants are better at speaking and understanding than at reading and writing English. One possible reason for this outcome is that immigrants acquire the skills most valued by the labor market. Another reason is that the costs of learning how to speak and understand English are lower than those of reading and writing. Consequently, because English-speaking and comprehension skills are learned during the initial twenty years in the United States, ESL courses might wish to revolve their curriculum around English-fluency skills for newly arrived immigrants so that they may reap the monetary rewards of these skills for the longest possible time. For older immigrants, ESL courses should concentrate on English reading and writing skills, as these are the skills which immigrants acquire after twenty-one years in the United States. The findings that proficiency in literacy skills increases after twenty years in the United States, and that improvements in oral skills diminish after this time, stress the importance of analyzing aspects of English proficiency other than speaking ability.

Although this study emphasized the monetary value of English skills as an incentive for immigrants to learn English, it found evidence that immigrants also learn how to read and write despite the relatively small rewards associated with literacy. One interpretation is that immigrants learn English for social, political, and other noneconomic reasons. If this interpretation is correct, it contradicts the perceptions that immigrants must be forced to learn English by making it the official language.

English acquisition is a dynamic process which continues many years after arriving in the United States. It is not true that current immigrants will not increase their proficiency in English. Over half of all immigrants who participated in the NALS arrived during the 1980s, and the English-proficiency rates in Table 9.1 partly reflect the fact that many of the immigrants are just beginning to acquire English skills. The political implications are clear:

if the English Only movement is based on the assumption that immigrants must be forced to learn English because its usage is not widespread, then such legislation is ill-advised. Immediate labor market rewards, time in the United States, high levels of education, and success in English-language courses increase the odds of proficiency. English-language acquisition has not stagnated. Just as turn-of-the-century immigrants (who represented a higher percentage of the U.S. population than today's immigrants) needed time to acclimate, recent immigrants must be allowed to undergo the same process.

Policymakers can serve this process not by legislating English, but by fostering programs that aid its acquisition. For example, rather than cutting back on English-language courses, more should be provided to accommodate the time schedules of immigrants who must work to support themselves and their families. These courses must also address any remedial education issues among the students and structure their curriculum to minimize dropouts. Since time is observed to affect proficiency, English-language courses should not be fast paced. These courses must be paced so that students can adequately absorb a lesson before proceeding to the next one. Accommodating the needs of students improves the learning experience, which in turn increases the likelihood of proficiency.

The results of this study, therefore, dispel the myth that immigrants are not learning English. Since an increase in proficiency rates among immigrants already in the United States is inevitable, the United States should not be concentrating on limiting multilingualism. The ability to communicate in various languages is a positive, not a negative, attribute, yet the majority of current policymakers would limit the number of languages to only one. The English Plus Resolution proposed by Congressman Jose Serrano, representing the 16th District in the South Bronx, New York, encourages the acquisition of English, plus the retention of all other languages in the United States, including indigenous languages. This type of legislation approaches the problem of English-language acquisition from a positive point of view and hence fosters greater ethnic unity than the majority of the proposed English Only laws. Greater facility in languages is a benefit, not only socially, but also in the new global economy.

Acknowledgments

The author would like to express his thanks to Ed Funkhouser, Jon Sonstelie, and Steve Trejo, who provided excellent comments and guidance, and to Stefanie Schmidt and Roseann Dueñas González, who also provided valuable comments on this chapter.

Works Cited

Borjas, George J. 1994. "The Economics of Immigration." *Journal of Economic Literature* 2: 1667–1717.

Carliner, Geoffrey. 1995. "The Language Ability of U.S. Immigrants: Assimilation and Cohort Effects." *NBER [National Bureau of Economic Research] Working Paper Series* No. 5222.

Chiswick, Barry R. 1991. "Speaking, Reading, and Earnings among Low-Skilled Immigrants." *Journal of Labor Economics* 9: 149–70.

Chiswick, Barry R., and Paul W. Miller. 1995. "The Endogeneity between Language and Earnings: International Analyses." *Journal of Labor Economics* 13: 246–88.

———. 1996. "Ethnic Networks and Language Proficiency." *Journal of Population Economics* 9: 19–35.

English Plus Resolution. H.Con.Res. 4. IH. January 7, 1997. Serrano.

Espinosa, Kristin, and Douglas S. Massey. 1997. "Determinants of English Proficiency among Mexican Migrants to the United States." *International Migration Review* 31: 28–50.

Funkhouser, Edward. 1996. "How Much of Immigrant Wage Assimilation Is Related to English Language Acquisition?" Unpublished manuscript, Department of Economics, UC Santa Barbara.

Greene, William H. 1993. *Econometric Analysis*. New York: Macmillian.

H.J. Res. 37. Proposing an amendment to the Constitution of the United States establishing English as the official language of the United States. February 4, 1997. Mr. Doolittle.

H.R. 123. English Language Empowerment Act. August 1, 1996. Bill Emerson.

H.R. 622. To amend title 4, United States Code, to declare English as the official language of the government of the United States. February 5, 1997. Mr. Stump.

H.R. 1005. To amend title 4, United States Code, to declare English as the official language of the government of the United States, and for other purposes. March 11, 1997. Mr. King.

Kominski, Robert. 1989. *How Good Is "How Well?" An Examination of the Census English-Speaking Ability Question.* Unpublished manuscript, Bureau of the Census.

McManus, Walter. 1985. "Labor Market Costs of Language Disparity: An Interpretation of Hispanic Earnings Differences." *American Economic Review* 75: 818–27.

———. 1990. "Labor Market Effects of Language Enclaves." *Journal of Human Resources* 25: 228–52.

McManus, Walter, William Gould, and Finis Welch. 1983. "Earnings of Hispanic Men: The Role of English Language Proficiency." *Journal of Labor Economics* 1: 101–30.

Rivera-Batiz, Francisco L. 1990. "English Language Proficiency and the Economic Progress of Immigrants." *Economic Letters* 34: 295–300.

———. 1991. "The Effects of Literacy on the Earnings of Hispanics in the United States." In Edwin Melendez, Clara Rodriguez, and Janis Barry Figueroa, eds., *Hispanics in the Labor Force: Issues and Policies.* New York: Plenum. 53–75.

S. 323. To amend title 4, United States Code, to declare English as the official language of the government of the United States. February 13, 1997. Mr. Shelby.

U.S. Department of Education, National Center for Education Statistics. 1997. *Technical Report and Data File Users Manual for the*

National Adult Literacy Survey, NCES 97-060, by Lynn Jenkins, Anne Campell, Kentaro Yamamoto, Irwin Kirsch, Norma Harris, Don Rock, Pat O'Reilly, Leyla Mohadjer, Joseph Waksberg, Huseyn Goksel, John Burke, Martha Berlin, Sue Reiger, James Green, Peter Mosenthal, and Andrew Kolstad. Washington, D.C.: U.S. Government Printing Office.

Veltman, Calvin. 1983. *Language Shift in the United States.* Berlin: Mouton.

WHAT DIFFERENCE DOES DIFFERENCE MAKE?

O ne crucial aspect of the Official English debate is that it forces us to revisit the discussion about the value of difference in society. As many critical analysts have pointed out, the proponents of Official English seem to either value homogeneity or wish to "remedy" differences by refurbishing various historically discredited concepts of unity. In this section, Rosina Lippi-Green addresses this issue when she asserts that the conflict of language in society cannot be simply dichotomized in terms of racism versus tolerance because the core question the American public has been trying to address in these language debates is whether social justice and equality require acceptance or elimination of differences.

The rationale for Lippi-Green's conclusion resides in the complexity of the language conflict she examines. As is well-known, in the most heated days of the Ebonics debate, many prominent public personalities of the African American community rejected the idea that African American Vernacular English and standard English be accorded equal attention in public education. The material Lippi-Green examines in this chapter challenges linguists and opponents of Official English politics with the same puzzling controversies: While linguists confidently define Ebonics, or for that matter any other non-standard language variety, as a neutral system of linguistic structures, nonlinguists, including many speakers of these stigmatized varieties, define language "on the basis of their personal relationship to the sociocultural context in which the language functions."

The inclusion of the Ebonics conflict in the Official English debate is important for two reasons: first, it forces us to deny easy answers; second, it is a warning sign that the political enforcement of a language standard threatens not simply the more recent immigrant population, but in fact a large group of U.S. citizens whose long historical struggle for equal rights and respect in this country is still not fully accomplished.

The social groups represented in Frances R. Aparicio's study grapple with similar language conflicts. This chapter portrays Hispanic/Latino students in the United States as caught between two incompatible worlds. As a result, they endure an unfair amount of social criticism both in school, where their accent betrays them as being different, and in their homes, where the elder members of their family perceive them as betraying their Spanish-language heritage. In both cases, the purity of standards is threatened by the presence of difference. One source of difference, Aparicio argues, is the conflicting social value of Spanish learned in the home as opposed to Spanish learned in school. Aparicio's discussion makes it easy to conclude that there is a dual market system operant in the United States in which the value of cultural capital (in the sense that Bourdieu uses this term) changes depending on the social status of the holder of this capital. If Spanish is learned at home, it is devalued; if Spanish is learned by an English speaker in the classroom, it is valued. Aparicio examines her students' painful personal experiences of dispossession in the broader social context of subtle and manipulative internal colonialization, which in the twentieth century has replaced the more brutal forms of classical colonialization by military intervention. If viewed through the lens of colonialism, Aparicio concludes, the project of defining social unity as linguistic homogeneity amounts to using language to control a culturally disparate citizenship.

The remaining chapters in this section are examples of successful pedagogical approaches to addressing cultural and linguistic difference in the classroom. Gail Y. Okawa teaches a survey course of linguistics for future teachers. Her students come from a monolingual environment, unaware of speakers of other languages and ignorant of their own linguistic history. Through a series of important realizations gained from the sociolinguistic literature and from the narratives of bilingual and bicultural individuals, Okawa's students become better prepared as teachers to empathize with the linguistically diverse population they will encounter in their classrooms. As this example shows, if well designed, even one class of linguistics can go a long way in changing prejudiced attitudes into positive language awareness.

Victoria Cliett and Louise R. Connal represent the large community of college-level writing teachers who face issues of language and diversity in their writing classes on a daily basis. Cliett reviews sociolinguistic literature to highlight the multidimensional nature of language, and argues that standard English is authenticated by a dominant social class as a neutral language for the purpose of disempowering those social groups whose language is legitimated for private and limited contexts only. The message that it is acceptable to be linguistically different as long as you keep it in the closet, however, not only hurts the groups whose language is thus deprived of social and public value, but it also deprives the public of the productive value of diversity. A similarly radical approach informs Louise Connal's pedagogy, which she terms "transcultural rhetoric." It is an experiment to enhance the productive and textual benefits of sharing language and discourse with "others" in the classroom. Connal's Puerto Rican roots foster her awareness of how diversity and difference shape the individual. To associate the colorful mix of languages and influences with impurity, as some cultural conservatives do, harms many without explaining anything. In Connal's classroom, students are encouraged to explore and exchange their differences for the purpose of enriching their writing "muscle" and to broaden their repertoire of styles, genres, and discourses.

As these examples of successful pedagogical interventions informed by postcolonial theory or sociolinguistic interpretations of language demonstrate, there are ways to incorporate both linguistic and cultural difference in education, but such efforts require more than English Only instruction. They require a study of the nature and origin of differences and a new concept of unity that derives from the understanding gained by facing diversity instead of denying or eliminating it.

CHAPTER TEN

That's Not My Language: The Struggle to (Re)Define African American English

ROSINA LIPPI-GREEN
Western Washington University

On October 9, 1998, a distinctive quarter-page advertisement appeared in the *New York Times*. In it, an African American figure reminiscent of Martin Luther King, Jr. stands with his back turned to a bold proclamation in white print: "I HAS A DREAM." The text makes its case by appealing directly to African Americans:

> Does this bother you? It should. We've spent over 400 years fighting for the right to have a voice. Is this how we'll use it? More importantly, is this how we'll teach our children to use it? If we expect more of them, we must not throw our hands in the air and agree with those who say our children cannot be taught. By now, you've probably heard about Ebonics (aka, black English). And if you think it's become a controversy because white America doesn't want us messing with their precious language, don't. White America couldn't care less what we do to segregate ourselves.
>
> The fact is language is power. And we can't take that power away from our children with Ebonics. Would Dr. Martin Luther King, Malcolm X, and all the others who paid the price of obtaining our voice with the currency of their lives embrace this? If you haven't used your voice lately, consider this an invitation.

SPEAK OUT AGAINST EBONICS

The National Head Start Association
1651 Prince Street, Alexandria, VA 22314

The National Head Start Association (NHSA) is a private, not-for-profit membership organization representing some two thousand federally funded Head Start programs across the country. These educational programs address the needs of poor children up to the age of five. The NHSA message is quite clear: to succeed, the African American community must assimilate linguistically. Allegiance to home and community by linguistic means is an acceptance of poverty, ignorance, and prejudice. The authorities called upon to give credence to this message are the men who gave their lives for equal rights. Here, Ebonics is not a fully functioning variety of English, a symbol of solidarity and allegiance, but a disaster for the African American community.

What is not generally known about this ad is that it was not conceptualized or written by the NHSA: it was the product of a collaboration between a group called Atlanta's Black Professionals and three prominent ad agencies. The ad won the 1998 grand prize of the annual Athena Award offered by the Newspaper Association of America; the *New York Times* ran it free, as a public service announcement.[1] According to executives at the ad agencies, the advertisement was popular when it first ran in Atlanta, and a poster-sized version was requested by schools from Miami to Richmond.[2]

It is clear that this advertisement follows directly from the national debate on what has come to be known as the Oakland Ebonics controversy.[3] What is unclear—and the far more important question—is this: How did we come to this place where successful African American professionals, a national education organization, and the most prominent daily newspaper in the United States not only collaborate to disseminate such divisive and exclusionary rhetoric, but also award each other for it? Does an organization dedicated to the education of poor children really intend to advocate that we turn our backs on speakers who cannot or will not assimilate to corporate conceptions of "good English"? And perhaps the most difficult question: What are linguists, parents, and teachers who are dedicated to the education of all children to do in the face of such beliefs and tactics?

The only place to begin this debate is at the very beginning, because at the bottom of this controversy lies a simple fact: we have no common definitions from which to depart. The variety of

English under debate has had many names, including Ebonics,[4] Black English (BE), Black English Vernacular (BEV), Black Vernacular English (BVE), African American Vernacular English (AAVE) and most recently, African American Language.[5] This multiplicity of terms may be confusing, but that is not surprising: we do not agree about what to call this language, what it is, or who speaks it. For the most part, we do not even seem to realize that we do not agree.

An attempt to define any language (such as English, Swahili, Tagalog) or variety of language (such as Cockney, Brooklynese, Hawai'ian Creole) will always be confounded by political and cultural complications. However objective *linguistic* definitions of a given language may be, no matter how detailed the description of phonology, intonation, lexicon, syntax, semantics, and rhetorical features, nonlinguists will define the language on the basis of their personal relationship to the sociocultural context in which the language functions. While we begin here with linguistic observations, it is important to remember that without an understanding of the political and social parameters of competing definitions, we can never hope to resolve differences of opinion.

Linguistic Definitions of AAVE

Linguists call AAVE "a variety of English" to avoid the political and ideological quagmire around terms such as "language" and "dialect." We can say without fear of immediate contradiction (by linguists) that AAVE is a variety of English with a structured, rule-governed grammar, spoken primarily (but not exclusively) by the majority of African Americans, usually in social contexts where other AAVE speakers predominate. Most recently, Mufwene, Rickford, Bailey, and Baugh (1998) provide a body of work which once again establishes AAVE as a variety of English with supraregional phonological and grammatical features, but also with significant social, stylistic, and regional variation, as is to be expected of any spoken language. That is, the language of African Americans living in the rural South is different from that of the Latino and European Americans who live alongside them, but it is also different from the AAVE spoken in urban centers in the South (Cukor-Avila 1995). Morgan and DeBerry (1995) provide insight into the way that African American youth integrated into urban hip hop culture must choose among grammatical, lexical, and phonological variables which identify them as aligned with either the West or East Coast.

AAVE is, in short, a functional spoken language which depends on structured variation to layer social meaning into discourse. Like all language, it is emblematic: it serves to encode all kinds of social information as part of the communicative process.

In linguistic terms, we can look at issues of pronunciation and intonation (phonetics and phonology), the ways in which words are constructed (morphology), sentence order (syntax), lexicon (vocabulary, which would include the popular concept of "slang"), and rhetorical devices. Some of these features will show similarity to other varieties of English; some seem to be particular to AAVE. For example, the substitution of /k/ for /t/ in /str/ clusters (street > [skrit]) is apparently unique to AAVE (Bailey and Thomas 1998, 89), while copula deletion—a very salient feature of AAVE—("She is gone" > "She gone") is also found in many other varieties of English (as well as in other languages, such as Russian).

Smitherman (1977) makes clear the complexity of defining AAVE when she points out that cultural and stylistic elements are just as important as phonology and syntax, and she provides examples of how these elements work together:

> Think of black speech as having two dimensions: language and style. Though we will separate the two for purposes of analysis, they are often overlapping. This is an important point, frequently overlooked in discussions of Black English. . . . Reverend Jesse Jackson preach[es]: "Africa would if Africa could. America could if America would. But Africa cain't and America ain't." Now here Reverend Jesse is using the language of Black Dialect when he says "ain't" and when he pronounced can't as "cain't". But the total expression, using black rhythmic speech, is the more powerful because the Reb has plugged into the style of Black Dialect. The statement thus depends for full communication on what black poet Eugene Redmond calls "songified" patterns and on an Afro-American cultural belief set. (3)

Given this perspective, it is difficult to claim that only poor or working-class African Americans are speakers of AAVE. Upper-middle-class blacks may seldom or never use grammatical features of AAVE, but such persons are often heard marking their language in a variety of ways to signal solidarity with the greater African American community. This may mean the use of AAVE intonation, tag questions, and address systems, or, more subtly, rhetorical features and discourse strategies. Smitherman's analysis of culturally specific rhetorical styles makes one thing very clear: even when no grammatical, phonological, or lexical features of AAVE are used, a person can, *in effect*, still be speaking AAVE by means of rhetorical devices. Thus, while the core grammatical features of AAVE may be heard most consistently in poorer black communities where there are strong social and communication networks, AAVE phonology (particularly intonation) and black rhetorical style are heard, on occasion, from prominent and successful African Americans in public forums.

Thus we have a body of empirical research which serves as a basis for defining the linguistic features of AAVE. In spite of this work, much of it done by African American scholars, there is little agreement in the black community about what AAVE is, or who speaks it.

From the Inside Out: AAVE as It Is Seen by Its Speakers

By the *linguistic* definition of AAVE, Oprah Winfrey, Clarence Thomas, and Reverend Jesse Jackson—all masters of public speaking—are AAVE speakers who, dependent on audience and topic, sometimes style-shift toward other varieties of English. But two of these African Americans have come out on numerous occasions with strong negative reactions to the very idea of AAVE. When the Oakland Ebonics controversy was at its height, Oprah Winfrey, Jesse Jackson, Maya Angelou, and other successful African Americans were not hesitant to reject AAVE in the harshest terms, using arguments similar to those in the "Speak out against Ebonics" NHSA advertisement.

It was in this situation that the rift in definitions became painfully clear. Jesse Jackson's quick and negative response to the

Oakland school board's resolution on Ebonics as "an unacceptable surrender bordering on disgrace . . . [that involves] teaching down to our children" was mysterious to many who perceive him both as a persuasive and eloquent public speaker and someone who uses AAVE intonation, rhetorical features, and phonology at all times, no matter how formal his subject or audience. In the mainstream media, this obvious contradiction was never raised by European American commentators. To point out a perceived discrepancy between Jackson's own language use and his professed beliefs about language in the African American community was a politically sensitive issue no one was willing to take on. It was only in a smaller newspaper produced by and for African Americans in San Francisco that the scholar Maulana Karenga noted, "It's unfortunate that Jesse Jackson made such intemperate remarks about Ebonics, especially . . . since he himself is a main speaker [of it]" (Boyd 1996, 28).

Many African Americans recite lists of prominent black leadership in their rejection of AAVE. Oprah Winfrey (DiMaio 1987) calls Martin Luther King, Jr., Whitney Young, and Mary McLeod Bethune speakers of "standard English." She cites Jesse Jackson as an example of someone who speaks AAVE but knows how to shift in his public discourse to a style appropriate for the most formal settings. She does not note the fact that Jesse Jackson strongly marks his public discourse with AAVE rhetorical devices; instead, she quotes Jackson's famous statement that "excellence is the best deterrent to racism," but she fails to discuss her equation between lack of excellence and the language of the African American community. For Rachel Jones, an African American woman writing an essay for *Newsweek* entitled "What's Wrong with Black English" (1990), Malcolm X, Martin Luther King, Jr., Toni Morrison, Alice Walker, James Baldwin, Andrew Young, Tom Bradley, and Barbara Jordan don't talk black or not black; they "talk right." This conclusion follows from her observation that none of these people employ or employed AAVE grammar or idiom in their public addresses—an assertion clearly countered by hard evidence.

In all these cases, those African Americans who serve as role models for black children are excluded as possible speakers of AAVE because of their leadership, contributions, and success.

This strategy moves the definition of AAVE out of the realm of the linguistic into the cultural and political. The puzzling gulf between Jesse Jackson's pronouncements on AAVE and his own usage of that variety of English originates in this artificial narrowing of the definition, whereby AAVE becomes a language of a particular kind of African American community, one from which Jackson, Jones, Winfrey, and Angelou, as well as Atlanta's Black Professionals, choose to separate themselves. In this approach, AAVE becomes the language of those African Americans who resist the priorities, politics, and view of the world of these prominent African Americans.

But theirs is not the only definition. While the mainstream media may ignore them, other prominent African Americans have refused to reject AAVE or its speakers and have argued for tolerance and acceptance. The most cited example is surely James Baldwin's (1979) moving editorial "If Black English Isn't a Language, Then Tell Me, What Is?" Another is June Jordan's (1985) essay "Nobody Mean More to Me Than You and the Future Life of Willie Jordan," which recounts the way her students faced this conflict head-on.

Many accept AAVE as a valid language even while they conclude that bidialectalism and selective assimilation to corporate English norms are practical realities. The fact that black children with aspirations outside their own communities must learn a language of wider communication (LWC) (Smitherman 1995) is usually acknowledged as a fact of life. Opinions on this range from sober utilitarianism and resignation to righteous anger:

> Pragmatic reality forces the burden of adjustment on groups who are outside positions of influence and power. It does little good to claim that street speech is a valid dialect—which it is—when the social cost of linguistic and other differences can be so high. (Baugh 1983, 122)
>
> JOHN BAUGH, *linguist*

> The worst of all possible things that could happen would be to lose that language. There are certain things I cannot say without recourse to my language. It's terrible to think that a child with five different present tenses comes to school to be faced with those books that are less than his own language. And then to be told things about his language, which is him,

that are sometimes permanently damaging. . . . This is a really cruel fallout of racism. I know the Standard English. I want to use it to help restore the other language, the lingua franca. (LeClaire 1994, 123–24)

TONI MORRISON, author, poet, Nobel Prize winner

Language is political. That's why you and me, my Brother and Sister, that's why we sposed to choke our natural self into the weird, lying, barbarous, unreal, white speech and writing habits that the schools lay down like holy law. Because, in other words, the powerful don't play; they mean to keep that power, and those who are the powerless (you and me) better shape up mimic/ape/suck-in the very image of the powerful, or the powerful will destroy you—you and our children. (Jordan 1989, 32)

JUNE JORDAN, poet, writer, political activist

But my opinion always has been that you have to learn to survive in the real world, and if you speak black English there's no way you're going to survive. There's no way you're going to get a job that you really want. There's no way that you're going to make an income that's going to make you live right. (Speicher and McMahon 1992, 399)

FEMALE UNIVERSITY STAFF

The greater African American community does not reject AAVE or redefine it in exclusionary terms, but for the most part it also accepts the inevitability of linguistic assimilation in certain settings. Along with this realization often comes deep unhappiness about this necessity. But this cannot be surprising. To make the two statements "I acknowledge that my home language is viable and adequate" and "I acknowledge that my home language will never be accepted" is to set up an unresolvable conflict:

Suspicion and skepticism are common Black reactions to Black users of LWC rhetorical styles. These perceptions exist simultaneously with the belief that one needs to master LWC in order to "get ahead." I call it "linguistic push-pull"; Du Bois calls it "double consciousness." The farther removed one is from mainstream "success," the greater the degree of cynicism about this ethnolinguistic, cultural ambivalence. Jesse Jackson knows about this; so did Malcolm X and Martin

Luther King; so does Louis Farrakhan. The oratory of each is LWC in its grammar but AVT [African Verbal Tradition] in its rhetorical style. (Smitherman 1995, 238)

The problem is this: while prominent and successful African Americans qualify their definitions of AAVE with social criteria outside of language, the rest of the country continues to use primarily linguistic criteria. To most non-black Americans, even the simplest intonation features signal AAVE, with all the attendant (and often overtly negative) associations.

Nonblack Reactions to African American Language

Broad condemnations of AAVE that extend to criticisms of African American culture and values are not difficult to document. AAVE seems to symbolize a willful and stubborn resistance to a cultural mainstreaming process. For nonblacks, this process is seen as the logical and reasonable cost of equality—and following from that, success—in other realms. AAVE evokes a kind of panic, a dread suspicion that desegregation has not done its job. The reasoning seems to be that the logical conclusion to a successful civil rights movement is the end of racism, *not because we have come to accept difference, but because we have eliminated difference.* There will be no need for a distinct African American culture or language because "those people" will have full access to, and control of, the superior European American one.

Expressions of this kind of logic are easy to find, as in this sports column:

Ungrammatical street talk by black professional athletes, and other blacks in public professions such as the music industry, has come to be accepted. Indeed, "Moses, you is a baaad damn shootin' individual" comes a lot closer to proper English usage than many public sentences uttered by black athletes. . . . But there's a problem here. Black athletes—and black musicians and TV performers, etc.,—are role models for young black children. We in the media have begun to pass on the street language of black "superstars" verbatim . . . and what this is doing is passing the message to a whole new generation of black children that it's OK to talk that way; more than OK, it's terrific to talk that way. . . . [T]he situation is compounded by leading black characters in several network television shows, who use street grammar to advance the feeling that they are young and cool.

The dilemma is that it doesn't make much difference for the black professional athletes, etc., who talk this way—they're wealthy men who are going to live well off their bodily skills no matter if they can talk at all, much less correctly. . . . [But] if a black child emulates one of the dumb-talking black athletes he sees being interviewed on TV, he is not going to be thought of as a superstar. He is going to be thought of as a stupid kid, and later, as a stupid adult. . . . They probably aren't talking that way because they think it's right; they're talking that way because it's a signal that they reject the white, middle-class world that they have started to live in the midst of. (Greene 1979)

Greene identifies two professions that he associates with successful African Americans: sports and entertainment. What these people have in common, in his estimation, is the fact that they speak AAVE, that they are in the public eye, and that they have the power to lead the black youth of America astray. His point, factually true, is that with the exception of these two groups, very few African Americans who achieve mainstream economic and social success are able to do so without the necessity of linguistic and, to some degree, cultural assimilation.

What seems to bother Greene so much is the fact that the gatekeeping mechanism is not perfect: it does not extend to all African Americans. Some have successfully evaded the language of what he freely identifies as that of the white middle class. It irritates him that these people have managed to become successful without "good language," but there is something even more upsetting. As a sports journalist, he finds himself compelled to pass on the language he hears from athletes, thus becoming complicit in letting the secret out to black children: not all African Americans give in linguistically, and yet they still get to the top.

Greene makes a series of factually incorrect assumptions. Black children learn AAVE not from television actors and sports figures but in their homes, as their first and native variety of U.S. English. More important, Greene assumes that the only role models African American children have are these sports and entertainment individuals, and further, that a good role model will not sound black. For him, the two are mutually exclusive. His message is clearly stated: "If you're a black child, and you're not one of the 100 or so best slam-dunkers or wide receivers in the world, you can go ahead and emulate the way you hear your heroes talk. But the chances are that you'll wind up as the hippest dude passing out towels in the men's washroom" (1979).

The stereotypes that underlie Greene's assumptions are disturbing, but there are other issues here which are more subtle and perhaps more damaging. His threats are real enough: black children who don't learn white English will have limited choices; what he claims is demonstrably true. But the inverse of this situation, the implied promise, is not equally true: black children who leave AAVE behind will not be given automatic access to the rewards and possibilities of the white middle-class world. Greene actually touches on the fallacy underlying this promise when he acknowledges later in his column that successful blacks who wear uniforms (such as airline pilots or army officers) in public places are often taken for service personnel.

While some prominent African Americans choose to deal with the conflicts inherent to public discussions of AAVE by redefining the language in the narrowest terms, there are non-African Americans who take the opposite strategy: AAVE is emblematic of the whole black community, its priorities and worldview.

Nonblack discomfort with AAVE is often externalized in a paternalistic voice, which can be seen to work in a variety of forums, including popular fiction. The novel is one of the most interesting points of access to current language ideology, because the way in which characters use language and talk about language can be revealing of white attitudes in the real world. The following excerpt from a romance novel titled *Family Blessings* provides a typical social construction of an idealized relationship between a middle-class, middle-American English speaker and an AAVE speaker. Here the hero, a young white police officer, has taken on the job of setting an African American child straight:

> "Yo."
> "What you talkin' like a black boy for?"
> "What *you* talkin' like a black boy for?"
> "I be black."

"You might be, but no sense talking like a dumb one if you ever want to get anywhere in this world. . . ."

"I could turn you in for dat, you know. Teachers in school can't even make us change how we talk. It's the rules. We got our culture to preserve."

"I'm not your teacher, and if you ask me, you're preserving the wrong side of your culture. . . . [L]isten to you, talking like a dummy! I told you, if you want to get out someday and make something of yourself and have a truck like this and a job where you can wear decent clothes and people will respect you, you start by talking like a smart person, which you are. I could hack that oreo talk if it was real, but the first time I picked you up for doing the five-finger discount over at the SA station, you talked like every other kid in your neighborhood. . . ."

"I'm twelve years old. You not supposed to talk to me like dat."

"Tell you what—I'll make you a deal. I'll talk to you nicer if you'll talk to me nicer. And the first thing you do is stop using that F word. And the second thing you do is start pronouncing words the way your first-grade teacher taught you to. The word is *that*, not *dat*." (Spencer 1995, 102–3)

Like Greene's sports column, the hero in this novel has both threats and promises for the African American child. The kind of authority cited is different: Greene draws on his own mastery of middle-class written English, as exemplified in his profession as a writer, whereas this fictional character has nothing more to underscore his pronouncements about language than his own observations and the trappings of his own success. "This is what you can have," he says, "if you start sounding like me. If you do not, you do so out of stubbornness and stupidity, and there is no hope for you."

Occasionally there is a public outpouring of pure emotion, without any of the commonsense arguments, complex rationalizations, or threats and promises which are such an integral part of more organized institutionalized subordination tactics. Such outpourings are useful, because they get right to the heart of the matter. A European American call-in viewer to the *Oprah Winfrey Show* declares, "I am sitting here just burning . . . the ones that want to speak or care to speak that way, they want to be different. I believe they put themselves that way to be separate" (DiMaio 1987).

The discourse becomes most complex—and most revealing—when African and European Americans attempt to discuss AAVE, each bringing to the discussion radically different definitions:

> BLACK WOMAN: So we gotta have our survival mechanism within our community. And our language is it. It lets us know that we all in this thing together.
>
> REPORTER: Black English is not standard English spoken badly—Black English is revenge. (*CBS Evening News*, December 5, 1985)

A black woman attempts to explain to a news reporter the positive and solidifying function of AAVE in her community. His response is at first at least partially accepting, but then he rejects her construction of the language as one with a positive function and recasts the language as a willful act of political resistance. The *Oxford English Dictionary* defines revenge as "The act of doing hurt or harm to another in return for wrong or injury suffered; satisfaction obtained by repayment of injuries" (*Oxford* 1989). AAVE is not seen as first and foremost a positive feature of a vibrant black community. Instead it is a willful act of rebellion: destructive, hurtful, and primitive in its motivations. The reporter attempts to construct an objective picture and definition of AAVE, but then falls back on more traditional views, seeing it as the weapon of excluded and resentful outsiders.

Nonblack attitudes toward AAVE are complex because AAVE taps into the most difficult and contentious issues surrounding race. AAVE makes us uncomfortable because it will not simply go away, no matter what we do to denigrate it and the people who speak it. We seek to embarrass its speakers, to ostracize them in public forums—and it persists. Even when we acknowledge its existence, our official policies toward this (and other) stigmatized varieties of language are policies of patronage and tolerance rather than acceptance. The irony is that AAVE is the distinct language of a cultural community we don't want to acknowledge as separate; at the same time, the only way we know how to deal with our discomfort about AAVE is to set it apart.

Conclusions

Definitions of AAVE are as fluid as language itself, serving purposes far beyond those on the surface. By shifting the definition of AAVE out of the realm of the linguistic into the cultural, some avoid hard questions about the costs of assimilation. Others define AAVE as broadly as possible, linking the language to the community in an attempt to censure both.

AAVE is a source of controversy between the African American community and the rest of the country, as well as within the African American community itself, because it throws a bright light on issues we do not want to face. Equal rights and equal access are good and important goals, but we demand high payment. Perhaps it is too high; certainly, AAVE persists in spite of stigmatization of the most direct and caustic kind, and despite repercussions in the form of real disadvantage and discrimination. Clearly, AAVE speakers get something from their communities and from each other that is missing in the world which is held up to them as superior.

What then is the purpose of the "Speak out against Ebonics" advertisement? Do those who subscribe to this approach truly believe that this language so closely linked to the African American community can be willed out of existence? Do they simply wish to distance themselves from it and the community it represents? Are they so focused on reinventing themselves that they are willing to turn their backs on those who hesitate to give up so much, for so little?

The advertisement won the praise of the mainstream media, but what concrete and positive steps will it bring about for the African American community? What is most disturbing about this advertisement and the reasoning behind it is the way it dismisses those who most need to be heard. "We're not wrong," says an exasperated AAVE speaker in response to criticism of himself and his language. "I'm tired of living in a country where we're always wrong" (DiMaio 1987).

Divisive rhetoric, exclusionary practices, and angry voices are strange tools to bring to such an important task as the education of young children. Teachers face a difficult task because parents do not send them a clear message. They hear "respect my culture" and at the same time they are encouraged to speak out against the language of that culture. The only hope for the students caught in the middle is a debate which begins with consistent and factual definitions. Definitions are the thorniest part of this particular controversy because they encapsulate the underlying conflicts in ideology. Thus it is no surprise that the larger issues of bi- and multilingualism in the schools seem unresolvable. With no common ground from which to depart, there can never be fruitful discussion. There is even a general lack of awareness that there is disagreement about an issue as basic as the definition of "English."

The proponents of ballot initiatives such as California's English for the Children never set foot in this difficult territory. Linguists, who are more willing to take on this topic, reject the idea of "standard" English outright and yet many of them ultimately consent to it, because while the definition is deficient in every factual way, it contains a powerful idea that most people subscribe to without thought: the belief that there is a homogenous, perfect language, a language stripped of ethnic, racial, economic, religious diversity—the one English that we should be teaching to our children, according to so many who take this as such a self-evident truth that they do not even bother to articulate it.

And here, of course, is the rub: not all Englishes are created equal in the world of English for the Children. Should one kind of linguistic diversity be wiped out, there are other battles to be fought. The other Englishes—English of the South Bronx, of Little Havana, of the Pine Ridge reservation—are the next battleground. And while we fight these battles, the real issues underlying lack of achievement go ignored, as pointed out by Cummins (1998):

> The reasons why some groups of culturally diverse students experience long-term persistent underachievement have much more to do with issues of status and power than with linguistic factors in isolation. Thus educational interventions that challenge the low status that has been assigned to a linguistic or cultural group are much more likely to be successful than those that reinforce this low status. It follows that a major criterion for judging the likely efficacy of any form of bilingual

education or all-English program is the extent to which it generates a sense of empowerment among culturally diverse students and communities by challenging the devaluation of students' identities in the wider society.

It is not possible to empower a people and a culture and simultaneously reject their language as less than perfect or acceptable. As James Baldwin pointed out twenty years ago: "It is not the Black child's language which is despised: It is his experience" (1979, E19).

Notes

1. The NHSA accepted as a donation some portion of the money that came along with the Athena Award, but it denies endorsing the advertisement for publication (Deputy Director Michael McGrady, personal communication).

2. My source for this information is a December 1998 telephone conversation with Lee St. James, who was head of the Ketchum agency in Atlanta when the ad was developed. Other corroborating information originates from e-mail correspondence with linguists who were concerned enough about the advertisement to investigate. My thanks to Geneva Smitherman, Orlando Taylor, Arthur Spears, Marcy Morgan, Rebecca Wheeler, and John Baugh.

3. The Oakland Ebonics controversy refers to the prolonged and sometimes hostile media responses and public discussions that followed the December 18, 1996, policy approval by the Oakland Unified School District (OUSD) Board of Education affirming standard American English development for all students. The policy mandated that effective instructional strategies must be utilized in order to ensure that every child has the opportunity to achieve English-language proficiency. The OUSD Board believed that recognition and understanding of the language structures unique to African American students, who comprised 53 percent of the students in the Oakland schools at the time, would enhance language development for these students.

4. Ebonics may be defined as "the linguistic and paralinguistic features which on a concentric continuum represent the communicative competence of the West African, Caribbean and United States slave descendant of African origin. It includes the various idioms, patois, argots, ideolects, and social dialects of black people" especially those who

have been forced to adapt to colonial circumstances. *Ebonics* derives its form from ebony (black) and phonics (sound, the study of sound) and refers to the study of the language of black people in all its cultural uniqueness (Williams 1975, ii).

5. I use AAVE here because it is the term currently most often used by African American linguists. The public now seems to have adopted "Ebonics" in the wake of the December 1996–February 1997 controversy surrounding the Oakland school board's pedagogical decisions, but because the term underwent almost immediate trivialization, even (or especially) in the mainstream media, many linguists avoid it.

Works Cited

Bailey, Guy, and E. Thomas. 1998. "Some Aspects of African-American Vernacular English Phonology." In Salikoko Mufwene, John Rickford, G. Bailey, and John Baugh, eds., *African-American English: Structure, History and Usage*. London: Routledge. 85–109.

Baldwin, James. 1979. "If Black English Isn't a Language, Then Tell Me, What Is?" *New York Times*. July 29: E19.

Baugh, John. 1983. *Black Street Speech: Its History, Structure, and Survival*. Austin: University of Texas Press.

Boyd, H. 1996. "Karenga on Jackson Criticism: 'Jesse Is Versed in Ebonics.'" [San Francisco] *Daily Challenge*. December 25: 27–29.

Cukor-Avila, Patricia. 1995. "The Evolution of AAVE in a Rural Texas Community: An Ethnolinguistic Study." Unpublished doctoral dissertation, University of Michigan, Ann Arbor.

Cummins, Jim. 1998. "Beyond Adversarial Discourse: Searching for Common Ground in the Education of Bilingual Students." Presentation to the California State Board of Education. University of Toronto, February 8.

DiMaio, D. (Producer). 1987, November 19. "Standard and 'Black English'" (J. McPharlin, Director). *Oprah Winfrey Show*. No. W309. Chicago: CBS.

Greene, Robert. 1979. Sports column. *Chicago Tribune*. December 3.

Jones, Rachel. 1990. "What's Wrong with Black English." In P. Eschholz, A. Rosa, and V. Clark, eds., *Language Awareness*. New York: St. Martin's Press. 93–95.

Jordan, June. 1985. *On Call: Political Essays*. Boston: South End Press. 123–39.

———. 1989. "White English/Black English: The Politics of Translation." *Moving Towards Home: Political Essays*. London: Virago Press. 29–41.

LeClair, T. 1994. "The Language Must Not Sweat." In Danille K. Taylor-Guthrie, ed., *Conversations with Toni Morrison*. Jackson: University Press of Mississippi. 119–28.

Morgan, M., and S. DeBerry. 1995. "Lexical Grammaticalization and Phonological Variation in Urban African American Hip Hop." Conference on New Ways of Analyzing Variation in English (NWAVE), Philadelphia. October.

Mufwene, Salikoko, John Rickford, Guy Bailey, and John Baugh, eds. 1998. *African-American English: Structure, History and Use*. London: Routledge.

Oxford English Dictionary, The. 1989. 2nd ed. New York: Oxford University Press.

Smitherman, Geneva. 1977. *Talkin' and Testifyin': The Language of Black America*. Detroit: Wayne State University Press.

———. 1995. "Testifyin', Sermonizin', and Signifyin': Anita Hill, Clarence Thomas, and the African American Verbal Tradition." In Geneva Smitherman, ed., *African American Women Speak Out on Anita Hill-Clarence Thomas*. Detroit: Wayne State Press. 224–42.

"Speak Out against Ebonics." 1998. *New York Times*. October 9: A19.

Speicher, B. L., and S. M. McMahon. 1992. "Some African-American Perspectives on Black English Vernacular." *Language in Society* 21(3): 383–407.

Spencer, LaVyrle. 1995. *Family Blessings*. New York: Jove.

Williams, R. L., ed. 1975. *Ebonics: The True Language of Black Folks*. St. Louis: Institute of Black Studies.

CHAPTER ELEVEN

Of Spanish Dispossessed

FRANCES R. APARICIO
University of Michigan

At first English was nothing
But sound
Like trumpets doing yakity yak
As we found meanings for the words
We noticed that many times the
Letters deceived the sound
What could we do
It was the language of a
Foreign land.

VÍCTOR HERNÁNDEZ CRUZ,
from "Snaps of Immigration," *Red Beans*

These verses describe the entry of Latino/Latina immigrants into English, the process of becoming bilingual, and the contradictory experience of gradually engaging in signification, in making meaning, through words whose sounds and phonetics are foreign and emerge from a dominant, outside culture. The poet's literary language, however, is English. Like most of Hernández Cruz's poetic oeuvre and U.S. Latino and Latina literary works, this poem today evinces the historical incorporation of Latinos/Latinas into the world of English in the aftermath of 1848 and 1898. "What could we do?" writes the Puerto Rican American poet, ironically commenting on the colonized subject's forced incorporation into the world of English, but eventually to speak, write, and think in English. As colonized subjects not unlike Shakespeare's Caliban, Richard Rodríguez in *Hunger of Memory* (1982) and Richard Rubio, the protagonist of *Pocho* (Villarreal 1959/1970), internalized the colonial values embedded in the learning of English, cannibalizing, absorbing, and appropriating the language of the colonizer. Today, for many U.S.-born Mexican Americans and Latinos/Latinas, English is not just their first and dominant language but also their only language. Other Latinos/Latinas, such as Tato Laviera, Víctor Hernández Cruz, and Alurista, have reaffirmed their bilingualism and the multidialectal textures of their bicultural experiences in their interlingual writings. Not unlike African writers who have been intellectually trained in the language of the imperial metropolis, U.S. Latino and Latina writers have been writing in English because that is the language of their intellectual formation, the language in which they have had to conceptualize their bicultural world.

In the centenary of 1898, and in the immediate aftermath of Proposition 227's electoral victory in California, a (post)colonial approach to the politics of language within the United States foregrounded how English, Spanish, and bilingualism for U.S. Latinos/Latinas constituted sites of struggle where cultural identity was reaffirmed, negotiated, and hybridized as a result of the colonial conditions in which their language acts are embedded. Since 1980, the English Only movement, attacks against bilingual education, the English for the Children initiative, anti–affirmative action legislation, and anti-immigrant laws have embodied racist forms of resistance to the institutional gains made by the civil rights movements. Because dominant forms of colonialism and military intervention would not be "democratic" or appropriate strategies for the United States to use within its own borders, the discourses of nationhood, social integration, and unity have been deployed instead, as (post)colonial arguments that racialize and exclude linguistic minorities from the body politic. Language, then, has emerged as a discursive site through which the United States, as a nation, reimagines itself as desirably homogeneous. Such a nation would necessitate one language to "glue" its culturally disparate citizens, argue the advocates of English Only and English for the Children, whose motto is "One Nation, One California" (1997). They consider the public use of Spanish and other "foreign" languages a symptom of a society balkanized by its cultural heterogeneity. By privileging language as a mutually exclusive icon of nationhood, these arguments ignore and displace the structural, socioeconomic, political, and racial factors that lead to social segregation and economic marginality.

Claiming to advocate for the social integration of immigrant children, Ron Unz and the supporters of English for the Children, including Latino/Latina public figures such as Jaime Escalante, have made learning English the sine qua non of social access to resources and to economic success (*English for the Children* 1997). The discourse in favor of dismantling bilingual education easily tapped into Latino/Latina and immigrant parents' desire to imagine their children's future success, symbolized in the possession and acquisition of English. Yet this logic ignores all of the other complex factors and social constraints that lead to, or limit, social mobility, such as "racial, class, gender, and occupational backgrounds; . . . the time, size, destination, and objectives of their immigrations; the history of their political relationship with the United States, and the economic infrastructure of the areas where they are located" (Zentella 1997, 265). In turn, Spanish has been associated with poverty and marginalization, domesticated as a language fit only for family life, undermined as a public language and as an intellectual tool, and defined as an obstacle to academic success (Aparicio 1998), a process parallel to what Alastair Pennycook has called "linguistic curtailment" (1994, 14). This discourse partly explains the overwhelming support for Proposition 227 on the part of Latino/Latina parents who have internalized these linguistic myths.

Learning and teaching English have become the symbolic torch for the internal, colonial forces of Americanization. As colonized subjects both outside and inside the imperial borders, U.S. Latinos/Latinas have been historically subjected to Americanization through policies in education, language, hygiene, and the criminal system, in the case of Puerto Ricans since 1898 and in the case of Mexican American communities after 1848. The current national language movement and the trends against bilingualism represent a continuation of the ideology of the Americanization programs previously implemented by the federal government but now spearheaded by special interest groups. In this sense, the politics of English in the U.S. Latino/Latina context reflects both the imperial expansionist and the nationalist uses of the language. According to Pennycook (1994), the discourse of English as an international language:

has moved from a rhetoric of colonial expansion, through a rhetoric of development aid to a rhetoric of the international free market. English and English teaching in these terms have been considered intrinsically good for the world, a key aspect of global development and a commodity freely traded on world markets. (6)

Arguably, the colonial presence of English in (former) British or U.S. colonies has not led to the dramatic language loss that occurs among U.S. minority groups. This difference is evident, for instance, in the strong, nationalist, and public value of Spanish on the island of Puerto Rico and its subordinated presence among mainland Puerto Ricans. Yet, as Pennycook demonstrates, even in foreign countries the imperial presence of English eventually leads to both linguistic curtailment and possible linguistic genocide. While it is true that in major U.S. cities, Spanish use has either increased or become more audible in public spaces, it is also true that U.S. Latinos/Latinas are becoming English-dominant by the second generation, a pattern that concurs with the European immigrant experience. As Ana Celia Zentella (1997) has observed, "an epidemic rate of anglicization is evident in the dramatic loss of Spanish by the second generation nationwide" (264). Yet, ironically, English Only proponents argue that English is being threatened as a national language. This either/or logic cannot account for the complexities of language use in bicultural subjects. Yet it continues to inform the debates about English and Spanish in the United States.

Moreover, the constructed primacy of English as a superior language and as the exclusive tool for achieving the American Dream continues to permeate media advertising, ESL teaching, educational policy, conflicts in the workplace, and legal and judicial decisions (Pennycook 1994; Lippi-Green 1997). Television advertisements for video and audio programs that teach English are quite common on Spanish cable television in the United States. Images of agricultural or construction workers are used to index a lack of English-language ability. Inversely, the image of a manager or executive appears as a result of having learned English, thus unequivocally equating English with economic success. It is not insignificant that these ads appear consistently during the transmission of *Sábado Gigante,* the most widely viewed Spanish program in the world.

The questions of how to learn English and how long it takes have displaced the concomitant issue of Spanish maintenance and bilingualism in the debates surrounding bilingual education and Proposition 227. A comparison here is productive. In Miami, for instance, according to Max Castro (1997), the "battle over language . . . is not about English versus Spanish but rather about English monolingualism versus bilingualism and about the eradication of Spanish or its survival" (292). In other words, what nativist English Only supporters are really struggling for is not making English per se the official language of the United States, but rather erasing Spanish within the domestic, national borders and silencing bilingualism as an option for bicultural citizens and subjects. As long as these "foreign" languages remain domesticated in the private sphere of the home, the family, and the neighborhood, they can be tolerated. Once they emerge as public languages, however, as has been the case of Spanish in Miami, Los Angeles, and other major U.S. cities where Spanish circulates in media, in the public space, and in the schools, then these so-called "foreign" languages become a social, political, and economic threat to English as both an imperial and national language. The public furor over the role of Ebonics in the classroom, triggered by pedagogical policies at the Oakland public schools, illustrated the U.S nationalist resistance to legitimate racialized forms of expression. As Rosina Lippi-Green (1997) argues, the arguments about linguistic "appropriacy" perpetuate the subordination of minority languages, while the division "between public and private languages" is also reproduced as teachers insist that standard English is the only acceptable register for public use. The message, according to Lippi-Green, is the following: "appreciate and respect the language of peripheral communities, but keep them in their place" (109).

The public voice of Latinos/Latinas who have argued against bilingual education, such as Richard Rodriguez, Linda Chavez, and Jaime Escalante, have preempted the argument that these movements are racist. By deploying Latinos/Latinas as spokespeople for English Only, U.S. English avoids being accused of ethnic warfare and promotes itself as a diverse movement interested in the social well-being of linguistic minorities and immigrants. Mario Mujica, a Chilean professional and immigrant who has been one of the most visible English Only advocates nationwide, exemplifies, precisely through his accented English, this mediating role. Ron Unz has also evoked his mother's history as an immigrant in order to legitimize his otherwise political interests as advocating for the interests of the Latino/Latina community (Bruni 1998, 24). Moreover, the participation of key Latino/Latina names in these movements' avant-garde legitimizes and authorizes these ideological positions for the larger Latino/Latina communities. These Latinos/Latinas are seen as experts because of their ethnic background and as successful immigrants who have achieved the American Dream, and this identity-based expertise displaces the research-based expertise and different perspectives that Latino/Latina scholarship brings to this debate.

Richard Rodriguez has been the most visible Latino to argue against bilingual education. U.S. audiences have had less access to the *testimonios* of diverse U.S. Latinos/Latinas than to the mainstreamed monopoly of Rodriguez's story of assimilation and cultural denial. The widely read *Hunger of Memory* (1983) is a complex and fascinating text, indeed speaking to the pain of linguistic and cultural loss. Rodriguez's logic of gaining cultural citizenship and a public identity only through English and through the inevitable loss of Spanish, however, represents only one way of negotiating the internal colonial experience of Mexican Americans. This narrative privileges the acculturation paradigm and precludes the heterogeneous experiences of young Latinos/Latinas who struggle with linguistic and educational colonial policies and attitudes and who construct their linguistic and cultural identities in other ways.

On Linguistic Dispossession

In this chapter, I examine narratives that trace the ways in which U.S. Latino/Latina students, from both college and high school, negotiate their bilingual and bicultural identities and give meaning to English and Spanish in their lives. The autoethnographic narratives written by thirty Latino/Latina college students at the University of Michigan, ten interviews with Latino/Latina high school students in southwest Detroit, and a focus group with eleven students from the same community constitute the qualitative information that forms the basis for this analysis. Together, they document the subtle workings of hegemony and the complexities of consent.

In this respect, my small sample contributes to the development of what Catherine Walsh (1991) has called "critical bilingualism," that is, "the ability to not just speak two languages, but to be conscious of the sociocultural, political, and ideological contexts in which the languages (and therefore the speakers) are positioned and function, and of the multiple meanings that are fostered in each." Walsh calls for "specific pedagogies that recognize and interrogate Puerto Rican [Latino/Latina] students' past and present realities, to include the experiences, perceptions, and voices that have traditionally been shut out, and to encourage movement toward critical bilingualism" (126–27). Here I foreground how the colonial dispossession of Spanish continues to be exercised through an educational and linguistic habitus, to use Pierre Bourdieu's term (1991). By establishing a linguistic habitus, that is, creating "a set of dispositions" that "generate practices, perceptions and attitudes" and that are "inculcated, structured, durable, generative and transposable" (Bourdieu 1991, 12), school systems domesticate Spanish and displace it onto the boundaries of family life. Moreover, dispositions such as linguistic accent and forms of speaking and writing reveal the body as "the site of incorporated history" (13). It is not coincidental that the tongue, the mouth, accents, and phonetics have been central physical, physiological, and metaphoric sites for linguistic repression. Confronting these inculcated values that are inscribed in their speech and bodies, Latino and Latina students strive to construct new cultural meanings out of the tensions between these institutional ideologies and their own personal selves, either by reclaiming Spanish or by reconstructing a bicultural identity through English.

In the context of Spanish-language use in the United States, I have been interested in exploring the national contradictions between the positively valued use of Spanish as a second, "foreign" language by European American students and the vexed experiences with Spanish that characterize the linguistic lives of many U.S. Latinos/Latinas. In my work, I have proposed the term "differential bilingualism" to argue that both additive and subtractive bilingualisms have been structurally used to maintain class stratification and privilege and to take away bilingualism as a source of cultural capital for linguistic minorities. As Walsh stated in 1991, "pedagogies that make use of students' voices can help promote critical awareness, an 'expert' understanding or reality, and the possibility for personal and collective transformation" (126–27). The "linguistic *autobiografías*" written by all students in my course The Politics of Language and Cultural Identity, which emerged as a critical tool for reflecting on the articulation of language and power, have formed the basis for my scholarly inquiry on this issue.

Here I limit myself to the linguistic experiences of U.S. Latino/Latina students. Collectively, these narratives contest, or at least problematize, the assumptions and myths that have informed the debates surrounding bilingual education. While public discourse has ignored the central role of Spanish and bilingualism in the lives of Latino/Latina immigrants and residents, these students' narratives speak not only to the cultural meaning and functions of Spanish, but also to its potential value as an economic, professional, and social asset. They also document how Spanish was taken away from them in both subtle and not so subtle effective ideological ways, while exploring the affective, social, and cultural conflicts that have ensued from this process of dispossession. While my use of the "Latino" rubric puts me at risk of generalizing about all national groups, I want to foreground that while these voices are unique in many ways, together they also reflect structural and historical colonizing processes that have had an impact on all groups. Obviously, for young Latinos/Latinas growing up in Michigan, where the Latino/Latina population constitutes about 4 percent of the state population, or for those from suburban areas where Spanish is not publicly practiced, the probability of losing their Spanish will be higher than for those growing up in cities such as Los Angeles, New York, Miami, or Chicago. Yet not all Latino/Latina students at the University of Michigan are in-state, and the autoethnographic narratives of out-of-state students, mostly from Hispanic/Latino states such as California and Texas, also detail stories about linguistic conflict and dispossession. Accounting for a complex web of factors—class, race, geographical, urban, suburban, gender, generational, and educational—that inform linguistic practice should not preclude examining the "web of coloniality" that structures Latinos/Latinas' lives (Lao 1997, 176).

The Nigerian writer Ngugi wa Thiongo (1986) describes the aims of hegemonic colonialism as controlling "the mental universe of the colonised, the control, through culture, of how people perceived themselves and their relationship to the world" (16). According to Ngugi, this involved "two aspects of the same process: the destruction or the deliberate undervaluing of a people's culture, their art, dances, religions, history, geography, education, orature and literature, and the conscious elevation of the language of the coloniser" (16). This double-edged colonial strategy continues to prevail in the case of Puerto Ricans, U.S. Puerto Ricans, and Mexican Americans. While Puerto Ricans on the island have faced both military and cultural occupations, U.S. Puerto Ricans have had to confront hegemonic manifestations of colonialism through educational policy. Both in its dominant and hegemonic manifestations, colonialism continues to inform the current political debates about the future status of the island, about official Spanish and English, and about the connection between English, education, and modernity. The 1998 vote on the Young Bill, which was approved by a margin of one vote in the House of Representatives, revealed that English will be considered a prerequisite for Puerto Rican statehood, a condition lobbied for by U.S. English. Pro-statehood speakers and politicians advocate for an "*estadidad jíbara*" (a Puerto Rican or *mestizo* statehood) yet also define English as the official language of education in order to insert Puerto Ricans into "modernity" and global economics. In other words, Puerto Rican subjects will not be deemed worthy of belonging to the United States' body politic unless they prove their competence in English and make it a public language on the island. To be sure, access to English needs to be democratized in Puerto Rico, where, as in postcolonial societies, English has been historically the privilege of the bourgeoisie and of an elite, professional sector. Yet the language of the Young Bill requires that English become the public and exclusive official language of the island. In this context, the term "bilingualism" has been deployed as a euphemism for English Only policies on an island where English is still resisted as a tool of empire.

In contrast, and as I have argued above, the U.S.-based movement against bilingual education has displaced bilingualism as a social and intellectual practice; instead, it has imposed English monolingualism as the only alternative for social and political belonging in the context of immigration and cultural difference. For Mexican Americans in California and the Southwest, the public role of Spanish was displaced in the aftermath of the U.S. occupation of the Southwest. The dispossession of lands also included the dispossession of culture and language through educational policies and Americanization programs. Throughout the twentieth century, Mexican American communities have consistently resisted colonialist ideologies that purposefully negate the cultural specificity of Mexican American students. The repression or suppression of Spanish in schools throughout the Southwest and the West has been documented (Valdez and Steiner 1972; *Piojo Narratives* 1994; Anzaldúa 1987; Padilla and Benavides 1992; Mirandé 1985; Meier and Stewart 1991; Valdés 1996). Forms of "linguistic terrorism," to use Gloria Anzaldúa's term (58–59), have included physical punishments, humiliation, segregation, and intellectual undervaluing. Mexican American adults have attested to the pedagogical practices by which they were publicly humiliated for the trace of Spanish sounds, accents, and phonetics in their English, candidly exposing the pernicious emotional and cultural effects of the colonial linguistic habitus in the educational context (*Piojo Narratives* 1994).

Alice Callaghan, the Episcopalian priest who led the boycott of seventy-five Latino/Latina families whose children attended a Los Angeles public school, demanding that the children be placed in mainstream classes, commented publicly that "the kids aren't learning English. Our kids want to be doctors and lawyers. They don't want to end up cleaning houses or selling tamales on the corner" (Terry 1998, n.p.). Echoing Texas Judge Kiser's controversial statements about Spanish some years ago, which Roseann D. González cites in the introduction to this volume, Ms. Callaghan's discourse reveals that Spanish continues to be associated with poverty and economic need. Instead of resorting to physical punishments such as washing the children's mouths with soap or corporal hitting, which have been outlawed and would violate human rights, European American–dominant society represses Spanish by evoking images of poverty and economic marginality. Such discourse inculcates in both parents and children linguistic perceptions that exert a particular symbolic violence on Spanish, delegitimizing it as a public language fit for professional and intellectual development. This process of racializing Spanish, or "ethnifying" it, turns this otherwise national and public language into a subordinate language dispossessed of cultural, economic, and symbolic capital (Aparicio 1998).

Concomitantly, the globalization of English renders the spread of English "natural, neutral and beneficial." This assumption finds echo in the arguments that immigrant children can learn English in only one year and that English for the Children was proposed for the benefit of the children and not as a political issue, which was indeed Unz's objective (Bruni 1998, 1). The teaching of English as a second language, however, as evinced in Africa, the Philippines, and India, really functions "as gatekeeper to positions of prestige in a society," reproducing class stratification rather than opening up economic opportunities (Pennycook 1994, 14). Within the United States, the dire socioeconomic conditions of many members of racial minorities who speak only English and the case of many Cuban Americans who have achieved economic success in and through Spanish and bilingualism belie the myth of English as the exclusive tool for economic success (Zentella 1997, 263–64). Economist Sherrie Kossoudji (1988), who has studied whether English-language ability determines higher income among Asian and Hispanic/Latino male immigrants, concluded that for Asians, knowledge of English was not associated with higher income, whereas for Latinos/Latinas, the lack of English kept them in lower occupational jobs and income levels. This difference had more to do with the economic enclave that characterizes the Asian American community, members of whom, like the Cuban exiles, did not need to speak English to participate in and benefit from commercial and business ventures. Thus Kossoudji's article reveals, through economic formulas, that English-language ability is directly correlated to income levels in the case of Latinos/Latinas. This supports the argument for teaching English as a vehicle for economic success. Yet the study also reveals that language is not the exclusive tool for achieving economic success in the United States, as the case of Asian immigrants clearly demonstrated. That English is correlated to income levels among Latinos/Latinas also suggests that assumptions and stereotypes about Spanish-speaking Latinos/Latinas may also play a part in undervaluing their job skills (Kossoudji 1988, 211). As Rosina Lippi-Green (1997) demonstrates in *English with an Accent,* the minimal trace of Spanish in one's English, or the lack of knowledge of English, predisposes the listener to consider the individual less intelligent and less apt than he or she really is (122–31). Thus it can be argued that the lack of English-language ability itself is not the exclusive constraint on economic success; instead, it is the consequence of exclusion based on the perceptions of others.

Racializing Spanish

Young Latino and Latina students consistently confront the dual ideological mechanism by which English is overdetermined as a superior language and Spanish is undermined as subordinate. A high school student in Detroit has been publicly shamed by European American students for having a Spanish accent in her English; yet, as this student observes, the same is not true when European American students speak Spanish with an accent: "*En la escuela se burlan de tu acento y que dices algo y luego lo repiten ellos como con lo, o sea que lo hacen notar que lo dijiste con acento y luego se rien y te quedas, pues te hacen sentir un poco inferior o te hacen sentir mal. Y bueno, nadie se burla de ellos cuando intentan hablar en español*" [At school others make fun of your accent, when you say something they repeat it, exaggerating your accent and then they laugh and you feel a bit inferior or they make you feel bad. But then, nobody makes fun of them when they try to speak in Spanish]. When I asked her who these students were who mocked her English, she replied "*los blancos, los estudiantes que saben inglés bien"* [whites, the students who know English well], conflating racial identity with English competence. The automatic attribution of linguistic competency to the racial identity of European Americans, however, is the supplementary inverse of the social construction of Latino/Latina students, who are mostly categorized as inferior or incompetent in their knowledge of both Spanish and English. Given that non-accented speech is an abstraction and not achievable by speakers who learn a second language, "of whom," Rosina Lippi-Green asks, "do we require the elimination of accents?" (1997, 50–51). This differential treatment by which accents and phonetics are marked foregrounds its racializing role.

If the trace of Spanish in their English already marks Latino/Latina students as inferior, this disposition is equally at work at the level of programs. Students entering bilingual education classes in high school are mocked by other students. As a Latino/Latina student remarked, *"yo nomás digo que les tenemos que tener mucha paciencia porque yo pasé por allí. De mí se rieron bastante también y pues yo me sentía mal y pues los comprendo cuando recién llegan, llegan a un grado que digamos high school, pues es más duro"* [I only say that we have to be patient with them, because I was in their place. Others laughed a lot at me also and I felt bad so I understand when they just arrive, when they enter a level like high school, it is much more difficult]. Indeed, many administrators, teachers, and students alike consider bilingual education programs remedial in nature, thus a priori rendering Spanish-speaking students intellectually inferior to others. The racially marked nature of these programs is strongly evident in a comment by a Detroit student who did not consider herself bilingual because, to her, bilinguals were only those students who first knew Spanish and later learned English. This assumption conflates bilingualism with Latino/Latina immigrants and reveals the racializing role of language. Because these values are inculcated in the culture of the schools, it is not surprising that many Latino/Latina parents do not want their children in bilingual education programs.

Those who mock recent Spanish monolingual immigrants are not just European Americans, but also young Mexican Americans who are U.S.-born or who have lived in the United States for a longer time. The feelings of superiority among English-speaking Mexican Americans, informed by nativist sentiments, lead them to draw boundaries between self and other and to establish hierarchies based on English competence:

> In 1980, as I started to grow up in the streets of Detroit, I was faced with discrimination that came from other Mexican kids, kids that were second- and even third-generation born in *Los Estados Unidos*. . . . Over the years, I experienced a lot of insults, fights, and bad looks from all kinds of people, even my own *raza*. Looks that if they could kill, I would probably be dead by now. To me, this became a way of life. I became used to it.

This young Mexican American student faced double discrimination from young Mexican Americans as well as from European American classmates who would tell him to "go back to Burrito land" for not understanding English. He grew up internalizing this violence, which in his case was not only symbolic but physical as well. Having later joined a gang, this student perpetuated the cycle of violence: "I began to do the same things to other Mexican kids who were just arriving from Mexico; I insulted them in the same manner that I had been insulted." Yet after witnessing the murder of his best friend by members of his own gang, he quit and began to study in order to go to college. Likewise, a young Mexican woman who grew up on the Texas-Mexico border indicated that she had been harassed by a light-skinned young Mexican American boy for not knowing English. The boundaries of self and other, then, are not only fueled by European American nativism, but also by racial and class conflicts within the Latino/Latina communities.

For a generation of Latino/Latina students who attended U.S. schools after bilingual education legislation had been implemented, the learning of English has not been "neutral," but rather accompanied by the undervaluing of Spanish and of Latino/Latina cultures. Unfortunately, the cultural-deficit model underlying many pedagogical decisions and attitudes is still quite prevalent. This, of course, creates a linguistic habitus that leads to self-silencing and loss of Spanish. Young Latino/Latina students "internalized feelings of linguistic and cultural defect" during the early stages of reading and speaking in English. A young Puerto Rican male student confessed that English and American culture were represented as utopian and that English speakers were considered *"mejores"* [better] because Puerto Ricans identified with European Americans, values that prevail among middle-class Puerto Rican youth. During junior high school, a young Latino man who grew up in New York "dreaded having to read aloud from a book for fear of sounding unintelligible or stupid." Another young man of Peruvian descent observed that at school when he learned English he also learned to be ashamed of his culture and language:

> I learned to be ashamed of speaking Spanish, which I thought of as a punishment; I was ashamed when my mother would speak to me in Spanish. It was a shame because my mother was a beautiful person in her own right but not within Anglo culture; I was ashamed because I was not like the other American kids. . . . Now I am ashamed of having been ashamed, but what can one do after such a great injustice?

Latino/Latina students who grew up in Anglophone communities, particularly in Michigan and the Midwest, stood out even more for speaking a foreign language that did not fit into the local and regional culture. A young Chilean American man remembers how he was the only student who spoke another language in his class, and when he would mistakenly utter a word or phrase in Spanish, all of his classmates would stare at him *"de forma bien rara"* [in a weird way]. This student, who wrote his linguistic autobiography in Spanish, used the verb phrase *"se me escapó una frase o palabra en castellano"* [a phrase or word in Spanish came out], suggesting that Spanish was repressed, not able to come out freely. This reveals that the Spanish language and the Latino/Latina cultural identity had to be kept at bay for the purposes of social and educational survival. Once Spanish came out, or "escaped," from the private realm of the individual or the family, it was considered a transgression of the social norm and of the particular linguistic habitus created by the school. By the second grade, this student remembered, he stopped speaking Spanish at home as well as in public. Later, he would return to it as he realized that it "could become an asset."

Likewise, a young Cuban American woman who grew up in Michigan also stopped speaking Spanish until her late teens. She recalls "no incidents of intended mockery—it was just that Spanish had no place in those worlds . . . there was something 'weird' about it, it was something I wanted to hide." She adds that

> the language itself, pure naked Cuban-brand Castillian, was never a barrier for me. What was a barrier was what I associated with *el idioma* [the language] in my North American experience: Ricky Ricardo, Speedy González, the simple bean-picking Juan Valdez. Taco Bell, Paul Rodríguez as the TV sitcom 'kooky Mexican-next-door.' *Miami Vice* drug lords. Poverty. Illegal aliens. . . . I could make a very long list. These are images I did not want to and couldn't identify with. So I let the Spanish go away.

These cases highlight the different ideological mechanisms by which Spanish is ultimately muted in the lives of Latino/Latina students through consent. Outright repression, mockery, and violence; the constructed "uselessness" of Spanish in monocultural settings; the need to develop self-defensive mechanisms against Latino/Latina stereotypes, that is, losing the language that could identify one as a social aberration; and self-silencing were indeed common among the Latino/Latina college students' autoethnographic narratives. From being called *"La Muda"* [the speechless one] by one's own relatives in Mexico to self-silencing due to linguistic discrimination in school, these otherwise personal linguistic decisions unveil the workings of hegemony and consent.

Erasing Spanish

It is redundant to state that most Latino/Latina students who attend the University of Michigan are literate in English. Yet, for many of these students, literacy in English also meant losing their identities as functional, bilingual Latinos/Latinas. Sixteen out of twenty-seven Latino/Latina students identified themselves as English-dominant, with varying degrees of fluency in Spanish as a second language. This is not surprising given the fact that the University of Michigan tends to recruit in suburban middle- and upper-class high schools throughout the state, the Midwest, and the nation. Yet not all of these English-dominant Latinos/Latinas are middle class with professional parents. Social class can work either to facilitate the maintenance of Spanish or to erase it (Sánchez 1994). Other factors inform the construction of these students' linguistic identity in English: students with European American mothers who spoke English at home; second- and third-generation students whose Latino/Latina parents were already English-dominant as a result of linguistic and educational policies; a suburban upbringing in which Spanish did not have a public presence; and growing up on U.S. military bases throughout Europe and the United States.

As a historical result of U.S. monolingual educational policy, the parents of these Latino/Latina students—in the Southwest, California, the Midwest, and the East Coast—experienced a gap between the linguistic practices in Spanish in their homes and the outside English-speaking linguistic market. The dominant linguistic dispositions that favor English over Spanish overshadowed the usefulness of Spanish as a social marker. Linguistic utterances, or a language for that matter, "can be understood as the product of the relation between a linguistic *habitus* and a linguistic market"(Bourdieu 1991, 17). Pierre Bourdieu asserts that speakers take into account the "value" that the market or "field" conditions will attribute to their linguistic expressions and internalize these constraints at the moment of production, that is, at the instance of the utterance. He exemplifies this process by arguing that the most "unequally distributed" forms of expression have the "greatest value" (19). If it is true that "the conditions for the acquisition of the capacity to produce" Spanish are restricted in the United States and that "the expressions themselves are relatively rare on the markets where they appear" (18), then Spanish would be of high value as linguistic capital, according to Bourdieu's logic. And indeed this is the case for European Americans who learn Spanish as a second language. For U.S. Latinos/Latinas, however, English represents the utterance of "greatest value" (19). Given the colonial conditions in which U.S. Spanish is embedded, the particular U.S. Spanish uttered by linguistic minorities does not assume value, but rather becomes useless. Indeed, what English Only advocates argue is that the more useful Spanish is within the United States, the more threatening it is for English and hence the more subordinated it should become.

Linguistic dispositions are durable, according to Bourdieu. Thus the internalization of the inferiority of Spanish and the superiority of English has been transmitted across generations. This durability moves from one body to another, from mother to daughter, from grandfather to grandson. In this context, the autoethnographic narratives serve as a critical tool of memory that traces that history of linguistic silencing within a family. A student from New Mexico wrote:

> Spanish was the first language of both my parents. When they entered first grade, they were punished if they were caught speaking it either on the playground or in the classroom. Because they did not know English, they relied on their friends who were bilingual to tell them what was going on. This was a horrifying experience for them as children. Since they did not want us to go through what they had been through, they believed that learning English as our first language was the only solution.

A Latina student from the Midwest recalls:

> My grandparents also pushed their children to speak English, for they needed to know English well to do well in school. My grandparents saw that a good education was the supreme equalizer in this country, and pushed their children to do well.

A Chicano student from California explained in detail how the marriage of his grandmother to his grandfather was invested in issues of respectability and pride and how this history informed linguistic decisions in the generations that followed:

> My grandfather had received a modest education in a nearby Franciscan seminary, and his plans to enter the priesthood were a source of pride for his devoutly Catholic family. A surprise and contested marriage to my grandmother obviously ruined those plans. From that day on, she represented the "barren branch" on the family tree.
>
> My grandmother countered with tenacity, however, and refused to bow to the power plays of my grandfather's

mother. Respectability would be hers and her family's. My grandparents raised seven children through some hard times, especially for Spanish speakers in California. . . . The English my grandfather had learned in the seminary placed him in an advantageous position as an organizer of Spanish-speaking field workers for the Sunkist citrus company. This ensured my family's survival during the Great Depression and exempted them from repatriation. Thus the value of speaking English was seared in the memory of my grandparents.

The linguistic behavior and dispositions that emerged in a historical time and social context before the implementation of bilingual education have been transmitted to younger generations who, ironically, do have more options after the late 1960s but who nevertheless are already predisposed to speak English by their parents' and grandparents' linguistic dilemmas. Moreover, the home becomes a central site for linguistic policing of the use of both Spanish and English. Parents and grandparents become complicit in reproducing what Rosina Lippi-Green (1997) has called standard language ideology (53–62), an ideology with multiple articulations for class and racial purity. Echoing Alicia Gaspar de Alba's experience described in "Literary Wetback" (1988), a Chilean American student wrote about how his parents from Chile insisted that he speak *"castellano"* [Castillian Spanish] rather than *"español"* [Latin American Spanish], the latter defined as the *mestizo*—an American and impure version of Castillian Spanish. A Mexican American female student from Detroit recalled that her mother, who had been a teacher in Mexico, constantly corrected their Spanish and also identified others' expressions as incorrect, stating: *"Mire que feo se oyó cuando hablan así; ustedes no me van a hablar se"* [Listen to that ugly way of speaking; you are not going to speak like that]. A Mexican student who had to learn English in U.S. schools remembers that her relatives humiliated her for not knowing English during a dinner conversation, talking about her without her knowledge. This traumatic experience motivated her to learn the language.

English-dominant Latinos/Latinas defy the nation-based homology between language and cultural identity. As they define themselves as bicultural without necessarily being bilingual, they interrogate the ways in which cultural identity has been historically linked to a national language, Spanish in their case. For a Mexican American young man who grew up in the suburbs of Sacramento to a Mexican father and a European American mother, his English monolingualism was the result of growing up in a European American neighborhood, attending a European American grade school, having mostly white friends and girl-friends, and listening only to English at home. His father's own linguistic history, tied to the search for social mobility, had already determined the monolingual setting for his children. The father lost his Spanish in order to improve "his working-class English by expanding his vocabulary." Eventually, the father, according to the son, "began thinking in English, and now struggles, much like me, to translate his thoughts into Spanish."

Likewise, a Mexican American young woman from Michigan attests to her father's growing assimilation into English and its impact on his children:

> Teaching my brothers and me Spanish was not really an option for my dad. Too many years of not using the language has left my dad monolingual. He can still carry on a conversation, but his Spanish is very forced and awkward sounding. He does remember speaking both languages, as a child, but English was his language of choice and definition.

Like her father, this young woman also identifies with English as her "first language," the language that "takes part in her self-definition." English offers her a confidence that she does not feel when she speaks in other languages. This confidence, according to her, "doesn't come from English being a 'better' language," but it is the one that she knows most. "I feel most secure with it; it is the language of my inner thoughts and dreams," she concludes in her personal reflection about the role of English in her life. When she speaks about English as the language "of choice and definition" for both her father and herself, however, it is clear that the degree of choice with which her father assimilated linguistically is debatable. Indeed, one of the most powerful linguistic myths surrounding English is its neutrality and naturalness, an assumption, according to Pennycook (1994), "that individuals and countries are somehow free of economic, political and ideological constraints when they apparently freely opt for English" (12). Thus the "failure to problematize notions of choice" (12) in discussions about the teaching and learning of English reproduces the political neutrality accorded this language in its global dissemination and its wide associations with Western, assumedly free and democratic societies.

In contrast, the linguistic history of a New Mexican family foregrounds the political, racial, and social values embedded in the teaching of English, an educational praxis far from neutral and unquestionably beneficial. This young woman described how her parents' Spanish was repressed in school through both physical punishment and symbolic violence. The linguistic disposition toward English was then transmitted to the children: "Since they did not want us to go through what they had been through, they believed that learning English as our first language was the *only* solution." Again, the exclusivity of English as a tool for social mobility becomes the ideological force behind linguistic assimilation. The father, who had believed that "his children would have a better life if they learned English" and "that his knowledge of English would open up better opportunities," soon realized that "he had been wrong." Facing both racism and linguistic discrimination at work, he realized that having taken Spanish away from his children was not going to protect them from racism. These two New Mexican parents taught their children "to be proud of [their] culture and heritage," however, instilling in them a strong bicultural foundation, albeit the absence of Spanish as the linguistic marker of identity.

Between Two National Imaginaries

Because of their "lack" of competence in Spanish, most English-dominant Latinos/Latinas have been excluded from consideration as *truly* Mexican or Hispanic. The complicity of parents, grandparents, and relatives in enforcing a construction of cultural identity linearly connected to fluency in the national language is clearly illustrated in numerous linguistic *autobiografías*. Caught between the European American monolingual construction of the United States as a nation and the parallel forces of Mexican or Puerto Rican nationalism, many U.S. Latinos/Latinas do not satisfy the social requirements that would allow them to belong entirely to either national body. English-dominant Latinos/Latinas who visit their relatives in Mexico or Puerto Rico, for instance, expressed linguistic anxieties and felt "intimidated" by their own family members. Indeed, a Latino high school student from Detroit mentioned that his Mexican relatives call him *"el hijo de Pete Wilson"* [Pete Wilson's son] because he speaks English. English, at the expense of Spanish, also foregrounds cultural conflicts within families. As a California Chicano student testified, when he was four years old his first memory regarding language issues had to do with the conflict between his great-grandmother and his grandmother regarding the fact that he did not speak Spanish:

> She [the great-grandmother] repeated her question, slower this time, but I did not respond. I did not know Spanish and had no clue what she was asking me. The three women turned to my grandmother and launched their attack. The once peaceful room filled with a flurry of words, fast and shrill. The sounds all rolled together in a wave of anger and indignity, plastering my grandmother to her chair. I could not understand what they were saying but I knew it was hurtful so I raced from the couch to her side. Holding her shaking hands, I stood between the angry women and their fusillade of words, and as forceful as a three- or four-year-old could, told them to "stop hurting my grandma"! As she broke into tears, I rushed into the kitchen and gathered my grandmother's cigarettes, handed them to her and told her to smoke, all the while wondering why these women had attacked her so angrily.

Particularly poignant, however, is the experience of a Chicana from the Midwest whose perceived lack of fluency in Spanish was considered a transgression by another Spanish-speaking Latino at an academic conference:

> As most of the presentations had been delivered in English or in interlingual Spanish/English, a discussion of language issues surfaced when an educator, fairly well-known in the community as a political activist and proponent of bilingual education, voiced his complaint that the conference was being held predominantly in English, rather than in Spanish. When a member of one of the panels attempted to explain that not all attendees, including Latino/a attendees and participants, were fluent in Spanish, the educator responded by saying that those

Latinos/as who were not Spanish-speakers—usually third-generation Latino/as who grew up in the period before bilingual education—constituted the lost generation, that things had changed and that the general population of Latinos/as shouldn't really be bothered with them. The educator delivered this opinion in Spanish, and although I had understood it, I remember sitting in that audience feeling marked and abandoned, feeling as though I'd been labeled as a member of "the lost generation" of Latino/as who, because my broken-*gringa* Spanish is less than adequate, should be left behind. Yet at that time in my life, as a high school English teacher, I was bringing works by Sandra Cisneros, Tomás Rivera, and Lorna Dee Cervantes into the school's curriculum, not without a fight, and teaching about Chicano/a culture to contextualize the literature. *A esta perdida le encantaba su cultura.*

That this educator excluded English-dominant Latinos/Latinas from the imagined community of U.S. Latinos/Latinas and labeled them "the lost generation" reveals the strong role of national languages in the construction of a national image. As an advocate for bilingual education, this individual should have been more sensitive to the structural, historical, and political factors that have produced English-dominant subjects within the Latino/Latina community rather than assuming that these were individual linguistic choices or "betrayals" on their part. This Chicana English teacher, however, proved that, despite her assumed lack of Spanish, which was contradicted by the very last, poetic sentence of the quote, she could still be a cultural activist and worker in English. Indeed, much of the Chicano activism during the 1960s and 1970s was articulated in English by what could be another *generación perdida*, yet Spanish was publicly deployed during the Chicano movement as an important symbolic marker of cultural identity (Sánchez 1994, 17).

Redefining Cultural Identity

Negotiating between their American-ness—their "being" in and through the English language—and their *Latinidad*, socially mediated through Spanish, Anglophone Latinos/Latinas redefine the role of language in the construction of their own, hybrid cultural identity. Some make a distinction between speaking fluent Spanish, mastering the grammar, and associating the language as part of their culture and family heritage. "My lack of facility with Spanish does not automatically preclude certain social, cultural, or political affinities," observed a student from California, who added that "Spanish evokes a deep, personal draw, a hard-to-define resonance which I associate with a history, a culture, a people." In other words, the linguistic knowledge and grammatical mastery that educators use as a basis for defining competency are not necessarily the criteria used by these students to define their connection to Spanish. They defined their "possession of the language" more in terms of symbolic and affective capital rather than of linguistic or grammatical criteria. The affective ties to the language remain in the lives of many Anglophone Latinos/Latinas. As the student from New Mexico observes, "While I didn't speak Spanish, it surrounded me. It was a part of my life and I was emotionally and socially attached to it." The Michigan woman who speaks English as her dominant language reevaluates the relationship between Spanish and Latino/Latina identity. After speaking about the affective and family values of the Mexican American culture, she concludes that "I don't need Spanish in order to feel Mexican, just as I don't have to hear 'I love you' to know I am loved." In other words, the implicit presence of Spanish continues to be a part of her family life and cultural identity, although it may not be verbally articulated on a day-to-day basis. This "underground," repressed presence of Spanish is also manifested in the high numbers of U.S. Latinos/Latinas who can understand the language, who have a receptive knowledge of it, but who feel anxious about speaking it in front of "native speakers," a result itself of the colonialist and racialized dispossession of Spanish in the United States. The silencing of the language, however, continues to be contested by the growing numbers of Latino/Latina students who try to reclaim the language at the college level, as adults, and by traveling abroad. These attempts at repossessing Spanish suggest that, contrary to assimilationist paradigms, language loss is not necessarily irreversible and that Latinos/Latinas continue to resist total linguistic assimilation. Yet feelings of inadequacy, ambivalence, and shame color their experiences of learning Spanish in the classroom, affective elements that reveal the impact of linguistic colonialism on individual lives.

Reclaiming Spanish as Cultural Capital

Out of the ten Latino/Latina high school students from southwest Detroit in this study, six attended bilingual education programs during their elementary school years. They spoke positively about their learning experiences in these classes, all of them indicating that the bilingual teachers explained the material in ways that were accessible to the students with a limited knowledge of English: "[T]he teachers in the bilingual education classes took out time to help you out, while in English [classes] we got to ask questions and it is like sometimes embarrassing 'cause it is the whole class." Students overall valued the bilingual education classes for the personal attention they received and for the ways in which teachers made the learning of English less traumatic and fearful than expected. Indeed, the positive valuation of bilingual education among students was evident some years ago when the school district decided to terminate the bilingual education program at Southwestern High School. As in other communities across the country, the Detroit Latino/Latina students organized a boycott; this one lasted thirty-nine days, and eventually the program was restored (Díaz Soto 1997). These fluent bilingual students who can read and write in both Spanish and English consider their bilingualism a "privilege," and they acknowledge with pride the symbolic and cultural capital that accompanies knowing two languages in one of the most monolingual societies in the world. As bilingual Latinos/Latinas, they see themselves as a "resource" for monolinguals and as a "bridge" between Spanish and English speakers. Unlike many of the Latino/Latina college students who experienced the loss of Spanish as a condition for educational achievement and social integration, these high school students see their Spanish as an asset and build their dreams for a professional and better future based on their double linguistic skills. Some spoke about using their bilingual skills in professions such as veterinary medicine, law enforcement, teaching, and immigration law. Bilingualism, not just learning English, represents for them an important skill that will allow them to enter a professional field. This attitude finds echo in Guadalupe Valdés's (1996) ethnographic work with Mexican immigrant families whose parents value English, but not at the expense of Spanish (136). Facing difficult living conditions and socioeconomic circumstances, perhaps many of these families value Spanish not just as symbolic capital, but also as a potential means for improving their economic and cultural capital.

The Detroit students' positive construction of Spanish is also the result of their experiences in bilingual education. Not only did they perceive that the teachers facilitated their learning, but they also conceptualized and engaged in intellectual and cognitive work in Spanish. By internalizing the intellectual, cognitive role of Spanish, students undermine its public domestication, its repression outside or inside the home. Many of these students do go back to Mexico or Puerto Rico to visit relatives, and they live in neighborhoods where Spanish is spoken and heard in restaurants, offices, and public spaces. These factors also reaffirm the public nature of their home language, in contrast to the invisibility of Spanish in the suburbs. Although the Detroit students have experienced their share of linguistic and racial discrimination, their vision of a balanced bilingualism in which English and Spanish stand on a more equal footing was stronger than any the Latino/Latina students at the University of Michigan expressed about their experiences with Spanish. The narratives from the English-dominant Latinos/Latinas suggest that learning English at the expense of Spanish is part of a persistent linguistic habitus that emerges from dispositions inculcated to some degree by family but mostly through the culture of the schools and the myths of social mobility. Bilingual education and Spanish-immersion programs threaten the national image of a European American United States and its dominant linguistic habitus by deploying Spanish as a public language and as a tool for cognitive development. Yet as long as Latino/Latina Spanish continues to be undermined as a public language and considered insignificant for, and even detrimental to, the intellectual and professional endeavors of U.S. minorities, the issue of equity through language teaching and learning will continue to haunt us.

Works Cited

Anzaldúa, Gloria. 1987. *Borderlands/La Frontera.* San Francisco: Spinsters/Aunt Lute.

Aparicio, Frances. 1998. "Whose Spanish, Whose Language, Whose Power?" *Indiana Journal of Hispanic Literatures* 12 Spring: 5–25.

Bourdieu, Pierre. 1991. *Language and Symbolic Power.* 1982. Edited and introduction by John B. Thompson. Translated by Gino Raymond and Matthew Adamson. Cambridge, MA: Harvard University Press.

Bruni, Frank. 1998. "The California Entrepreneur Who Beat Bilingual Education." *New York Times.* June 14. 1, 14.

Castro, Max J. 1997. "The Politics of Language in Miami." In Mary Romero, Pierrette Hondagneu-Sotelo, and Vilma Ortiz, eds., *Challenging Fronteras: Structuring Latina and Latino Lives in the United States.* New York: Routledge. 279–96.

Díaz Soto, Lourdes. 1997. *Language, Culture, and Power: Bilingual Families and the Struggle for Quality Education.* Albany: State University of New York Press.

English for the Children. 1997. Available: http://www.onenation.org.

Gaspar de Alba, Alicia. 1988. "Literary Wetback." *The Massachusetts Review* 29(2): 242–46.

Hernández Cruz, Víctor. 1991. "Snaps of Immigration." *Red Beans.* Minneapolis: Coffee House Press.

Kossoudji, Sherrie A. 1988. "English Language Ability and the Labor Market Opportunities of Hispanic and East Asian Immigrant Men." *Journal of Labor Economics* 6(2): 205–28.

Lao, Agustín. 1997. "Islands at the Crossroads: Puerto Ricanness Traveling between the Translocal Nation and the Global City." In Frances Negrón Muntaner and Ramón Grosfoguel, eds., *Puerto Rican Jam: Rethinking Colonialism and Nationalism.* Minneapolis: University of Minnesota Press. 169–88.

Lippi-Green, Rosina. 1997. *English with an Accent: Language, Ideology, and Discrimination in the United States.* London: Routledge.

Meier, Kenneth J., and Joseph Stewart Jr. 1991. *The Politics of Hispanic Education: Un paso pa'lante y dos pa'trás.* Albany: State University of New York Press.

Mirandé, Alfredo. 1985. *The Chicano Experience: An Alternative Perspective.* Notre Dame: University of Notre Dame Press.

Ngugi wa Thiong'o. 1986. *Decolonizing the Mind: The Politics of Language in African Literature.* London: James Currey.

Padilla, Raymond V., and Alfredo H. Benavides. 1992. *Critical Perspectives on Bilingual Education Research.* Tempe, AZ: Bilingual Press.

Pennycook, Alastair. 1994. *The Cultural Politics of English as an International Language.* London: Longman.

Piojo Narratives. 1994. Available Bitnet: MCLR-L@msu.edu.

Rodriguez, Richard. 1983. *Hunger of Memory: The Education of Richard Rodríguez.* New York: Bantam Books.

Sánchez, Rosaura. 1994. *Chicano Discourse: Socio-historic Perspectives.* Houston: Arte Público Press.

Terry, Don. 1998. "Bilingual Education Facing Toughest Test" [Online]. *New York Times.* March 10. http://www.nytimes.com/archives.

Valdés, Guadalupe. 1996. *Con respeto: Bridging the Distances between Culturally Diverse Families and Schools.* New York: Teachers College Press.

Valdez, Luis, and Stan Steiner, eds. 1972. *Aztlán: An Anthology of Mexican-American Literature.* New York: Vintage Books.

Villarreal, José Antonio. 1970. *Pocho.* New York: Doubleday. (Original work published 1959.)

Walsh, Catherine E. 1991. *Pedagogy and the Struggle for Voice: Issues of Language, Power, and Schooling for Puerto Ricans.* Toronto: OISE Press.

Zentella, Ana Celia. 1997. *Growing Up Bilingual: Puerto Rican Children in New York.* Malden, MA: Blackwell.

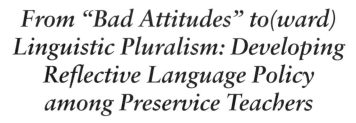

CHAPTER TWELVE

From "Bad Attitudes" to(ward) Linguistic Pluralism: Developing Reflective Language Policy among Preservice Teachers

GAIL Y. OKAWA
Youngstown State University

Up until these last few months, I didn't really think about the language that I spoke or the languages that others spoke. . . . I thought that my use of language was correct and everyone that didn't speak the way I did was wrong. Much of this way I once thought was influenced by my parents, my community, and my own closed-mindedness.

ALLEN, Language Autobiography

O ver the last forty years, more and more English language arts teachers in the United States have taught students from backgrounds culturally and linguistically different from their own. This was a diversity prompted in the 1950s by movements toward educational equity and desegregation and, more recently, by new patterns of immigration from Latin America, the Caribbean, Africa, Asia, and eastern Europe. Such language differences between teacher and student and among students resulted initially in theories of "verbal deprivation" among psychologists such as Arthur Jensen (1969), and Carl Bereiter and Siegfried Englemann (1966)—gross misunderstandings about standard and nonstandard dialects that were countered by linguists such as Geneva Smitherman (e.g., 1977, 1981), William

Labov (1982), James Sledd (1983), and professional organizations such as NCTE's Conference on College Composition and Communication (CCCC 1974).[1] Since 1981 exclusionist forces such as U.S. English and its precursors have responded to linguistic diversity by promoting English Only policies throughout the nation. Many opponents see these policies as constitutional violations (e.g., ACLU 1996; CCCC 1993; Daniels 1990; and especially González 1990) and not too thinly veiled attempts to use linguistic chauvinism and imperialism to racist ends (Daniels 1990; Louie 1998; Stroud 1997). Such forms of what González (1990) refers to as "'linguicism,' or racism on the basis of language" (50) are not unlike methods used in the Hawaiian Islands from 1924 to 1948 with the establishment of an English Standard school system.[2] Whether derived from dialects or languages, linguistic differences have revealed our deepest—often our most unexamined yet aggressive—feelings of ethnocentrism.

As of December 18, 1996, we have had to add "Ebonics" to the list of controversies—not the pan-African meaning that Robert Williams originally intended to convey by the term in 1973, nor even the African American Vernacular English (AAVE) that it might linguistically designate, but rather the conflicting emotional responses among both African Americans and non–African Americans that the word evokes. Perhaps widespread English Only attitudes had intensified the climate of intolerance leading up to the most recent Ebonics controversy.

Nowhere are the repercussions of such controversies felt more acutely than by students in the nation's classrooms. Previous and current language-attitude research involving teachers and preservice teachers reflects negative attitudes toward and linguistic stereotyping of limited-English-proficient (LEP) and AAVE speakers (Gere and Smith 1979; Hughes 1967; Shuy 1973; Williams 1970; Williams, Hopper, and Natalicio 1977; Bowie 1994; Byrnes and Kiger 1991, 1994). The case of *Lau v. Nichols,* in which non-English-speaking Chinese students sought equal educational opportunities from the San Francisco Unified School District, provides a classic example of how "sink or swim" attitudes and instruction have created educational inequality for LEP children, such that these practices were declared a violation of the Fourteenth Amendment by the U.S. Supreme Court in 1974

(Jiménez 1992, 251–55; see also Crawford 1996). Similarly, the *King Elementary School Children v. Ann Arbor School District* case in the late 1970s brought to light how African American children were being ill-treated because of their home language, leading to the decision by Judge C. W. Joiner in 1979 to extend the *Lau v. Nichols* ruling to "children who speak a minority dialect of English" (Jiménez 1992, 255; see also Labov 1982; Smitherman 1981). The autobiographical narratives of scholars such as Keith Gilyard (1991), Victor Villanueva, Jr. (1993), and Haunani-Kay Trask (1993) further reflect the psychic costs paid by students from linguistic and cultural minority groups and amplify our responsibility as teachers in the process. Despite precedent-setting laws and ample evidence of damage done, the "bad attitudes" persist among the most recent generations of would-be teachers.

In this context, how do we encourage informed language attitudes and decisions among inservice and preservice teachers based on linguistic knowledge rather than on language myths? How can we provoke a questioning of negative attitudes— blatant and latent discrimination—among those potentially or currently in the teaching force? Such questions have continued to plague me over the past few years. Having worked with hundreds of education students, I have observed that ignorance of language as systematic social behavior with historical roots is one of the greatest co-conspirators of linguistic chauvinism and internalized linguistic imperialism. This ignorance produces language attitudes that shore up the English Only movement, fuel the Ebonics controversy, and provoke other forms of linguistic intolerance or shame among aggressors or victims, colonizing or colonized. As U.S. school populations continue to grow more diverse, and as linguistically diverse students grow in number, it is increasingly imperative that pre- and inservice teachers in the English/language arts field recognize the social and political consequences of our daily decisions regarding language. We need to understand how we ourselves make language policy on a daily basis—and how individually culpable we are in silencing or encouraging the linguistic growth of our students.

"Bad Attitudes": Sources and Consequences

I teach an English course called Introduction to Language at a state university in what some automobile manufacturers have referred to as the "heartland of America." Located in the heart of a small midwestern city in the Rust Belt, the university is a commuter campus, and students with few exceptions stop by, pick up their education, and return to the surrounding provincial communities where English Only and standard English are often upheld, whether or not these varieties are actually spoken.

Intro to Language is an infamous sophomore-level course required of and designed primarily for preservice (mainly elementary) education majors. When I began this teaching assignment upon arrival at the university over six years ago, I had developed my syllabus, in a kind of vacuum, as an introduction to language in social context. I had designed the course to provide prospective teachers with knowledge of language as dynamic, socially constructed, and changing; with an understanding of language acquisition; and with experience as language observers and "researchers." We would study how language is influenced by culture, class, geography, and gender, producing its myriad varieties and controversies, as well as matters of language policy. A generic introduction to language. After teaching fifteen sections of this course on a ten-week quarter system, however, I have become more familiar with the region and its students and now adapt course material to this particular linguistic and social context.

The institution's approximately 12,000 students are predominantly Euro-Americans from the city and surrounding suburban and rural communities. Many of them are children, grandchildren, and great-grandchildren of the steel mill workers who immigrated to the area from eastern and southern Europe during steel's heyday. Students in my classes have cited such cultural and linguistic heritages as Italian, Slovak, Polish, Greek, Croatian, and Hungarian, in addition to Irish, Scottish, English, German, and French, with the occasional student of color being African American or Puerto Rican. Between 1977 and 1981, many mills shut down, leaving thousands jobless and leading to the closing of hundreds of businesses. The consequences of these events continue to be felt two decades later. In analyzing the challenges they have encountered while teaching at the same university in the early 1990s, Sherry Linkon and Bill Mullen (1995) describe in *Radical Teacher* the socioeconomic and political context:

> Economic depression and the strong, steadfastly separate ethnic cultures of Youngstown have contributed to the development of a generally divisive, conservative culture in the region. By far the strongest and most hostile division has developed between whites and blacks. Historically, this may be traced to the role African Americans played as company-imported strikebreakers and competitors in the labor pool as early as the 1930s. More recently, the division reflects de facto segregation caused by white flight. . . . [W]hite students, many of whom attended all-white suburban high schools, often encounter blacks for the first time in the classroom and on campus. (27–28)

In addition to Euro-Americans and African Americans, Latinos primarily of Puerto Rican background have had a presence in the region since the 1940s.

In the classroom, many of these tensions play out in negative attitudes toward different languages and dialects, views which are inseparable from unexamined social attitudes toward those of different races, ethnicities, and classes. The repercussions of such intolerance are often manifested in prescriptive approaches to language; overconcern with standard English, grammar, and correctness; frustration with speakers of other languages and/or dialects; and a suspiciousness of any kind of difference.

In so highly charged a social context, my own outsider status further complicates the classroom dynamics. Although a third-generation American not unlike many of my students, I am a Japanese American woman from Hawai'i and look unfamiliar to many, even "foreign," perhaps "alien" to some, for the relative invisibility of Asians and Asian Americans in this community leads to ready stereotyping. Some students, for example, have encountered only foreign-born Asian professors "with accents" and assume they will also have difficulty understanding me (cf. Okawa 1998, 1999). Then, too, as Glenn Omatsu (1995) asserts, "anti-Asian racism has been a defining feature of American labor history" (33) and, in a region steeped in labor culture and attitudes, my Asian background may factor in negatively for some students as well.

While developing a newfound understanding of my students through my classes over the years, I have become increasingly committed to confronting language attitudes as a fundamental concern of the course—not only to identify them, but also to see where they originate. By deconstructing their attitudes and understanding where they come from, students may realize that they have choices in perpetuating or changing their attitudes, especially in the context of teaching young children. Language attitudes thus become an increasingly visible text of the class as students interrogate their experience and assumptions through reading, class discussion, and writing assignments.

The Course: Topics and Readings

The stated approach to the course is fairly general and nonthreatening:

> Our goal will be to understand *language as a phenomenon that is alive and changing,* not rigid and exclusionary. We will examine its role in our lives:
>
> ◆ how we, as human beings, acquire it and use it
>
> ◆ how we shape (and are shaped by) language, socially, culturally, and politically
>
> Through lecture, discussion, and group work, we will seek to understand language from a multicultural perspective.

To guide prospective teachers in understanding language through a multicultural lens as a dynamic, changing phenomenon, I use a historical approach to explore how we might arrive at a particular point in our language development in a given social context. The U.S. experience becomes a case in point: We begin with a macro-level framework of linguistic and cultural "acquisition" in this country's language history, which exemplifies the pervasiveness of multilingualism and the concept of language variation, despite the emergence of English as the lingua franca (Molesky

1988; Heath 1980). Through our brief study of the layering of languages, beginning with the hundreds of tongues spoken by native peoples, "colonial languages" such as English, Spanish, French, and German (Molesky 1988), African languages such as Hausa, Ibo, and Yoruba (Smitherman 1977), and numerous immigrant languages and dialects during different waves of immigration, we learn that English has not been the only language in and of the United States and that in many ways there is more than meets the eye in the students' backgrounds as well. In discussing "language maintenance," "shift," "loss," and "death," using examples from the American Indian experience of conquest and the students' ethnic/linguistic heritages, some students begin to see the homogenizing effects of assimilation in their family language histories. They discover both their heritages and losses. Jeanine,[3] for example, describes the process of language shift and loss in her family over several generations:

> My great grandfathers came to Ellis Island searching for the American dream, a better life. When they arrived in this ethnocentric world they learned that the Italian language was thought to hold less intelligence than English does. As a result, they changed their names to sound more American. . . .
>
> As a small child I began to speak Italian fluently but was strongly discouraged by my great-grandparents [from doing] so. I thought I was doing something terribly wrong when I spoke Italian, since I was scolded. From that point on, they never spoke Italian in front of me unless they were speaking about something they did not want me to know about—Christmas presents, swear words, or other family members' turmoil. The family suffered a language loss because my dad and aunt were not allowed to speak Italian either. They learned it, though, from listening to their parents and grandparents speak. Recently I asked my grandparents why they did not want anyone in the family to speak Italian besides them. They said that they did not want me to have to suffer [as] they did because of the way I spoke when I was going to get a job. They continued to say that people are thought to be more important and intelligent if they speak "standard English." They wanted their family to be accepted and respected in an English-speaking society that thought speakers of other languages were less intelligent.

In effect, we must reverse the course of unquestioned assimilation and break down the polarizing identity of "whiteness" outlined by Linkon and Mullen. At the same time, the actual regional and cultural variations in American English—as well as stereotypes and attitudes about them—are introduced in a visually and audibly explicit way as we view examples in the video "American Tongues."

Having sketched out the country's language history to illustrate the increasing complexity of U.S. multilingualism, I move the class to a micro-level study of individual linguistic and cultural acquisition, and assign readings on some basic language-acquisition research in this context of language varieties. In this way, students can begin to see the relationships between culture and language, between environment and linguistic behavior; they become familiar with the universality of the process—and the particularity of the circumstances—of acquiring the grammars (phonology, syntax, semantics, pragmatics) of any given language variety. As they learn how any child acquires language, they come to understand how inextricable culture and language are; as they see how they themselves become language users within a sociocultural context, they can appreciate more readily how this happens with others. They also learn about ethnocentricity and how naturally they may become ethnocentric through language and about language.

We examine more closely the relationships between different cultures and language, using Shirley Brice Heath's (1983) seminal research in *Ways with Words*, particularly her work on questioning, which was carried out in the black community of Trackton and the white community of Roadville. Through the research described in "Questioning at Home and at School: A Comparative Study" (Heath 1982), many students see how cultural context and assumptions may shape our use and expectations of discourse differently—in this case, the discourse routine of questioning/answering—and appreciate the profound implications that such differences in assumptions may have for students and teachers in a classroom setting.

In order to understand more clearly the intersections among language, culture, and identity, we explore examples from the

African American language experience, primarily because the city's schoolchildren are predominantly African American. Again, I use a historical framework to give students a context for current language practices. We watch "Black on White" (1986) an hour-long documentary from the Story of English series, which traces the origins of Black English (BE, now AAVE [African American Vernacular English]) and the influences of BE on dialects spoken by other Americans. We read Smitherman's (1998) "It Bees Dat Way Sometime" and William Labov's (1994) "The Study of Non-standard English" to make salient the film's point about the rule-governed nature of this language variety and to dispel myths of "verbal deprivation."

Perhaps more important for prospective teachers, we read Keith Gilyard's *Voices of the Self: A Study of Language Competence* (1991) so that the students, many of whom will do internships and student teaching in urban schools, become aware of the complexities of a bidialectal child's language experience. Through Gilyard's autobiographical narrative and analysis, they can see language acquisition, communicative competence, code switching, and language politics, among other things, at play in concrete terms. They see Keith becoming Raymond as he switches codes and identities to survive his different environments. In this case, my best-laid plans seem to have the desired effect, for some students explicitly comment on the insights they have gained through this reading. In an overview of the course one quarter, Lonnie, a Head Start teacher, wrote:

> I really think that it was essential to read Gilyard. It is important to know that language varieties, [such] as Black English, are rule-governed and have structure. Gilyard's book also showed how teachers can affect a student's learning through their acceptance of all aspects of the student.

Others, like Helen, refer more broadly to major epiphanies regarding the language varieties of others:

> This class has changed everything I once believed about Black English. I now see it with specific rules of grammar and its own unique system. The key I suppose is not to judge the language but to find a common place for when to use it. I am

aware [that] I was very ethnocentric and felt like other people just did not understand "how to speak." After reading Gilyard and seeing the way his mom used code switching, I see that it simply is an issue of when to use one's native language. All in all, because of the awareness this class has raised in me and the various authors who dedicated their lives to bring language awareness to people, I have changed [the] beliefs I once held about Black English as well as language as a whole. I feel I can be a more inspiring teacher because of this experience. . . . My value judgements had to do with my parents, friends, and teachers and just being ignorant [of] language's complexity.

Even those who struggle to some degree with understanding and mastering various linguistic concepts may conclude that *Voices of the Self* is interesting, even enjoyable reading, that "[Gilyard] was a good example of everything we learned." This terrain is not traveled without difficulty, however, for negative attitudes can be entrenched, and some students resent the attention paid to Black English, dismiss it on their evaluations as my "bias," or show their disapproval in other ways.

To emphasize the significance of social, political, and geographical context in language development from another perspective, I also draw a parallel between the history and experience of Black English speakers and that of Hawai'i Creole English speakers. While West Africans were brought to North American plantations enslaved and generally isolated from others who spoke the same languages to prevent insurrection, Asians from China, Japan, Korea, and the Philippines were brought to the Hawaiian Islands—along with thousands from Portugal and Puerto Rico, fewer from Norway, Germany, and other European countries (Takaki 1983) —as contract labor. These groups were segregated by language and ethnic group to discourage pan-ethnic resistance to harsh plantation conditions. In both situations, a white English-speaking oligarchy maintained a position of authority so that speakers of different native languages adapted to the English-speaking environments using pidgin English forms.[4] Pidgin English speakers and their Creole-speaking descendants in both the Islands and the mainland United States have been stigmatized, especially with regard to education, although Dell Hymes (1971) referred to pidgin languages as "creative adaptations" epitomizing the very "interdependence of language and society" (3). On this topic, we discuss both Gilyard's code switching and the development of pidgin and Creole forms as creative linguistic phenomena exemplifying "verbal agility" (my term for verbal acumen), metalinguistic awareness, and the inherent relationships between language and identity.

Hawai'i's creole vernacular, still referred to regionally as Pidgin English, serves as a clear example of how language is influenced by social class and region and leads into our discussion of the students' regional dialects. Here their natural ethnocentricity is tested again. Discussions about language and gender usually stir some interest and prompt candid examples as we look at how gender may influence our language use, sense of linguistic identity, and treatment in a classroom.

When we look specifically at language attitudes in terms of language change and language policy in the later weeks of the quarter—particularly in light of the controversy on dialect differences that prompted the *Students' Right to Their Own Language* document (CCCC 1974) and the national uproar on Ebonics, and controversies on multilingualism versus English Only that prompted the CCCC *National Language Policy* statement (1993)—I point out how language attitudes produce language policy on a large scale. More important, some prospective teachers in my classes make connections between teachers' language attitudes and students' self-esteem, identity, and language development. They begin to understand the gravity of their own attitudes in future classroom policymaking—how teachers set language policy with each decision they make regarding their students' and their own language use.

Developing a Reflective Language Policy

In essence, the course asks the questions, how is language a dynamic, human phenomenon and how did we get to this point of multilingual complexity as a nation and as individuals? Over the ten weeks, the course provides basic tools for the students' investigation. Their personal exploration culminates in a language autobiography,[5] an opportunity to synthesize, internalize, and situate much of their learning about language in their own experience, to do "some research and much contemplation," according to Denny, a particularly thoughtful student. I provide the following guidelines for this writing assignment:

> This project asks you to explore your personal language development in a reflective narrative. You will need to dig into your language "roots" like a detective and cover the following topics: (a) your family language history, (b) your own acquisition of language, (c) your language development, and (d) the development of your own language attitudes and awareness. You may need to interview family members in your search.

In the course of this autobiographical narrative and other writing, many students identify their "bad attitudes" themselves, in terms of closed- or narrow-mindedness, stereotyping, prejudices, immaturity, ignorance, and/or ethnocentricity on the one hand, and shame or embarrassment on the other. Indeed, both African American and Euro-American students may find that they have been victims of linguistic ignorance and intolerance in very different ways. Miriam, for one, realizes that she had internalized social attitudes stigmatizing Black English speech:

> One thing I have acquired from this class is a sense of pride concerning my race's language. I must admit, I started the quarter with a hidden shame of my language. A shame born from a lack of knowledge regarding my history. Black English has widely been rejected by society for a long time. That rejection has fostered a prejudice toward and within the Black race itself. We have been made to feel not only shame of our language but also of how we speak our language. I believe this is the reason that we as Black people are skeptical to admit [that] "when we let our hair down," the majority of us do speak Black English.
>
> A lot of Blacks, including myself, try unsuccessfully to code switch. This code switching can take considerable effort if we are placed in a particular situation. This class has taught me that my language is something to be proud of. It is a Language, not ignorant lazy speech produced by a group of people. It is who I am.
>
> Gilyard held the answer for me. I must strive to be "two-way strong." I must continue to master standardized English, but hang on to my heritage as well. This is the motivation I

will take from this class and place in the hearts of my students. If students are educated early about their own language history, they may not form as many prejudiced judgments regarding someone else's language.

Others, like Avis, an African American woman in her forties, find the experience of writing their language autobiography to have a more generalized effect of healing. In class one day, Avis observed that the language autobiography, which she had struggled with and worked on tirelessly, helped her to "see herself" in a new and meaningful way.

From another perspective, Allen, a secondary English major of Euro-American background from one of the small communities outside Youngstown, refers in his language autobiography to his own intolerance:

> Up until these last few months, I didn't really think about the language that I spoke or the languages that others spoke. Like many others, I had a very [simplistic] view on what I thought the appropriate language in society should be. I thought that my use of language was correct and everyone that didn't speak the way I did was wrong. Much of this way I once thought was influenced by my parents, my community, and my own closed-mindedness. . . .
>
> Although my parents provided a good basis for learning and understanding the English language, the town in which I grew up kept me closed-minded to how others spoke. Aside from one black family, Leetonia, my hometown, is an entirely white community. Everyone that I grew up with speaks the same and virtually acts the same. The only time I was subject to different dialects was when I occasionally caught *Mr. Belvedere* on television. It sounds funny now but because *Mr. Belvedere* was a comedy, I thought that other dialects were humorous. My idea was that the language I spoke should be the only language. My friends and I felt others were stupid or ignorant if they spoke differently than we did. W. F. Bolton describes this type of view as a form of ethnocentricity. . . .

By exploring his family language history and his own language development, Allen comes to understand the nature and origin of his attitudes toward his language and those of others outside his community. Recognizing his inherited ethnocentric views, he can go about the business of exercising choice in any given situation:

> After taking nine weeks of English 651, I no longer have the same ethnocentric view that I once had. This class has taught me a lot about my language history and about how immature my views of others' language were. It has taught me more about language in nine weeks than I've learned in twenty-one years of growing up. I now see others' language as being different, but equal. I also see them to be far from ignorant.
>
> Keith Gilyard's book, *Voices of the Self: A Study in Language Competence,* provided an example for me. Since the book [is] autobiographical, I could put myself in his shoes. Sometimes it was hard for me to relate to the examples being set forth in the classroom. All the articles and authors we've covered didn't provide the illustration that I needed. Gilyard's tribulations and triumphs in the classroom were instrumental to my changed feelings. Since I aspire to become a high school teacher, I want to be able to reach every child, not just the ones I share the same dialect with.

With such insights about prescriptive approaches to their own language and its dialectal variations (and realizing that they have been victims of prescriptivism themselves, in some cases), students can begin to understand linguistic chauvinism/protectionism/restrictionism in more personal terms. Perhaps Jeanine put it best:

> The attitudes I had were that anyone who spoke English even remotely differently [from] myself must have been lacking some important education. That people who spoke differently were less intelligent or [that they were] funny. It was not until this class that I realized how off-target my language attitudes were. In addition, how stupid I was to think that just because they spoke differently they must be less intelligent. I was too quick to judge and now feel my awareness has heightened. I feel that I have become a "cultural relativist." This view can only make me more aware of the responsibility I have to educate my students and debunk the social myth that just because you speak differently you are less intelligent. My attitudes have grown since I discovered and resurfaced the roots behind the closed-minded attitudes. . . . [A]s you resurface the roots of your language attitudes you can begin to change them. We

grow up in an ethnocentric world and this is where we learn how to speak and develop our linguistic skills. I believe it is important to learn where your ethnocentric behavior stems from.

Developing a sociolinguistic knowledge base gives students a rationale from which to make informed decisions so that they finally may be more able to comprehend the issues and implications surrounding the English Only controversy as well as the anti-exclusionary and pluralist purpose of the CCCC *National Language Policy* (CCCC 1993) statement, passed by the CCCC membership in March 1988 and, more recently, by the NCTE membership in November 1998: "This policy would enable everyone to participate in the life of this multicultural nation by ensuring continued respect both for English, our common language, and for the many other languages that contribute to our rich cultural heritage." Moreover, they can be more receptive to its three-pronged approach to language:

1. To provide resources to enable native and nonnative speakers to achieve oral and literate competence in English, the language of wider communication.

2. To support programs that assert the legitimacy of native languages and dialects and ensure that proficiency in one's mother tongue will not be lost.

3. To foster the teaching of languages other than English so that native speakers of English can rediscover the language of their heritage or learn a second language. (n.p.)

Most students say they have "never thought about these things [issues] before"; some wish they had never had to; some say the course should be required of all university students. With all of this said, my greatest hope is that when these students go into their own classrooms, they will have the background:

◆ to become language observers/researchers (as Heath [1982] and others have encouraged us to do)

◆ to identify verbal agility more than correctness among their students

- ◆ to select literature that celebrates dialects, languages, and verbal agility
- ◆ to use autobiographical narrative to develop students' self-esteem and unique voices, and to develop teachers' understanding of students' language experiences
- ◆ to respect the language rights and identities of their students, to recognize how they set language policy every school day

In an (ungraded) overview for a recent class, Chris candidly describes her growing awareness of dialects and languages in terms of her future as a teacher:

> It's really fascinating to find out how languages actually evolved. More importantly, and for this I am truly grateful, I found out something so crucial for future teachers like myself: how important it is to understand languages and how important they are to a person's identity. I didn't know I was closed-minded when I started this class, but I think I was. I'm ashamed to say I would have probably accepted only standard English in my classroom and discouraged the use of any other language. Now, thankfully, I have been made aware that other dialects and different forms of speech are not wrong just because they are different from my own. You have taught me that I should acknowledge and respect every student's language, and realize that it can be used to teach in a variety of ways. I believe the concepts in this class will prove invaluable to me, not only in the classroom, but in everyday life.

In a relatively nonthreatening learning environment based on descriptive deconstructions of language behavior, students can often confront threatening and uncomfortable issues—admit to ignorance and ethnocentricity—and act on that understanding. For Jeanine, Lonnie, Helen, Denny, Miriam, Allen, Chris, and their students, these reflections can become a profound beginning of revised attitudes about language, identity, and culture.

Notes

1. In response to the controversy over students' language varieties and the role of those language varieties in education, a specially appointed committee of the CCCC was charged in 1971 with preparing a position

statement on students' dialects. The document, *Students' Right to Their Own Language,* took the following strong stand on the issue:

> We affirm the students' right to their own patterns and varieties of language—the dialects of their nurture or whatever dialects in which they find their own identity and style. Language scholars long ago denied that the myth of a standard American dialect has any validity. The claim that any one dialect is unacceptable amounts to an attempt of one social group to exert its dominance over another. Such a claim leads to false advice for speakers and writers, and immoral advice for humans. A nation proud of its diverse heritage and its cultural and racial variety will preserve its heritage of dialects. We affirm strongly that teachers must have the experiences and training that will enable them to respect diversity and uphold the right of students to their own language. (2–3)

The resolution on language was adopted by the CCCC membership in April 1974.

2. "Linguistic chauvinism" refers to the belief in the superiority of one's own language, while "linguistic imperialism" refers to the policy of imposing one language or dialect in dominance over another. As Fuchs (1961) maintains, racial and linguistic elitism among the white English-speaking sugar plantation oligarchy became the basis for Hawai'i's English Standard school system, wherein linguistic segregation served as a veneer for racist school segregation for almost a quarter of a century. Linguist Charlene Sato (1985) asserts that "the major effect of this system was the further stratification of Hawaiian society along ethnic lines by means of discrimination along linguistic ones. By institutionalizing linguistic inequality in this way, the ES [English Standard] schools legitimized the negative stereotyping of HCE [Hawai'i Creole English] speakers" (264).

3. In order to ensure student anonymity, pseudonyms have been used for all student names.

4. See Dillard (1972) and Smitherman (1977) on the historical background of Black English/African American Vernacular English; see Carr (1972), Reinecke (1969), Sato (1985), and Takaki (1983) on the development of Hawai'i Pidgin English and Hawai'i Creole English.

5. Note on writing assignments: Writing assignments are based on theories of reflection from Paulo Freire's work (1970); concepts of "situated (vs. universal) knowledge" from feminist theorists such as Haraway (1991); and the extensive body of literature on narrative and

autobiographical writing in education (see Cazden and Hymes [1978]; DiPardo [1990]; Graham [1991]; Haroian-Guerin [1999]; and Rosen [1986])—how this writing develops both reflection and "situatedness" among writers. During some terms, I ask students to keep a Language Experience Journal that will enhance their reflective and observational skills. They write two types of journal entries: (1) entries that ask students to write reflections on their personal language learning, behavior/use, and attitudes, and to relate them to their readings and class discussion; and (2) entries that ask them to describe and analyze examples of language use they observe in others. During other terms, I ask students instead to keep a Language Log, running entries of terms and concepts with examples and observations similar to those kept in the Language Experience Journal.

Works Cited

American Civil Liberties Union. 1996. "English Only." *ACLU Briefing Paper* [Online]: http://www.aclu.org/library/pbp6.html. January 14, 1999.

Bereiter, Carl, and Siegfried Englemann. 1966. *Teaching Disadvantaged Children in the Preschool.* Englewood Cliffs, NJ: Prentice-Hall.

"Black on White." 1986. The Story of English Series. Dir./Prod. William Cran. Chicago: Films Incorporated.

Bowie, Carole. 1994. "Influencing Future Teachers' Attitudes toward Black English: Are We Making a Difference?" *Journal of Teacher Education* 3(1).

Byrnes, Deborah A., and Gary Kiger. 1991. "Teacher Attitudes about Language Differences." ERIC document 340 232.

———. 1994. "Language Attitudes of Teachers Scale (LATS)." *Educational and Psychological Measurement* 54(1).

Carr, Elizabeth. 1972. *Da Kine Talk: From Pidgin to Standard English in Hawaii.* Honolulu: University Press of Hawaii.

Cazden, C., and D. Hymes. 1978. "Narrative Thinking and Story-Telling Rights: A Folklorist's Clue to a Critique of Education." *Keystone Folklore* 22: 22–35.

Conference on College Composition and Communication. 1974. *Students' Right to Their Own Language* [Special issue]. *College Composition and Communication* 25: 1–32.

————. 1993. *The National Language Policy* [Brochure]. Urbana, IL: NCTE.

Crawford, James. 1996. "Summing Up the *Lau* Decision: Justice Is Never Simple." In *Revisiting the* Lau *Decision—20 Years After: Proceedings of a National Commemorative Symposium Held on November 3–4, 1994, in San Francisco, California.* Oakland, CA: ARC Associates. Available: http://ourworld.compuserve.com/homepages/JWCRAWFORD/summing.htm.

Daniels, Harvey A., ed. 1990. *Not Only English: Affirming America's Multilingual Heritage.* Urbana, IL: National Council of Teachers of English.

Dillard, J. L. 1972. *Black English: Its History and Usage in the United States.* New York: Random House.

DiPardo, Anne. 1990. "Narrative Knowers, Expository Knowledge: Discourse as a Dialectic." *Written Communication* 7(1): 59–95.

Freire, Paulo. 1970. *Pedagogy of the Oppressed.* Trans. Myra B. Ramos. New York: Continuum.

Fuchs, Lawrence. 1961. *Hawaii Pono: A Social History.* New York: Harcourt, Brace & World.

Gere, Ann, and Eugene Smith. 1979. *Attitudes, Language, and Change.* Urbana, IL: National Council of Teachers of English.

Gilyard, Keith. 1991. *Voices of the Self: A Study of Language Competence.* Detroit: Wayne State University Press.

González, Roseann Dueñas. 1990. "In the Aftermath of the ELA: Stripping Language Minorities of Their Rights." In Harvey A. Daniels, ed., *Not Only English: Affirming America's Multilingual Heritage.* Urbana, IL: National Council of Teachers of English. 49–60.

Graham, R. J. 1991. *Reading and Writing the Self: Autobiography in Education and the Curriculum.* New York: Teachers College Press.

Haraway, Donna. 1991. *Simians, Cyborgs, and Women: The Reinvention of Nature.* New York: Routledge.

Haroian-Guerin, Gil, ed. 1999. *The Personal Narrative: Writing Ourselves as Teachers and Scholars.* Portland, ME: Calendar Islands.

Heath, Shirley Brice. 1980. "Standard English: Biography of a Symbol." In Timothy Shopen and Joseph M. Williams, eds., *Standards and Dialects in English.* Cambridge, MA: Winthrop. 3–32.

———. 1982. "Questioning at Home and at School: A Comparative Study." In G. Spindler, ed., *Doing the Ethnography of Schooling*. New York: Holt, Rinehart, and Winston. 105–33.

———. 1983. *Ways with Words: Language, Life, and Work in Communities and Classrooms*. New York: Cambridge University Press.

Hughes, Anne E. 1967. *An Investigation of Certain Sociolinguistic Phenomena in the Vocabulary, Pronunciation, and Grammar of Detroit Pre-School Children, Their Parents and Teachers*. Unpublished doctoral dissertation, Michigan State University, East Lansing.

Hymes, Dell. 1971. Preface. In Dell Hymes, ed., *Pidginization and Creolization of Languages*. New York: Cambridge University Press. v–viii.

Jensen, Arthur. 1969. "How Much Can We Boost IQ and Scholastic Achievement?" *Harvard Educational Review* 39: 1–123.

Jiménez, Martha. 1992. "The Educational Rights of Language-Minority Children." In James Crawford, ed., *Language Loyalties: A Source Book on the Official English Controversy*. Chicago: University of Chicago Press. 243–57.

Labov, William. 1982. "Objectivity and Commitment in Linguistic Science: The Case of the Black English Trial in Ann Arbor." *Language in Society* 11: 165–201.

———. 1994. "The Study of Non-Standard English." In Virginia P. Clark et al., eds., *Language: Introductory Readings*. New York: St. Martin's Press. 555–62.

Linkon, Sherry, and Bill Mullen. 1995. "Gender, Race, and Place: Teaching Working-Class Students in Youngstown." *Radical Teacher* 46: 27–32.

Louie, Tom. 1998. "The Facts Behind the Debate on Bilingual Education." *Peacework* Magazine 290 (November): 8–9.

Molesky, Jean. 1988. "Understanding the American Linguistic Mosaic: A Historical Overview of Language Maintenance and Language Shift." In Sandra Lee McKay and Sau-ling Cynthia Wong, eds., *Language Diversity: Problem or Resource?* New York: Newbury House. 29–68.

Okawa, Gail Y. 1998. "Re-seeing Our Professional Face(s)." *English Journal* 88: 98–104.

———. 1999. "Lotus Blossom and the Rust Belt." Paper presented at the Conference on College Composition and Communication, Atlanta, GA, March 26.

Omatsu, Glenn. 1995. "Racism or Solidarity? Unions and Asian Immigrant Workers." *Radical Teacher* 46: 33–37.

Reinecke, John. 1969. *Language and Dialect in Hawaii: A Sociolinguistic History to 1935.* Honolulu: University of Hawaii Press.

Rosen, H. 1986. *Stories and Meanings.* London: National Association for the Teaching of English.

Sato, Charlene. 1985. "Linguistic Inequality in Hawaii: The Post-Creole Dilemma." In N. Wolfson and J. Manes, eds., *Language of Inequality.* New York: Mouton. 255–72.

Shuy, Roger. 1973. "Language Variation in the Training of Teachers." In Johanna S. DeStefano, ed., *Language, Society, and Education: A Profile of Black English.* Charles A. Jones Publishing.

Sledd, James. 1983. "In Defense of the 'Students' Right.'" *College English* 45: 667–75.

Smitherman, Geneva. 1977. *Talkin' and Testifyin': The Language of Black America.* Boston: Houghton Mifflin.

———. 1981. "'What Go Round Come Round': *King* in Perspective." *Harvard Educational Review* 51: 40–56.

———. 1998. "It Bees Dat Way Sometime." In Virginia P. Clark et al., eds. In *Language: Readings in Language and Culture.* New York: St. Martin's Press. 328–43.

Stroud, Kim. 1997. "English-Only Laws Reflect Prejudice, Not Patriotism." *Detroit Free Press,* June 30. 9A.

Takaki, Ronald. 1983. *Pau Hana: Plantation Life and Labor in Hawaii.* Honolulu: University of Hawaii Press.

Trask, Haunani-Kay. 1993. *From a Native Daughter: Colonialism and Sovereignty in Hawai'i.* Monroe, ME: Common Courage Press.

Villanueva, Victor, Jr. 1993. *Bootstraps: From an American Academic of Color.* Urbana, IL: National Council of Teachers of English.

Williams, Frederick. 1970. "Psychological Correlates of Speech Characteristics: On Sounding 'Disadvantaged.'" *Journal of Speech and Hearing Research* 13: 472–88.

Williams, Frederick, Robert Hopper, and Diana S. Natalicio. 1977. *The Sounds of Children.* Englewood Cliffs, NJ: Prentice-Hall.

CHAPTER THIRTEEN

Between the Lines: Reconciling Diversity and Standard English

VICTORIA CLIETT
Wayne State University

Ravi Coltrane, son of saxophonist John Coltrane, in discussing the significance of following in his father's footsteps, said that playing the notes was not enough; it was the experience behind the notes that made his father or any musician distinctive (Mandel 1998). I use the music analogy to address standard English (SE) and its pedagogy in the writing classroom: standard English defines the rich and complex act of good writing the same way that playing the notes defines the rich and complex act of making good music. Another musical analogy that helps us clarify the relationship between writing and standard English comes from the movie *Bird* (1989). In this film, the character of Charlie "Bird" Parker (played by Forest Whitaker) is watching a longtime mentor and saxophone player perform at a rock and roll concert. Disgusted, Parker runs onto the stage, snatches the saxophone from his mentor, and begins to play. He is thrown out of the theatre into the alley, and his mentor asks Parker what is wrong with him. Parker responds that he wanted to see if the saxophone could still "play more than one note at a time."

"Playing more than one note at a time" is not just another ethereal jazz credo; it also explains the complexity of language and culture, for every synchronic construction of language reflects a historical influence or diachronic change. Students come into the classroom shaped by their diverse histories and past experiences through their language, but they are confronted with standard English as monolithic, acontextual, and ahistorical. To reconcile the relationship between standard English, culture, and history in the classroom, we must realize that standard English is not just a "one note" language; it mediates between culture, history, and experience. This essay presents a few conceptual approaches to the reconciliation of standard English with the multicultural classroom.

The Dimensionality of Standard English

In the writing classroom, students do not interact with language in a linear way although the writing process itself might be straightforward. Between the initial assignment and the final paper, the students recall history and consider their shifts in opinion. Writing is an easy or a difficult task depending on whether students can direct the undercurrents of culture and history permeating their language into a coherent essay that is composed through standard English. Standard English is one of the factors that make the written discourse taught in our classrooms monolithic, ahistorical, and acontextual. Louise Wetherbee Phelps (1988) criticized this model and proposed three criteria that a less static model of written discourse should meet:

> First, it must be *dynamic*, accounting for change and development in a structure over time, both as it is composed and as it is read. Second, it must be *relativistic or perspectival*, allowing interpretation to vary with alternate perspectives or gestalts of meaning according to contextual factors. Third, it must account for *the constitution or reconstitution* of structure as a process in which the observer plays an interactive role as participant in a communication event. (141)

Keeping this dynamic model of writing and the jazz analogy in mind, we can construct a three-dimensional model of standard English as depicted in Figure 13.1.

Imagine a picture in a frame; we know that the picture is only a representation of someone, not the real person. The two-dimensional element represents standard English—context is the picture frame, so to speak. The subject in the picture could provide more detailed information about when and where the picture was taken, age, circumstances, and so forth. We would know that this

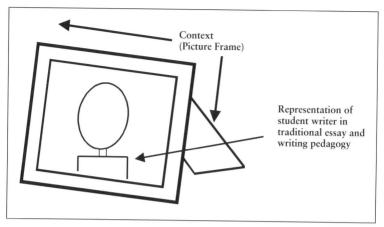

FIGURE **13.1.** *Three-dimensional model of standard English.*

snapshot is only a moment in the subject's life, and it does not represent much of his or her entire richness. Picking up the jazz analogy once again, jazz music is known for its artists' varied interpretations. In the music itself, whole measures of notes represent singular melodies. In a best-case education scenario, standard English might be used in a multicultural setting in the same manner as jazz music; standard language in its linear structure offers possibilities for interpretation of the culture behind the words. In other words, everyone might interpret the picture in a different way. The student from a diverse background does not sacrifice her own culture as long as she maneuvers her language behind standard English. Unfortunately, standard English is often given primacy in the classroom as the end to a means; its mastery is the proof of writing competency, which makes this student's maneuvering so difficult. Standard English is looked on as the actual goal or end of writing instruction rather than as the means by which subjects can interpret the story behind the picture.

There is an ongoing conflict over the dominant role of standard English in the writing classroom, which is also reflected in the conflict between traditional and multicultural writing instruction. The multicultural approach to writing has naturally challenged the dominance of standard English, which invited complaints by conservatives as well as understandable reservations from well-known composition theorists. Linda Flower

(1989) argues that writing should be "grounded in specific knowledge about real people writing in significant personal, social, or political situations." She also believes that "if we would understand how cognition and context interact, we cannot remain satisfied with speculative theories based only on abstract social or political imperatives" (283). Heather MacDonald (1995), however, looks on composition teachers' interest in the context of writing much less favorably:

> For years, composition teachers have absorbed the worst strains in both popular and academic cultures. The result is an indigestible stew of 1960's liberationist zeal, 1970's deconstructivist nihilism, and 1980's multicultural proselytizing. The only thing that composition teachers are not talking and writing about these days is how to teach students to compose clear, logical prose. (3–4)

MacDonald's remarks reclaim a more traditional writing instruction that is disappearing with the explosion of unconventional writing pedagogy in recent years. George Will's statement (1995), which piggybacks MacDonald's article, could be considered more severe:

> In 1966, the City University of New York began the first academic affirmative action program. Open admissions would soon follow, as would the idea that it is cultural imperialism to deny full legitimacy to anything called "Black English." Simultaneously came the idea that demands for literacy oppress the masses and condition them to accept the coercion of capitalism. . . . The smugly self-absorbed professoriate that perpetuates all this academic malpractice is often tenured and always comfortable. The students on the receiving end are always cheated and often unemployable. (3)

MacDonald and Will clearly associate less emphasis on standard English with less concern for good writing, or "clear, logical prose."

Left Margins: Cultural Studies and Composition Pedagogy (Fitts 1995) is an anthology of relatively current ideas and pedagogy in writing instruction that have been criticized by conservatives such as George Will and Heather MacDonald. The pedagogy demonstrated in *Left Margins* exhibits a persistent if not desperate attempt to rip away the public/academic masks students need to wear in the classroom, in the belief that scrupulous interrogation of private values and racial, gender, or class identities will open the door to instant mastery of composition. The new cultural studies–based pedagogy is an attempt to gain access to the undercurrents of culture held back by traditional writing instruction. For example, two teachers, Joseph C. Bodziock and Christopher Ferry (1995), characterize their teaching experience as the story of "two white, middle-income men trying to represent a world full of difference to a group of largely white, middle- and lower-income students" (39). Both are cognizant of the fact that when the issue of difference was introduced into class, students tended to "shut down" because they had learned to see themselves in their own universe without locating the self "in a larger communal and cultural sphere" (42). Colleen M. Tremonte (1995) introduces the pedagogy of "gravedigging" to "enable students to contextualize their investigation so as to examine how socially constructed and politically situated myths affect their personal lives" (57). Kathleen Dixon (1995) exposes White students to 2 Live Crew and Queen Latifah in spite of resistance (103–4). Christopher Wise (1995) uses contemporary criticism on *Pee-Wee's Playhouse* to teach writing (129). This is the pedagogy that has put MacDonald and Will on notice, but it does not sit well with composition scholars such as Gary Tate (1995) either:

> I am not surprised to see cultural studies used to fill the seemingly empty space that is college composition, even though we have learned in the last thirty years that if we are serious about teaching *writing* rather than literature or politics or religion, we can—should—make the writing of our students the focus (content) of the course. Only one or two of the authors in this book even hint that they are interested in such a focus. (270)

The opinions of those who advocate the values of traditional academia have haunted me for most of my undergraduate and graduate career in English. I remember as an undergraduate student taking a course in Old English literature, a required class for English majors. During the introduction of the course, the instructor emphasized that we must learn Old English not only because of its extinction as a language, but also to understand the history of the American language. I pointed out to the instructor that as an African American I did not share the same history. She told me that as long as I was an American, the same history applied. I could not relate to Anglo-Saxon as a direct ancestor of standard English based on the way I used English. When I took sociolinguistics a couple of years later, I related easily to the theories of creolization and the study of the Gullah languages, which were situated within the African American culture and engaged my interrogation of language and the history of standard English. All of this is to say that the English language's Anglo-Saxon lineage should not be considered the only legitimate history of standard English.

It is not standard English, however, that is necessarily oppressive, but the stifling of the undercurrents of history, context, and culture concomitant with the practice of valorizing standard English. History has shown that standard English is a tool of oppressive, (neo)colonial practices; this reason alone validates the need for multicultural writing instruction. Standard English has been used by the dominant culture to maintain the power of the Western world. In his discussion of popular culture, Henry Giroux (1992) outlined the practices of the dominant culture, interpreting the theory of Antonio Gramsci by appropriating Gramsci's theory of hegemonic power as a "political and pedagogical process," stressing that "every relation of hegemony is necessarily an educational relationship" (186). Through this educational relationship, the dominant culture gains the consent of the subordinate culture, yet the popular culture of the subordinate groups "cannot be defined around a set of ideological meanings permanently inscribed in particular cultural forms" (187).

Black English, for example, is accepted as a "dialect of English," but it is not an acceptable use of language in a job interview (Gee 1991, 131). Black English is accepted and legitimized only in a specific cultural practice and context. Standard English, on the other hand, is assumed to function in any context, but only because its use is authenticated and therefore legitimized by the dominant culture. When a dominant cultural practice, such as the use of language, is authenticated, it is "saved," so to speak, from diachronic or synchronic shifts and appears as "objective" knowledge.

This practice of the dominant culture has filtered through the tradition of academia: the literacy of the dominant cultural practice has been distanced from the social experience behind standard English. Through standardized tests and proficiency exams, this literacy has been suspended from the experience of everyday life and presented as a literacy without a particular culture or value system. The example of Black English demonstrates how standard English, in its false claim to be acontextual, automatically transforms the literacy of the subordinate culture into a delegitimized object.

In its two-dimensional structure, standard English also represents the result of a dominant culture's colonization practices. When Donaldo Macedo (1991) documented the quest for a new literacy program in the Republic of Cape Verde, a Portuguese colony, he used this experience to illustrate the process of emancipatory literacy. Cape Verde was a colony that became independent in 1975 (148). The struggle to initiate a new pedagogy was hampered by the decision about whether to use the subordinate language of Capeverdean or the dominant language of Portuguese. Capeverdean educators ultimately resorted to teaching the natives in the colonizing language of Portuguese, a decision that negated the Freirean intentions of helping the Capeverdeans reconstruct a new national identity (154).

In the U.S. educational system, the "native" language is not quite so distinct. A dialect such as Black English, however, is recognized only as a language of a resistant culture; it would not be acceptable for use outside of the Black culture. The use of standard English, on the other hand, has been transformed into a practice of prescriptive rules and stylistic form. The dominant culture transforms its contextual, specific hegemony into a pedagogy that can be disseminated, textualized, and reproduced again and again in the classroom, disguised as an acontextual language. Students of the subordinated culture must put standard English back into its proper historical and political context in order to locate their own literacy.

The erasing of history as part of the dominant culture's linguistic practices has long been recognized in linguistic and anthropological circles. Brian Street (1994) points out that in assessing the literacy of Fiji natives, Clammer characterized the natives as primitive, using an autonomous model of literacy as a standard. Street states that Clammer fails to account for the "social upheavals" that took place on the islands and the "significance of the response to colonisation" (6). Clammer's false claim of knowledge about Fiji natives is constructed through the erroneous belief that standard English is acontextual.

In the discipline of sociolinguistics, a "standard" language is upheld in an attempt to establish a uniformity in which language change can be measured. A consequence of this decision is that non-standard dialects are seen as "incorrect, irregular, ungrammatical and deviant" (Milroy 1992, 7). James Milroy asserts that in reality, no language can ever achieve stability; it is in a constant state of change. To make any assessment of literacy at all, language should always be observed in the speech community in which it is used (7):

> The belief that language change is dysfunctional is most clearly expressed in popular attitudes to language. These commonly conceive of languages as ideal and perfect structures, and of speakers as awkward creatures who violate these perfect structures by misusing and corrupting "language.". . . So strong is this intolerance of speaker-variation and change that in many countries academies have been set up to enforce a uniform "correct" usage and to prevent uncontrolled divergence. . . . There are, of course, socio-political and economic reasons for these attitudes. . . . They are powerful and deep seated and they cannot be ignored. (32)

In the early history of the composition classroom, the pedagogy of writing was also based on the use of "ideal and perfect structures," or, to use Phelps's (1989) words, on "objectivist conceptions of text, textuality, meaning" (141). As it became the new national language, standard English became the fixed measuring stick for language competence. Immigrants who flooded into the United States during the nineteenth century would throw away their own culture and become new citizens.

The cultural dominance of standard English was reinforced by the dominance of literature-trained teachers in the early-instruction composition courses. Literature implied an elite canon and the promotion of its values. It is irrefutable that there are "standards" imposed through "English" that simultaneously impose the dominant culture on the student. Moreover, standard English does not allow for the three-dimensionality of history and culture, but it does allow for a detached frame of reference and means to communicate through context.

Context

How do context and standard English interact? Because the contextuality of standard English is detached, it is important to remember that students who are considered competent writers have a social advantage that stems from socioeconomic and curricular changes that took place in the teaching of writing in the late nineteenth century. At that time, reading and writing made the shift from a cultural rhetoric to a gatekeeping standard for college applicants and immigrants. In the last half of the nineteenth century, an expanding economy created new professions outside of the "elitist" professions of "law, medicine, and church." The university began to offer "upward mobility through certification in such professions as agriculture, engineering, journalism, social work, education, and a host of other new professional pursuits" (Berlin 1987, 21). Standard English became the litmus test for new first-year students:

> [T]he test in English ensured that the new open university would not become too open, allowing the new immigrants, for example, to earn degrees in science or mathematics without demonstrating by their use of language that they belonged in the middle class. However, establishing the entrance test in composition suggested that the ability to write was something the college student ought to bring with him from his preparatory school, a place which was more and more likely to be one of the new public high schools that were now appearing everywhere. (23)

The socioeconomic shift in education that took place a hundred years ago continues to have serious reverberations today as the gap between public and private schools has recreated an elitist class segregated from the disadvantaged minorities and immigrant populations.

Standard English is a set of comprehensible rules and forms only for those who already understand cultural semantics. Those who are culturally disenfranchised must find a way to make meaning of standard English from the previous cultural experiences of others since their own experience cannot be found in standard English. Disenfranchisement does not necessarily run along racial lines but strongly correlates with socioeconomic status, which is overdetermined by race.

James Gee (1991), a linguist, defined three systems in the construction of language which are essential in order for the speaker and hearer to understand each other. The referential system incorporates literal meaning, the contextualization system incorporates social relations, and the ideological system incorporates values, beliefs, and worldviews. Furthermore, these systems inseparably overlap in any piece of language. Gee's research on oral texts illustrated how these three systems are represented in different patterns of language.

Gee told "The Alligator River Story" to lower- and lower-middle-class students, Black and White. The story was about two lovers, Abigail and Gregory, who were separated by a river of man-eating alligators. In order to get across the river, Abigail had to sleep with Sinbad, a riverboat captain. After initially refusing Sinbad's offer, Abigail goes to Ivan, a friend, for advice. Ivan refuses to get involved, leaving Abigail to sleep with Sinbad. When Abigail makes it across the river, she tells Gregory about the incident, at which Gregory refuses to have anything to do with her. Abigail tells another friend, Slug, what has happened. Slug, sympathizing with Abigail, beats up Gregory.

Gee asked a group of Black students and a group of White students—all from lower- to lower-middle-class backgrounds—to rank the characters from "most offensive to least offensive," allowing one student from each group to represent them. Both groups ranked Sinbad and Gregory as most offensive, but the Black student placed more importance on social interaction, context, references, and ideology, as well as considering the teacher "someone who shares knowledge with him [the student] and who is part of the overall task" (Gee 1991,127). The White student was more autonomous, using "reason" and "psychology." These findings support the theories of the dominant culture in which the act is separated from the meaning. Gee points out that the White student considered Sinbad offensive not because he "asked Abigail to sleep with him, but because he 'wanted' to sleep with her, the actual act having little significance on Sinbad's guilt" (128).

Gee then told the story to upper-class White students, who also chose a spokesperson to respond to Gee's questions. He noticed that in the upper-class White student's language, social relationships between the characters are "attenuated"; the characters never confront each other. The upper-class White student was much more detached than either the lower-middle-class White or Black student. The upper-class students spoke with complete autonomy and with no reference to the social world at all (129). The upper-class students were in effect "abstracting" the story from the traditional practice of the dominant culture.

This autonomy of the upper-class students is characterized by what Phelps (1988) outlines as the Cartesian principle of dividing the world into subject and object. Phelps distinguishes two strands in this process, in which it is first necessary to determine subject and object as two "stable and determinate wholes," and then, as a result, to establish the "ontological independence of objects from the consciousness and situation of individual observers" (136). These principles are the tradition of Western classical science and hence are a credo of the dominant culture which upholds the philosophy of Western civilization. The socioeconomically disadvantaged student, on the other hand, who is an object within the political structure, finds him- or herself in the position of trying to find autonomy in the text through fragmented, subjective reality, as Phelps points out:

> Written discourse is patently a communication transaction involving experiences by writer and readers that are life events for both. When the text is detached both from composing acts and from correlative reading acts and is transformed into an autonomous, context-free object in which meaning has somehow been fixed as "content," there is no way to explain its

participation as a mediating element in the felt event of communication initiated by the writer and consummated uniquely by each successful reading act. The text and the acts of the discourse event become ontologically incompatible within a static concept of discourse structure. (1988, 141)

Life experiences are necessary in order for a student to write. A step toward becoming a critical thinker involves not only the organization of the essay but also stepping back from standard English, adding a third dimension to language, and relieving the tension created by the flattening of experience in traditional pedagogy. On the other hand, the skill in writing the essay requires that disadvantaged students overcome their subjectivity in order to abstract the personal world.

William Labov and Wendell A. Harris's (1986) study of de facto segregation in Philadelphia, which demonstrated how context and language interact, provides another approach to context. Labov and Harris wanted to study how linguistic traits cross racial lines in the city of Philadelphia. I want to emphasize how context and standard English interact, by using the study's comparison between social networks and social histories. Social networks are based on the personal, occupational, family, or other connections among the members of a community. Labov and Harris found that these networks play an important role in the use of certain linguistic mannerisms. When comparing the absence of the third singular /s/ by social networks, however, Labov and Harris saw inconsistencies and concluded that social networks may not be the biggest influence on language. When subjects were grouped by social types (e.g., musicians, activists) or social histories (e.g., Southerners, Puerto Ricans in the Black community), Labov and Harris found more consistent similarities and concluded that "while it is true that close social ties can intensify linguistic similarities, social networks mirror linguistic structure only when speakers share a common social history" (1986, 9). Plotting Labov and Harris's study into the cubical conceptual model, I assume that social networks operate on a two-dimensional level, not depending so much on culture or history. But it is also important to note that language use is represented more accurately when shared histories are accounted for.

The lesson to be learned in composition is that as we cut across race, gender, and class lines, it does not pay to cling to these superficial or static categories without critically interrogating them in the classroom. In writing, it is not only the positive lines of style or structure that count, but also how students see the gaps between the lines, or how they interpret the notes of the music, if you will. The cultural studies–based writing instruction represented in *Left Margins* has, perhaps, been scrutinized for the wrong reasons. While it is good that race, class, and gender can be taken into account in the writing classroom, we cannot make these social matrices the only means by which students can engage in the type of critical thinking that will enable them to write standard English.

Linda Flower's (1989) view of composition may be more agreeable when she says that an understanding of cognition and context is needed, for, using Ravi Coltrane's statement on music, underneath the clean and simple understanding of standard English there is indeed a complex and rich cultural interpretation of the essay, and of writing in general.

The Dimensionality of Culture

In *The Beatles Anthology, Volume 1* (1996), Paul McCartney recounts how, in learning to play the guitar, he, along with John Lennon and George Harrison, traveled to the other side of Liverpool to learn to play a chord they had heard on a blues album. I often read music reviews by critics who dub a group "The New Beatles" or the "Beatles of the 90s." But how can one, through musical notes, duplicate the experience of four working-class youths, born during World War II, who grew up listening to Black R&B and blues musicians? As Ravi Coltrane stated, linear notes have an undercurrent of knowledge and personal experience that play a part in the construction of a single song. Yet the artists who are considered "Beatlesque" are called so because they duplicate notes which stand in for that original experience, which has now become flattened into a genre or type of music. I use the Beatles analogy to demonstrate how a unique sound or expression can become stylized. Stylistic categories such as rap, country, or heavy metal provide some context in which to assess or understand music. The Beatles' originality arose from their significant divergence from accepted categories of music, while at the same time owing something to the historical convergence of the R&B and skiffle music they listened to as teenagers. But the Beatlesque sound does not invoke this previous history. Likewise, it is helpful for student writers to become aware of the rhetorical categories imposed on them, if only to deviate from these categories and deconstruct them in a meaningful way by looking at the spaces between the lines.

In her early research, Linda Flower (1979) compared writing processes between effective and ineffective writers. Effective writers "do not simply *express* thought but *transform* it in certain complex but describable ways for the needs of a reader" (19). Flower also states the two most important stylistic goals that writers of formal written discourse must meet:

> One goal might be described as stylistic control, that is, the ability to choose a more embedded or more elegant transformation from variations which are roughly equivalent in meaning. The second goal is to create a completely autonomous text, that is, a text that does not need context, gestures, or audible effects to convey its meaning. (29)

Furthermore, she describes effective writers as the ones who are able to retrieve information within the reader/writer context and have a complex system of semantic memory. Ineffective writers, on the other hand, produce "writer based" prose, in which the needs of the reader are put aside and the writers are caught within their own experiences instead of writing for the reader (34–35). The problem is that ineffective writers are considered such because they do not share the cultural norms that influence academic writing. Students from subordinate-culture groups are writing from a marginalized position, from which it is impossible to write through an "objective," "context-free" author identity. Writing reader-oriented prose is not necessarily a question of being effective or ineffective; it is a question of which sociopolitical identities allow students to use their cultural repertoires of meaning and engage them autonomously.

I see the reservations of composition theorists not as a rejection of culture in the classroom but as a reaction to culture being used in an uncritical way. I present the examples from *Left Margins* as an illustration of multicultural pedagogy being used in confrontational and unproductive ways. How do these methods and introduction of various media teach the writing act other than to provoke reflexive rather than reflective responses? Culture does not have to fall solely within the boundaries of race, class, and gender; culture can be any environment that provides the primary source of history by which a subject engages in critical thinking and writing. A subject does not always have to positively identify with a particular culture; language can betray and affirm dominant beliefs of the self and others. It is in the recognition of these contradictory undercurrents that critical thinking and writing take place.

In academic politics, students from subordinated groups are often looked on as writers who have not been initiated into the Cartesian process of separating subject from object either at all or in the same way that students from the dominant culture have. Therefore all of their independent, autonomous strategies are disabled because the subordinate-culture groups have no prior knowledge or history of which problem-solving strategies to use. Subordinate-culture groups are forced to stay within the immediate, concrete contexts of the two-dimensional frame to learn. As we have seen from Gee's (1991) research, however, those contexts are determined by sociopolitical hegemonic practices.

But there are ways of reconciling different cultures in the composition classroom. Paulo Freire (1991) discusses word versus world contexts and describes reading the world as an intimate process that occurs naturally and as opposed to an attenuated process in which words are "superimposed" onto the context of meaning. But Freire also emphasizes that he learned to reread his world, undertaking the "archaeology of . . . understanding the complex act of reading in [his] own existential experience" (143). The same holds true for the disadvantaged students who must historicize their "reading" experience. In reality, literacy is not about writing; it is about the author locating him- or herself within various frames in the classroom, including standard English versus his or her own language.

In composition research, Carol Lee's (1993) study of scaffolding and African American texts reinforces the need to reattach standard English to culture. Standard English does have a culture and a history, but this culture and history are disguised as literacy, whereas languages from other cultures are not considered literate. While tutoring a Black student in one of my English classes, I tried to give him some idea how to write a research paper. I tried to convey the detachment from the social world that research papers need in order to sound authentic, but how do you tell a student to write like an upper-class White male if that is not the primary culture through which he acquires knowledge? This brings me to the practice of signifying, a word that Geneva Smitherman, Henry Louis Gates Jr., and other humanities scholars have now made familiar in composition studies. To quote Carol Lee (1993), "The social practice is signifying, a ritualized form of talk in the African-American community, and the school task is literary interpretation" (9). As we shift from social communities to the classroom, the names may change but the task remains the same. As Lee states, signifying requires "to reason or infer metaphorically," and it also "involves establishing an unstated relationship between the topic and the vehicle of the metaphor and the building levels of parallel associations that extend to the topic of the metaphor" (12–13). In short, students who are able to "signify" understand not only the codes of their own language, but also the codes of standard English, and can use varying and complex types of metaphors. They can not only play the notes, but they can also interpret them. Signifying is a legitimate writing practice that teachers do not recognize in the classroom, but as we can see it draws on prior social knowledge and history that builds a scaffold to standard English. To visualize signifying, imagine a cloth draped over a figure or person. The cloth is no longer flat and two-dimensional but takes on shape and definition. In Black English, it is not uncommon to take a term such as "bad," "cool," or "sweet" and transform the original meaning in standard English to one popular in Black English. The Black English meaning, then, actually crosses over to mainstream speech, and two meanings are acknowledged. In Lee's (1993)study, scaffolding takes place when students able to understand that "bad" in their culture means something else in mainstream language; they are able to scaffold or bridge to standard English in a productive way. Traditionally, standard English has been "one size fits all." In other words, context, like a picture frame, encompasses some likeness or representation of someone; it is not a real person, there is not a body attached to this frame. Standard English as used by the dominant culture will not acknowledge any history or culture that would allow for expression of a real person. (This picture was taken of me when I was sixteen at Yellowstone Park. It had been a wonderful day . . . the sun was shining. . . . etc.).

When students are able to signify, they appropriate standard English to their experiences rather than let standard English make them fragmented writers; they accomplish more critical and complex work in writing. Lee's scaffolding practice actually entails a "reattaching" of language to history and culture, as illustrated in Figure 13.2.

Composition Classroom 2000

When imagining the writing classroom in the new millennium, we should consider the following three principles in writing pedagogy:

1. A dynamic pedagogy as outlined by Phelps's (1988) work must not allow canonized texts to remain untouched by history; these texts cannot be viewed as representative of any time period

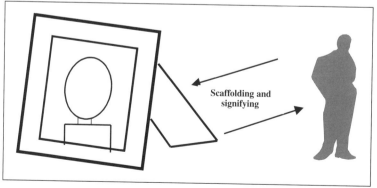

FIGURE 13.2. *Reattaching language and history to culture.*

or culture. In accounting for change over time, students' past experiences should be brought to these texts, and all students should be allowed to engage in problem solving and constructing knowledge.

2.   A context-based pedagogy must encompass the historical and sociopolitical background of both academic literacy and the literacy of marginalized cultures. Based on Phelps's (1988) principle of relativity, such pedagogy acknowledges that written discourse can be assigned meaning only in its particular historical, social, or political context; it cannot have universal meaning. This principle underlines the idea of historicizing standard English and allows students to see the distance between language and meaning. Phelps adapts Einstein's theory to composition when she states that "all measurements of time and space depend on the observer's frame of reference—that is, they are relative rather than absolute. Events appear different to observers in different coordinate systems" (143). Standard English must be understood as related to its own sociopolitical context rather than as a universal standard of language use.

3.   Students must be encouraged to write about the sociopolitical shifts they perceive between themselves and the text. They must be encouraged to bring their local literacy into the classroom and understand how they use their language as signifiers. This third principle, identified by Phelps (1988) as (re)constitution, embraces the idea of emancipatory literacy, discussed extensively by Paulo Freire (1991). In emancipatory literacy, language emerges as a tool of resignification, recreation, and hence liberation. Students are allowed to make new meaning in the world to change language in the classroom.

   With these three principles in mind, we can take a different approach to writing the essay. The essay cannot be seen as a composition of introductory paragraph, supporting statements, and conclusion. The composition essay is a narrative working within the dimensions of history and context (going back to our frames). Students who are beneficiaries of the dominant culture are perceived as competent writers since their past cultural experiences derived from history are co-opted in the composition classroom.

Students from subordinate cultures are forced to leave their culture and history behind, making them fragmented writers since they have to write without the advantage of previous knowledge. Effective writers are critical subjects. Critical subjects are never positioned on positive planes; instead, they write about the gaps between the lines rather than about the actual lines. This is only possible through historicizing. It is deceptive to think that an effective essay can be positively defined by a formula; its coherence comes from the subjects' ability to write from a historical continuum along the lines of past, present, and future within the context of culture. If no histories other than that of the dominant culture are allowed, then the disadvantaged student is indeed trapped within a two dimensional "frame." And when we look at the construction of the essay, we can see a progression from present (thesis statement), to past (supporting statements), to future (conclusion). If we focus on this alternative structure, then meaning as it applies to writing will allow for difference and erase expectations of being an "effective" writer; language and culture can be accounted for.

It is clear that new initiatives must be pursued in our writing programs. We must now understand literacy as a sociopolitical foundation in this country; it is no longer separable as acontextual. We must historicize rather than politicize. We must historicize because we have no choice—this is how we create narratives. Changing the sociopolitical structure in this country may be out of reach for now, but we can start by changing what writing means in the university. The hegemony of the dominant culture can no longer be allowed to hide behind process-oriented pedagogy. The education of our students has been compromised for too long.

Works Cited

Beatles Anthology, The, Volume 1. 1996. Dir. Geoff Wonfor. Apple Corps.

Berlin, James A. 1987. *Rhetoric and Reality: Writing Instruction in American Colleges, 1900–1985.* Carbondale: Southern Illinois University Press.

Bodziok, Joseph C., and Ferry Christopher. 1995. "Teaching 'Myth, Difference and Popular Culture.'" In Karen Fitts and Alan W. France, eds., *Left Margins: Cultural Studies and Composition Pedagogy*. New York: SUNY Press. 39–51.

Dixon, Kathleen. 1995. "Making and Taking Apart 'Culture' in the (Writing) Classroom." In Karen Fitts and Alan W. France, eds., *Left Margins: Cultural Studies and Composition Pedagogy*. New York: SUNY Press. 99–114.

Bird. 1989. Dir. Clint Eastwood. Perf. Forest Whitaker. Warner Home Video.

Fitts, Karen, and Alan W. France, eds. 1995. *Left Margins: Cultural Studies and Composition Pedagogy*. New York: SUNY Press.

Flower, Linda. 1979. "Writer-Based Prose: A Cognitive Basis for Problems in Writing." *College English* 41: 19–37.

———. 1989. "Cognition, Context, and Theory Building." *College Composition and Communication* 40: 282–311.

Freire, Paulo. 1991. "The Importance of the Act of Reading." Trans. Loretta Slover. In Candace Mitchell and Kathleen Weiler, eds., *Rewriting Literacy: Culture and Discourse of the Other*. New York: Bergin and Garvey. 139–45.

Gee, James Paul. 1991. "Discourse Systems and Aspirin Bottles: On Literacy." In Candace Mitchell and Kathleen Weiler, eds., *Rewriting Literacy: Culture and Discourse of the Other*. New York: Bergin and Garvey. 123–35.

Giroux, Henry. 1992. *Border Crossings: Cultural Workers and the Politics of Education*. London: Routledge.

Labov, William, and Wendell A. Harris. 1986. "De Facto Segregation of Black and White Vernaculars." In David Sankoff, ed., *Diversity and Diachrony*. Philadelphia: John Benjamins. 1–24.

Lee, Carol D. 1993. *Signifying as a Scaffold for Literary Interpretation: The Pedagogical Implications of an African American Discourse Genre*. Urbana, IL: National Council of Teachers of English.

MacDonald, Heather. 1995. "Why Johnny Can't Write." *Public Interest Quarterly* 120: 3–13.

Macedo, Donaldo. 1991. "The Politics of an Emancipatory Literacy in Cape Verde." In Candace Mitchell and Kathleen Weiler, eds.,

Rewriting Literacy: Culture and Discourse of the Other. New York: Bergin and Garvey. 147–59.

Mandel, Howard. 1998. "Louder Than Words: The Enduring Legacy of John Coltrane." *Downbeat* (June): 20–27.

Milroy, James. 1992. *Linguistic Variation and Change.* Oxford: Blackwell.

Phelps, Louise Wetherbee. 1988. *Composition as a Human Science: Contributions to the Self-Understanding of a Discipline.* New York: Oxford University Press.

Street, Brian V. 1994. *Literacy in Theory and Practice.* Cambridge: Cambridge University Press.

Tate, Gary. 1995. "Empty Pedagogical Space and Silent Students." In Karen Fitts and Alan W. France, eds., *Left Margins: Cultural Studies and Composition Pedagogy.* New York: SUNY Press. 269–73.

Tremonte, Colleen M. 1995. "Gravedigging: Excavating Cultural Myths." In Karen Fitts and Alan W. France, eds., *Left Margins: Cultural Studies and Composition Pedagogy.* New York: SUNY Press. 53–67.

Will, George. 1995. "Subtracting from National Literacy." *Detroit News,* July 2. B3.

Wise, Christopher. 1995. "Pee-Wee, Penley, and Pedagogy, or, Hands-on Feminism in the Writing Classroom." Karen Fitts and Alan W. France, eds., *Left Margins: Cultural Studies and Composition Pedagogy.* New York: SUNY Press. 129–38.

CHAPTER FOURTEEN

Transcultural Rhetorics for Cultural Survival

LOUISE RODRÍGUEZ CONNAL
University of Arizona

Theoretical discussions concerning English Only, hybridity, identification, and cultures frequently are confronted with praxis in U.S. classrooms. The U.S. population is diverse, and from the very beginning, it has been a nation that experiences hybridity but feels uncomfortable with it. People from different countries have immigrated and added their languages and ways of thinking and speaking to the U.S. culture. These linguistic events sometimes smoothly blend in, but sometimes they clash violently with the standard American English taught in schools throughout the country. Moreover, the acknowledgment of diversity still does not include diverse or multiple language use in our classrooms, where English Only laws and pedagogical practices are typically advocated.

One of the many questions this situation raises is how the students who carry the cultural and linguistic marks of diversity can flourish in the classroom and benefit from knowing—and working with and across—two or more languages and rhetorical styles. What follows is an attempt to respond to this question using my experience as a Puerto Rican woman and a writing teacher, as well as insights from postcolonial theory and feminist writing.

Looking for the connection between my identities as a woman who is both Puerto Rican and American, I have had to face the myths handed down to me by my mother and father. My parents believed that if I spoke English without an accent, I could succeed. Based on their life stories, my parents believed, as many others do, that fluency in English would lead to a better life in the United States. Teachers around the country drum out "bad" English for reasons similar to those held by my parents, for they understand that skillful use of "proper" English correlates with success in U.S. society. However, is this correlation accurate?

Juan Flores in *Divided Borders: Essays on Puerto Rican Identity* (1993) also mentions the myth that connects English-language proficiency to success. Specifically, the chapter titled "'La Carreta Made a U-Turn': Puerto Rican Language and Culture in the United States" discusses the connections linking success in society with issues of identity, politics, rhetoric, and English Only. I draw on Flores because he precisely sums up the Puerto Rican minority experience on the U.S. mainland:

> For language minorities in the United States, the acquisition of standard English is presumed to signal both a willingness to assimilate and an effort to take the most crucial first step to gain the knowledge and skills that enable social advance. Learn the language, it is said, and the doors of the "larger" society will swing open. (160)

Flores, however, also points out the hypocrisy of claims that success comes from language skills, and he alleges that "the language-as-lever rationale is riddled with contradictions" (160). Namely, such an argument blatantly ignores that other factors such as race, class, education, and gender have an impact on the degree of social and monetary success that people can achieve. Those of us who have experiences with bilingualism (the knowledge and use of two languages or two varieties of a language) and with issues of social justice for minorities realize, along with Flores, that regarding English as the sole prerequisite of success in U.S. society is a rationalization that informs public policy much too often.

The rationalization comes in the form of the idea that in order to be part of their country, all people must speak from one voice, in one language. English Only implies that unity comes from sharing a single linguistic code. Therefore many minorities within the United States feel coerced into assimilation by the prevailing practices of our educational system. As Flores (1993) asserts, "the element of coercion . . . runs through the entire history of language contact under colonial conditions" (160), and, indeed, many of the language-instruction practices that minority students experience in schools can be illuminated by the concepts constructed by postcolonial scholars.

In order to successfully interact with the colonial power, the colonized must agree to use the language of the colonizer. Hence a call for English Only in a context such as Puerto Rico is coercive. Puerto Rico has a long history of linguistic and cultural hybridity, and the imposition of one linguistic code that is very different from Spanish is at best difficult to enforce. When demands for English are connected to a permanent change in status, English Only becomes an implement of colonization. Puerto Ricans, whether on the island or on the mainland, are caught in a colonial relationship with the United States. The invitation to end Puerto Rico's colonial status is a convenient cover for the "long-term imposition of English in Puerto Rico," which in the same colonial logic implies that Puerto Ricans have an obligation to give up their Spanish and its varieties for standard English (Flores 1993, 160). Such an invitation erases the actual transcultural and hybrid experiences, including the use of many varieties of Spanish English, in both the United States and Puerto Rico.

The politics of education, as seen through the lens of English Only rhetoric, similarly imply that there is a need for a unifying language in our diversely populated country. Therefore, so the advocates of English Only believe, colonized countries must assume English as their national language. This fear of the Other translates into the belief that other dialects or languages have negative influences that compromise the citizenship of our country. In the United States, however, it would be difficult to "return to" or to develop a purified state of language, and the plea for English Only is based on assertions that contradict the dynamic nature of language learning, linguistic change, and growth. Although English Only proponents believe there is one proper and unchanged dialect of English, a language education that allows for various uses of language is more congruent with the everyday linguistic experience of the citizens of the United States.

Transcultural Rhetoric—The Pedagogical Alternative

Issues of English Only concern me because I see the limitations that teaching only standard English has on many students in my composition classes. Among my first observations of writing students were their fear, insecurity, and lack of confidence about the language used in their writing. I observed minimal use of the first person; a dependence on the standard five-paragraph essay format; and fear of directly addressing an audience. As a rule, students tend to use strategies that help them hide their (or others') differences or identities. Another feature of many of my students' writing is their reluctance to connect their personal knowledge with public, or researched, knowledge. They seem to prefer standard, or "objective," knowledge and language to the significant insights of their particular lives or cultural experiences. This is especially true for women of color and students representing other minority groups with family backgrounds different from those of mainstream, middle-class America. The fear of making errors that would label them as ignorant or less intelligent than others mutes these students' expression of what they know. Minority students, in my teaching experience, are among the most silent in class. Since this silence can be construed as limited intelligence or consent to dominant-language policies, the positive aspects and potential of knowing more than the standard dialect are often hurtfully ignored.

By arguing for the acknowledgment and inclusion of what is nonstandard, I do not mean that we should not teach standard uses of English. We should, however, wholeheartedly acknowledge that there are many "englishes." Awareness of variety in accents, dialects, and rhetorical styles helps the writer/speaker to address a variety of rhetorical situations and audiences that require different uses of spoken and written language.

The transcultural rhetoric I use in my teaching can loosely be defined as a rhetoric that crosses and includes multiple languages, genres, and styles. Transcultural rhetoric expresses the sensibilities of people whose cultures are hybridized—people who affiliate with two or more cultures, languages, or dialects. Transcultural rhetoric is an argument for using and appreciating the different critical and cultural awarenesses that hybrid people can contribute to our society and knowledge base. Although not all of my students would consider themselves "hybrids," they all can benefit from the flexibility of writing that utilizes variety in form and content. Students can benefit from gaining critical awareness of the ingredients that comprise the world in which they live. As many of my students reported, transcultural rhetoric helped them to develop writing "muscle." I encourage my students not only to read, analyze, and write, but also to collaborate as they engage their writing tasks, because transcultural rhetoric, of necessity, requires a willingness to cross into another person's style, point of view, and so forth.

The Theory Link: Postcolonial and Hybridity

When exploring the theoretical sources of resistance to monolithic language use, I found postcolonial theory and the concepts of hybridity developed within that framework useful. One of the concepts in postcolonial studies is to see issues of language and culture through the lens of difference in power relations. These complex relations can be located in what Mary Louise Pratt calls "contact zones." Pratt (1991) defines these zones as "social spaces where cultures meet, clash and grapple with each other, often in contexts of highly asymmetrical relations of power, such as colonialism, slavery, or their aftermaths as they are lived out in many parts of the world today" (34). The difference in power relations often implies the imposition of language and customs on the groups with less power. In that sense, discussions of postcolonial power directly relate to the English Only public debate, for English Only imposes the language of the most powerful social group on all people within U.S. boundaries.

The experiences of the colonized population in other countries mirrors the experiences of many minority groups in the United States. While many immigrants came here from Europe, many more are members of groups whose lands and people were taken by force of war. Mexican Americans, Native Americans, Puerto Ricans, and Hawaiians have experienced territorial conquest and cultural conflicts the same way the indigenous populations of many Third World countries did. As Edward Said (1993), one of the most eloquent scholars of postcolonialism, puts it, the United States can be seen as "an immigrant settler society super-imposed on the ruins of considerable native presence" (xxv). This similarity makes the work of postcolonial scholarship relevant for the U.S. context, too. Insofar as these "colonized" minority groups seek to make changes or exchanges with the U.S. govern-ment in their struggle to maintain their cultures, it could be argued that they are entering a postcolonial state characterized by hybridized languages, cultures, and identities.

Another useful concept postcolonial scholars focus on is the hybridity of identities developed in the contact zones. This con-cept closely relates to issues of rhetoric and language choice in the classroom and in society. For example, Said (1993) explains how his experience of maintaining his Muslim and Arab identity while living in countries that are colonizers of his homeland results in a new, complex identity: "I grew up as an Arab with a Western edu-cation. Ever since I can remember, I have felt that I belonged to both worlds, without being completely of either one or the other" (xxvi). Said also notes that the U.S. identity is hybridized from its inception and acknowledges that there is "ideological concern over identity," which he says is "understandably entangled with the interests and agendas of various groups—not all of them oppressed minorities—that wish to set priorities reflecting these interests" (xxv).

The concept of hybridity as it engages with the concept of identity is relevant to the development and interruption of hier-archies among cultures. According to Ashcroft, Griffiths, and Tiffin (1995), the idea of national identity is "often based on nat-uralized myths of racial or cultural origin. . . . [I]t was a vital part of the collective political resistance which focused on issues of separate identity and cultural distinctiveness" (183). Hybridity undermines the concept of separate and pure identities. Hybrids construct places in the contact zone which challenge the natural-ized myths of racial or cultural beginnings, especially those transmitted through the "proper" or "pure" language. The chal-lenge to the notion of cultural and linguistic purity or concepts such as English Only makes hybridity a useful alternative in cul-tural and linguistic education. Ashcroft, Griffiths, and Tiffin (1995) point out that in postcolonial writing, the "hybridized nature of post-colonial culture is viewed as a strength rather than as weakness" (183).

Another, slightly different approach to hybridity is expressed in Homi Bhabha's work. Homi Bhabha (1994) argues that the interplay among cultures takes place in the interstices of cultural structures. While Pratt (1991) presents a model of "contact zones" where cultures overlap in order for cultural exchanges to take place, Bhabha focuses on the "in between spaces [that] provide the terrain for elaborating strategies of selfhood—singular or communal—that initiate new signs of identity, and innovative sites of collaboration and contestation, in the act of defining the idea of society itself" (2). He further argues that minority groups in the interstitial places where negotiation occurs must contend with cultural authority. That is, they should resist those who essentialize or expect a set of pregiven traits to represent minority groups in the "ongoing negotiation that seeks to authorize cultural hybridities" (2).

These concepts demonstrate the interaction among differing cultures and languages. English Only concepts erase the possibility for the kinds of cultural and linguistic negotiations that Bhabha, Pratt, Said, and other scholars discuss. English Only proponents frequently are in positions of power or in positions to wield influence over the political implementation of education. Hence they attempt to stifle "contact zone" conflicts that contradict their views of language learning in the United States. The fear of "englishes" spoken with a different sound or "flavor" strongly motivates the one-English-fits-all thinking. Ironically, language issues such as English Only sometimes arise out of the need and desire of formerly colonized or immigrant peoples to partake in the dominant culture of the United States. In addition, the pedagogies needed to help those who are interested in maintaining their home languages and cultures while acquiring the dominant language and culture are often derided and attacked by uninformed politicians and the public as well. The common element in all these phenomena is the lack of even a minimal understanding of how languages change as a result of cultural-linguistic contact or other natural linguistic evolutionary processes.

From my experience as a Puerto Rican American and from contact with Puerto Ricans raised on the mainland of the United States, I recognize our lack of knowledge of the history of Puerto

Rico. This lack of knowledge is an important factor in fostering a colonial or imperial mentality. But presenting the dominant culture as the superior culture creates problems leading to lack of confidence or lowered self-esteem among those from cultures whose histories are erased or otherwise suppressed. Adding to a confusing sense of identity is the fact that citizenship did not prevent Puerto Ricans who came to the mainland from experiencing the racism and other forms of marginalization accorded to other U.S. citizens with a different skin hue. Their *íngles* was not U.S.-flavored, and all Puerto Ricans, whether white or black, were racialized—that is, they were treated as a colonized subject, or Other. The idea of English Only seeks to eradicate differences that exist as a consequence of enslavement, immigration, and colonization of other nations. Yet these differences exist, and the pedagogy and language we use should address them.

The Rhetorics of Crisis

Fear of those who appear or sound different seems to drive much of the rhetoric of crisis in the public media, too. These rhetorics of crisis recurrently surround discussions about the quality of education in the United States, focusing specifically on issues of language education because of the emotion attached to the topic.

Those of us in English Studies have long heard calls from Allan Bloom, E. D. Hirsch, William Bennett, and others to teach a common language and a common literary canon. Issues such as English Only usually arise in a context that exhibits great concern over what to include and exclude in the canon of literature we teach in schools, or over what and whose history should be taught. The effectiveness or ineffectiveness of bilingual education is frequently discussed as part of these concerns. As increasing numbers of working-class students of color enter the school system, the crisis rhetorics lamenting the decline of education intensify. Evaluating and responding to accusations of literacy crisis, John Trimbur states:

> The resonance of the two terms—"literacy" and "crisis"—have taken on a certain formulaic, self-explanatory quality. Just to utter the phrase is to perform the act, putting literacy in

crisis by releasing diffuse but widely shared anxieties about deteriorating educational standards, drops in test scores, the permissiveness of the 1960s, black English, the effects of television and video games, John Dewey and progressive education, and the failure to compete economically with the Japanese. The rhetorical power of the phrase "literacy crisis" resides in its ability to condense a broad range of cultural, social, political, and economic tensions into one central image. (277)

Trimbur rightly points to the power of the phrase "literacy crisis" to excite people into (frequently thoughtless) actions that affect our students. Many politicians use the phrase at every election to plant fear in the minds of voters. Fear and elitism frame such discussions. Unfortunately, fear and elitism do not provide an environment in which the educational needs of our students can be addressed in a reasonable manner.

Those of us who teach while keeping the diverse student populations of our classrooms in mind need to hear the opinions of those who respect and use the differences our students bring to the classroom. Of course, much of what I allude to has begun in multicultural classrooms across the country. But the purpose of using or adding materials and techniques that originate outside the teaching traditions beloved by those whose life experiences differ from today's students is often misunderstood.

We should not confuse multiplicity with deficiency. Differences in the ways we use language or in our accents or in the dialects in which we speak and write should not label people as inferior, substandard, or deficient members of our society. The existence of hybridized student populations in our classes, indeed throughout the world, call for teaching that crosses barriers. As teachers we should practice the "pedagogical arts of the contact zone" (Pratt 1991, 40). In other words, difference and diversity should not be interpreted as signs of crisis. Instead, they should be embraced and celebrated in both our rhetoric and our pedagogy.

Hybridity, Writing, and the Female Voice

Members of society must have access to language education that relates to their realities. Additionally, the ability to negotiate differences in "englishes" is important to the construction of the means to engage with others' points of view and methods of representing diverse experiences. Writing provides one method for accomplishing this. Women writers, many of whom are also minorities, lend valuable insight into the processes of artistic creation of texts through acknowledging difference and listening to many voices. As Trinh T. Min-ha (1989) states, "Writing, in a way, is listening to the others' language and reading with the others' eyes. The more ears I'm able to hear with, the farther I see the plurality of meaning and the less I lend myself to the illusion of a single message" (30). In *Reclaiming Medusa: Short Stories by Contemporary Puerto Rican Women,* Diana L. Vélez (1997) explains this complexity in the writing and language use of the anthology's female contributors: "as the writer inscribes her desire through the symbolic order of language, she weaves narratives which, in their imaginative relation to her life, undercut its suffocating reality" (ii). Gloria Anzaldúa (1987) joins these women writers when she points out how "a multitude of dialects interweave to form a generally comprehensible linguistic continuum" (39). Ashcroft, Griffiths, and Tiffin (1989) further point out that, as a world language, English is a "continuum of 'intersections' in which the speaking habits in various communities have intervened to reconstruct the language" (39–40).

Women have conflicts not only with imposed language standards but also with the standards of patriarchy. Speaking out from a position that lacks authority in a male-dominant society is a problem Spivak (1988) addresses in her essay "Can the Subaltern Speak?" Her answer "no" to the question posed in the title stems from her observation that a subaltern's speech frequently is misread because of her political powerlessness. The subaltern is not in a politically viable position to make herself heard. What she says is likely to have little or no effect, if it is heard at all. Spivak claims that the subaltern is defined by the "first world," and she is perceived or inscribed with definitions constructed by the first world. These misrepresentations skew the context, stories, and meanings she presents. Until the subaltern can move into a position where she has some political standing, she will not be able to control the interpretation of her message. If the subaltern remains mute or does not break through the misrepresentations, some will assume that the first world's views of the Other—i.e., the population of Third World nations—are indeed correct. In order to resist this misreading, women of color must speak and write the authentic representations of their lives, beliefs, and histories.

Like Spivak, Anzaldúa (1987) is aware that people of color are rendered invisible and silent. In *Borderlands/La frontera: The New Mestiza*, Anzaldúa advocates the assertive stance of taking pride in our heritage and speaking out for ourselves. She also says we must learn to use hybridity in positive actions because

> at the confluence of two or more genetic streams, with chromosomes constantly "crossing over," this mixture of races, rather than resulting in an inferior being, provides hybrid progeny, a mutable, more malleable species with a rich gene pool. From this racial, ideological, cultural, and biological cross-pollinization, an "alien" consciousness is presently in the making—a new *mestiza* consciousness, *una conciencia de mujer*. It is the consciousness of the Borderlands. (77)

Many of us can reclaim our heritage and take our place in the "contact zone" through the languages we choose. In Anzaldúa's (1987) words: "There is no one Chicano language just as there is no one Chicano experience. A Monolingual Chicana whose first language is English or Spanish is just as much a Chicana as one who speaks several variants of Spanish" (59). Once we have given up on the idea of a standard English, our only recourse is to develop and use a language and writing style that communicate and represent the realities of our lives: "For a people who are neither Spanish nor live in a country in which Spanish is the first language; for a people who cannot entirely identify with either standard (formal Castilian) Spanish nor standard English, what recourse is left to them but to create their own language?" (Anzaldúa 1987, 55). This experience of the borderline identity and language is the one I feel I should tap into when I teach my students to write in a language that expresses their identity rather than simply meets the requirements of standard English.

Women experience patriarchal, cultural, and other influences on their lives. It is therefore important that the political, social, economic, and psychological conflicts be understood through the stories and ways we use language—written or spoken. We understand the relationship between the authority to speak and the languages we use to do so. Anzaldúa (1987) teaches us that we must resist or defy cultural losses by using the languages that contribute to our multiplicity:

> The new mestiza copes by developing a tolerance for contradictions, a tolerance for ambiguity. She learns to be Indian in Mexican culture, to be Mexican from an Anglo point of view. She learns to juggle cultures. She has a plural personality, she operates in a pluralistic mode—nothing is thrust out, the good the bad the ugly, nothing rejected, nothing abandoned. (101)

Just as Anzaldúa's new mestiza reconstructs her identity by taking stock in what she inherits from a multiplicity of cultures and by making selections appropriate to her needs, I think we should encourage our students to use their rich and diverse cultural and linguistic inheritances for survival and growth. In doing this, we experience the process of transculturation and understand hybridization. Writing classrooms can be "safe houses" in the contact zone for women as well as for minorities to move away from the culturally imposed rhetoric of submissiveness to the standard. The students who are exposed to transculturation through writing compose representations that address their need for survival and identity instead of composing essays that meet imposed requirements.

Maria Lugones is another minority woman writer who has helped me articulate the concept of transculturation. Lugones (1994) accurately points out the futility in what she calls the "exercise in purity," since no language is unaffected by the other languages or cultures in the contact zone. She likens language and cultural influences not to a contact zone but to a kitchen activity—the separation of the egg white from the yolk. No matter how great our effort at separating both parts of the egg, contends Lugones, the white sticks to the yolk. Likewise, the influence of languages on each other lingers. I believe the same difficulty with separation occurs in both the lives of those of us caught between two or more cultures and languages and in the emerging writing of those of us who experience transculturation.

The concept of transcultural rhetoric is important because it reveals the creative practice that is in fact already a part of the composing processes we teach in our composition classrooms. Additionally, it helps students view language and writing through different cultural lenses. The project I use, for example, gives my students and mestizas permission to break silence about their lives' stories.

Transcultural Writing for the Composition Classroom

Teaching transcultural rhetoric requires that I convey to my students the different ways in which we persuade others about things that matter to us. Specifically, I work to have students think about how language and culture intersect and what such an intersection means in our understanding of others and ourselves, or of the world in which we live. I teach students to explore their relationship to language and learning through the effects of language in all of our lives. While I have developed assignments that allow for historical explorations, I find that personal explorations are equally helpful in teaching transcultural rhetoric.

In teaching advanced composition, I use a unit developed by Sandra Florence, who works at the University Composition Board at the University of Arizona. Through Florence's Intertextual Collaboration Unit (ITC), I encourage students to reach into their classmates' experiences in ways that validate the ideas, style, and knowledge held by all of them. The ITC unit includes an exercise in which all students must select material from their peers and integrate the "borrowed" material into their own drafts. This aspect of the exercise requires students to reflect on and engage with the material borrowed before it is put into another context. In addition, students must keep track of the ways the material was originally used and changed once students integrated it into their drafts. The reflection on the changes in use allows students to see aspects of life through other people's perspectives. More important, the forced borrowing demonstrates the difficulties of creating a seamless work out of differing experiences. In order to make this exercise fit more closely with Pratt's pedagogical arts of the contact zone, I strongly encourage students to see where the borrowed material and ideas lead them. In this assignment, we all become sensitive to the difficulties of superimposing or appropriating one writer's experience. The assignment works as a perfect transcultural model, however, because it encourages creation of work that literally crosses and blends the variety of student experiences and writing styles within the context of a single writing project.

The process of transculturation is a means of survival in a world frequently inhospitable to difference. By teaching students to develop a hybrid or mestiza consciousness, and by using a language and rhetoric of our own, we compose a place for ourselves. The clashing elements of this rhetoric often come together naturally. Those of us who understand the cultural contexts of languages should consider accepting the uncertainty and chaos that Anzaldúa advocates. Doing so can lead us to teaching strategies that allow for multiplicity of language, style, experiences, and purposes for communication. More important, teaching a multiple and transcultural rhetoric can help us to break the silence of minority and women students as well as the imposition of English Only and standardized language use.

Works Cited

Anzaldúa, Gloria. 1987. *Borderlands/La frontera: The New Mestiza.* San Francisco: Aunt Lute.

Ashcroft, Bill, Gareth Griffiths, and Helen Tiffin. 1989. *The Empire Writes Back: Theory and Practice in Post-Colonial Literatures.* London: Routledge.

———. 1994. *The Post-Colonial Studies Reader.* London: Routledge.

Bhabha, Homi K. 1994. *The Location of Culture.* London: Routledge.

Flores, Juan. 1993. *Divided Borders: Essays on Puerto Rican Identity.* Houston: Arte Publico Press.

Lugones, Maria. 1994. "Purity, Impurity, and Separation." *Signs: Journal of Women in Culture and Society* 19(2): 458–79.

Minh-ha, Trinh T. 1989. *Woman, Native, Other: Writing, Postcoloniality, and Feminism.* Bloomington: Indiana University Press.

Pratt, Mary L. 1991. "Arts of the Contact Zone." *Profession*. New York: Modern Language Association. 33–40.

Said, Edward W. 1979. *Orientalism*. New York: Vintage Books.

———. 1993. *Culture and Imperialism*. New York: Alfred A. Knopf.

Spivak, Gayatri Chakravorty. 1988. "Can the Subaltern Speak?" In Cary Nelson and Lawrence Grossberg, eds., *Marxism and the Interpretation of Cultures*. Urbana: University of Illinois Press. 271–313.

Trimbur, John. 1991. "Literacy and the Discourse of Crisis." In Richard Bullock, John Trimbur, and Charles Schuster, eds., *The Politics of Writing Instruction: Postsecondary*. Portsmouth, NH: Boynton/Cook. 277–95.

Vélez, Diana L., ed. 1997. *Reclaiming Medusa: Short Stories by Contemporary Puerto Rican Women*. Rev. ed. San Francisco: Aunt Lute.

On English Only

VICTOR VILLANUEVA
Washington State University

So what have I learned by reading this book? I have learned that the push to a de jure official language is just another manifestation of a U.S. history of xenophobia, that history has shown that single-language legislation is attached to colonialism and even to multiculturalism (in terms of deciding who gains access and who remains exploited). I have learned that there are ramifications to curing social fears with laws. I have learned that rather than single-language legislation and the maintenance of old colonialism, there really needs to be a move toward hybridity. This book supplied an abundance of detail to things I had long ago intuited and verified other things already known.[1] And how I think of those things known is as a number of prevalent myths that enjoy a great deal of popular currency.

Myth 1: Earlier New Americans Accepted English

America had known hundreds of native languages before Europeans arrived. And after four hundred years, many indigenous languages remain, despite officious attempts at their elimination through Bureau of Indian Affairs schools (de Groat, personal communication, November 20, 1998; West 1992). Colonists brought Dutch and some Swedish to the New York-Delaware area. The Holland Tunnel remains, along with Rutgers University. The Huguenots brought French to Louisiana, an officially bilingual state to this day. The Spaniards brought Spanish to Florida, the Southwest, and the West. Germans brought their language to Pennsylvania. Pennsylvania "Dutch" (really Deutsche) remains a distinct dialect, its German influence still present.

Germans did not quietly accept the primacy of English. Those who were in the colonies during the Revolutionary War era were in no hurry to learn English. In much the same way that John Tanton's memo points to his fear of a Spanish takeover of the United States, Benjamin Franklin in 1751 showed a distrust of the numbers of Germans and of their remaining together.

But despite the anger and the fear, the founding fathers figured more unity could be had in pluralism than in subjugation. The Germans would be necessary allies in a revolution. Government documents were published in German. After the war, during the drafting of the Constitution, the new nation's designers still decided not to officiate English, despite the perceived threat of a German primacy. The nation builders believed that principles of freedom should include linguistic freedom—even the freedom to speak what the founding fathers believed to be an inferior tongue (Heath 1976). German remained America's semiofficial second language until this century.

It was a semiofficial second language in that there were some instances of official German in the United States. In 1795 Germans petitioned the new Congress to have laws published in German as well as English. The petition of the Virginia delegation made it through committee, falling to defeat by only one vote. In the years between 1830 and 1890, 4.5 million more Germans came to the United States. In 1837, seven years after the first wave, Pennsylvania legislated that the public schools be conducted in English and German—legislated that German would have equal status with English. By 1840 Ohio's public schools were bilingual German-English. Some schools in Minnesota, Maryland, and Indiana were conducted exclusively in German (Fallows 1987). Publicly funded German schools existed through much of the nineteenth century (Conklin and Lourie 1983).

The schools did not completely die out until World War I. Then the German Americans quieted and quickly assimilated (nearly two hundred years after their first arrival). After World War I, the push for "100 percent Americanization" saw bilingual education give way to something like current teachings of English as a second language. Mexican Americans were included in a nationwide push to Americanize the "immigrant"—the Italians, Yugoslavs, Poles, and Rumanians who were living in ghettos.

The public believed they were refusing to learn English (Hakuta 1987). The California Commission on Immigration and Housing outwardly declared its endorsement of "Americanization propaganda" (Fallows 1987, 378). Intensive English instruction was mandated and instituted. Penalties were imposed on those who spoke other languages. Successful learning of English was gauged by students' abilities to speak like the Anglo middle class. The success of these programs was measured by standardized achievement tests and IQ tests. These and other criteria determined students' high school curricula, with people of color and immigrants consistently finding their way into trade-oriented schools rather than college preparatory schools. This is a story I know—intimately—though by the time I was ready for high school, I could no longer consider myself quite bilingual, still having competence in understanding my first language but no longer adept at producing it.

Myth 2: English Only Simply Codifies the Status Quo

The rationale goes that since English is the de facto official language, making it the de jure official language would be inconsequential, really. And among the responses we read in this volume is the question of which English will represent the English-speaking middle class. This isn't even a matter of racially specific dialects. Within the middle-class white male world there is Jimmy Carter's English and Bill Clinton's and John F. Kennedy's. And though no one here mentioned it, there are markers of women's ways with words. Which white middle-class U.S. English will it be (since British, Australian, Canadian, and African American would surely be out)?

Once the question of which standard English to officiate is solved, we would need to follow the ways of the French Academy by establishing a U.S. English Language Academy and enforcing its policies. This becomes involved—and it is not preposterous, not only because such laws exist elsewhere, but also because Dade County, Florida, has already piloted such legislation here: "English-Only law in Dade County, Florida is construed to prohibit signs in the zoo which identify animals by their genus and species (in Latin)" (Califa 1991, 7). Although a couple of the essays in this collection call for a linguistic hybridity in which English would embrace its many cultures, the irony is that that has always been the case. If the United States really sought to purify the language (as in a U.S. English Academy modeled after the French Academy), it would have a monumental task ahead. Some states would have to change names to rid them of their foreignness: Vermont (French), Illinois (a French rendering of an American Indian name), Mississippi (American Indian), Colorado (Spanish), Texas and New Mexico (Spanish renderings of Aztecan), and so on. Most states do not have English names. Even Pennsylvania is only part English. English state names include Washington and New York and only a few more.

And once we've changed the names of the majority of our states to conform to a pure English, we'd have to change names of cities and streets. I grew up on Bedford-Stuyvessant. Stuy would need to change. Near Kowalski Street. That's out. So much for El Camino Real in California, or cities such as Los Angeles, or even Manteca or Massapequa. And while we're in the government building where English is the only language to be spoken, we'll have to make that call for pizza clandestinely so that no one hears us utter the Italian word; and we'll need to be careful about that hot dog (which will never again be a frankfurter)—no kraut on that dog. And the American hamburger will become the meat patty, never mind tacos and burritos. Preposterous? No more than Dade County's attempt at zoology. But more significant, an English Only law would be an attempt to deny the very hybridity which comprises our language and our country.

Myth 3: People Are Refusing to Learn English

So there are many ghettos in the United States full of Spanish-speaking people (never mind various Asian groups and Russians and others). And the numbers are greater than in any time past. But most Latinos and Latinas are not new immigrants; most were never immigrants at all, but natives to this country, long ago learning to move between Spanish and English. Latinos and Latinas are only partly the descendants of Spain; we are also of the indigenous peoples of these lands before the Spaniards and (at least for the Caribbean Latino/Latina) of the West Africans who came to this continent as slaves. Only Native Americans have been on this continent longer than the descendants of Spain.

The New World belonged to Spain, claimed by Columbus (an Italian—which should remind us that the continent will also have to be renamed, since the A in USA represents an Italian derivative). Columbus was "Colón" to the Spaniards. Colón is still a common surname among Caribbean Latinos and Latinas. In 1513 Ponce de León discovered Florida. In 1565 the Spaniards established their first colony in St. Augustine. By 1540 Francisco Vásquez de Coronado had conquered the Aztec empire and explored what are now Arizona, Texas, Colorado, and New Mexico. In 1598 Juan de Onate founded Gabriel de los Españoles, the Chamita of New Mexico who still claim a direct lineage to Spain. In the Caribbean, the Arawak and Boricua languages of the Taino Indians of Puerto Rico and the native Indian tongues of Cubans were erased by the Spaniards. We are many groups united in having been subjected to Spanish Only mandates for four hundred years.

The numbers of Spanish-speaking ghettos may be great, but the numbers resistant to English learning are negligible. Ninety-eight percent of Latinos/Latinas responding to a national survey believed it essential for their children to learn to read and write "perfect" English (Hakuta 1987).

The fear of Hispanics/Latinos outnumbering Euro-Americans that John Tanton, former president of U.S. English, betrayed in his infamous 1986 memo is too silly, so silly that I am amazed at the need for this book at all. How does the periphery—the Third World—hope to overturn the core? If numbers alone dictated which language holds superior, English would not have been the language of the United States. English would not be the language of the globe. And yet English is the global lingua franca, though the populations of the United States, Canada, England, and Australia combined do not constitute a majority of the world population. I have seen Arafat, the chairman of the PLO, trouble to speak to U.S. news reporters in English; I have heard the ambassador of Iraq speaking English, as well as the prime minister of Israel, who was likely elected in part for being bilingual in

Hebrew and English. Years ago the PBS television series *The Story of English* noted that an Air Italia commercial jet flying over Italian air space, making a routine local run, piloted by Italians speaking to an exclusively Italian ground crew, must nevertheless speak in English. If a student in Beijing or Liberia or Mexico City recognizes the need for English, surely the American or would-be American recognizes the need. There might well be U.S. ghettos in which little English is spoken. That has been the case for most of this century, and such ghettos have proven to be way stations on the path to full participation in U.S. society.

Myth 4: Bilingual Education Doesn't Work

Of all the myths that pervade the English Only debate, this is the most complicated and the most soundly debunked in this collection. Still, even if we assume that bilingual education doesn't work, how would English Only legislation help those learning English to acquire it more quickly? A law cannot speed up cognitive processes. A mandate cannot press someone to acquire a language faster than the mind can assimilate the new information. Yet a law that ends bilingual education dooms non-English-speaking children to empty sounds, sounds without meaning, during the period of acquisition, a time when others are gathering meaning. We think in terms of immersion, the way we learned French during that trip to Montreal, or the way we learned Spanish in Puerto Vallarta. But did we learn how to engage in academic subjects? Did we learn concepts never before known? We learned how to deal with a menu. Doing away with bilingual education means denying opportunities to learn at the same rate as those who already possess the language of instruction.

"Sink or swim" suggests a resignation to let some sink. But too many already do—and we blame it on the first language, when the issue is much more complicated. We blame bilingual education for the phenomenal failure rate of Boston and New York Puerto Ricans, when the overwhelming majority have received only English instruction since first entering school— whether in Boston, New York, or Puerto Rico, where bilingual education in English and in Spanish is mandated. And when they sink, these children tend not to blame a system that fails them; they blame themselves. Those who swim all too often find that they have lost sight of their homelands. Some neither sink nor swim: they are alienated from their culture of origin and not quite a part of the new culture—the plight of so many of America's people of color. Surely it is better to have two cultures than one; surely two is better than none.

Bilingual education does not doom children; the lack of it does. If we do away with bilingual education, we will have to replace it with something. Returning to what didn't work for so many during the fifty years or so when there was no bilingual education, when the overwhelming majority of first-generation immigrants had no opportunities to catch up with their English-speaking peers, doesn't sound like a sound solution. If we're to go back to the good ol' days, we should go back to the days of the later nineteenth century and early twentieth century when western European immigrants were allowed to learn while they acquired the language of power—*those* days of bilingual education. Children of the Southern and Eastern Hemispheres ought to be afforded the opportunities once realized by those of the West.

A Musing

The other morning I spoke with Ceci, my friend the Cuban English professor. Her husband said something to me over the phone that I had to unravel quickly, making an immediate translation from my first language to my only language, slipping the Spanish into the English to understand. Their baby, I'm told, translates into Spanish for her mother when someone speaks English at home; the child translates the English into Spanish so that the English professor will understand. Cute.

During that phone conversation, I tried to come up with a familiar Spanish saying. It was there, just at the tip of the mind. But I couldn't grasp it. I said it in English. Ceci then said it in Spanish. Quickly. Then again more slowly. I heard it. I understood it. I recognized it. I still feel unsure that I could produce it. My Spanish is limited to single sentences, never extended stretches of discourse. I can't. At least I don't believe I can. And I listen to salsa and mambo and bomba and plena—the music of my childhood. But I can't dance to it in front of anyone. And phrases from the CDs slip by me, untranslated. I am assimilated. I am not.

There was a time when a person came to the United States to begin a life separated from the homeland, having to give it all up, everything that came before. This voluntary loss is what separated us from the peoples of the Eurasian continent. They crossed borders and languages but were always near the homeland, so that they acquired a language if they needed to stay in some country and culture other than home, but without giving up home, because there would be reasons to return sometimes. So Europeans remain multilingual. So Asians remain multilingual. Mr. Fawlty on the TV comedy speaks a bit of French, pokes some fun at German, and speaks a broken Spanish to Manuel, the Spanish waiter, who in turn speaks a broken English. And though there is always the presumption of the superiority of English in an English TV show, though the studio audience laughs at the parochial Mr. Fawlty, an archaism, there is the general assumption among that audience that languages will cross.

Today the rest of the world is a few hours away. Some might have to scrimp and save for a year before affording a flight home to Germany or Russia or Cuba, but the fare is rarely really out of reach. And a week's vacation can be spent in the homeland. No one—no one, whatever the race—needs to give up the home tongue anymore, now that the world is small. And most of the world knows English, and most of the world knows another language, at least one more.

So I was driving home from some chore or other on the afternoon of the morning I had spoken to Ceci. And in the midst of a left turn, I thought: "I'm fifty now, with maybe a third of my life left. I wonder if I'll die without ever being fluent in the language that first met my ears." English is the only language I know, really. Yet Spanish is the language of my ear, of my soul. And I try to pass it on to my children. But I am inadequate.

For any other value—anything—a parent would not deny his or her children what he or she had been denied. We wish our children to know and enjoy those things we lacked. It's what motivates most of us. We teachers are even in the business of legacy, of passing on. I'm saddened by my loss. I'm saddened by my sister's lack, she who has even less of the family legacy than I. The loss wasn't necessary—Ceci stands as an indicator. One gives up nothing by being adept at two languages or more. One gains. So many have had to give up so much to be part of the United States. It was the price we paid, when going back meant prison or famine, or at best an expensive and long trip on a steamship. That price is no longer necessary. Why deny the children a richness simply because it had been denied the parents? The story that begins "my grandfather had to" is wrongheaded. We don't limit on the basis of our ancestors' limits. We break through the limitations of the past. Our children—the children—will learn English. There is no stopping it. Why should the learning be painful? The new residents of this land will learn English. There is no stopping it. Why should their rights be denied during the process of acquiring this new language? Why legislate a kind of assimilation that no longer obtains, is no longer necessary, and was never not painful?

Note

1. Parts of the following essay have previously appeared in slightly different form in "Solamente Inglés and Hispanics" in Harvey Daniels, ed., *Not Only English: Affirming America's Multilingual Heritage* (Urbana: NCTE, 1990, 77–85), and in *Bootstraps: From an American Academic of Color* (Urbana: NCTE, 1993), reproduced with the permission of the publisher.

Works Cited

Califa, Antonio J. 1991. *The Attack on Minority Language Speakers in the United States.* Unpublished manuscript.

Conklin, N. F., and M.A. Lourie. 1983. *A Host of Tongues: Language Communities in the United States.* New York: Free Press.

Fallows, J. 1987. "Bilingual Education." In H. Knepler and M. Knepler, eds., *Crossing Cultures*. New York: Macmillan. 378–88.

Hakuta, Kenji. 1987. Public testimony to the Connecticut State Legislature. March 30.

Heath, Shirley B. 1976. "A National Language Academy? Debate in the New Nation." *International Journal of the Sociology of Language* 11: 9–43.

West, Peter. 1992. "Indians Work to Save a Language—Their Heritage." *Education Week* 12(4): 1, 16, 17.

INDEX

Editors

Roseann Dueñas González is currently professor of English, the first Mexican American woman to attain such distinction at the University of Arizona. She has been a faculty member and administrator at the University of Arizona for twenty-five years, working in the areas of minority education, second-language acquisition, language policy, and interpreter training and testing. She is founder and director of the Writing Skills Improvement Program and the Summer Institute for Writing and Thinking, two programs dedicated to supporting the intellectual and writing development of minority students. After directing the graduate program in English Language and Linguistics for ten years, González co-founded and developed the Second Language Acquisition and Teaching (SLAT) doctoral program at the University of Arizona. She is currently director of the National Center for Interpretation: Testing, Research, and Policy and directs the Federal Court Certification Program that certifies Spanish-English interpreters for use in federal courts throughout the United States, providing due process for non-English-speaking Hispanic Americans. She has written and lectured widely in the areas of minority education, language policy, language discrimination, and judicial interpreter training and testing, and has held a variety of posts in NCTE.

Ildikó Melis is currently a doctoral student in the Rhetoric, Composition, and the Teaching of English (RCTE) program of the University of Arizona, where she also teaches first-year composition classes and works on language policy–related research projects. She earned her M.A. in English and Hungarian at Eötvös Loránd University (ELTE), Budapest, Hungary, and an M.A. in ESL in 1989 at the University of Arizona. From 1990 to 1996, she was director of the first-year composition program and assistant professor of English applied linguistics in ELTE's School of English and American Studies, teaching courses in applied linguistics and academic writing. She has also co-authored two course texts on writing in English, *The Joy of Reading* (1994) and *The Little Red Writing Book* (1996), both published by the Hungarian National Educational Publisher Company.

CONTRIBUTORS

Frances R. Aparicio is Arthur F. Thurnau Professor and associate professor of Spanish and American culture at the University of Michigan, Ann Arbor, where she has also directed the Latina/o Studies Program. Author of *Versiones, interpretaciones, creaciones* (1991) and *Listening to Salsa: Gender, Latin Popular Music and Puerto Rican Cultures* (1998), Professor Aparicio has also published essays on the politics of language in the U.S. Latino/Latina context and on teaching Spanish to U.S. Latinos/Latinas.

Elsa Roberts Auerbach is associate professor of English at the University of Massachusetts Boston. She has coordinated several university-community literacy collaborations, including the UMass English Family Literacy Project, the Bilingual Community Literacy Training Project, the UMass Student Literacy Corps Project, and the Community Training for Adult and Family Literacy Project. She is author of numerous articles and books on adult ESOL and literacy.

Victoria Cliett is coordinator of the Reading Programs at Wayne State University in Detroit, Michigan. She was a recipient of the Conference on College Composition and Communication (CCCC) Scholar for the Dream Travel Award in 1996. She also serves on the CCCC Language Policy Committee as well as on the NCTE Advisory Committee of People of Color. She is a doctoral candidate at Wayne State University.

Louise Rodríguez Connal completed her doctorate in rhetoric, composition, and the teaching of English in August 1999 from the University of Arizona. Her dissertation is *Toward Transcultural Rhetorics: A View from Hybrid America and the Puerto Rican Diaspora*. Rodríguez Connal has published poems in the *Pacific Review,* and she contributed to the forthcoming *Encyclopedia of Rhetoric and Composition* and *Who's Who of Women Writers*. She teaches a variety of writing courses at the University of Arizona. Her research focuses on transcultural rhetorics and hybridity, and her interest in teaching focuses on the needs of minority, high-risk students and reentry students. In 1993 she received the

Scholars for the Dream Award from the Conference on College Composition and Communication.

James Crawford is an independent writer based in Washington, D.C., who specializes in education and language policy. His books include *Bilingual Education: History, Politics, Theory, and Practice* (4ᵗʰ ed., 1999); *Hold Your Tongue: Bilingualism and the Politics of "English Only"* (1992); and *Language Loyalties: A Source Book on the Official English Controversy* (1992). He has also worked as a writer-consultant to organizations such as the National Association for Bilingual Education, Teachers of English to Speakers of Other Languages, and the Stanford Working Group on Federal Programs for Limited-English-Proficient Students. Previously, he served as Washington editor of *Education Week*. Crawford also maintains an extensive language policy Web site at http://ourworld.compuserve.com/homepages/jwcrawford/.

Jim Cummins is a professor in the Department of Curriculum, Teaching, and Learning at the Ontario Institute for Studies in Education of the University of Toronto. His research has focused on the nature of language proficiency and second-language acquisition, with particular emphasis on the social and educational barriers that limit academic success for culturally diverse students. Among his publications are *Negotiating Identities: Education for Empowerment in a Diverse Society* (1996) and *Language, Power, and Pedagogy: Bilingual Children in the Crossfire* (2000).

Eugene E. García is dean of the Graduate School of Education and professor of education at the University of California, Berkeley. He has published extensively in the area of language teaching and bilingual development. He served as a senior officer and director of the Office of Bilingual Education and Minority Languages Affairs in the U.S. Department of Education from 1993 to 1995, and he is conducting research in the areas of effective schooling for linguistically and culturally diverse student populations.

Arturo Gonzalez is assistant professor at the Mexican American Studies and Research Center at the University of Arizona. He was the winner of the Lancaster Award for best dissertation of 1996–1998 in the social sciences. Professor Gonzalez's research focuses on the education and labor market outcomes of immigrants and Latinos in the United States. Along with Adela de la Torre and John A. Garcia, he co-authored "Minority Student Achievement and Workforce Success in Arizona" in 1998 for the Arizona Minority Education Policy and Analysis Center. He has also published on the topics of Mexican enclaves and English-language acquisition. His current research project examines the role of community colleges in the postsecondary education and labor market experience of Latinos.

Elliot L. Judd is associate professor of English and director of the M.A. TESOL program at the University of Illinois at Chicago. Previously, he taught at Ohio University and SUNY Cortland. Judd has also been a consultant to adult and elementary/secondary ESL programs in New York, Ohio, and Illinois. He was a visiting Fulbright lecturer in Venezuela in 1988 and an invited lecturer in Yugoslavia in 1998. Judd was the founding editor of *TESOL Journal* and has published in the areas of language policy, ESOL methodology, and the sociopolitical aspects of ESOL instruction.

Stephen D. Krashen is currently professor of education at the University of Southern California. He is best known for his work in establishing a general theory of second-language acquisition, as the co-founder of the Natural Approach, and as the inventor of sheltered subject matter teaching. His recent books include *Under Attack: The Case against Bilingual Education* (1996), *Foreign Language Education: The Easy Way* (1998), and *Condemned without a Trial: Bogus Arguments against Bilingual Education* (1999).

Rosina Lippi-Green is associate professor of linguistics and creative writing in the English department at Western Washington University. She has written numerous articles on language ideology and language subordination, as well as a book, *English with an Accent: Language, Ideology and Discrimination in the U.S.* (1997). Her work on Title VII national-origin discrimination linked to language trait is widely used in the legal community.

Gail Y. Okawa, associate professor of English at Youngstown State University, teaches and writes about multicultural literacy, cultural rhetorics, sociolinguistics, and teaching force issues, and is especially interested in the representation and use of autobiographical narrative in such studies. Her recent publications include essays in several book collections and in *English Journal*. She is currently working on a study of mentoring among senior scholars of color and a book tentatively titled *Carving Our Own Faces: The Making of Language and Literacy Teachers of Color*. Okawa serves on the Language Policy Committee of the Conference on College Composition and Communication (CCCC) and chairs the CCCC Scholars for the Dream Travel Award Committee and the Committee on the Smithsonian Project.

Carol Schmid is professor of sociology at Guilford Technical Community College in Jamestown, North Carolina. She has recently completed a manuscript on the politics of language in the United States, Canada, and Switzerland and is author of *Conflict and Consensus in Switzerland* (1981) and many articles on the legal and sociolinguistic status of language in the United States, Canada, and Switzerland. She is also an attorney in North Carolina.

Thomas Scovel was born and raised in China and has spent many years living and working in bilingual environments in Asia. He is a professor in the MATESOL program at San Francisco State University, where he teaches courses in applied linguistics and ESL. His main research interests concern second-language acquisition and psycholinguistics, and he has published many articles and several books in these fields. In his real life, Tom is a grandfather and participates in triathlons.

Victor Villanueva is professor of English at Washington State University, where he teaches rhetoric and composition studies and directs the Composition Program. An intellectual, activist, and scholar, he writes about politics of rhetoric and its effects on people of color. *Bootstraps* is a classic memoir from the perspective of an "American Academic of Color." He is a major figure in NCTE and is a past chair of the Conference on College Composition and Communication.

Dorothy Waggoner is the editor and publisher of the newsletter *Numbers and Needs: Ethnic and Linguistic Minorities in the United States*. As a program officer in the U.S. Department of Education, she worked in the Bilingual Education Program and in the National Center for Education Statistics. She chaired the subcommittee on language of the federal Advisory Committee on Race and Ethnicity for the 1980 census that devised the census language questions used in 1980, 1990, and 2000. She has written extensively on the need for programs to assist limited-English-proficient populations.

This book was typeset in Sabon
by Precision Graphics.
Typefaces used on the cover include
Formata and Futura.
The book was printed on 50-lb. offset paper
by Versa Press.